SYNGRESS®

WarDriving

Drive, Detect, Defend

A Guide to Wireless Security

Chris Hurley aka Roamer

Frank Thornton
Michael Puchol
Russ Rogers   Technical Editor

KEY	SERIAL NUMBER
001	DJYN754VGP
002	PO9879887U
003	8292JHSWWW
004	273JK8LMV6
005	CVPLQ6WQ23
006	JHGHGH7566
007	HJJELL9833
008	29WMKREWFH
009	GIIYTE3789
010	IMWT6TDFFY

PUBLISHED BY
Syngress Publishing, Inc.
800 Hingham Street
Rockland, MA 02370

WarDriving: Drive, Detect, Defend   A Guide to Wireless Security

Printed in the United States of America
1 2 3 4 5 6 7 8 9 0
ISBN: 1-931836-03-5

Acquisitions Editor: Christine Kloiber
Technical Editor: Russ Rogers
Page Layout and Art: Patricia Lupien

Cover Designer: Michael Kavish
Copy Editor: Mike McGee
Indexer: Rich Carlson

Distributed by O'Reilly & Associates in the United States and Jaguar Book Group in Canada.

Acknowledgments

We would like to acknowledge the following people for their kindness and support in making this book possible.

Ping Look and Jeff Moss of Black Hat for their invaluable insight into the world of computer security and their support of the Syngress publishing program. A special thanks to Jeff for sharing his thoughts with our readers in the Foreword to this book, and to Ping for providing design expertise on the cover.

Syngress books are now distributed in the United States by O'Reilly & Associates, Inc. The enthusiasm and work ethic at ORA is incredible and we would like to thank everyone there for their time and efforts to bring Syngress books to market: Tim O'Reilly, Laura Baldwin, Mark Brokering, Mike Leonard, Donna Selenko, Bonnie Sheehan, Cindy Davis, Grant Kikkert, Opol Matsutaro, Lynn Schwartz, Steve Hazelwood, Mark Wilson, Rick Brown, Leslie Becker, Jill Lothrop, Tim Hinton, Kyle Hart, Sara Winge, C. J. Rayhill, Peter Pardo, Leslie Crandell, Valerie Dow, Regina Aggio, Pascal Honscher, Preston Paull, Susan Thompson, Bruce Stewart, Laura Schmier, Sue Willing, Mark Jacobsen, Betsy Waliszewski, Dawn Mann, Kathryn Barrett, and to all the others who work with us. And a thumbs up to Rob Bullington for all his help of late.

The incredibly hard working team at Elsevier Science, including Jonathan Bunkell, AnnHelen Lindeholm, Duncan Enright, David Burton, Rosanna Ramacciotti, Robert Fairbrother, Miguel Sanchez, Klaus Beran, and Rosie Moss for making certain that our vision remains worldwide in scope.

David Buckland, Wendi Wong, Daniel Loh, Marie Chieng, Lucy Chong, Leslie Lim, Audrey Gan, and Joseph Chan of STP Distributors for the enthusiasm with which they receive our books.

Kwon Sung June at Acorn Publishing for his support.

Jackie Gross, Gayle Voycey, Alexia Penny, Anik Robitaille, Craig Siddall, Iolanda Miller, Jane Mackay, and Marie Skelly at Jackie Gross & Associates for all their help and enthusiasm representing our product in Canada.

Lois Fraser, Connie McMenemy, Shannon Russell, and the rest of the great folks at Jaguar Book Group for their help with distribution of Syngress books in Canada.

David Scott, Tricia Wilden, Marilla Burgess, Annette Scott, Geoff Ebbs, Hedley Partis, Bec Lowe, and Mark Langley of Woodslane for distributing our books throughout Australia, New Zealand, Papua New Guinea, Fiji Tonga, Solomon Islands, and the Cook Islands.

Winston Lim of Global Publishing for his help and support with distribution of Syngress books in the Philippines.

Author

Chris Hurley (aka Roamer) is a Principal Information Security Engineer working in the Washington, DC area. He is the founder of the WorldWide WarDrive, an effort by information security professionals and hobbyists to generate awareness of the insecurities associated with wireless networks. Primarily focusing his efforts on vulnerability assessments, he also performs penetration testing, forensics, and incident response operations on both wired and wireless networks. He has spoken at several security conferences, been published in numerous online and print publications, and been the subject of several interviews and stories regarding the WorldWide WarDrive. He is the primary organizer of the WarDriving Contest held at the annual DefCon hacker conference. Chris holds a bachelors degree in computer science from Angelo State University. He lives in Maryland with his wife of 14 years, Jennifer, and their 7-year-old daughter Ashley.

Contributors

Frank (Thorn) Thornton runs his own technology-consulting firm, Blackthorn Systems, which specializes in wireless networks. His specialties include wireless network architecture, design, and implementation, as well as network troubleshooting and optimization. An interest in amateur radio has also helped him bridge the gap between computers and wireless networks. Frank's experience with computers goes back to the 1970s when he started programming mainframes. Over the last 30 years, he has used dozens of different operating systems and programming languages. Having learned at a young age which end of the soldering iron was hot, he has even been known to repair hardware on occasion. In addition to his computer and wireless interests, Frank was a law enforcement officer for many years. As a detective and forensics expert he has investigated approximately one hundred homicides and thousands of other crime scenes. Combining both professional interests, he was a member of the workgroup that established ANSI Standard ANSI/NIST-CSL 1-1993 Data Format for the Interchange of Fingerprint Information. He resides in Vermont with his wife.

Michael Puchol, (BEng, Hons) is the founder of Sonar Security, a small enterprise that has become the leading source of wireless security knowledge in Spain, and which provides consultancy in the design, deployment, and security of wireless communications systems. He pioneered WarDriving in Europe, and is the creator of StumbVerter, the most widely used tool for mapping and analysing WiFi access points and their geographical distribution.

Marius Milner is a software engineer working for a startup in Silicon Valley, CA. He likes to explore the intricacies of wireless networking and is the author of the award-winning tool Netstumbler, as well as its smaller counterpart, MiniStumbler. He has had a passion for technology since he got his first LEGO set at the age of 4. He has a masters in mathematics from the University of Cambridge. He lives in Palo Alto, CA, with his wife, Liz, and his children Abigail, Emily, and Thomas.

Technical Editor and Contributor

Russ Rogers (CISSP, CISM, IAM) is a Co-Founder, Chief Executive Officer, Chief Technology Officer, and Principle Security Consultant for Security Horizon, Inc; a Colorado-based professional security services and training provider. Russ is a key contributor to Security Horizon's technology efforts and leads the technical security practice and the services business development efforts. Russ is a United States Air Force Veteran and has served in military and contract support for the National Security Agency and the Defense Information Systems Agency. Russ is also the editor-in-chief of 'The Security Journal' and occasional staff member for the Black Hat Security Briefings. Russ holds an associate's degree in Applied Communications Technology from the Community College of the Air Force, a bachelor's degree from the University of Maryland in computer information systems, and a master's degree from the University of Maryland in computer systems management. Russ is a member of the Information System Security Association (ISSA), the Information System Audit and Control Association (ISACA), and the Association of Certified Fraud Examiners (ACFE). He is also an Associate Professor at the University of Advancing Technology (uat.edu), just outside of Phoenix, Arizona.

Contents

Foreword

When I was thirteen years old and my father got an IBM PC-2 (the one with 640k!) at a company discount, my obsession with computers and computer security began. Back then the name of the game was dial-up networking. 300-baud modems with "auto dial" were in hot demand! This meant that you didn't have to manually dial anymore!

You could see where this was going. It would be possible to have your computer dial all the phone numbers in your prefix looking for other systems it could connect to. This was a great way to see what was going on in your calling area, because seeing what was going on in long distance calling areas was just too expensive!

When the movie "War Games" came out, it exposed *War Dialing* to the public, and soon after it seemed everyone was dialing up a storm. The secret was out, and the old timers were complaining that the *newbies* had ruined it for everyone. How could a self-respecting hacker explore the phone lines if everyone else was doing the same thing? Programs like ToneLoc, Scan, and PhoneTag became popular on the IBM PC with some that allowed dialing several modems at one time to speed things up. Certain programs could even print graphical representations of each prefix, showing what numbers were fax machines, computers, people, or even what phone numbers never answered. One friend of mine covered his walls with print outs of every local calling area he could find in Los Angeles, and all the 1-800 toll free numbers! In response, system operators who were getting scanned struck back with Caller ID verification for people wanting to connect to their systems, automatic call-back, and modems that were only turned on during certain times of the day.

War Dialing came onto the scene again when Peter Shipley wrote about his experiences dialing the San Francisco bay area over a period of years. It made for a good article, and lured some people away from the Internet, and back to the old-school ways of war dialing. What was old was now new again.

Then, along came the Internet, and people applied the concept of war dialing to port scanning. Because of the nature of TCP and IPV4 and IPV6 address space, port scanning is much more time consuming, but is essentially still the same idea. These new school hackers, who grew up on the Internet, couldn't care less about the old way of doing things. They were forging ahead with their own new techniques for mass scanning parts of the Internet looking for new systems that might allow for exploration.

System operators, now being scanned by people all over the planet (not just those people in their own calling region) struck back with port scan detection tools, which limited connections from certain IP addresses, and required VPN connections. The pool of people who could now scan you had grown as large as possible! The battle never ceases.

Once wireless cards and hubs got cheap enough, people started plugging them in like crazy all over the country. Everyone from college students to large companies wanted to free themselves of wires, and they were happy to adopt the new 802.11, or WiFi, wireless standards. Next thing you knew it was possible to accidentally, or intentionally, connect to someone else's wireless access point to get on their network. Hacker's loved this, because unlike telephone wires that you must physically connect to in order to communicate or scan, WiFi allows you to passively listen in on communications with little chance of detection. These are the origins of WarDriving.

I find WarDriving cool because it combines a bit of the old school world of dial up with the way things are now done on the net. You can only connect to machines that you can pick up, much like only being able to War Dial for systems in your local calling area. To make WarDriving easier, people developed better antennas, better WiFi scanning programs, and more powerful methods of mapping and recording the systems they detected. Instead of covering your walls with tone maps from your modem, you can now cover your walls with GPS maps of where you have located wireless access points.

Unlike the old school way of just scanning to explore, the new WiFi way allows you to go a step further. Many people intentionally leave their access points "open," thus allowing anyone who wants to connect through them to the Internet. While popular at some smaller cafes (i.e., Not Starbucks) people do this as all over the world. Find one of these open access points, and it could be your anonymous on-ramp to the net. And, by running an open access point you could contribute to the overall connectedness of your community.

Maybe this is what drives the Dialers and Scanners. The desire to explore and map out previously unknown territory is a powerful motivator. I know that is why I dialed for months, trying to find other Bulletin Board Systems that did not advertise, or were only open to those who found it by scanning. Out of all that effort, what did I get? I found one good BBS system, but also some long-term friends.

When you have to drive a car and scan, you are combining automobiles and exploration. I think most American males are programmed from birth to enjoy both! Interested? You came to the right place. This book covers everything from introductory to advanced WarDriving concepts, and is the most comprehensive look at WarDriving I have seen. It is written by the people who both pioneered and refined the field. The lead author, Chris Hurley, organizes the WorldWide WarDrive, as well as the WarDriving contest at DEF CON each year. His knowledge in applied WarDriving is extensive.

As WarDriving has moved out of the darkness and into the light, people have invented WarChalking to publicly mark networks that have been discovered. McDonalds and Starbucks use WiFi to entice customers into their establishments, and hackers in the desert using a home made antenna have extended its range from hundreds of feet to over 20 miles! While that is a highly geek-tastic thing to do, demonstrates that enough people have adopted a wireless lifestyle that this technology is here to stay. If a technology is here to stay, then isn't it our job to take it apart, see how it works, and generally hack it up? I don't know about you, but I like to peek under the hood of my car.

—*Jeff Moss*
Black Hat, Inc.
www.blackhat.com
Seattle, 2004

## Chapter 1

Learning to WarDrive

Solutions in this Chapter:

- The Origins of WarDriving
- Tools of the Trade or "What Do I Need?"
- Putting It All Together

☑ Summary

☑ Solutions Fast Track

☑ Frequently Asked Questions

Introduction

Wireless networks have become a way of life in the past two years. As more wireless networks are deployed, the need to secure them increases. This chapter provides background on one effort to educate users of wireless networks about the insecurities associated with wireless networking. This effort is called WarDriving.

This chapter presents a brief history of WarDriving and the terminology necessary to understand what WarDriving is all about. This includes information on why the activity of driving around discovering wireless access points is called WarDriving, some misconceptions associated with the term, and the truth behind the idea of WarDriving. This chapter also discusses the legality of WarDriving.

In order to successfully WarDrive, there are some tools, both hardware and software, that you will need. These tools are presented along with cost estimates and some recommendations. Since there are hundreds of possible configurations that can be used for WarDriving, some of the most popular are presented to help you decide what to buy for your own initial WarDriving setup.

Many of the tools that a WarDriver uses are the same tools that could be used by an attacker to gain unauthorized access to a wireless network. Since this is not the goal of a WarDriver, the methodology that you can use to ethically WarDrive is presented.

WarDriving is a fun hobby that has the potential to make a difference in the overall security posture of wireless networking. By understanding WarDriving, obtaining the proper tools, and then using them ethically, you can have countless hours of fun while making a difference.

The Origins of WarDriving

WarDriving is an activity that is misunderstood by many people. This applies to both the general public, and to the news media that has reported on WarDriving. Because the name "WarDriving" has an ominous sound to it, many people associate WarDriving with a criminal activity. Before the discussion of how to WarDrive begins, you need to understand the history of WarDriving and the origin of the name. The facts necessary to comprehend the truth about WarDriving, as well as why the media has incorrectly reported on WarDriving are provided.

What's in a Name?

WarDriving is the act of moving around a specific area and mapping the population of wireless access points for statistical purposes. These statistics are then used to raise awareness of the security problems associated with these types of networks (typically wireless). The commonly accepted definition of WarDriving among those who are actually practitioners is that WarDriving is not exclusive of surveillance and research by automobile – WarDriving is accomplished by anyone moving around a certain area looking for data. This includes: walking, which is often referred to as WarWalking; flying, which is also referred to as WarFlying; bicycling, and so forth. WarDriving does NOT utilize the resources of any wireless access point or network that is discovered without prior authorization of the owner.

The Terminology History of WarDriving

The term WarDriving comes from WarDialing, a term you may be familiar with being that it was introduced to the general public by Matthew Broderick's character, David Lightman, in the 1983 movie, *WarGames*. WarDialing is the practice of using a modem attached to a computer to dial an entire exchange of telephone numbers (often sequentially—for example, 555-1111, 555-1112, and so forth) to locate any computers with modems attached to them.

Essentially, WarDriving employs the same concept, although it is updated to a more current technology: wireless networks. A WarDriver drives around an area, often after mapping a route out first, to determine all of the wireless access points in that area. Once these access points are discovered, a WarDriver uses a software program or Web site to map the results of his efforts. Based on these results, a statistical analysis is performed. This statistical analysis can be of one drive, one area, or a general overview of all wireless networks.

The concept of driving around discovering wireless networks probably began the day after the first wireless access point was deployed. However, WarDriving became more well-known when the process was automated by Peter Shipley, a computer security consultant in Berkeley, California. During the fall of 2000, Shipley conducted an 18-month survey of wireless networks in Berkeley, California and reported his results at the annual DefCon hacker conference in July of 2001. This presentation, designed to raise awareness of the insecurity of wireless networks that were deployed at that time, laid the groundwork for the "true" WarDriver.

WarDriving Misconceptions

These days, you might hear people confuse the terminology WarDriver and Hacker. As you probably know, the term *hacker* was originally used to describe a person that was able to modify a computer (often in a way unintended by its manufacturer) to suit his or her own purposes. However, over time, owing to the confusion of the masses and consistent media abuse, the term hacker is now commonly used to describe a criminal; someone that accesses a computer or network without the authorization of the owner. The same situation can be applied to the term WarDriver. WarDriver has been misused to describe someone that accesses wireless networks without authorization from the owner. An individual that accesses a computer system, wired or wireless, without authorization is a criminal. Criminality has nothing to do with either hacking or WarDriving.

The news media, in an effort to generate ratings and increase viewership, has sensationalized WarDriving. Almost every local television news outlet has done a story on "wireless hackers armed with laptops" or "drive-by hackers" that are reading your e-mail or using your wireless network to surf the Web. These stories are geared to propagate Fear, Uncertainty, and Doubt (FUD). FUD stories usually take a small risk, and attempt to elevate the seriousness of the situation in the minds of their audience. Stories that prey on fear are good for ratings, but don't always depict an activity accurately.

An unfortunate side effect of these stories has been that the reporters invariably ask the "WarDriver" to gather information that is being transmitted across a wireless network so that the "victim" can be shown their personal information that was collected. Again, this has nothing to do with WarDriving and while a case can be made that this activity (known as sniffing) in and of itself is not illegal, it is at a minimum unethical and is not a practice that WarDrivers engage in.

These stories also tend to focus on gimmicky aspects of WarDriving such as the directional antenna that can be made using a Pringles can. While a functional antenna can be made from Pringles cans, coffee cans, soup cans, or pretty much anything cylindrical and hollow, the reality is that very few (if any) WarDrivers actually use these for WarDriving. Many of them have made these antennas in an attempt to both verify the original concept and improve upon it in some instances.

Notes from the Underground...

Warchalking Is a Myth

In 2002, the news media latched onto something called warchalking. Warchalking is the act of making chalk marks on buildings or sidewalks to denote the presence and availability of wireless networks. Playing off of the practice of hobos during the Great Depression who would mark homes or areas to communicate information about the area to other hobos, warchalkers use a series of symbols to alert others as to what type of wireless network they will find in that area. Three primary symbols used by warchalkers are illustrated in the following figures. Figure 1.1 indicates an open node, or one in which WEP encryption is not utilized and individuals are encouraged to use. The Service Set Identifier (SSID) or network name is chalked above the symbol and the available bandwidth speed is chalked below the symbol.

Figure 1.1 The Open Node

Figure 1.2 The Closed Node

Figure 1.2 indicates a closed node. One that is not open for public use. The SSID or network name is chalked above the symbol and nothing is chalked below the symbol.

Continued

Figure 1.3 The WEP Node

The symbol in Figure 1.3 indicates a node with WEP encryption enabled. This should be viewed as an unequivocal stop sign. The SSID and contact information to arrange for authorized access are chalked above the symbol and the available bandwidth is chalked below the symbol. Aside from hot spots such as Starbucks, there have been very few actual sightings of warchalked wireless networks. Despite the media hype surrounding warchalking, it is generally viewed as a silly activity by WarDrivers. A recent poll on the NetStumbler forums (https://forums.netstumbler.com) was unable to find even one person that had actually chalked an access point. The results of the survey can be seen in Figure 1.4. More information on the NetStumbler Forums and other online WarDriving Communities is presented in Chapter 8 of this book.

Figure 1.4 Results of the NetStumbler Forums Poll about Warchalking

Do you warchalk? You have already voted on this poll.		
Yes ▪	0	0%
No ▬▬▬▬▬▬▬▬▬▬▬▬▬▬▬	48	100.00%
Total: 48 votes		100%

The Truth about WarDriving

The reality of WarDriving is simple. Computer security professionals, hobbyists, and others are generally interested in providing information to the public about security vulnerabilities that are present with "out of the box" configurations of wireless access points. Wireless access points that can be purchased at a local electronics or computer store are not geared toward security. They are designed so that a person with little or no understanding of networking can purchase a wireless access point, and with little or no outside help, set it up and begin using it.

Computers have become a staple of everyday life. Technology that makes using computers easier and more fun needs to be available to everyone. Companies such as Linksys and D-Link have been very successful at making these new technologies easy for end users to set up and begin using. To do otherwise would alienate a large part of their target market. In Chapter 10, a step-by-step guide to enabling the built-in security features of these access points is discussed.

The Legality of WarDriving

According to the FBI, it is not illegal to scan access points, but once a theft of service, denial of service, or theft of information occurs, then it becomes a federal violation through 18USC 1030 (www.usdoj.gov/criminal/cybercrime/ 1030_new.html). While this is good, general information, any questions about the legality of a specific act in the United States should be posed directly to either the local FBI field office, a cyber crime attorney, or the U.S. Attorney's office. This information only applies to the United States. WarDrivers are encouraged to investigate the local laws where they live to ensure that they aren't inadvertently violating the law. Understanding the distinction between "scanning" or identifying wireless access points and actually using the access point is understanding the difference between WarDriving, a legal activity, and theft, an obviously illegal activity.

Tools of the Trade or "What Do I Need?"

This section will introduce you to all of the tools that are required in order to successfully WarDrive. There are several different configurations that can be effectively used for WarDriving, including:

- Getting the hardware
- Choosing a wireless network card
- Deciding on an external antenna
- Connecting your antenna to your wireless NIC

The following sections discuss potential equipment acquisitions and common configurations for each.

Getting the Hardware

You will need some form of hardware to use with your WarDriving equipment. There are two primary setups that WarDrivers utilize:

- The Laptop Setup
- The PDA Setup

The Laptop Setup

The most commonly used WarDriving setup utilizes a laptop computer. To WarDrive with a laptop, you need several pieces of hardware (each of which is discussed in detail in this chapter) and at least one WarDriving software program. A successful laptop WarDriving setup includes:

- A laptop computer
- A wireless NIC Card
- An external antenna
- A pigtail to connect the external antenna to the wireless NIC
- A handheld global positioning system (GPS) unit
- A GPS data cable
- A WarDriving software program
- A cigarette lighter or AC adapter power inverter

Because most of the commonly used WarDriving software is not resource intensive, the laptop can be an older model. If you decide to use a laptop computer to WarDrive, you need to determine the WarDriving software you plan to use as well. For instance, if you do not feel comfortable with the Linux operating system, you will have to rely on tools that are supported in a Microsoft Windows environment. Because NetStumbler only works in Windows environments (and Kismet only runs on Linux), your choice of software is limited. A typical laptop WarDriving setup is shown in Figure 1.5.

Figure 1.5 A Typical Laptop Computer WarDriving Setup

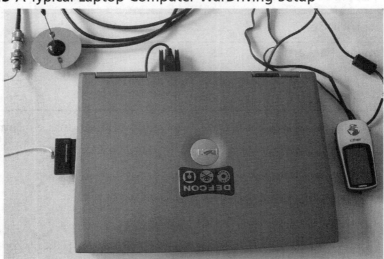

The Personal Digital Assistant (PDA) Setup

PDAs are the perfect accessory for the WarDriver because they are highly portable. The Compaq iPAQ (see Figure 1.6), or any number of other PDAs that utilize the ARM, MIPS, or SH3 processor can be utilized with common WarDriving software packages. See Table 1.1.

Figure 1.6 A Typical PDA WarDriving Setup

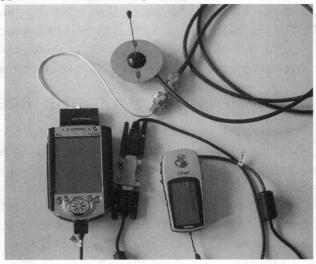

Table 1.1 PDA Processors

Manufacturer/Model	Processor
Compaq/Hewlett Packard iPAQ PDAs	ARM
Hewlett Packard Jornada PDAs	SH3
CASIO PDAs	MIPS

As with the laptop setup, the PDA setup requires additional equipment in order to be successful:

- A PDA with a data cable

- A wireless NIC Card

- An external antenna

- A pigtail to connect the external antenna to the wireless NIC

- A handheld global positioning system (GPS) unit

- A GPS data cable

- A null modem connector

- A WarDriving software program

Similar to the laptop configuration, the software package you choose will affect your choice of PDA. MiniStumbler, the PDA version of NetStumbler, works on PDAs that utilize the Microsoft Pocket PC operating system. The HP/Compaq iPAQ is one of the more popular PDAs among WarDrivers that prefer MiniStumbler. WarDrivers that prefer to use a PDA port of Kismet are likely to choose the Sharp Zaurus since it runs a PDA version of Linux. There are also Kismet packages that have specifically been designed for use on the Zaurus.

Choosing a Wireless Network Interface Card

Now that you have chosen either a laptop or a PDA to use while WarDriving, you will need to determine which wireless NIC card to use. Most of the wireless networks that are currently deployed are 802.11b networks. You will find more access points if you use an 802.11b NIC. 802.11g access points, which transfer data at nearly five times the speed of 802.11b (54 MBps as opposed to 11 MBps) are gaining popularity and it is likely that an 802.11g card will soon supplant an 802.11b card as the favorite of WarDrivers. This is not likely to happen, however, until WarDriving tools catch up and offer more extensive 802.11g support. In addition to increased speed, the 802.11g standard supports WiFi Protected Access (WPA) encryption. Once effectively deployed, WPA will help to improve the overall security posture of wireless networks. Some 802.11a cards are currently supported by WarDriving software under certain conditions. These conditions will be discussed throughout the book; specifically in Chapters 2 through 6.

As a general rule, 802.11a (or any 802.11a/b/g combo) cards are not recommended for WarDriving. This is because 802.11a was broken into three distinct frequency ranges: Unlicensed National Information Infrastructure (UNII)1, UNII2, and UNII3. Under Federal Communications Commission (FCC) regulations, UNII1 cannot have removable antennas. Although UNII2 and UNII3 are allowed to have removable antennas, most 802.11a cards utilize both UNII1 and UNII2. Because UNII1 is utilized, removable antennas are not an option for these cards in the United States.

When Kismet and NetStumbler were first introduced, there were two primary chipsets available on wireless NICs: the Hermes chipset and the Prism2 chipset. Although there are many other chipsets available now, most WarDriving software is designed for use with one of these two chipsets. As a general rule NetStumbler works with cards based on the Hermes chipset. Kismet, on the other hand, is designed for use with cards based on the Prism2 chipset. This is not a hard and fast rule since some Prism2 cards will work under NetStumbler in certain configurations. Also, with appropriate Linux kernel modifications, Hermes cards can be used with Kismet.

Types of Wireless NICs

In order to WarDrive, you will need a wireless NIC. Before purchasing a wireless card, you should determine the software and configuration you plan to use. NetStumbler (see Chapters 2 and 3) offers the easiest configuration for cards based on the Hermes chipset (for example, ORiNOCO cards). NetStumbler offers support for the following cards:

- Lucent Technologies WaveLAN/IEEE (Agere ORiNOCO)
- Dell TrueMobile 1150 Series
- Avaya Wireless PC Card
- Toshiba Wireless LAN Card
- Compaq WL110

- Cabletron/Enterasys Roamabout
- Elsa Airlancer MC–11
- ARtem ComCard 11Mbps
- IBM High Rate Wireless LAN PC Card
- 1stWave 1ST-PC-DSS11IS, DSS11IG, DSS11ES, DSS11EG
- Some Prism2-based cards will work under Windows XP.

Kismet (described in detail in Chapters 4 through 6) works with both Prism2- and Hermes-based cards. However, most Linux and BSD distributions require kernel and driver patch modifications and recompiles in order for Hermes-based cards to enter monitor mode as required by Kismet. Kismet offers support for the following cards:

- Cisco
  1. Aironet 340
  2. Aironet 350
- Prism 2
  1. Linksys
  2. D-Link
  3. Zoom
  4. Demarctech
  5. Microsoft
  6. Many others
- ORiNOCO
  1. Lucent ORiNOCO-based cards such as the WaveLAN
  2. Airport
- AIRPORT
  1. Airport cards under Mac OS X using the Viha drivers
- ACX100
  1. Dlink 650+

In order to maximize your results, you will want a card that has an external antenna connector (Figure 1.7). This will allow you to extend the range of your card by attaching a stronger antenna to your WarDriving setup.

Figure 1.7 ORiNOCO External Antenna Connector

Many WarDrivers prefer the ORiNOCO Gold 802.11b card produced by Agere or Lucent (see Figure 1.8) because it is compatible with both Kismet and NetStumbler and because it also has an external antenna connector. This card is now produced by Proxim and no longer uses the Hermes chipset, nor does it have an external antenna connector. The Hermes-based card is still available; however, it is now marketed as the "ORiNOCO Gold Classic."

Figure 1.8 The ORiNOCO Gold Card

I highly recommend the ORiNOCO Gold (now the Gold Classic) card. This card is outstanding for both everyday use and for WarDriving. Also, as previously noted, this card can be configured for use in both NetStumbler and Kismet. This is particularly useful when using a laptop computer that is configured to dual boot both Linux and Windows. This allows you to utilize the wireless NIC in both operating systems as well as most common WarDriving software in both environments without having to change hardware.

Other Cards

Cisco Aironet 350 Series (see Figure 1.9) cards provide a unique functionality in that some models are available with two external antenna connectors. This is particularly useful in areas with tall buildings because you can attach two directional antennas and manually sweep them up and down buildings on both sides of the road at the same time. (Note: this will probably require two passengers to operate the antennas.)

Figure 1.9 Cisco Aironet 350 Series Card with Dual MMCX Connectors

The "store bought" cards that you find at most major retailers (Linksys, SMC, and so forth) are generally not good cards to use while WarDriving because they do not have external antenna connectors. Most of these cards are based on the Prism 2 chipset (see Figure 1.10).

Figure 1.10 A Prism2-Based Card

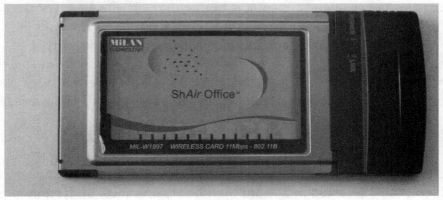

A slightly out-of-date, but still useful listing of wireless NICs, and the chipsets they use was put together by Seattle Wireless and can be found at: www.seat-tlewireless.net/index.cgi/HardwareComparison.

External Antennas

In order to maximize the results of a WarDrive, an external antenna should be used. An antenna is a device for radiating or receiving radio waves. Most wireless network cards have a low power antenna built in to them. An external antenna will increase the range of the radio signal detected by the wireless network card. Many different types of antennas can be used with wireless NICs: parabolic antennas, directional antennas, and omni-directional antennas are just a few. Because of their size, parabolic antennas (see Figure 1.11) are not overly practical antennas for WarDriving.

Figure 1.11 A Parabolic Antenna Isn't Good for WarDriving

Many WarDrivers use either an external omni–directional antenna or an external directional antenna in conjunction with their wireless network card. Both of these are available in many different sizes and signal strengths. There are many factors that need to be considered when determining what type of antenna to use. This book will not cover specific in–depth details on radio and antenna theory, but will provide some basic information on how antennas work. There are numerous references both online and in print that go into radio and antenna theory in depth.

NOTE

If you are interested in a more than basic, user-level understanding of the previous concepts, you should investigate the following two resources, *Building a Cisco Wireless LAN* (ISBN: 1-928994-58-X) and *Designing a Wireless Network* (ISBN: 1-928994-45-8), both available from Syngress Publishing (www.syngress.com). Other books include *Jeff Duntemann's Drive-By WiFi Guide* (Paraglyph Publishing, ISBN: 1-932111-74-3), *802.11 Wireless Networks: The Definitive Guide* (O'Reilly & Associates, ISBN: 0-596001-83-5).

The Amateur Radio Relay League (www.arrl.org) also provides some excellent information on antennas and antenna theory. Although this information is geared primarily toward amateur, or HAM, radio, the theories presented are the same regardless of the radio spectrum you are transmitting in.

There are some basic terms you should understand when determining what type of antenna should be used while WarDriving:

- **Decibel (dB)** A decibel is the unit of measure for power ratios describing loss or gain, normally expressed in watts. A decibel is not an absolute value—it is the measurement of power gained or lost between two communicating devices. These units are usually given in terms of the logarithm to Base 10 of a ratio.

- **dBi value** This is the ratio of the gain of an antenna as compared to an *isotropic* antenna. The greater the dBi value, the higher the gain. If the gain is high, the angle of coverage will be more acute.

- **Isotropic antenna** An isotropic antenna is a theoretical construct that describes an antenna that will radiate its signal 360 degrees to cover the area in a perfect sphere. It is used as a basis by which to describe the *gain* of a real antenna.

- **Line of sight** Line of sight is an unobstructed straight line between two transmitting devices. You will most often see the need for a line of sight path for long-range directional radio transmissions. Due to the curvature of the earth, the maximum line of sight for devices not mounted on towers is six miles (9.65 km).

Omni-Directional Antennas

As the name indicates, omni-directional antennas "see" in all directions at once. An omni-directional antenna is best used when driving alone, and can be purchased for $50.00 and up depending on the gain and mounting mechanism. One common misconception is that the stronger the gain of the antenna, the better your WarDriving results will be. This is not entirely true, however. The important thing to understand from the preceding definition of dBi value is the last sentence: "If the gain is high, the angle of coverage will be more acute." Because the signal of an omni-directional antenna is shaped roughly like a donut, the higher (or larger) the gain, the "shorter" the donut. The opposite is true as well. A smaller gain antenna has a "taller" donut.

Figure 1.12 shows the signal donut of a 5 dBi gain omni-directional antenna (see Figure 1.10) compared to that of an 8 dBi gain omni-directional antenna. The signal donut of the 5 dBi is taller than the signal donut of an 8 dBi gain omni-directional antenna. This is illustrated in the side view. What this means is that although it has a "weaker" signal, as indicated in the overhead view, a 5 dBi gain omni-directional antenna is likely to provide better results in a neighborhood with tall buildings such as an urban downtown area. Also, because these antennas rely on line-of-sight communication, a 5 dBi gain antenna works very well in residential areas where homes and other buildings provide obstructions between your antenna and any wireless access points.

Figure 1.12 Signal Donut Comparison of 5 dBi and 8 dBi gain Omni-

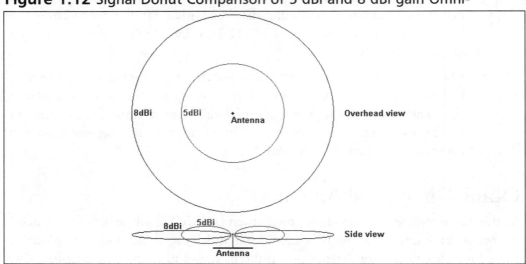

Another advantage of the 5 dBi gain antenna is that many are available with a magnetic base. This means that you can simply put it on the roof of your car and the magnet will hold it in place while driving; no additional mounting brackets are required.

An 8 dBi gain (see Figure 1.13), or higher, antenna is excellent for use on longer drives in open areas with few obstructions such as interstate highways. These antennas are very effective when businesses or residences are farther away from your vehicle and there is a large field or roadway between you and any potential access points. It is more difficult to find magnetic mounted antennas that are stronger than 5 dBi gain (see Figure 1.14). These antennas usually require some form of external mounting bracket.

Figure 1.13 An 8 dBi Gain Omni-Directional Antenna

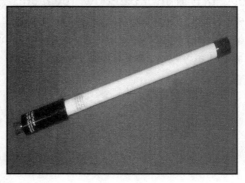

Figure 1.14 A 5 dBi Gain Magnetic Mount Omni-Directional Antenna

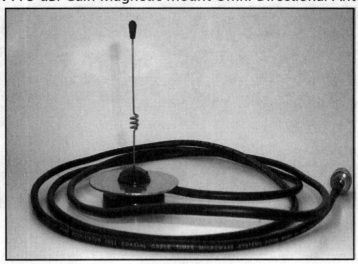

Regardless of the dBi gain antenna you use, an omni-directional antenna is usually going to be the best choice for WarDriving. This is primarily because it radiates its signal in all directions at once. Because these antennas do rely on line-of-sight communications, it is not necessary to continually sweep the antenna in the direction of potential access points in order to discover them. There are, however, situations where a directional antenna is more effective.

Directional Antennas

Directional antennas also rely on line of sight to transmit; however, unlike omni-directional antennas, they can only "see" in the direction they are pointed. Directional antennas are excellent for use in areas with tall buildings. From a stationary position near the base of the building, you can sweep the antenna up and down the length of the building and detect access points that would have been missed with an omni-directional antenna. Additionally, directional antennas can have a much stronger dBi gain in a shorter (not necessarily smaller) package. For example, a 14.5 dBi gain directional antenna, as shown in Figure 1.15, is just slightly longer than the 8 dBi gain omni-directional antenna shown in Figure 1.13, but has a significantly stronger dBi gain.

Figure 1.15 A 14.5 dBi Gain Directional Antenna

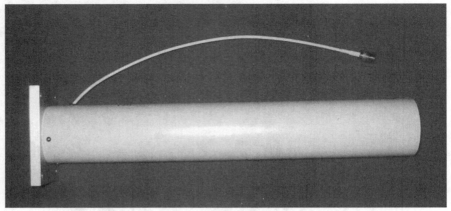

There are several types of directional antennas such as yagis, parabolic grids, and so forth. However, the most commonly used antenna is the yagi antenna since these can be purchased relatively inexpensively and provide a large dBi gain.

Notes from the Underground…

The Pringles "Cantenna"

One of the most fun things you can do is build your own antenna. With a small investment (usually less than $10), you can build a very strong directional antenna. Although this will probably not be an antenna that you will use extensively for WarDriving, taking the time and effort to build your own antenna can teach you many concepts of antenna theory that will be very useful when determining the type of antenna you want to use while WarDriving.

There are a number of online resources that detail the step-by-step methodology for building a "homebrew" antenna. Probably the best is Rob Flickenger's guide at www.oreillynet.com/cs/weblog/view/wlg/448.

The first thing you will need is a hollow cylindrical object such as a Pringles can (emptied of course), a coffee can, an old soup can, or anything with a similar shape. This will provide the housing for the second piece of the antenna, the collector rod. You will need to build the collector rod from parts you can purchase at any Radio Shack.

Continued

The most interesting part of the process is determining the length of the collector rod. This is where you will learn the most. The basic formula is:

$$W = 3.0 * 10^8 * (1 / LEF) * 10^{-9}$$

In this equation, W is the wavelength frequency and LEF is the Low End Frequency of the channel the antenna should transmit on. Because 802.11b transmits in channels 1–11 of the 2.4 GHz spectrum, if you use the channel 1 LEF of 2.412 and the channel 11 LEF of 2.462, you can determine both the longest (channel 1) and shortest (channel 11) rod you will need. Unless you want the antenna to specifically work on one channel, a much more exacting process, you can keep your rod length between these two values.

After you have determined the longest and shortest wavelength, simply cut your rod to a quarter of those values. In the case of a 2.4 GHz antenna, you will want to keep your rod between 1.2" and 1.22". Once the rod is cut, it is merely a matter of assembling the components and trying it out. (See Figure 1.16.)

Figure 1.16 The Pringles "Cantenna"

Before attempting to make your own antenna, you should be aware of the risks involved. An improperly constructed antenna could destroy any equipment you connect it to. Also, if your antenna rod lengths are calculated incorrectly, you could transmit outside of the allowable 2.4 GHz spectrum and find yourself on the wrong side of an FCC investigation.

Connecting Your Antenna to Your Wireless NIC

In order to connect your antenna to the external antenna connector on your wireless NIC you will need the appropriate pigtail cable (see Figure 1.17). Most antennas have an N–Type connector but the wireless NIC usually has a proprietary connector. When you purchase your card you should verify with either the retailer or the card manufacturer what type of external antenna connector is built into the card.

Figure 1.17 Pigtail for Use with ORiNOCO Cards and N-Type Barrel Connectors

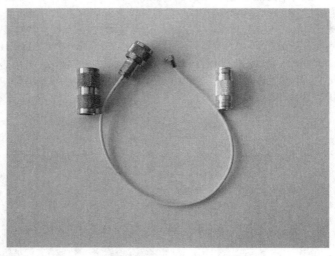

   Once you have identified the type of external connector your card has, you will need to purchase a pigtail that has both the correct connection for your card as well as the correct N–Type connector. Some antennas ship with male N–Type connectors and others ship with female N–Type connectors. Because the pigtails are expensive (around $30) you should verify whether your antenna has a male or female connector, and purchase the opposite connection on your pigtail. For instance, if you purchase a 5 dBi magnetic mount omni–directional antenna with a female N–Type connector for use with your ORiNOCO Gold card, you will need a pigtail that has a Lucent proprietary connector as well as a male N–Type connector. This will allow you to successfully connect your antenna to your wireless NICs external antenna connector. Since you may have multiple antennas with both male and female N–Type connectors, it might also be a good idea to purchase barrel connectors that will allow you to attach your pigtail to either a male or female N-Type Connector.

Global Positioning System (GPS)

Most WarDrivers want to map the results of their drives. To do this, a portable GPS capable of National Marine Electronics Output (NMEA) is required. Some WarDriving software supports other proprietary formats (such as Garmin). For instance, NetStumbler supports the Garmin format. The Garmin format "reports" your current location to your software every second, whereas NMEA only reports your location once every two seconds. Using the Garmin format increases the accuracy of the access-point locations. Unfortunately, Kismet (and other WarDriving software) only supports NMEA output. By purchasing a GPS capable of NMEA output, you provide yourself with the flexibility to switch between WarDriving software without requiring additional hardware.

When choosing a GPS, several factors should be considered. As mentioned earlier, making sure it is capable of NMEA output is a must. It is also important to find out which accessories come with the GPS unit. For instance, there are several models in the Garmin eTrex line of handheld GPSs. The base model, simply called the eTrex (see Figure 1.18) retails for about $120. This unit has all of the functionality required for a WarDriver and is capable of NMEA output. When you compare this to the eTrex Venture, which retails for $150, the initial indication would be to go with the cheaper model. However, once the accessories included with these two are looked into, you will notice that the Venture comes with the PC Interface cable, whereas the base model doesn't. Because this cable costs about $50, the Venture is a better purchase. In addition to the PC Interface cable, you get additional functionality with the Venture that, while not required for WarDriving, can be fun to play with, all for $20 less.

Figure 1.18 The Garmin eTrex Handheld GPS

You should also determine if your laptop computer has a serial port. Most PC Interface cables have a serial interface. If your laptop doesn't have a serial interface, you can purchase a serial to Universal Serial Bus (USB) cable for use with your GPS.

In order to use your GPS with a PDA, you will need a null modem connector and the proper connection cables for your PDA. The proper configuration for this setup is PDA | Proprietary connector/serial conversion cable | Null Modem Connector | GPS PC Interface cable. This setup is depicted in Figure 1.19.

Figure 1.19 PDA GPS Cable Connections

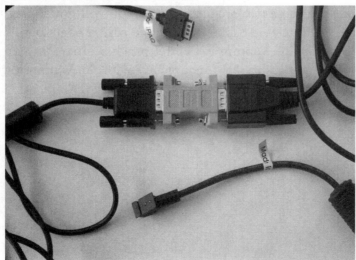

Putting It All Together

Once you have selected your WarDriving gear and understand what WarDriving is, you are almost ready to begin. You now know that you want to go out and identify wireless access points and map them out, but before you can do this you need to make sure you aren't going to inadvertently connect to one or more of the wireless networks you discover. Because so many access points are set up in the default configuration, this is a real possibility.

Many wireless access points that are available today also include a built-in cable or DSL router to allow multiple hosts to access a single cable or DSL modem and get to the Internet. While this combination does help the end user quickly gain access to the Internet, both on wired and wireless networks, it also increases the potential ways that an attacker can easily compromise the network. This is primarily because, in their default configurations, the wireless access point will allow any card to connect to it without requiring any configuration on the client side, and the router has a Dynamic Host Configuration Protocol (DHCP) server enabled. The DHCP server will automatically assign a valid IP address to any host that requests one from it. When coupled with a wireless access point that grants access to any host, the DHCP server completes the connection process. At this point, an attacker has complete access to all services available on the network.

This is not an issue when using Linux software such as Kismet or AirSnort since these programs operate in monitor mode. A device in monitor mode will merely sniff all traffic without making any connections. In order to avoid accidentally connecting to these networks when using Windows, however, you will need to make a few simple configuration changes before you begin WarDriving. These steps are described in the following section.

Tools and Traps…

One thing to be aware of when WarDriving is a tool from Black Alchemy called FakeAP (www.blackalchemy.to/project/fakeap/). FakeAP can be configured to generate hundreds or thousands of "fake" access points. A WarDriver that is in range of a system configured with FakeAP will notice a large number of access points quickly being detected. This is because FakeAP generates 802.11b beacon frames with SSIDs and MAC addresses randomly chosen from the FakeAP dictionary.

On a typical WarDrive, it is virtually impossible to detect that access points you have discovered were actually generated by FakeAP. There are several reasons for this. First, by default, FakeAP generates only four fake SSIDs per second. Driving by a system configured with FakeAP is unlikely to register because by the time enough fake access points have been generated for you to notice an anomaly, you will be out of range. Second, FakeAP can be configured to use any dictionary wordlist. This means that the SSIDs will appear to be normal SSIDs. There is no pattern that can be picked out or set of words that can be automatically discounted as FakeAP-generated. Finally, FakeAP can be configured to generate both WEP-encrypted and unencrypted fake access points. In short, this means that because FakeAPs beacons are so random and realistic, it cannot be detected.

In most cases, FakeAP will not be a serious problem for WarDrivers; however, if you happen to get stopped at a traffic light in range of FakeAP, you will have a large number of non-existent access points in your logs that you will either want to remove, or which will cause you to stop your WarDriving application and restart it after you are safely out of range of the system running FakeAP.

Disabling the TCP/IP Stack in Windows

By disabling the TCP/IP stack in windows, your laptop will not have the functionality to connect to any network. This is a very simple process that you will need to perform before each WarDrive.

1. In Windows 2000/XP, right-click **Network Neighborhood** icon and then choose **Properties**, as shown in Figure 1.20.

Figure 1.20 Disabling the TCP/IP Stack Step One

2. This will open the Network and Dial-Up Configurations window.
    There may be several network adapters listed here. Locate your wireless
    network card and right-click it, then choose **Properties** again, as shown
    in Figure 1.21.

Figure 1.21 Disabling the TCP/IP Stack Step Two

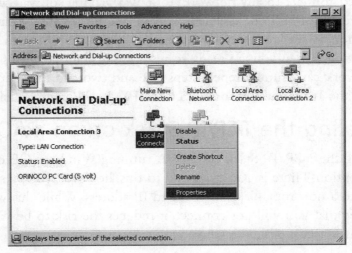

3. This will open the Properties for your wireless network card. Next,
    simply remove the check from the **Internet Protocol (TCP/IP)**
    checkbox and then choose **OK**. The before and after views of the dialog
    box can be seen in Figure 1.22.

Figure 1.22 Disabling the TCP/IP Stack Step Three

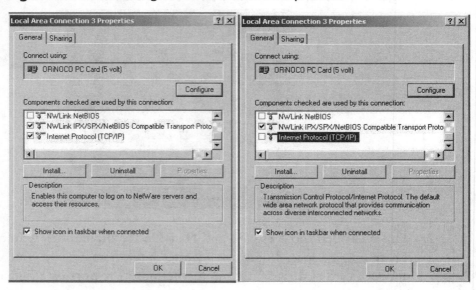

Your TCP/IP stack is now disabled and your wireless network card will not be able to connect to any network. Your WarDriving software will function perfectly even with TCP/IP disabled but you will not expose yourself to possible legal action by inadvertently connecting to a network that you discover while WarDriving. When you are ready to resume normal operations with your wireless network card, simply repeat steps one and two and then replace the checkmark in the **Internet Protocol (TCP/IP)** checkbox and click **OK**.

Disabling the TCP/IP Stack on an iPAQ

Disabling the TCP/IP Stack on a PDA running Windows CE or Pocket PC is not an option. There is a workaround to this, however; you can set your IP address to a non-routable, non-standard IP address. While this won't absolutely guarantee that you will not connect, it reduces the risk to be virtually non-existent. This is accomplished in three easy steps.

1. Click **Start | Settings** and then choose the **Connections** Tab, as shown in Figure 1.23.

Figure 1.23 Setting a Non-Standard IP Address on a Pocket PC
Step 1

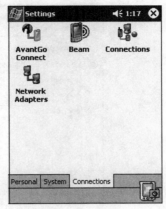

2. Next, click the **Network Adapters** icon. This will bring up a listing of the network adapters that are installed on the handheld device. Select the **HP Wireless Network Driver** and click **Properties** (see Figure 1.24).

Figure 1.24 Setting a Non-Standard IP Address on a Pocket PC
Step 2

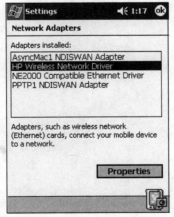

3. Finally, select the **Use Specific IP address** radio button. In the IP address field, set the IP address to **0.0.0.1** and the subnet mask to **255.0.0.0**. Leave the default gateway field blank. Your window should look similar to the window shown in Figure 1.25. Once these values have been set, click **OK**.

Figure 1.25 Setting a Non-Standard IP Address on a Pocket PC Step 3

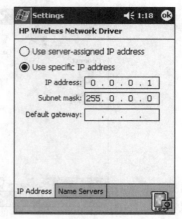

After you have clicked **OK**, a pop-up window will appear letting you know that your settings will take effect the next time the adapter is used. Simply click **OK** and then remove and reinsert the PCMCIA card. You can now begin your WarDrive without worrying about connecting to an access point inadvertently.

Summary

WarDriving, despite the negative connotations that some media outlets have attached to it, is an activity that is not only fun, but that can provide a valuable source of security information to the user community. By WarDriving an area and generating maps and statistical analysis of the security posture of the wireless networks in that region, the residents or businesses there can determine what steps they need to take to secure their wireless networks. Providing this general information can help generate an awareness of the necessity to enable the built-in security measures available on most access points.

If you decide to WarDrive using a laptop computer configuration, you will need to determine the operating system and WarDriving software package you plan to use. Once you have loaded these, you need to insert your wireless NIC card into a PCMCIA slot on your laptop. Next, attach the handheld GPS unit to the serial or USB port on the laptop. Using the appropriate pigtail, connect your choice of an omni-directional antenna, directional antenna, or both to your wireless NIC. If you don't want to run on battery power, connect your laptop computer's power cable to a power inverter. Next, disable the TCP/IP stack if you are using Windows to avoid inadvertent connections to any poorly configured wireless networks. Once all of your connections are in place and you have a power source for the laptop, simply start up your WarDriving software and begin your WarDrive.

Using a PDA setup is a similar process. Insert your wireless NIC into a PCMCIA sleeve for the PDA. Next, attach your external antenna(s) by connecting them to the appropriate pigtail for your wireless NIC. Connect your GPS to its data cable and the serial cable to a null modem connector. Following this, you will need to connect your PDA's proprietary cable to your PDA input slot and the other end to the null modem connector. If you don't want to risk losing power on your PDA in the middle of the drive, you should connect your PDA to a cigarette lighter power source. Next, set your IP Address to 0.0.0.1 with a subnet mask of 255.0.0.0 and no default gateway. Now, simply turn on the PDA and start your WarDriving software.

Solutions Fast Track

The Origins of WarDriving

☑ WarDriving is the act of moving around a certain area and mapping the population of wireless access points for statistical purposes and to raise awareness of the security problems associated with these types of networks. WarDriving does not in any way imply using these wireless access points without authorization.

☑ The term WarDriving refers to all wireless discovery activity (WarFlying, WarWalking, and so forth).

☑ The term WarDriving originates from WarDialing, the practice of using a modem attached to a computer to dial an entire exchange of telephone numbers to locate any computers with modems attached to them. This activity was dubbed WarDialing because it was introduced to the general public by Matthew Broderick's character, David Lightman, in the 1983 movie, *WarGames.*

☑ The FBI has stated that WarDriving, according to its true meaning, is not illegal in the United States.

Tools of the Trade or "What Do I Need?"

☑ There are two primary hardware setups for WarDriving:

a. A laptop computer

b. A Personal Digital Assistant (PDA)

☑ In order to WarDrive, you will need:

a. A wireless network interface card (NIC), preferably with an external antenna connector.

b. An external antenna of which two types are primarily used:

i. Omni-directional antennas are used to WarDrive when you want to pick up as many access points as possible in all directions.

ii. Directional antennas are used to WarDrive when attempting to pinpoint particular access points in a known location or direction.

c. A pigtail with the proper connectors for use in attaching your antenna to your wireless network card.

d. A handheld GPS capable of NMEA output.

e. An external power source such as a power inverter or cigarette lighter adapter is beneficial.

Putting It All Together

☑ When using Windows operating systems, you should disable the TCP/IP stack to avoid inadvertently connecting to misconfigured wireless networks.

☑ When using a Pocket PC or Windows CE, you should set a non-standard IP address and subnet mask to avoid inadvertently connecting to misconfigured wireless networks.

☑ Because the tools for use in the Linux operating system use monitor mode, no additional configuration is necessary.

Frequently Asked Questions

The following Frequently Asked Questions, answered by the authors of this book, are designed to both measure your understanding of the concepts presented in this chapter and to assist you with real-life implementation of these concepts. To have your questions about this chapter answered by the author, browse to **www.syngress.com/solutions** and click on the **"Ask the Author"** form. You will also gain access to thousands of other FAQs at ITFAQnet.com.

Q: Since store-bought wireless NICs don't have external antenna connectors, where can I purchase cards that have them?

A: Both Wireless Central (www.wirelesscentral.net) and Fleeman, Anderson, and Bird Corporation (www.fab-corp.com) sell cards with external antenna connectors. They also sell pigtails, antennas, and other wireless accessories.

Q: What is the difference between using the NMEA standard when WarDriving and the Garmin proprietary standard?

A: The NMEA standard reports its signal to your WarDriving software every two seconds. The Garmin standard reports its signal once each second. The Garmin standard can provide a more accurate location for each access point found while WarDriving.

Q: Why can't I find an 802.11a PCMCIA NIC with an external antenna connection?

A: Because 802.11a cards that are sold today use both UNII1 and UNII2. The FCC has ruled that any UNII1 devices may not be connected to an external antenna. These restrictions obviously apply only in the United States.

Q: What are the frequencies used by of each of the 2.4 GHz channels?

A: There are 11 channels used in the United States and Canada and 13 channels in Europe on the 2.4 GHz spectrum starting with Channel 1 at 2.412 GHz and incremented by 0.005 GHz for each channel. See Table 1.2 for additional details.

Table 1.2 Frequency Assignments for 2.4 GHz Band

Channel	GHz
Channel 1	2.412
Channel 2	2.417
Channel 3	2.422
Channel 4	2.427
Channel 5	2.432
Channel 6	2.437
Channel 7	2.442
Channel 8	2.447
Channel 9	2.452
Channel 10	2.457
Channel 11	2.462
Channel 12	2.467
Channel 13	2.472

Q: Both 802.11a and 802.11g networks support speeds of up to 54 Mbps. What is the difference between the two standards?

A: There are many differences between the two standards. Two primary ones are that 802.11a operates in the 5.0 GHz spectrum while 802.11g operates in the 2.4 GHz spectrum. Because of the frequency spectrum they're associated with, 802.11g networks support greater distances than 802.11a networks.

Q: Are there any good online information resources that WarDrivers should check out?

A: User-supported forums are an excellent place to both learn and exchange information with other WarDrivers. Two of the best are the NetStumbler Forums (http://forums.netstumbler.com) and the Kismet forums (www.kismetwireless.net/forum.php). Topics ranging from specific hardware issues to ethics to topical news discussions can be found at both sites.

Chapter 2

NetStumbler and MiniStumbler: Overview

Solutions in this Chapter:

- How NetStumbler and MiniStumbler Work
- Wireless Ethernet Cards that Work with NetStumbler and MiniStumbler
- Minimum System Requirements
- Installation
- Running NetStumbler
- NetStumbler Menus and Tool Icons
- Running MiniStumbler
- MiniStumbler Menus and Tool Icons

- ☑ Summary
- ☑ Solutions Fast Track
- ☑ Frequently Asked Questions

Introduction

NetStumbler is *the* application for WarDrivers who use Microsoft Windows as their operating system. While the term "killer application" is often overused to describe programs, NetStumbler certainly comes close to that description for many wireless network users. It has helped thousands of networking and security specialists in their jobs, and its ease of use has certainly advanced the popularity of WarDriving as a hobby.

If you are interested in locating wireless local area networks (WLANs) for professional use or have taken up the hobby of WarDriving, then you have probably heard of NetStumbler. NetStumbler has taken the wireless networking world by storm. From network administrators to law enforcement officials and every WarDriver in between, NetStumbler has become the wireless network tool of choice for thousands of users. It has a straightforward interface that most new WarDrivers can readily use, yet it is sophisticated enough to have radio frequency (RF) and networking tools to satisfy both computer networking and radio professionals.

NetStumbler has so influenced the world of Wireless LAN discovery that many users no longer call the activity "WarDriving," but instead refer to it as "netstumbling" or simply "stumbling."

So what is NetStumbler? Network Stumbler (the official name) is a wireless network detector and analysis tool. Marius Milner, the writer of the application, created the first version in early 2001, just as the price of 802.11b wireless networking devices were starting to become affordable on the consumer markets. While Peter Shipley of San Francisco is generally credited with creating the first WarDriving PERL scripts in April of 2001, Marius Milner was right behind Mr. Shipley, releasing the first beta version of NetStumbler a month later in May, 2001.

NetStumbler detects wireless local area networks (WLANs) that are based on the 802.11b and 802.11g data formats in the Industrial Scientific and Medical (ISM) radio band and Unlicensed National Information Infrastructure (U–NII), a band using 802.11a data formats. Furthermore, it provides radio frequency (RF) signal information and other data related to the peculiarities of combining computers and radios. NetStumbler may also provide information on the band and data format being used, depending on what wireless networking card is being implemented: 802.11b, 802.11a, or 802.11g. Since the first version, Marius has continued to improve the application, adding features and refinements to each release.

NOTE

There are several parts to the wireless standard known as IEEE 802.11. Here's a quick summary:

- **802.11** Has data speeds of up to 2 megabits per second (Mbps) and uses either Frequency Hopping Spread Spectrum (FHSS) or Direct-Sequence Spread Spectrum (DSSS) transmission techniques. Even though both are based in the ISM radio band, FHSS and DSSS devices cannot network with each other.
- **802.11a** Has data speeds of up to 54 Mbps and uses the Orthogonal Frequency Division Multiplexing (OFDM) technique in the U-NII radio band.
- **802.11b** Has data speeds of up to 11 Mbps and uses only the DSSS technique in the ISM radio band. It's backward-compatible with 802.11 DSSS devices.
- **802.11g** Has data speeds of up to 54Mbps and uses both OFDM and DSSS techniques in the ISM radio band. Use of the DSSS allows it to be backward-compatible with 802.11b and 802.11 DSSS devices.

While 802.11 debuted in the mid-1990s, wireless networking didn't become a big consumer item until the introduction of inexpensive 802.11b equipment in 2001. Even though the 802.11a standard was ratified just prior to 802.11b, most manufacturers made "b" equipment first. 802.11a has a very short range in comparison to any of the other standards due to the U-NII band, and has never gained much popularity. The newest standard, 802.11g, was ratified in 2003, and is backward-compatible with 802.11b and 802.11 DSSS equipment. For these reasons, 802.11b enjoys the most popular use, with 802.11g catching up quickly.

If you want to learn more about the standards, www.hpl.hp.com/personal/Jean_Tourrilhes/Linux/Linux.Wireless.std.html has some detailed information on how they came about.

The next two chapters will introduce you to NetStumbler and how to use it to your fullest advantage in your WarDriving endeavors. We will also discuss MiniStumbler, the PocketPC version of NetStumbler. Much of what is covered involves both programs, and in areas where those programs differ, there will be information specific to each application. As of this writing, the current release of both NetStumbler and MiniStumbler is v.0.4.0.

How NetStumbler and MiniStumbler Work

Both NetStumbler and MiniStumbler are active wireless network detection applications (see the sidebar *"'Active' versus 'Passive' WLAN Detection"* for more details). NetStumbler does not passively listen for, or receive, beacons.

Tools & Traps...

"Active" versus "Passive" WLAN Detection

NetStumbler is an "active" wireless network detection application. This means the program takes a specific action to accomplish the WLAN detection. The action is to send out a specific data probe called a *Probe Request*. The Probe Request frame and the associated Probe Response frame are part of the 802.11 standard. Applications that employ the "passive" detection procedure do not broadcast any signals. Instead, these programs listen to the radio band, waiting to hear any 802.11 traffic that may be within range of the wireless card, but do not initiate such traffic on their own. Much like the Windows versus Linux debate, the proponents of both detection methods at times get involved in intense debates over which method is better. Suffice it to say, both approaches have their good and bad points. Therefore, tools using both techniques deserve their proper place in your WarDriving toolkit.

At the default rate of approximately once per second, NetStumbler sends out a Probe Request frame, and then listens for any responding Probe Response data frames from access points or ad-hoc networks that are in range. In simple terms, the request is an electronic "Hello! Is anyone there?" while the Probe Response is the answer to that question. When it answers, the access point (AP or peers in an ad-hoc network) responds with certain information such as the wireless network name, called the Service Set Identifier (SSID) and Machine Access Code (MAC) numbers. The response is the 802.11 equivalent of: "Oh, hello! I'm here! My MAC is 00:00:00:00:00:00 and my SSID is MySSID." If the request receives any response, then NetStumbler logs the information and reports it to the user via the interface.

If it detects an infrastructure wireless LAN, NetStumbler will then request the AP's name, if it uses the ORiNOCO or Cisco naming convention. When it finds an ad-hoc WLAN, it will request the names of all the peers it sees if they behave like an ORiNOCO or Cisco access point.

In addition, the interface of NetStumbler provides filtering and analysis tools for the user. These tools allow the user to filter out the number of access points and WLANs based on criteria such as those networks that are using encrypted traffic.

Damage & Defense...

Disabling the Beacon

NetStumbler transmits a "Broadcast Request" probe to discover the WLAN. Most access points will respond to a Broadcast Request by default. When it responds, the AP transmits its SSID, MAC number, and other information. However, many brands and models of AP allow this feature to be disabled. Once an AP ceases to respond to the request, NetStumbler can no longer detect it. If you don't want your wireless LAN to show up on the screen of another NetStumbler user, disable the SSID broadcast on your access point. Check your AP manual for "Disable SSID Broadcast", "Closed SSID," or similar features.

   The one caveat to this is if the SSID that the WarDriver enters for NetStumbler happens to have the same SSID as your network, then your AP will still respond to the probe. This is another good reason to change the default SSID. This material will be further described in Chapter 10 (Basic Wireless Network Security).

Wireless Ethernet Cards that Work with NetStumbler and MiniStumbler

To use NetStumbler or MiniStumbler, you need a wireless Ethernet card. There are a wide variety of makes and models available, and every day new models are released, so the question becomes: Which ones work with NetStumbler? Generally, the best cards are those that use the Hermes chipset. Primarily, this refers to the ORiNOCO Gold or Silver "Classic" cards or "re-badged" versions of those cards. The big disadvantage to these cards, however, is that they only work with 802.11b data. "Re-badges", are made by manufacturers such as ORiNOCO, but sold under another brand name, such as Dell. The marking decals or "badge" is changed to reflect the new brand, hence the term "re-badge." Table 2.1 contains a list of the Hermes cards. Most of these are re-badged ORiNOCO brand cards.

Table 2.1 Common Hermes Chipset Cards

Lucent Technologies WaveLAN/IEEE (Agere ORiNOCO)
Dell TrueMobile 1150 Series (PCMCIA and mini-PCI)
Avaya Wireless PC Card
Toshiba Wireless LAN Card (PCMCIA and built-in)
Compaq WL110 Cabletron/Enterasys Roamabout
Elsa Airlancer MC-11
ARtem ComCard 11Mbps
IBM High Rate Wireless LAN PC Card
1stWave 1ST-PC-DSS11IS, DSS11IG, DSS11ES, DSS11EG

NetStumbler 0.4.0 also has expanded support for the following types of cards: 802.11a cards, 802.11a/b dual-mode cards, and 802.11a/b/g tri-mode cards (all based on the Atheros chipset), and 802.11b cards based on the Intersil Prism, Atmel, Broadcom, and Centrino chipsets.

The ORiNOCO cards still offer one major advantage that many other brands and models of cards do not have: An external antenna connection. While it is possible to perform a hardware hack and add a connector to almost any card, it is much easier for the user and the card to use a connector installed by the manufacturer.

MiniStumbler 0.4.0 will work with the built-in WiFi of the Toshiba e740. In the CompactFlash (CF) format, the Dell TrueMobile 1180 and the Buffalo AirStation WLI-CF-S11G both work. The D-Link DCF-650W CF format will function if the Buffalo CF driver is used with it. In the PC form factor, these cards will work: the Proxim/Agere ORiNOCO (also known as the Lucent WaveLAN/IEEE), the Compaq WL110, the Dell TrueMobile 1150 (using the

ORiNOCO driver), the Buffalo Airstation WLI-PCM-L11GP (also using the ORiNOCO driver), and the Senao NL-2511CD. For those cards using the ORiNOCO driver, version 7.*x* or later of the driver must be used.

NOTE

One caution about the ORiNOCO cards: In mid-2003 the Proxim company, which produced a rival brand of wireless cards, purchased the ORiNOCO line. They then began a new line of cards, utilizing a new chipset, but calling them ORiNOCO Silver and Gold. This caused much confusion among wireless users, as many applications and hardware (including some ORiNOCO brand Access Points) were not working correctly with the new cards. The older cards quickly became know as the "Classics" by those involved in wireless networking. If you are going to be purchasing an ORiNOCO card, make sure you get the correct model numbers. Model 8410 is for the "Classic" Hermes-based cards (FCC ID: IMRWLPCE24H), while the new cards are marked as Model 8420 (FCC ID: IMRPC2411B). Aside from the different model numbers, the newer cards are marked with a logo of waving businessman, and display the name "Proxim" in addition to the name ORiNOCO. At the antenna end of the card, which extends out of the laptop, they are also marked "Proxim."

Fortunately, NetStumbler and MiniStumbler 0.4.0 do work with the new cards, so WarDrivers can now use either the new cards or the "Classics."

New cards and chipsets are coming out all the time, and users naturally want to know if they will work with NetStumbler. The answer is a definite "maybe." It depends on the chipset, operating system, and the drivers. Users of Windows 95, Windows 98, and Windows ME are only able to use the wireless cards listed in the README file, which are mostly Hermes chipset cards. Users of Windows 2000 or XP *may* use cards based on other chipsets. Usually, this will require use of the Network Device Interface Specification (NDIS) version 5.1 drivers. However, sometimes these card and driver combinations will not work with NetStumbler at all. Other times, users report initial success using a particular card, only to find it later fails for some unknown reason. Additionally, most users of NDIS 5.1 say that some of the features of NetStumbler do not work properly. More information about this is detailed in Chapter 3. According to the README file, Windows NT 4.0 has not been tested with NetStumbler, and is therefore not recommended as an

OS. However, at least one user on the NetStumbler discussion forums http://forums.netstumbler.com reported that NetStumbler works with WinNT 4.0 and Service Pack 5.

Minimum System Requirements

There are no official minimum system requirements for NetStumbler. However, the executable file of Version 0.4.0 is only 532KB in size. With the program and ancillary files consuming only 2 megabytes of disk space, the whole package is rather tiny by today's standards. Obviously, you will need a PC. Most WarDrivers prefer a laptop or micro PC such as a Libretto, although some hardy individuals have been known to equip their vehicles with full-size tower systems.

Some members of the NetStumbler forums have setups that are rather minimal in terms of computing power. The lowest end system I personally know of is a 75MHz Pentium I with 16MB of RAM, running Window95. My personal "stumbling rig" is an IBM ThinkPad, Model 355CD. It is a 100MHz Pentium I, with 16MB of RAM, and is running Windows98SE. While not quite ready for a PC museum, it is hardly state-of-the-art. There are few programs produced within the last five years that this machine could comfortably run, yet it handles "stumbling" just fine.

To run MiniStumbler, you must have a handheld or mobile device running Windows Handheld PC 2000, Pocket PC 3.0, or Pocket PC 2002. Windows Pocket PC 2003 is not yet supported. If a PC Card or Personal Computer Memory Card International Association (PCMCIA) wireless card is to be used with the handheld, then an expansion pack or other device capable of attaching the card to the mobile device is required.

The one option that most WarDrivers use is the Global Positioning System (GPS) satellite receiver. These devices determine your position on the earth by triangulating off satellite signals. Both NetStumbler and MiniStumbler will talk to many GPS receivers via a serial link, and record the location of a wireless network based on the data from the GPS.

The second optional device that most WarDrivers have is an external antenna for their vehicle. These come in a variety of shapes, sizes, and power gain levels. In addition to a laptop (or handheld) PC, wireless card, and the optional GPS and antenna, you will likely need different cables, power supplies, and adapters to successfully conduct a WarDrive. Those items will be covered in detail in Chapter 3.

Installation

Installation of both NetStumbler and MiniStumbler is straightforward. First, download the appropriate installer package from www.netstumbler.com or Marius Milner's page at www.stumbler.net. The download for the NetStumbler installer is 1.08MB, and 1.17MB for MiniStumbler. While it may seem odd that the "mini" version of the program has a larger download, the reason is simple. The MiniStumbler installer actually carries a payload containing six slightly different versions of the program, one for each of the most popular processors and operating system combinations used in handheld PCs. They are

- PPC2000 running on the ARM processor
- PPC2000 running on the MIPS processor
- PPC2000 running on the SH3 processor
- HPC2000 running on the ARM processor
- HPC2000 running on the MIPS processor
- PPC2002 running on the ARM processor

NetStumbler Installation

Once downloaded, run the installer. The installer starts by asking you which options you would like to install. See Figure 2.1.

Figure 2.1 Installation Options

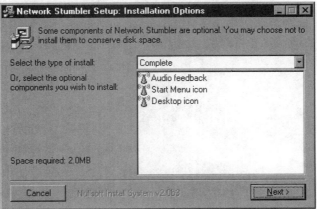

For convenience, I recommend installing the complete package. The Audio Feedback sounds may be turned off via either software or hardware, and the icons and Start menu can be deleted or rearranged as you deem necessary.

The installer then asks the user for an installation folder, as seen in Figure 2.2. Unless you have a need for a different directory, stick with the default folder of C:\Program Files\Network Stumbler.

Figure 2.2 Installation Folder

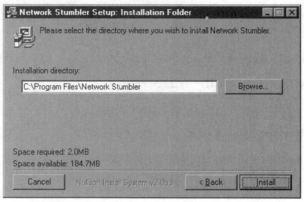

A progress bar then appears, showing how the installation is proceeding. As you can see in Figure 2.3, when the setup is complete, a Show Details button is enabled.

Figure 2.3 Completed Installation

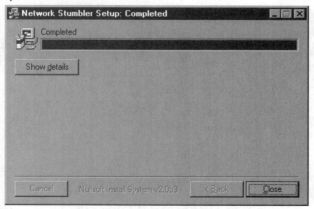

Figure 2.4 shows that by clicking the **Show Details** button, you can see exactly what files were extracted and the directory where each one was placed.

Figure 2.4 Installation Details

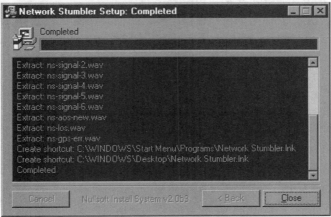

At the completion of the setup, the Installer program asks if you would like to see the readme file, as per Figure 2.5. It's strongly recommended that you read it. It is relatively short as readme files go, and contains important information about running and using NetStumbler.

Figure 2.5 The Option to View the readme File

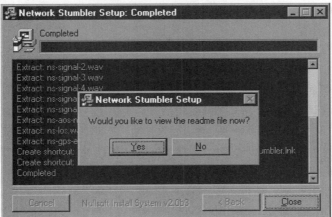

MiniStumbler Installation

Installing MiniStumbler is similar to the NetStumbler installation process. First, make sure that the handheld is in communication with the host PC, and then run the MiniStumblerInstaller.exe program.

Figure 2.6 shows the installer running. First, the installer displays a status bar as the PC communicates with the handheld PC. You may see the Add/Remove program for the handheld running in the background.

Figure 2.6 The MiniStumbler Installer Running

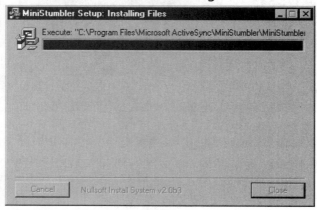

Next, the Installer prompts you for the default installation directory, as seen in Figure 2.7. Again, unless you have good reason to change it, use the default directory.

Figure 2.7 Directory Selection

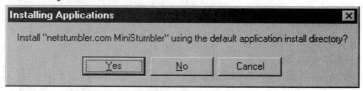

Figure 2.8 shows a second status bar, which opens as the installer actually places the executable and support files on the handheld device.

Figure 2.8 Installation Progress

You will be prompted to read the readme file, as seen in Figure 2.9. Taking the few minutes to review its contents may save you hours of effort later.

Figure 2.9 View the readme File

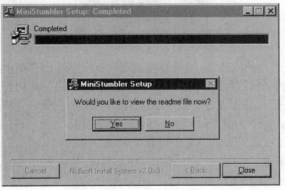

Once it has completed that step, the Installer reminds you to check the hand-held device to make sure no other steps are needed to complete the installation. The reminder is displayed in Figure 2.10.

Figure 2.10 The Reminder

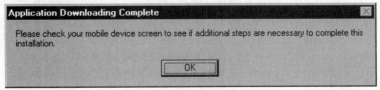

Once the Installer has finished, MiniStumbler should be fully installed on your mobile PC and ready for use.

Running NetStumbler

To start NetStumbler, select the **Network Stumbler** desktop icon seen in Figure 2.11, or choose **Network Stumbler** from the **Start | Programs** menu.

Figure 2.11 The Network Stumbler Desktop Icon

When NetStumbler starts, it immediately attempts to locate a usable wireless card and a GPS receiver. The application also opens a new file, with the extension of NS1. The extension NS1 simply stands for NetStumbler1. The file name is derived from the date and time when NetStumbler was started, and is in the format YYYYMMDDHHMMSS.ns1. If a wireless card is located, then the program begins to scan for nearby access points. The data from any located APs are immediately entered into the new file.

Two splash screens open, one after the other, when NetStumbler starts. Both look the same as Figure 2.12, with the exception that the second one has information regarding the installed wireless card that NetStumbler has detected. Information such as the MAC number and Firmware revisions will show, depending on the specifics of the cards installed, and which one was detected initially.

Figure 2.12 Opening Splash Screens

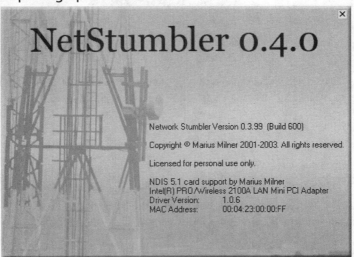

Notes from the Underground...

Registry Entries

When NetStumbler v.0.4.0 starts, it checks the Registry for the following listed entries. If they are not present, the program will create them. Many of the Registry entries have empty or zero values and data when using the default setting. A value is added only if the default is changed. While few users will have any reason to actually go into the Registry to change these settings, they have been included here for completeness.

```
[HKEY_CURRENT_USER\Software\Bogosoft]

[HKEY_CURRENT_USER\Software\Bogosoft\NetStumbler]

[HKEY_CURRENT_USER\Software\Bogosoft\NetStumbler\Recent File List]

"File1"="C:\\Program Files\\Network Stumbler\\20031027113735.ns1"

"File2"="C:\\Program Files\\Network Stumbler\\20031026103653.ns1"

"File3"="C:\\Program Files\\Network Stumbler\\20031022065233.ns1"

"File4"="C:\\Program Files\\Network Stumbler\\20031021071721.ns1"

[HKEY_CURRENT_USER\Software\Bogosoft\NetStumbler\Settings]
```

Continued

```
"Auto Save"=dword:00000001

"Auto Configure"=dword:00000000

"View
Defaults"=hex:01,00,00,00,c8,00,00,00,00,00,00,00,00,00,00,00,00,00
,00,\
00,00,00,00,00,00,00,00,00,00,00,00,00,00,00,00,00,00,00,00,00,00,0
0,00,00,\00,00,00,00,00,00,00,00,00,00,00,00,00,00,00,00,00,00,00,0
0,00,00,00,00,13,\
00,00,00,00,00,00,00,01,00,00,00,10,00,00,00,6e,00,0b,00,01,00,76,0
0,0c,00,\02,00,5a,00,0f,00,03,00,28,00,1d,00,04,00,3c,00,19,00,05,0
0,28,00,13,00,06,\00,28,00,16,00,07,00,28,00,1a,00,08,00,37,00,1b,0
0,09,00,2d,00,1c,00,0a,00,\2d,00,0d,00,0b,00,50,00,0e,00,0c,00,50,0
0,11,00,0d,00,46,00,12,00,0e,00,46,\00,14,00,0f,00,2d,00,15,00,10,0
0,2d,00,17,00,11,00,28,00,18,00,12,00,32,00,\00,00,00,00,00,00,00,0
0,00,00,00,00,00,00,00,00,00,00,00,00,00,00,00,00,\00,00,00,00,00,0
0,00,00,00,00,00,00,00,00,00,00,00,00,00,00,00,00,00,00,\00,0
0,00,00,00,00,00,00,00,00,00,00,00,00,00,00,00,00,00,00,00,00,00,00
,00,\00,00,00

"GPS Port"=dword:00000001

"Font"=hex:f3,ff,ff,ff,00,00,00,00,00,00,00,00,00,00,00,00,bc,02,00
,00,00,00,\
00,00,01,02,01,22,4d,53,20,53,61,6e,73,20,53,65,72,69,66,00,07,00,5
0,10,57,\
17,08,00,40,41,a7,16,02,00,ae,37,ac,50

"Get AP Name"=dword:00000001

"Auto Start Scan"=dword:00000001

"Auto Speed"=dword:00000001

"Speed"=dword:00000003

"Script Type"=dword:00000001

"Midi Enable"=dword:00000000

"Midi Channel"=dword:00000000

"Midi Patch"=dword:00000000

"Midi Transpose"=dword:00000014

"Device"="wUson48.VXD"

"Device Key"="0005"

"Device Type"=dword:00000003
```

Figures 2.13 though 2.18 show NetStumbler data captured from a typical WarDriving session using NetStumbler 0.4.0. The data shown here was recently captured "live and in the wild." Using this data, we will explore how to operate the NetStumbler user interface. The screen shots were made after the WarDriving session. As a result, the status bar at the bottom of the screen shows that the NetStumbler was not actively scanning for networks, and that the GPS was disabled at the time.

In Figure 2.13, you can see that a total of 16 wireless networks were found.

Figure 2.13 Captured Data Using NetStumbler

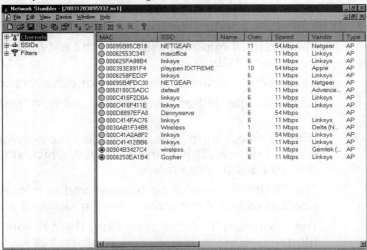

First, you will notice that the screen is divided into two panes. The pane on the left has a familiar tree structure, consisting of three levels: Channels, SSIDs, and Filters. The right pane has a list of detected networks. Each row in the right pane is for a single AP, an infrastructure network, or peer in an ad-hoc network. The rows are divided into 23 columns, containing much of the associated data that NetStumbler was able to determine about the AP or peer. Each column represents one item about a given access point or peer network. On most computers used for WarDriving, the screen setting will not allow all 23 columns to be displayed. Simply moving the scroll bar will allow you to view all the columns. The column headings and their associated meanings are detailed in Table 2.2.

Table 2.2 Right Pane Column Headings

Column Name	Description
MAC	Machine Address Code; a unique address for each Ethernet device. Preceding each MAC is a small circular icon. The icon will change according to several factors. Please see Table 2.3 for details.
SSID	Service Set Identifier; also known as the "Network Name."
Name	Access point name. Often blank, as it is not used by all brands of wireless equipment.
Chan	Channel number the network is operating on. In 802.11b communications, 1 to 14.
Speed	The reported maximum speed of the network, in megabits per second (Mbps).
Vendor	Equipment manufacturer's name or other brand identifier.
Type	Network type; either AP for access point, or peer for peer-to-peer.
Encryption	If the wireless traffic is encrypted on the network by the wireless devices, it is marked as WEP, which stands for "Wired Equivalency Privacy."
SNR	The RF signal-to-noise ratio; measured in microvolt deciBels (dBm). Only active when in range of a network.
Signal+	The maximum RF signal seen from the network device in dBm.
Noise-	The minimum RF noise reported at the device in dBm.
SNR+	The maximum RF signal-to-noise ratio reported at the device in dBm.
IP Addr	The reported Internet Protocol address, if any.
Subnet	Any reported network IP subnet, if any.
Latitude	Latitude as reported by the GPS receiver when NetStumbler saw the network.
Longitude	Longitude as reported by the GPS receiver when NetStumbler saw the network.
First Seen	The time when NetStumbler first saw the network.
Last Seen	The time when NetStumbler last saw the network.
Signal	The current RF signal level in dBm. Only active when in range of a network.

Continued

Table 2.2 Right Pane Column Headings

Column Name	Description
Noise	The current RF noise level in dBm. Only active when in range of a network.
Flags	802.11 flags from the network in hexadecimal (Base 16) code.
Beacon Interval	The interval of the beacon broadcast from the AP.
Distance	The distance to where you were when the best SNR was seen.

The terms in the column descriptions will be covered in more detail in Chapter 3.

As mentioned in the description for MAC in Table 2.2, small circular icons appear next to each Machine Address Code. The icons change color according to the radio signal strength, as listed in Table 2.3. Also, if the network is encrypted, then the icon will contain a padlock symbol, as shown in Figure 2.14. However, Figure 2.14 shows enlarged versions of the icons, so that you may compare the Open versus the Encrypted or locked icons.

Table 2.3 Encryption and Signal Icons

Color	Meaning
Grey No	signal
Red Poor	signal
Orange	Fair signal
Yellow	Good
Light Green	Better
Bright Green	Best

Figure 2.14 The Open and Encrypted Network Icons

The Channel indicators have three states, which you may see change as you are WarDriving:

- A channel number alone (for example, 5) means that NetStumbler located a given network on that channel.

- A channel number followed by an asterisk (for instance, 6★) means that NetStumbler is currently associated with a network on that channel.

- A channel number followed by a plus sign (say, 8+) means that NetStumbler recently associated with a network during this NS session.

The current and recent associations are not saved to the file.

Starting with the tree structure used in the left pane of Figure 2.15, let's look at how you can make use of the data. We can see the left pane has three items on the tree marked as Channels, SSIDs, and Filters. Beneath each one of those items you are able to selectively filter the data collected by NetStumbler to make better use of it. Both "Channels" and "SSIDs" consist of lists of the SSIDs and the Channels in use by the APs or networks that NetStumbler located. For example, this use of NetStumbler found 16 access points (none were ad-hoc networks.). By selecting **Channels** in the left pane, we can see that, of the 16 APs seen by NetStumbler, all of them were on only four channels: 1, 6, 10, and 11. By selecting **6**, we can see how many of those APs were on Channel 6, and the MAC of each AP. In this particular case, 13 of the access points were on just this one channel. (Manufacturers typically use Channel 6 as the default channel for access points.)

Figure 2.15 Filtering by Channels

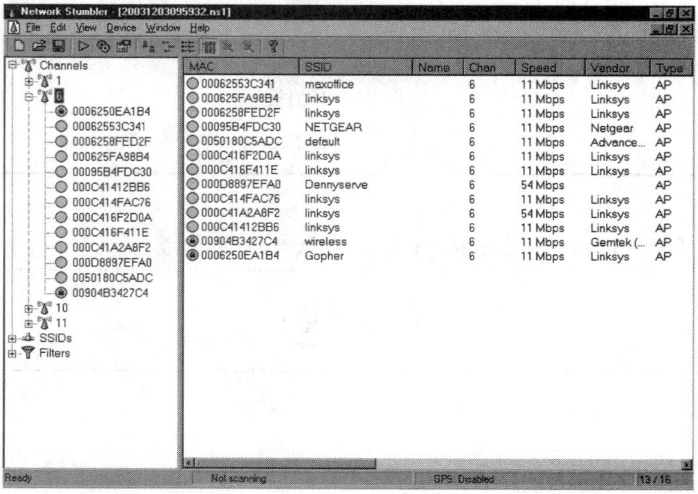

Also, if you look at the lower-right corner of the status bar, you will see the numerals 13/16. These two numbers represent the amount of APs in the current filter, and the total number of APs found. This is a quick way of determining the results of using a given filter. It is especially nice when filtering large amounts of data.

In the same way, selecting **SSIDs** will filter by the network names, as shown in Figure 2.16.

Figure 2.16 Filtering by SSID

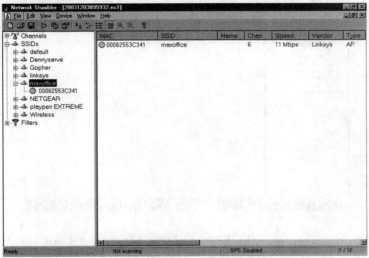

First, the SSID level is selected, and then the SSID of "maxoffice." Only one AP is seen here, as only one AP was located with that SSID, and the status line says 1/16.

Finally, the last level on the right pain is marked "Filters" and has nine standard filters for viewing the wireless networks you have found. These filters are

- Encryption Off
- Encryption On
- ESS (AP)
- IBSS (Peer)
- CF Pollable
- Short Preamble

- PBCC

- Short Slot Time (11g)

- Default SSID

We'll show two common examples of the filters here. First, Figure 2.17 shows filtering by networks using encryption.

Figure 2.17 Filter: Encryption On

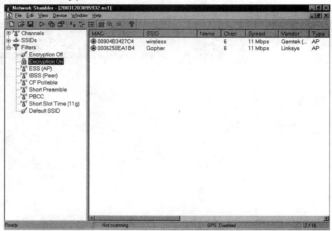

In the second example of the Filters use, in Figure 2.18, we see the APs using the default SSIDs that were set at the factory. While the program does not contain a complete list of all manufacturers and APs, it does have many of the most popular brands.

Figure 2.18 Filter: Default SSID

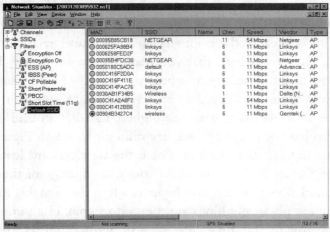

In each example of using the Filters, note that in the lower-right corner of the status bar, the number of networks meeting the filter criteria is shown in comparison to the total number of networks found.

Finally, going back to the Channels level of the tree for a moment, Figure 2.19 shows what happens when a MAC is selected under a particular channel. The standard right pane is replaced with a Signal-to-Noise Ratio graphic display.

Figure 2.19 Signal-to-Noise Ratio Graphic Display

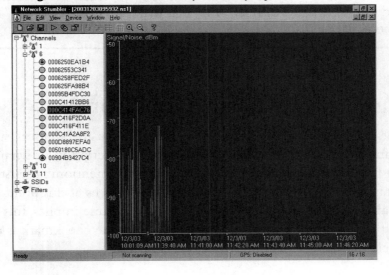

Signal Strength bars are in red and green. The upper (green) portion of the bars shows the RF signal above the noise, while the lower (red) section of each bar shows the noise level. You will notice that the deciBels are expressed in negative numbers. This is because the numbers measure power relative to one milliWatt (mW). The power level that your card receives is usually below a milliWatt, so most of the time, the numbers are negative. In this particular case, the noise level was running at approximately −97dBm to −99dBm, and the signal was, on average, about −80dBm, with the highest signal at around −66dBm. .

There are also bars of purple, which are difficult to see in Figure 2.19, but are there. Purple bars indicate the point at which the wireless card lost the radio signal. This usually occurs when the card passes out of range of the particular wireless network. However, it can also happen when the signal is momentarily lost due to an object physically blocking the radio signal. The radios used in wireless networks usually require a clear Line of Sight, often referred to as LOS, between antennae. When large objects such as a semi-trailer or building blocks the Line of Sight, many times the signal is lost.

NOTE

One word of caution about the term "Line of Sight." While LOS is usually a clear line that you can see from Point A to Point B, it isn't always true. Transmitted and received radio waves don't always behave in the manner we think they should, and the way in which they propagate is a whole science in and of itself. Just use the term "Line of Sight" with a grain of salt.

NetStumbler Menus and Tool Icons

Most of the menus used in NetStumbler will be familiar to PC users, such as File, Edit, and Windows, and will not need any real description or detailed instruction for use. However, several menus are worth mentioning. First, there is one non-standard item on the File menu that concerns us at this point. This is **File | Enable** scan, as shown in Figure 2.20. As the name implies, this enables or disables the scanning for wireless networks. When the checkmark is displayed, then the network card is scanning.

Figure 2.20 Enabling a Scan for Networks in NetStumbler

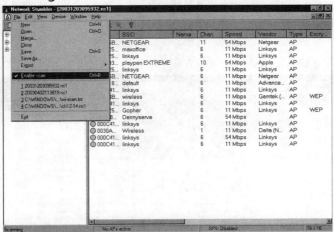

First, **View | Options** opens a dialog box containing many of the items needed to configure NetStumbler. This dialog box is shown in Figure 2.21. Chapter 3 will cover how and why you will be configuring those options to optimize your use of NetStumbler.

Figure 2.21 NetStumbler Options

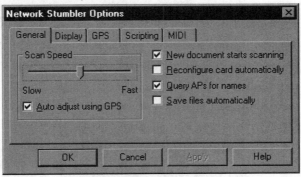

The other menu we should talk about is the Device menu, seen in Figure 2.22. Opening the Device menu shows a list of all network interface cards (NICs) detected on the computer. Some of those NICs will be grayed out if NetStumbler understands that they are network devices, but does not recognize them as wireless cards. Network devices that NetStumbler recognizes as wireless cards will be listed in black. At the bottom of that menu, is the **Use Any**

Suitable Device option. Checking this option allows NetStumbler to automatically select the first wireless device on the menu, if one has been detected when the program started.

Figure 2.22 The Device Menu

Toolbar Icons

In much the same way as the menus, most of the icons in the toolbar should be familiar to Windows users. The standard icons such as New, Open, and Save are all visible. Three new icons are present however, as you can see in Figure 2.23. There is a green arrow pointing to the right, two over-lapping gears, and a hand holding a menu.

Figure 2.23 New Toolbar Icons

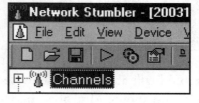

The green arrow icon enables or disables the wireless card from scanning for networks, the same as **File | Enable** scan menu item. The gears automatically configure the wireless card for scanning, and the hand-holding-the-menu symbol opens the same Options dialog box we saw in Figure 2.21. These options will be expanded upon in Chapter 3 when we cover the actual configuration and setup for WarDriving.

Running MiniStumbler

MiniStumbler is NetStumbler's "little brother." Where NetStumbler needs a full-fledged PC or laptop to run, MiniStumbler only requires a handheld Windows computer such as an iPAQ PocketPC. Due to the physically smaller size of the package, using MiniStumbler is much more versatile. Obviously, you are able to carry an operating PocketPC in places where it would be awkward or even impossible to carry a laptop. This versatility does come at a price, however. Owning to the nature of the mobile package, some of the features of NetStumbler have been left out of MiniStumbler.

The fact that MiniStumbler is a stripped down version of NetStumbler should not dissuade you from using it. It records all the same data as its big brother. If you want to employ filtering on captured data, it is a simple matter of transferring the data to a PC, and doing the needed analysis with NetStumbler. Figure 2.24 shows the user interface for MiniStumbler.

Starting MiniStumbler is done by tapping the Start menu on the mobile. If you let the installer use the default values, then MS should be on the Start menu. Otherwise, it should be under Start Programs.

Figure 2.24 Captured Data Using MiniStumbler

The MiniStumbler user interface is essentially the same as the Right Pane of NetStumbler. It contains the same columns as NetStumbler. You may want to refer back to Table 2.2, for a quick refresher on all of them. Since there is no left pane, there are no filters for the user to apply on the captured data.

Also, there is no secondary right pane. You have to do without the graphic Signal-to-Noise function when using MiniStumbler.

Like NetStumbler, when MiniStumbler starts, it immediately attempts to locate a usable wireless card and a GPS receiver. MiniStumbler then opens a new file, with the extension of NS1. Just like its big brother, the file name is based on the date and time, and is in the format YYYYMMDDHHMMSS.ns1. After finding the wireless card, MiniStumbler scans the airwaves for nearby WLANs. The data from any located networks is immediately entered into the new file.

MiniStumbler Menus and Tool Icons

Looking at the bottom of Figure 2.24, you can see there are two menus, File and View, and the same three special tool icons. The File menu performs the standard functions such as opening, and saving files, and has an added checkmark next to "Enable Scan" as shown in Figure 2.25. As the name implies, this box enables or disables the scanning for networks. **View | Options** brings up the MiniStumbler Options screen, which will be covered in Chapter 3. The Options screen is seen in Figure 2.26.

Figure 2.25 Enabling a Scan for Networks in MiniStumbler

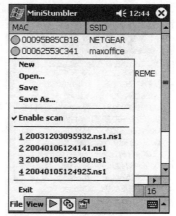

Figure 2.26 MiniStumbler Options

The tool icons perform exactly the same functions as their NetStumbler counterparts. The green arrow icon enables or disables the wireless card from scanning, while the gears automatically configure the wireless card for scanning. The hand–holding–the–menu symbol opens the same Options screen.

Summary

NetStumbler and MiniStumbler are the applications of choice for WarDrivers that use the Windows operating systems. Both programs quickly and easily detect wireless networks, and supply the user with a wealth of needed information. This chapter has introduced the basic operation of both NetStumbler and MiniStumbler, and should get you up and running with either version of the program. We have discussed installation procedures for both programs, the user interface for both NetStumbler and MiniStumbler, and some of the menus and features unique to the applications.

Solutions Fast Track

How NetStumbler and MiniStumbler Work

- ☑ Both NetStumbler and MiniStumbler are active applications.
- ☑ About once per second, NetStumbler transmits a Probe Request frame. The program then listens for any responding Probe Response data.

Wireless Ethernet Cards that Work with NetStumbler and MiniStumbler

- ☑ Wireless cards use the Hermes chipset.
- ☑ NetStumbler 0.4.0 also has expanded support for cards based on the Atheros, Intersil Prism, Atmel, Centrino, and Broadcom chipsets.

Minimum System Requirements

- ☑ NetStumbler: Windows 95 or later, that's capable of supporting a wireless card (Windows XP recommended).
- ☑ MiniStumbler: Windows Handheld PC 2000, Pocket PC 3.0, or Pocket PC 2002, that's capable of supporting a wireless card.
- ☑ Antennae and GPS receivers are optional requirements.

Installation

- ☑ The installer package can be downloaded from either www.netstumbler.com or www.stumbler.net.

- ☑ The first step after downloading the package is to run the installer program.

- ☑ View the readme file for any needed information.

Running NetStumbler

- ☑ NetStumbler has two panes: right and left.

- ☑ The left pane contains the Filter tree.

- ☑ The right pane holds the discovered network information.

- ☑ The secondary right pane contains radio signal/noise graphing.

NetStumbler Menus and Tool Icons

- ☑ There are two menus unique to NetStumbler to select devices and options.

- ☑ NetStumbler also has three unique tool buttons to control and configure the application.

Running MiniStumbler

- ☑ The running MiniStumbler has a single pane, containing discovered network information.

- ☑ There are no filters in the running MiniStumbler.

MiniStumbler Menus and Tool Icons

- ☑ MiniStumbler contains several unique menu items to select devices and options.

- ☑ Three unique Tool buttons in MiniStumbler can be used to control and configure the program.

Frequently Asked Questions

The following Frequently Asked Questions, answered by the authors of this book, are designed to both measure your understanding of the concepts presented in this chapter and to assist you with real-life implementation of these concepts. To have your questions about this chapter answered by the author, browse to **www.syngress.com/solutions** and click on the **"Ask the Author"** form. You will also gain access to thousands of other FAQs at ITFAQnet.com.

Q: I want to view my MiniStumbler files on my laptop or desktop computer. Are the .ns1 files produced by MiniStumbler the same and compatible with NetStumbler?

A: Yes. Simply copy or move the files from the mobile device to your desktop or laptop, and NetStumbler will read them without any modifications or conversion.

Q: Does NetStumbler detect ORiNOCO Central Outdoor Routers (COR), Remote Outdoor Routers (ROR), or ORiNOCO equipment running Karlnet?

A: No. The data frames and formats used by the COR, ROR, and Karlnet are not 802.1b compliant, even though they are using identical equipment and the ISM radio band. Due to those differences, such equipment will not respond to the 802.11 broadcast request and will not be detected.

Q: Should NetStumbler be run while my PC is connected to a wireless network?

A: No. NetStumbler is designed to find networks. Due to the nature of how it does this, by generating packets and requests, it may degrade the network performance by interrupting valid network traffic.

Q: Can NetStumbler along with my wireless configuration and control program (usually called a Client Manager) run at the same time?

A: It is best to disable any wireless controls when running NetStumbler. Most of these programs will conflict with NetStumbler's operation.

## Chapter 3

Operating NetStumbler and MiniStumbler

Solutions in this Chapter:

- Operational Details
- Option Settings
- Disabling Network Protocols
- Additional RF Equipment: Antennae and Cables
- Using a GPS receiver with NetStumbler and MiniStumbler
- Putting It All Together: The Complete "Stumbling Setup"
- Exporting NetStumbler Data
- Additional Resources

- ☑ Summary
- ☑ Solutions Fast Track
- ☑ Frequently Asked Questions

Introduction: "Welcome to the Real World."

The character Morpheus from the movie, *The Matrix,* is quoted here for good reason. What we have discussed about NetStumbler thus far is good, but it has really been little more than theory. Now, we are about to put the theory into practice. As always, real life tends to be more complicated and has more "gotchas" than pure theory. From this point on, we'll be talking about the steps to actually implement WarDriving using NetStumbler. Like Neo, to whom Morpheus was speaking, you are about to find out that some things are probably not quite what you expected.

We first need to discuss some of the options and operating details that were touched upon in Chapter 2. In this chapter, we'll talk about many of the options, buttons, and details that will help you get the best out of your WarDriving experience using NetStumbler.

Second, many users have an expectation that they can immediately use NetStumbler or MiniStumbler with little more than a laptop or handheld PC and a wireless network card. This is certainly how most people start, at least for the first use. However, to obtain the best possible results, most users quickly find that they need (and want) extra equipment.

Most of the information in this chapter will cover both NetStumbler and MiniStumbler. Their differences will be noted, as will how they apply to each application.

Operational Details

First, let's go into detail on some of the items we touched on in Chapter 2, including the use of different wireless card drivers and the columns used for the captured data. Next, we'll discuss a control that's new to NetStumbler 0.4.0 for looking up Domain Names from the Access Point's IP address. Then comes a detailed look into the Options and how to set them for optimum NetStumbler operation. Also, we'll talk about turning off any networking protocols to avoid connecting to wireless local area networks (WLANs) and why you should avoid connecting to networks that are not yours, or that you do not have permission to access.

Notes from the Underground...

Running a Copy of NetStumbler on Your Desktop PC

Even if your desktop PC is not equipped with a wireless card, keeping a copy of NetStumbler installed there makes a lot of sense. Since most desktop machines have more storage space, long-term storage of all the files accumulated from WarDriving is a lot easier to manage. And, since most desktop PCs have much faster and more powerful processors, this also allows you to run operations such as merging multiple NS1 files into a large single file without using a slower laptop.

NDIS 5.1 Drivers, Wireless Cards, and NetStumbler

NDIS stands for "Network Driver Interface Specification." The NDIS 5.1 driver functions as a software bridge between the Windows 2000 or Windows XP Operating System and the card hardware. This allows the driver to pass information from a program to the card and back.

Unfortunately, most of the wireless card NDIS drivers seem to have some bugs. People who have cards that need the NDIS 5.1 drivers to work with NetStumbler usually say that some features of NetStumbler do not work properly. The most commonly reported problem with NDIS 5.1 cards is that the NDIS drivers always report the Noise measurement as −100dBm; no matter what the Noise level might be in actuality. The result in this case is an inaccurate Signal-to-Noise Ratio (SNR) measurement. For general WarDriving this may not be a big issue, but if you are attempting to fine-tune a WLAN or locate a rogue AP, the lack of accurate information may be detrimental

Other commonly reported problems with NDIS drivers are similar in nature. For example, a common problem with Version 0.3.30 of NetStumbler involved the D-Link AG650+ 802.11a/b/g card and NDIS combination reporting the correct noise level, but it did not clear from the "AP Active" area on the Status Line at the bottom of the screen when the detected AP went out of range. Fortunately, version 0.4.0 of NetStumbler now clears these APs from the Status Line after a few seconds. Users of other card and driver combinations say that a fixed Signal level is reported no matter how near or far they are from an AP.

Two other common problems associated with the NDIS drivers involve NetStumbler shutting down when an AP is discovered, and NetStumbler starting and then immediately quitting.

Tools & Traps…

Disabling the Client Manager

Most wireless cards come with a control program that enables the user to configure the card for such things as the Service Set IDentifier (SSID), encryption settings, and other WLAN parameters. Most, if not all of the programs used will interfere with NetStumbler's operation, and should be disabled while running NetStumbler. Typically, these applications are called the "Wireless Client Manager," "Wireless Configuration Utility," or something similar. Whatever name the manufacturer of your card calls it, in order to obtain the best results while WarDriving, it is usually better to avoid conflicts with NetStumbler.

In order to get consistent behavior, the best practice is to create a "NetStumbler" or "MiniStumbler" confirmation profile that will allow you to set up the card quickly for use with NetStumbler. To do this, enter the wireless card program, and create a new profile. Set the SSID to "ANY" (without quotes) and turn off the encryption. Save this configuration, naming it "NetStumbler" or "MiniStumbler" as is appropriate. Alternately, use the SSID (ANY) as the profile name, so you immediately know what network uses which SSID.

Now, whenever you are about do a WarDrive, open the wireless card control application, and select this configuration profile. Then *exit*, do not minimize, the control program. This will place the card in the ideal configuration for WarDriving, yet prevent the control from causing any interference with NetStumbler.

For users of Windows XP, use NetStumbler's "Reconfigure card automatically" under View | Options | General tab. This will stop XP's Wireless Zero Configuration (WZC) service. If this is not done, then WZC attempts to control the card, and it will conflict with NetStumbler's control (the NetStumbler Options are discussed in detail further in this chapter). WZC can also be permanently turned off through the Services applet under the Windows XP Control Panel. Stop WZC and then disable the Startup option.

Right Pane Column Headings

As mentioned in Chapter 2, here is a more detailed account of each of the column headings seen in the right pane (see Figure 3.1). Rather than repeat explanations for some of these headings, related items have been placed together with a full explanation.

Figure 3.1 The Right Pane Has Several Columns

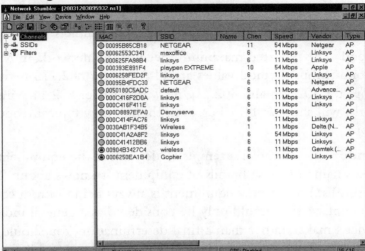

- **MAC** The Machine Address Code (MAC) is a unique address for each Ethernet device, comprised of a twelve-digit hexadecimal number. The first six digits are the vendor portion of the name, assigned by the Institute of Electrical and Electronics Engineers, Inc. (IEEE). The last six digits are the serial number of the device. You may obtain a text list of vender codes from the IEEE at: http://standards.ieee.org/regauth/oui/oui.txt. This list contains company addresses as well as names. However, it is limited to those companies that allow their information to be made public. Having an updated list may help you figure out the manufacturer of a given device if NetStumbler is not able to determine the maker's name.

- **SSID** This is the Service Set IDentifier; also known as the "Network Name." The SSID is a part of the 802.11 standards. Many times, the default SSID is set to the manufacturer's name. For example, "linksys" is the default SSID for most Linksys brand equipment. The SSID is case-sensitive, so a name of "BillsNetwork" is a different network than "billsnetwork."

- **Name** The Access Point's name. NetStumbler only detects the name of those APs using the ORiNOCO and Cisco naming protocol. Most of the time, this data is blank, or has no value, even when it is filled in at setup.

- **Chan** This is the channel number the network is operating on. See the Channels sidebar for more information on the channels numbers and which countries allow operations on what channels.

- **Speed** The reported maximum speed of the network, in MegaBits per second (Mbps). Typical values are 11 Mbps for 802.11b networks and 54 Mbps for 802.11a and 802.11g networks. Older 802.11 wireless networks will show as 11 Mbps, even though they typically operate at 2 Mbps.

- **Vendor** NetStumbler attempts to determine the equipment manufacturer's name of those brands of equipment it knows about. (See **MAC** on this list.) Since new equipment is always being introduced to the marketplace, this should only be considered as a general indicator of the device's maker, rather than a final determination. You should also recall that some brands are "rebadged." That is, someone else manufactures the actual working parts, and the company whose name is on the products markets the device.

- **Type** This is the reported network type of either: "AP" for Access Point, or "Peer" for Peer-to-Peer. Access Point–based networks are also known as "Infrastructure" networks, and Peer-to-Peer WLANs are often referred to as "ad-hoc" networks. Most often, Infrastructure WLANs are connected to other networks and the Internet though the AP. Ad-hoc networks are usually just a collection of independent laptops without outside connections.

- **Encryption** If WLAN has the wireless traffic as encrypted, NetStumbler marks it as Wired Equivalency Privacy (WEP). If WEP is being displayed, you cannot connect to the network without knowing the encryption key. Some keys are static and are rarely changed. Other systems allow for dynamic key rotations and can change up to several times per second. Newer WLANs may use the "WiFi Protected Access"

(WPA) encryption scheme, which was released in the last year. However, NetStumbler will mark all encrypted WLANs as "WEP."

- **Signal**, **Noise**, and **SNR** The Signal is the current Radio Frequency (RF) Signal in milliwatt deciBels (dBm), while the Noise is the amount of that signal which is not usable. Similar to audio static on an AM/FM radio, when there is a clean radio signal and less static, the signal is heard well by the listener. This same principal applies to WLAN signals. The better the Signal, and the less Noise, the better the data will be transmitted and received over the WLAN. The Signal-to-Noise Ratio is the amount of Signal, minus the Noise level. These levels are only active when in range of a network.

- **Signal+**, **Noise-**, and **SNR+** These columns are exactly the same as the **Signal**, **Noise**, and **SNR**, with one difference. Where the Signal, Noise, and SNR display the current levels when receiving information from a WLAN, the Signal+, Noise-, and SNR+ show the maximum levels for Signal and SNR and the lowest Noise level seen for a given wireless network.

- **IP Addr** and **Subnet** This is the reported Internet Protocol (IP) Address and IP Subnet, if any. These are listed together, as they are interrelated. When NetStumbler associates with a wireless network, two things happen. First, you may be assigned an address via the Dynamic Hosting Control Protocol (DHCP). This will also yield the subnet. If so, the Address Resolution Protocol (ARP) cache is queried with the Basic Service Set IDentifier (BSSID). This will yield the IP address if the Access Point is the DHCP server or default gateway for that network. Second, if the network is an ORiNOCO or Cisco network, the request for the name may also yield an IP address. If there is no dynamic addressing via DHCP, or it is not an ORiNOCO or Cisco network, no information will be displayed in these columns. Also, if the TCP/IP protocol is disabled, as discussed further along in the chapter, then these columns will not contain any information.

- **Latitude** and **Longitude** This is the Latitude and Longitude at the time when NetStumbler saw the strongest signal, as reported by the Global Positioning System (GPS) receiver. This data is the position of the GPS receiver, *not* the actual location of the WLAN. The **View | Options** dialog box controls how these two figures are displayed, and is discussed further along in this chapter.

- **First Seen** and **Last Seen**   These columns are exactly what they appear to be: the Hour, Minutes, and Seconds when NetStumbler first and last saw the wireless network. These times are based on the PC's system clock.

- **Flags**   The Flags are information about the network in hexadecimal code. The codes are:

  - 0001 indicates the Extended Service Set (ESS) or Infrastructure mode.

  - 0002 shows the Independent Basic Service Set (IBSS) or Ad-Hoc mode. This is the inverse of the ESS mode.

  - 0004 designates that the network uses the Contention-Free (CF) Pollable protocol. This protocol requires that stations on the WLAN first sense the medium before transmitting, by sending a "Request to Send" data frame, and then wait for a "Clear to Send" reply from other network devices before broadcasting.

  - 0008 is the Contention-Free (CF) CF-Poll Request, used by the CF-Pollable protocol.

  - 0010 shows that encryption ("WEP") is enabled on the WLAN.

  - 0020 indicates that the WLAN is using the Short Preamble. This allows a WLAN to improve the efficiency of some "real-time" applications such as streaming video or Voice-Over-IP (VoIP) telephony applications.

  - 0040 this flag is for when Packet Binary Convolutional Code (PBCC) is being used on the network. PBCC is a Texas Instruments (TI) 22 Mbps version of IEEE 802.11b (sometimes referred to as "802.11b+").

  - 0080 indicates Channel Agility, which allows the network to change channels automatically, if interference is seen from other devices.

  - 0400 The 0400 flag is part of the newly finalized 802.11g standard, and indicates a Short Time Slot.

  - 2000 indicates Direct-Sequence Spread Spectrum (DSSS) Orthogonal Frequency Division Multiplexing (OFDM) modulation.

  - DB00 is the area of the Flags reserved for future use.

- **Beacon Interval** This is the amount of time between beacon transmissions from the AP, measured in kilomicroseconds (units of 1.024 milliseconds). This time sequence is needed by various WLAN functions such as the power saving mode. For WarDriving, it may only be of general interest, but knowing this information may help diagnose specific problems on a wireless network.

- **Distance** This is the distance from the point at which the highest signal was received from the WLAN. If you are moving toward the signal source wireless network, this reading should be continuously decreasing. Heading away from a signal source will make this reading increase. Note that in order to have any distance information, a GPS receiver must be connected and configured properly. Again, use of a GPS receiver is discussed further along in this chapter.

Notes from the Underground…

Channels

In 802.11b and 802.11g communications, there are 14 channels defined internationally. Channels 1 through 11 are the channels used in the United States, as allowed by the Federal Communications Commission (FCC). Channels 1 through 13 are used in most of Europe. Channel 14 is the only channel used in Japan. Other countries usually follow one of these conventions, but may add other restrictions for specific use. For example, Canada uses the same channels as the United States. In comparison, Mexico allows Channels 1 through 8 to be used indoors only, while Channels 9, 10, and 11 can be used both indoors and outdoors, while Israel allows use only on Channels 3 to 9. In addition, some people have reportedly purchased surplus equipment that is designated for other countries or have hacked the firmware to add additional channels. Because of this, you may occasionally see channels 12, 13, or 14 in the U.S. or Canada, where you normally wouldn't see anything above 11. Just a note of caution: running such equipment in a country where the equipment isn't compliant with the regulations may be illegal.

Continued

> For 802.11a there are 16 channels, using these designations: 34, 36, 38, 40, 42, 44, 46, 48, 52, 56, 60, 64, 149, 153, 157, and 161. Internationally, 802.11a channels are restricted to indoor use only. In the United States, the FCC allows indoor and outdoor usage on Channels 52, 56, 60, and 64.

IP Address Look Up

You can see the context menu and the Look Up options for NetStumbler in Figure 3.2 and for MiniStumbler in Figure 3.3. On the right pane, selecting a MAC address and then right-clicking it opens a separate Context menu. Normally, this context menu displays the SSID of the select MAC, and allows you to **Select All** or **Delete** any selected MACs and all associated information. However, this menu has an added function. If you select an active MAC that has an IP address or Subnet assignment, then the menu will display three additional "Look up" options for the address block. There is one for each of the American Registry for Internet Numbers (ARIN), Réseaux Internet Protocol Européens (RIPE), the European version of ARIN, and Asia Pacific Network Information Centre (APNIC).

Figure 3.2 Context Menu and Look Up Options in NetStumbler

Figure 3.3 Context Menu and Look Up Options in MiniStumbler

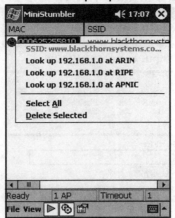

These "Look up" options run what is known as a WHOIS query. WHOIS is a common network utility, usually found on Unix or Unix-type systems. It is used to look up Domain Name and IP address information, including Ownership, and other information such as associated organizations or customers.

However, in this case the WHOIS is performed via a web interface to a search engine maintained by ARIN, RIPE, or APNIC. Clicking one of these options will open the default Internet browser and run a standard WHOIS request on the corresponding server. A screenshot of the sample output from ARIN is shown in Figure 3.4 for NetStumbler, while Figure 3.5 shows the corresponding screenshot for MiniStumbler.

Figure 3.4 Look Up Results in the ARIN WHOIS in NetStumbler

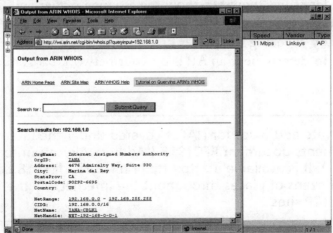

Figure 3.5 Look Up Results in the ARIN WHOIS in MiniStumbler

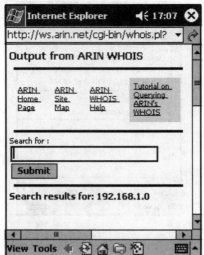

To use the Look Up function, the network connection must include access to the Internet and specifically the World Wide Web. The results of the WHOIS query shows the owner of the IP address, the range of addresses that are owned, and the assigned customer (if any).

Readers who are used to dealing with IP addresses will no doubt realize that those used in these examples are from a private address range. This is due to the fact that this particular WLAN uses Network Address Translation (NAT), as this WLAN is isolated from the wired network for security reasons. As such, the WHOIS lookup really shows very little information. Using the lookup on an actual public address will, however, show the assigned owner and user.

This is a very useful tool for determining if you have a rogue Access Point on your network. By checking the owner or customer name of a given address, you should be able to determine if an AP is on your network backbone.

NOTE:

Using private addresses for NAT is covered under the Internet Request For Comments document RFC1918 ("Address Allocation for Private Internets"). It is available at: ftp://ftp.arin.net/rfc/rfc1918.txt and is mirrored in dozens of places throughout the Internet, via the World Wide Web and FTP sites.

As you can see, some of the information collected by NetStumbler is very detailed. If you are WarDriving as a hobby, you may not have much use for a lot of the information that NetStumbler collects other than the MAC, SSID, and location data. However, professionals locating rogue APs or fine-tuning WLANs quickly appreciate that having the extra data saves them time and effort.

Option Settings

To get the optimum use from NetStumbler, many of the functions must be set up correctly. Many of those options are located in the Network Stumbler Options dialog box under **View | Options**. It has four main tabs, and multiple suboptions.

The General Tab

The General Tab is seen in Figure 3.6. It controls the Scan Speed and several other functions, including the wireless card automatic configuration.

Figure 3.6 General Tabs for NetStumbler and MiniStumbler

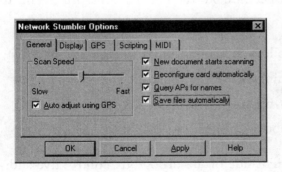

The Scan Speed program of NetStumbler has an internal timer that fires every 0.25 seconds (4 times per second). This timer has an associated trigger number for the number of cycles before NetStumbler sends out a Broadcast Request for the Beacon. On the default setting, the Beacon Request broadcast is sent out every fourth time this timer is fired or once every second.

This trigger number is under the direct control of the user, by using the Scan Speed slider. The slider has five positions, though by default, the slider is set to the center position, which makes 4 the value of the trigger. The full range of the slider settings, the associated number of cycles that are needed to send out the Broadcast Request, and the resulting times that the Broadcast Request is transmitted, are listed in Table 3.1.

Table 3.1 Broadcast Request Settings and Cycles

Setting	Number of Cycles to Trigger	Time
Slower	6	1.5 seconds
Slow	5	1.25 seconds
Medium*	4	1 seconds
Fast	3	0.75 seconds
Faster	2	0.5 seconds

*Default setting

On the NetStumbler Forums, many people have suggested a variety of settings for different activities they've successfully used during their WarDriving. Opinions vary as to some of the specifics, but the general consensus seems to be

- **Slower** For walking
- **Slow** When jogging, rollerblading, or skating in crowded areas
- **Medium** For rollerblading, skating, and biking
- **Fast** For low-speed driving up to 25MPH (40KM/h)
- **Faster** When driving above 25MPH (40KM/h)

The checkboxes on the right side of the dialog box control five additional options. They are:

- **Auto adjust using GPS** Using this option allows the speed reported by your Global Positioning System receiver to vary the frequency of this timer. Additional information on using a GPS unit with NetStumbler with be further explained later in this chapter. As the GPS unit reports faster speeds to NetStumbler, the timer frequency increases within the range of 2 to 6 times per second so that NetStumbler doesn't miss any

AP's. Of course, as the GPS reports slower speeds, the time frequency is automatically decreased.

- **New Document Starts Scanning** Enabling this checkbox allows the wireless card to start scanning whenever a new document is opened—for example, when NetStumbler starts.

- **Reconfigure Card Automatically** This option allows NetStumbler to configure your wireless card using a null SSID and Basic Service Set (BSS) mode. This does not change any WEP settings you may have enabled. In this mode, it will occasionally disconnect you from any currently associated AP. This is done to allow NetStumbler to perform accurate network scans.

- **Query APs for Names** This option lets NetStumbler ask the AP if it is an ORiNOCO or Cisco access point, or whether it supports naming like either of those brands. If so, it asks the AP for its name. This is what appears in the Name column on the right pane of NetStumbler, and why any name data is seen rather infrequently. Only those two brands are supported at present. If NetStumbler sees another network that has a better signal than the one you're associated with, it will disconnect the current association so it can get the new AP name.

- **Save Files Automatically** This saves the current .NS1 file every five minutes. It also saves the .NS1 file if you close the file or exit NetStumbler.

The Display Tab

The Display tab has one control, as seen in Figure 3.7. This is a pull-down list for the display of the GPS Latitude and Longitude data in the Right pane. The default format is Degrees and Minutes to the one-thousandth (D°MM.MMM).

Figure 3.7 Display Tabs for NetStumbler and MiniStumbler

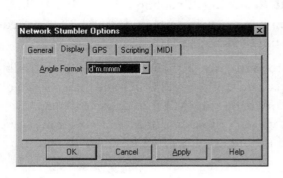
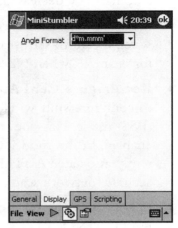

Other options include Degrees shown to ten-thousandths (D.DDDD°); Degrees expressed to hundred-thousandths (D.DDDDD°); Degrees and Minutes, with the Minutes displayed down to ten-thousandths (D°MM.MMMM), Degrees, Minutes, and Seconds (D°M'S"); and Degrees, Minutes, and Seconds, with the Seconds expressed to one-hundredths (D°M'S.SS").

The GPS Tab

The GPS tab sets the options for communicating with a GPS receiver, as seen in Figure 3.8. Various options are available to set the protocol, communications port, the bits per second, the number of data bits, the number of stop bits, and the parity. NetStumbler accepts data in the NMEA 0183 protocol by default. Four additional proprietary GPS formats Garmin Binary, Garmin Text, Tripmate, and Earthmate are also available as options for users who have the Garmin, DeLorme Tripmate, or DeLorme Earthmate GPS receivers.

Figure 3.8 GPS Tabs for NetStumbler and MiniStumbler

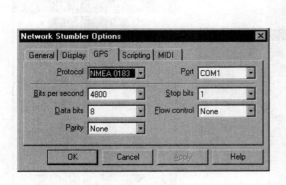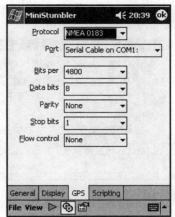

By default, the GPS communications settings for NetStumbler are 4800 bits per second, 8 Data Bits, No Parity Bit, and 1 Stop Bit. This conforms to the default communications settings of most brands of GPS. The communications serial port is disabled by default. To use this setting, choose an available communications port. In NetStumbler, this is COM1 through COM16. The actual ports will vary according to the individual PC.

In MiniStumbler, the available ports are a Serial Cable on COM1, Bluetooth Serial ports on COM7 or COM8, and a Serial Cable on BT. Again, the availability will depend on the individual PocketPC.

The Scripting Tab

NetStumbler includes the ability to run script programs. The Scripting tab is seen in Figure 3.9. This allows the user to add to and extend the utility of NetStumbler well beyond the built-in functions. Scripts can be written in any scripting language installed on your computer. Common script engines that run scripts on Windows machines are Visual Basic Script Edition (also known as VBScript), JScript, Windows Script Components, Windows Script Host, and Windows Script Runtime Version. Other script languages, such as PERL, may be installed on your computer.

Figure 3.9 Scripting Tabs for NetStumbler and MiniStumbler

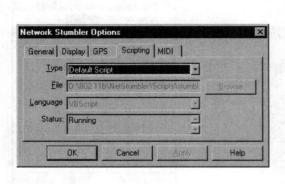
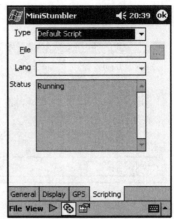

To run a script, you must first install the scripting engine and any desired scripts. Then, go to the **View | Option** dialog box, and look at the Scripts tab. Select the **Type** of script, the **File** name of the script and the engine that will run it. NetStumbler loads the script into the engine, and then the script executes. As various conditions are met, the script performs the associated action. For example, in the following script segment, when the subroutine **OnEnableScan** is called, it plays the "SSROAM" wave file.

```
'Sub OnEnableScan
'  PlaySound "SSROAM.WAV"
'End Sub
```

While the default script is VBScript, you may use any other scripting language and engine that is loaded on your system. For example, if you have Jscript and VBScript on your PC, both would show up in the Scripting dialog box. You could select the language that you prefer, or whichever one would run a given script.

If you are interested in writing your own custom scripts, start with the reference page at www.stumbler.net/scripting.html. It has a complete list of all Functions called by NS, and the only requirement is that any script you write must call the same function names (for example, OnEnableScan) as the default script.

Before you start writing your own scripts, you should also look at the Scripts Forum on the NetStumbler forums located at http://forums.netstumbler.com/forumdisplay.php?s=&forumid=24. The Scripts Forum has many user-written scripts, and there may be one that does exactly what you want. Scripts written and submitted by various members of the forums range from controlling an external Liquid Crystal Display (LCD) character-based display to providing live tracking on different map programs. Even if you don't find a script that accomplishes exactly what you want to do, the other scripts are a great resource to help you write your own script programs.

The default script that is built into NetStumbler is included here for reference:

```
On Error Resume Next

'Sub OnEnableScan
' PlaySound "SSROAM.WAV"
'End Sub

'Sub OnDisableScan
' PlaySound "SSROAM.WAV"
'End Sub

'Sub OnScanStart
' PlaySound "Windows XP Balloon.WAV"
'End Sub

'Sub OnScanResult(SSID, BSSID, CapFlags, Signal, Noise, LastSeen) ' NOT YET
' SSID : String : SSID (Network name)
' BSSID : String : BSSID (MAC address)
' CapFlags : Integer : 802.11 capability flags
' Signal : Integer : signal level (dBm)
' Noise : Integer : noise level(dBm)
' LastSeen : Time : When this BSSID was last seen
'End Sub

Sub OnScanComplete(FoundNew, SeenBefore, LostContact, BestSNR) ' NOT YET
' FoundNew : Integer : Count of new BSSIDs
' SeenBefore : Integer : Count of not-new BSSIDs
```

```
' LostContact : Integer : Count of BSSIDs missed since last scan
' BestSNR : Integer : SNR of strongest signal (dBm)

' MsgBox "OnScanComplete " & FoundNew & " " & SeenBefore & " " &
LostContact & " " & BestSNR
If FoundNew>0 Then
PlaySound "ns-aos-new.WAV"
ElseIf LostContact>0 Then
PlaySound "ns-los.WAV"
ElseIf SeenBefore>0 Then
' Still seeing some
If BestSNR >= 60 Then
PlaySound "ns-signal-6.WAV"
ElseIf BestSNR >= 50 Then
PlaySound "ns-signal-5.WAV"
ElseIf BestSNR >= 40 Then
PlaySound "ns-signal-4.WAV"
ElseIf BestSNR >= 30 Then
PlaySound "ns-signal-3.WAV"
ElseIf BestSNR >= 20 Then
PlaySound "ns-signal-2.WAV"
ElseIf BestSNR >= 10 Then
PlaySound "ns-signal-1.WAV"
Else
PlaySound "ns-signal-0.WAV"
End If
Else
' Nothing seen
' PlaySound "ns-tick.WAV"
End If
End Sub

Dim GPSOk
GPSOk = True

Sub OnGPSTimeout
```

```
If GPSOk Then
GPSOk = False
PlaySound "ns-gps-err.WAV"
End If
End Sub


Sub OnGPSNoFix
If GPSOk Then
GPSOk = False
PlaySound "ns-gps-err.WAV"
End If
End Sub


Sub OnGPSPosition (Lat, Lon, Alt)
' Lat : double : Latitude, degrees east
' Lon : double : Longitude, degrees north
' Alt : double : Altitude above sea level, meters
GPSOk = True
End Sub


'Sub OnGPSSpeed (Speed)
' Speed : double : Speed, knots
'End Sub
```

The MIDI Tab

Many laptops today come with a Musical Instrument Digital Interface (MIDI) built in to the computer's motherboard. The MIDI tab allows NetStumbler to play musical tones in response to the SNR readings, via the MIDI interface. This may be used as an alternative to using the NetStumbler sound files. You will recall from Chapter 2 that installing the sounds is an option. If you did not install those files, this still allows for some sound functions.

You may enable this function using this tab, and also change the MIDI Channel, Patch, and Transpose. If a MIDI driver and device is not detected on the laptop, then these options are visible but not available. The checkbox will be grayed out, as seen in Figure 3.10.

Figure 3.10 The NetStumbler MIDI Tab

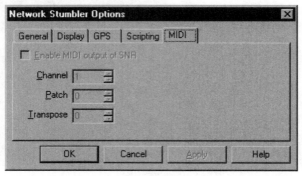

The MIDI tab is not available in MiniStumbler.

Playing Sounds

When you are WarDriving, NetStumbler will play sounds as certain actions occur. NetStumbler comes with ten sound files; each is associated within the program for a specific action. For example, every time a new wireless network is discovered, one particular sound (-ns-aos-new.wav) is played. As we noted in Chapter 2, these files are a default installation option. They are located in C:/Program Files/Network Stumbler if the default installation folder is chosen. The file names are:

- ns-signal-0.wav
- ns-signal-1.wav
- ns-signal-2.wav
- ns-signal-3.wav
- ns-signal-4.wav
- ns-signal-5.wav
- ns-signal-6.wav
- ns-aos-new.wav
- ns-los.wav
- ns-gps-err.wav

The files **ns-signal-0.wav** through **ns-signal-6.wav** are associated with the RF Signal strength readings. **Ns-aos-new.wav** plays when a new WLAN is seen, and **ns–los.wav** plays when a WLAN's signal is lost. If there is an error condition with the GPS, such as a timeout, then **ns-gps-err.wav** will play. These sounds may also be called from scripts.

Notes from the Underground…

Alternative Sounds

Almost any .wav file can be used in NetStumbler or MiniStumbler to indicate when an AP or ad-hoc network is detected. While most people leave the default sounds in place, many WarDrivers like to use alternative sound files.

Some sounds seem to have better acoustics in a moving vehicle, while others can be just for fun. Typically, I use a series of submarine sonar "pings" for routine use, because the high pitch is easy to hear above tire and road noises. However, one of my favorite sounds when showing NetStumbler to new users is an audio clip from the Three Stooges. In it, Moe yells: "Quiet numbskulls, I'm broadcasting!"

Changing sounds is very easy to do. Simply rename the sound file you'd like to use to the appropriate NetStumbler sound file name. For example, suppose you want to have a voice telling you to check the GPS in case of an error, rather than the default low frequency tone. First, record someone saying "Check GPS" or "GPS error!" Then save that sound file as "ns-gps-err.WAV" in your NetStumbler folder. Now, whenever a GPS error condition occurs, the new sound file will play.

If you are using MiniStumbler, you may want to convert the file to a Pulse Code Modulation (PCM) format before transferring to your PocketPC. A PocketPC reportedly cannot play the Adaptive Delta Pulse Code Modulation (ADPCM) format, which is a common file format used on many desktop and laptop Windows PCs. Additionally, some users on the NetStumbler Forums report that 16-bit mono is preferred since they find that an 8-bit mono file sounds too scratchy.

Disabling Network Protocols

In many jurisdictions, simply connecting to any computer network without prior permission may be illegal. To avoid any inadvertent illegal action on your part, or any action that be might perceived as illegal, you should prevent your computer from communicating through any APs that you stumble across. The simplest way to accomplish this is to turn off the Transmission Control Protocol / Internet Protocol (TCP/IP) as well as any other network protocols that you may be running. On most computers that use Internet access, TCP/IP is the standard installed protocol. Disabling all installed protocols will prevent the wireless card from transmitting those protocols, and then using them to connect. If the card doesn't transmit the network protocols, then the network will not allow a connection, and the card cannot use the network, even accidentally. Note that you don't have to delete the protocols, just disable them. That way, you may enable them later, when you need them but aren't WarDriving.

Users of DHCP can quickly disable the TCP/IP protocol by using the *IPCP-NFIG.EXE* command, as seen in Figure 3.7. The *IPCONFIG.EXE* command is available in the following Microsoft Operating Systems: Windows 95, Windows 98/98SE, Windows ME, Windows 2000, and Windows XP. In Figure 3.11, you can see how entering IPCONFIG with the argument /RELEASE_ALL on the command line (MS-DOS prompt or Command Prompt), releases all current TCP/IP network configuration values and sets the IP address to 0.0.0.0 for all Ethernet devices.

Figure 3.11 Using IPCONFIG.EXE to Disable TCP/IP

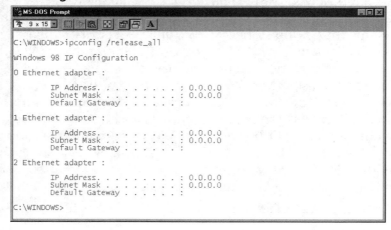

For further information on IPCONFIG.EXE, type **IPCONFIG /?** at the command prompt, or search the Microsoft Knowledge Base at http://search.microsoft.com.

WINIPCFG is the Graphic User Interface equivalent for the *IPCONFIG* command, seen in Figure 3.12. It is available in Windows Millennium Edition (ME), Windows 98/98SE, and Windows 95.

Figure 3.12 Using WINIPCFG.EXE to Disable TCP/IP

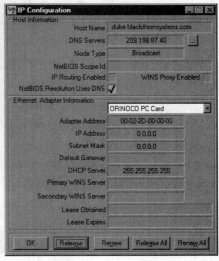

Using the controls, you may either select an adapter using the drop-down list, or press the **Release All** button to disable TCP/IP on all Ethernet devices. WINIPCFG has a standard window (seen on the left in Figure 3.12), and an expanded window (seen on the right). The standard window is enlarged to the expanded window when the **More Info...** button is pushed.

Windows NT, 2000, and XP do not have a graphical equivalent to the WINIPCFG command. On those systems, you can use Network Connections to modify an IP address. To disable the TCP/IP on Windows NT, 2000, and XP, open **Network Connections** on the Control Panel, and right-click the desired network connection. **Select Status**, and then click the **Support** tab. Enter an IP address and subnet of **0.0.0.0** and **0.0.0.0**, respectively, in the TCP/IP Properties.

The TCP/IP protocol must be disabled manually on a Pocket PC. To disable TCP/IP on a PocketPC, go to **Start | Setting | Network Adapters**. Select your wireless card, and press the **Properties** button. Select the radio button for **Use specific IP address** and enter **0.0.0.0** for the IP address, subnet mask, and default gateway as seen in Figure 3.13.

Figure 3.13 Disabling TCP/IP on a PocketPC

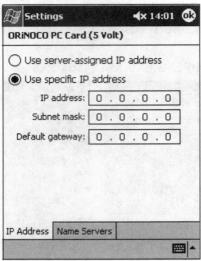

Additional RF Equipment: Antennae and Cables

The steel and aluminum body panels in most auto and light truck bodies block radio signals very effectively. As a result, most WarDrivers will want an external antenna on their vehicle to improve the detection of APs. An external antenna for WarDriving functions in the same way as the AM/FM radio antenna on your car. It allows a weak signal, which otherwise might not penetrate the car body, to be brought in where the receiver is located. Conversely, it also allows the transmitted portion of the signal to extend past the card body. Because of these reasons, usually an antenna is the first accessory purchased for the WarDriving kit.

Generally, an antenna capable of transmitting and receiving the signal equally in all directions is preferred. These antennae are known as omni-directional, or omni for short. Most WarDrivers use an omni antenna in the 3dBi to 8dBi range, as these give the best compromise on signal gain and pattern. Commonly, this type of omni-directional antenna has a magnetic base that sticks readily to a steel car body roof. Such "mag mounts" as they are known, allow the antenna to be transferred between different vehicles without a complicated installation. Figure 3.14 shows a typical 3dBi mag mount antenna.

Figure 3.14 3dBi Omni-Directional Antenna with Magnetic Mount Base

Most antennae of this type come with an attached 10- to 20-foot cable. This cable allows the signal to be carried easily inside the car or truck. The cable end opposite the antenna usually terminates in a Type N-Male connector. If the attached cable is too short or absent, a cable of the appropriate length will have to be purchased.

In addition to an omni, directional antennae of different types are available from a wide variety of sources. A directional antenna is confined to sending and receiving in a single direction, as the name implies. Directional antennae also come in different gain levels, and usually are described as having a particular "beam width" in degrees. Think of it like a flashlight beam of light. The beam width on a directional is the area the antenna will send and pick up radio signals.

Due to the narrow focus of the "beam," directional antennae are of limited use for general WarDriving, since the signal is confined to sending and receiving in only one area. Most times while WarDriving, you are attempting to find as many APs as possible, in all directions. However, a directional is a must if you are attempting to locate a specific AP. For example, when attempting to locate an unauthorized or "rogue" AP on a company network, a directional antenna is an indispensable tool.

Pigtails

The frequencies used by 802.11 WLANS fall into the microwave area of the radio spectrum. In order not to lose too much of the radio energy in the connectors, the connectors must be of the proper type and rated for microwave use. The "N" type connector is one of the most commonly used for microwave RF communications, and is seen on many brands of antennae and cables. Unfortunately, an N connector is huge in comparison to the average WLAN cards. The combined weight of the cable and the connector would almost certainly destroy most cards in short order. For this reason, the card manufacturers use tiny connectors on the cards. To convert from the tiny connector used on the card to the N connector, we need what is known as a "pigtail" cable.

The term "pigtail" comes from radio engineering and ham radio. A pigtail is nothing more than a short piece of antenna cable, with different connectors on each end. They are used to convert one connector type to another. Usually, the cable used for a pigtail is a smaller diameter and type than the main cable, but this is not always true. The exact origins of the term seem to be lost, but since most small diameter coaxial cables curl rather tightly after being unwound from a cable spool, it seems reasonable that the name came from the fact that a small length of cable might resemble the curled tail of a pig.

The most common pigtail used for WarDriving is the ORiNOCO proprietary connector (Type MC) to a Type N-Female connector, which is a reflection of the popularity of the ORiNOCO card, as seen in Figure 3.15. However, there are others pigtail types. Another fairly common pigtail is the Type MMCX connector to a Type N-Female connector. When purchasing a pigtail, you must determine the connectors that you need on each end of the cable. This will depend on the brand and model of your card, and the connector on the antenna cable. If you have more than one card that you will be using for WarDriving, most likely you will need more than one pigtail. Most pigtails will be about 12 to 18 inches (30 to 45cm) in length. Longer pigtails may be found, but are generally best avoided. This is because the thin cables have a high signal loss, and the longer the cable, the more signal is lost before it gets to the radio card.

Figure 3.15 Pigtail (Type N to Type MC)

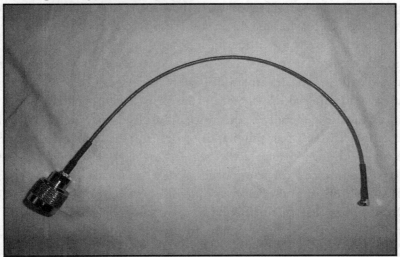

Using a GPS Receiver
with NetStumbler and MiniStumbler

In order to physically locate an access point (AP) or to map AP locations, you have to know where you are when the AP is detected. While this may seem to be simplistic, it is true. So how do you track where you are when an AP is detected? One option would be for you to take notes, writing down your exact location every time NetStumbler finds an Access Point. But, this could be rather difficult; getting a precise location might involve making measurements, along with detailed notes. For instance, "35 feet north of the 'No Parking' sign in front of 23 Main St.; five feet from the edge of the sidewalk." Using such a technique might be tedious, and you would proceed fairly slowly.

However, there is a much easier way to do this, with a level of precision within approximately 25 feet. By simply attaching a Global Positioning System (GPS) satellite receiver to your computer, NetStumbler will automatically log your location every time it receives a Probe Response frame.

GPS units are radio receivers that measure a signal from several different Global Positioning satellites. By using triangulation, the receiver calculates its location on the surface of the Earth using those signals. The location is reported in terms of the Latitude, Longitude, Altitude, and other data. Most GPS units continuously update their location information. The unit then sends out this position data over a serial data link, typically about once a second. In turn, NetStumbler reads this serial link data. It then records the Longitude and Latitude from the GPS whenever a Probe Response frame is heard.

Because of this *ease of use* in recording the location of a detected AP, a GPS is the second accessory that most WarDrivers add to their "Stumbling Rig."

Features of GPS receivers vary, but generally they fall into two categories: those that have an integral display and those that have no display. Those that are without a display are generally referred to as "mouse" or "puck" styles since they tend to resemble either a computer mouse or a hockey puck. Mouse or puck GPS receivers without a display are generally less expensive, but they need to be connected to a computer (or some other device) to work properly. Those with displays can function in a standalone mode. If you plan on using your GPS solely for WarDriving, a mouse or puck style may be fine. However, if you plan on using the GPS for other activities such as hiking, then you should buy one with a display. Figure 3.16 shows three common GPS units. The two on either end have a built-in Liquid Crystal Display (LCD), while the center one is a "puck" without a display.

Figure 3.16 Typical GPS Receiver Models

Typical GPS Problems

There are several potential "stumbling" blocks you may come across when using your GPS receiver with NetStumbler. First and foremost is the requirement to use a GPS unit that will transmit its data over some manner of communications link. Most GPS receivers will output location data in the National Marine Electronics Association (NMEA) 0183 data protocol, using a serial cable. Technically, the NMEA 0183 output is EIA-422A data, but for all practical purposes it is the same as RS-232 serial data. This means a GPS that sends NMEA 0183 data will talk to the serial communications (COM) ports used on most computers. Some newer GPS units use Bluetooth low-power radio communications to transmit the NMEA data.

Before you attempt to use the GPS receiver with NetStumbler or MiniStumbler, you must go through an initialization procedure. The procedure needs to be done before the GPS will send out the correct location data. Be sure to read the instructions for your GPS, and go through the setup.

The serial ports on both the computer running NetStumbler and the GPS receiver must be set to use the same settings that NetStumbler uses. As we saw in the section covering the GPS tab of the NetStumbler Options dialog box, the default GPS communications settings for NetStumbler are 4800 baud, 8 Data Bits, No Parity Bit, and 1 Stop Bit. This is because these are the default settings for many NMEA devices. Again, the port and communication settings may be changed as needed via the GPS tab on the **View | Options** dialog box. NetStumbler will look for NMEA data on whichever serial port is set under the GPS settings. It will also adjust the speed and other data setting on the chosen serial port to the settings found under this tab.

The Map Datum from the GPS should be set to World Geodetic System of 1984 or WGS84. This is the default setting for most GPS receivers, but occasionally the data output is set to the North American Datum of 1927 (NAD27). While the two data sets are very similar, there can be a difference in location of over 100 meters (320 feet) in different sections of the United States. Using the NAD27 setting therefore may result in inaccurate location information. This error will become very apparent if any mapping is done using the NetStumbler data.

A second problem is that some GPS brands and models need to lock on to the satellite signals and establish their location *before* they send any serial data. More than one person has started checking cables and connections, and analyzing RS-232 data protocols, only to realize that the receiver had just not seen enough satellite signals to establish a location, and had not sent anything out of the serial port.

Conversely, many GPS units will send out data, but it may not be very accurate if the receiver has not locked onto the satellite signals. One chipset, the Sony

CXD2931R, used in some popular GPS units is known to initialize itself to Tokyo if it cannot see any satellite signals. That's fine if you happen to be in Tokyo when you start your WarDrive, but will probably not be very accurate otherwise.

The lesson here is to make sure your GPS receiver has a satellite lock before you head out on your first WarDrive. GPS satellite signals are relatively weak since the satellites are in high orbit, and the GPS receiver may need several minutes to figure out where it is on the Earth's surface. If you are inside a building, moving outdoors will help speed up this process, as the receiver will have better "Line of Sight" to the satellites, and therefore have better signal reception. Also, anything that blocks the GPS receiver's clear view of the sky, from heavy tree cover to a city's "concrete canyons," can hinder the capability of the receiver to determine location. While WarDriving, try to keep the GPS where it can see the sky. In most vehicles, this will be an area on the dashboard under the windshield, or near another window. For the sake of safety, make sure the GPS receiver (or any other device) does not obstruct the driver's field of view.

Tools & Traps…

Troubleshooting GPS Problems

If NetStumbler does not seem to be communicating with your GPS receiver, it is sometimes difficult to determine if the fault lays with the NetStumbler settings, the GPS unit itself, or something else such as the cables and connectors.

To check if the GPS is sending data, use a terminal emulator program. A common terminal emulator is HyperTerminal, which comes with Windows. Start by changing the Communications settings in the Device Manager to the GPS serial settings. For most brands of GPS receiver, the default communications settings are 4800 baud, 8 Data Bits, 1 Stop Bit, and No Parity. Don't forget to choose the communications port that is connected to the GPS.

Make sure that the GPS has a clear view of the sky to get proper signals. If the GPS receiver is working properly, and the communications settings are correct, then you should see NMEA sentences in the terminal emulator. NMEA sentences should look similar to the following, although the data will differ slightly according to your location.

Continued

```
$GPGSV,3,1,10,17,78,216,38,23,63,311,42,26,56,051,41,15,52,303,43*7
E

$GPGSV,3,2,10,18,46,295,49,09,36,152,,29,36,053,,03,09,317,*7C

$GPGSV,3,3,10,10,08,097,,06,04,203,,,,,,,,,*7C

$GPGLL,4422.2935,N,07313.8332,W,005702.969,A*21

$GPGGA,005702.97,4422.2935,N,07313.8332,W,1,05,2.7,00075,M,,,,*3E

$GPRMC,005702.97,A,4422.2935,N,07313.8332,W,00.0,000.0,150303,15.,W
*67

$GPGSA,A,2,17,23,26,18,15,,,,,,,,2.7,2.7,*13
```

If you see information similar to this, then the GPS is working properly, and you may need to adjust the NetStumbler settings. If you see characters that make no sense, then one or more communications settings are incorrect. Double-check the settings on both the GPS and the PC.

No characters showing at all in the terminal window indicates a probable cable issue. In this case, you may need to purchase a Null Modem, which will swap the connections of several common lines used in serial connections. Null Modems for serial cables can be obtained at most Radio Shack stores for under $10.

For advanced GPS diagnostics, you might want to look at the VisualGPS freeware program at www.visualgps.net/. For iPAQ users, there is VisualGPSce for the ARM processor.

A third issue is that RS-232 serial data has its own pitfalls. Almost all serial connections on the GPS receivers are proprietary, so most users will need to purchase a cable from the GPS manufacturer. The plugs and sockets for the PC end of the cable are usually DB9 subconnectors on most laptops, but sometimes those are also proprietary. Encountering a plug (or socket) on both the laptop and the GPS requiring the purchase and use of gender-changer plugs or sockets in order to just get the equipment to connect to each other is quite common. Another common difficulty with the RS-232 standard is finding that a null modem is required to switch the location of the data lines within the connectors. A gender changer and a null modem are shown in Figure 3.17.

Figure 3.17 A "Gender Changer" Plug and a Null Modem Needed to Connect Various GPS Cables

The final common problem with using a GPS is that many laptops produced in the last few years lack RS-232 serial ports. Instead, the serial ports have been replaced with the faster and more flexible Universal Serial Bus (USB) ports. However, the current version of NetStumbler does not support USB data for the GPS data. This will require the use of a serial-to-USB converter, and assigning a virtual serial communication (COM) port to the USB input.

Putting It All Together: The Complete "Stumbling Setup"

At this point, you should have collected all the pieces. Hopefully, you have been able to configure everything, and confirmed that it's all working. No doubt, you are about to head out on your first WarDrive. Before you do, however, look over these setups and make sure you are ready. You can see a typical NetStumbler setup in Figure 3.18. Most setups will include the following, or very similar, items:

- A laptop with PC Card or PCMCIA slot(s)
- An ORiNOCO Classic Gold wireless network interface card
- An antenna pigtail
- A portable omni-directional antenna in the 3dBi to 8dBi range, with magnetic mount base
- GPS
- Serial communications cable for GPS
- GPS cradle mount

Figure 3.18 A Complete NetStumbler WarDriving Rig: Laptop, GPS Receiver, Omni Antenna, and Pigtail

A laptop carrying case (shoulder bag or backpack) is not shown in the photo, but is certainly an item that you don't want to overlook. It helps make carrying all the equipment around a lot easier.

A typical MiniStumbler setup is shown in Figure 3.19. It includes:

- An iPAQ PocketPC
- A PC card expansion pack
- ORiNOCO Classic Gold wireless network interface card
- An antenna pigtail
- An omni-directional antenna
- GPS
- A serial communications cable for GPS
- A Belkin USB/Serial "Y-Sync" synchronization cable for iPAQ
- A Radio Shack Male DB9–Male DB9 Gender Adapter
- A Radio Shack Null Modem Adapter

Figure 3.19 A Complete MiniStumbler WarDriving Rig: PocketPC, GPS Receiver, Omni Antenna, and Pigtail

If you have a MiniStumbler kit, you might want to consider having a minimal setup to use while walking or bicycle riding. A possible "WarWalking" kit could consist of items similar to this list:

- An iPAQ PocketPC
- A PC card expansion pack
- ORiNOCO Classic Gold wireless network interface card
- "Puck"- or "Mouse"-style GPS
- A serial communications cable for GPS

With a minimal setup such as this, you can usually carry a whole "Stumbler Setup" in a large camera case or fanny pack. You can see how compact the whole assembly is in Figure 3.20.

Figure 3.20 A Minimal MiniStumbler "WarWalking" Rig: PocketPC and GPS Receiver Only

Three other accessories that may you may find useful are: a mobile power supply for the laptop or PocketPC, multiple socket cigarette lighter adapter, and a DC–AC power inverter. The multiple cigarette lighter socket adapter allows you to have extra 12-Volt power sockets in your vehicle without rewiring, and a DC–AC converter allows you to power devices that you might not own an automotive power supply for, such as a laptop. Independently or together, these two accessories allow you to have a flexible electrical power arrangement in your vehicle.

Belkin makes a USB/Automotive Power Adapter that powers an iPAQ in a vehicle while connected to a GPS. This allows the iPAQ to be powered in a vehicle via a Synchronization cable. The adapter actually comes with a Belkin mobile synchronization cable, but it seems to work well with most USB cables, including the Serial/USB Y-cable.

Exporting NetStumbler Data

After you've returned from your WarDrive, you will have some data. Depending on your area, and the number of WLANs there, you may have a lot of data! If you are inclined to perform any kind of analysis, you may want to use the data in other programs such as spreadsheets or databases. To help you do this, NetStumbler includes the capability to export the collected data in three formats:

Summary, Text, and Wi-Scan. However, MiniStumbler does not include an export function. To extract text data from a file compiled by MiniStumbler, the file must first be opened in MiniStumbler.

The export functions are located in the **File** menu under **File | Export | Summary**, **File | Export | Text**, and **File | Export | wi-scan**. All three are very similar in that they export the information as text files. They differ only in the amount of information that they export. Using the original NetStumbler file used in Chapter 2, we'll see how the information is exported

As the name implies, **Summary** exports a single line summary of each WLAN detected in a Tab delimited format. Most of the column headings are the same or similar to the graphical NetStumbler display. Here is the top of a Summary file, and the one line from the first detected AP:

```
# $Creator: Network Stumbler Version 0.4.0
# $Format: wi-scan summary with extensions
# Latitude    Longitude    ( SSID )    Type    ( BSSID )    Time (GMT)    [
SNR Sig Noise ]    # ( Name )    Flags    Channelbits    BcnIntvl
DataRate
# $DateGMT: 2003-12-03
N 44.3702500    W 73.2314583    ( linksys )    BBS    ( 00:0c:41:41:2b:b6 )
14:59:51 (GMT)    [ 28 81 53 ]    # ( )    0005    00000040    100    110
```

The **Text** file format exports the same information, but gives all readings recorded for a particular AP. In this example, the Text file has reported six lines of data for the same AP that was seen in the Summary example.

```
# $Creator: Network Stumbler Version 0.4.0
# $Format: wi-scan with extensions
# Latitude    Longitude    ( SSID )    Type    ( BSSID )    Time (GMT)
[ SNR Sig Noise ]    # ( Name )    Flags    Channelbits    BcnIntvl
DataRate
# $DateGMT: 2003-12-03
N 44.3718317    W 73.2304633    ( linksys )    BBS    ( 00:0c:41:41:2b:b6 )
14:59:51 (GMT)    [ 7 59 52 ]    # ( )    0005    00000040    100    110
N 44.3718317    W 73.2304633    ( linksys )    BBS    ( 00:0c:41:41:2b:b6 )
14:59:51 (GMT)    [ 7 59 52 ]    # ( )    0005    00000040    100    110
N 44.3717967    W 73.2303550    ( linksys )    BBS    ( 00:0c:41:41:2b:b6 )
14:59:58 (GMT)    [ 7 59 52 ]    # ( )    0005    00000040    100    110
N 44.3717800    W 73.2304183    ( linksys )    BBS    ( 00:0c:41:41:2b:b6 )
15:00:00 (GMT)    [ 0 53 53 ]    # ( )    0005    00000040    100    110
```

```
N 44.3717800     W 73.2304183     ( linksys )    BBS    ( 00:0c:41:41:2b:b6 )
15:00:00 (GMT)    [ 6 59 53 ]    # ( )    0005    00000040    100    110
N 44.3717750     W 73.2304417     ( linksys )    BBS    ( 00:0c:41:41:2b:b6 )
15:00:28 (GMT)    [ 7 58 51 ]    # ( )    0005    00000040    100    110
```

Finally, the **wi-scan** file format exports the multiple readings for each AP, but has fewer columns. This format is compatible with the data from several other WLAN scanning programs. In this example, you can see the same six data lines as in the Text example. However, the Number, Name, Flags, Channel Bits, Beacon Interval and Data Rate columns are not included.

```
# $Creator: Network Stumbler Version 0.4.0
# $Format: wi-scan
# Latitude    Longitude    ( SSID )    Type    ( BSSID )    Time (GMT)    [
SNR Sig Noise ]
# $DateGMT: 2003-12-03
N 44.2230990     W 73.1382780     ( linksys )    BBS    ( 00:0c:41:41:2b:b6 )
14:59:51 (GMT)    [ 7 59 52 ]
N 44.2230990     W 73.1382780     ( linksys )    BBS    ( 00:0c:41:41:2b:b6 )
14:59:51 (GMT)    [ 7 59 52 ]
N 44.2230780     W 73.1382130     ( linksys )    BBS    ( 00:0c:41:41:2b:b6 )
14:59:58 (GMT)    [ 7 59 52 ]
N 44.2230680     W 73.1382510     ( linksys )    BBS    ( 00:0c:41:41:2b:b6 )
15:00:00 (GMT)    [ 0 53 53 ]
N 44.2230680     W 73.1382510     ( linksys )    BBS    ( 00:0c:41:41:2b:b6 )
15:00:00 (GMT)    [ 6 59 53 ]
N 44.2230650     W 73.1382650     ( linksys )    BBS    ( 00:0c:41:41:2b:b6 )
15:00:28 (GMT)    [ 7 58 51 ]
```

Using the Exported Data

If you plan on using the Summary, Text, or Wi-Scan text exports for any kind of analysis or mapping, there are several things you need to know about them. First, the text output always shows the Signal Strength data as a positive number. To determine the correct dBm reading, you must subtract 149 from the reading in the text file. This is due to the manner in which the card drivers internally record the numbers.

The second piece of information you need to know is the way that the data is encoded in the *Flags* and *Channelbits* columns. As previously noted, the Flag column contains the 802.11 capability information in hexadecimal (base 16). This is also true of the *Channelbits* field. To determine what data has been recorded in these two fields, you may need to perform some hexadecimal arithmetic. If you don't understand how to do addition or subtraction in hexadecimal, then you should consider reading up on the subjects. It is not particularly difficult, but it is more complicated than we have space for here

To determine the values contained in the Flags field, you need to perform the hexadecimal operation AND. For example, you scan an AP; the Flags are shown as 0011. Using AND against 0011 for all the possible values, only 1 and 10 would return TRUE (or 1).

- **0001** ←
- 0002
- 0004
- 0008
- **0010** ←
- 0020
- 0040
- 0080
- 0400

Since **0001** indicates Extended Service Set (ESS) or Infrastructure mode, and **0010** indicates privacy or encryption, you therefore can conclude that you have detected a wireless network that is infrastructure-based (it uses an access point) and which has encryption turned on.

A flag of 0035 would be computed as:

- **0001** ←
- 0002
- **0004** ←
- 0008
- **0010** ←
- **0020** ←
- 0040

- 0080
- 0400

Base on this, you can determine that the WLAN is running in Infrastructure mode, the AP is CF-Pollable, it is using a Short Preamble, and encryption is turned on, as **0001** indicates ESS mode, **0004** designates that the network uses the Contention-Free (CF) Pollable protocol, **0010** shows that encryption is enabled, and **0020** indicates that the WLAN is using the Short Preamble.

The 802.11b channel numbers and corresponding *Channelbits* hexadecimal codes are shown in Table 3.2.

Table 3.2 Channels and the Channel Bits

Channel	Channel Bits
1	0002
2	0004
3	0008
4	0010
5	0020
6	0040
7	0080
8	0100
9	0200
10	0400
11	0800
12	1000
13	2000
14	4000

Again, these are encoded as hexadecimal numbers. If multiple channels are encountered, then hex arithmetic will have to be performed to determine the channels from the *Channelbits* columns.

Additional Resources

The NetStumbler Web site, www.netstumbler.com, and the NetStumbler Forums, forums.nestumber.com, are great places to exchange information with other people who use NetStumbler and MiniStumbler. Sometimes Marius Milner, the author of NetStumbler and MiniStumbler, even shows up to let everyone know the latest information on the two applications. You should definitely consider looking around, and join in. One word of caution: the forums tend to be long on information, and short on newcomer's feelings. If you want to participate in the Forums, please read the FAQs and use the built-in forum Search function before asking questions. Few threads attract flames faster then a "newbie" who hasn't searched and asks a common question.

Marius Milner also maintains his own Web site: www.stumbler.net. There you can find out about things such as the newest versions of NetStumbler.

Several other resources on the Web include:

- NetStumbler listserv: www.michiganwireless.org/lists.html
- NetStumbler listserv archive: www.michiganwireless.org/archive/mail-list.html
- National Marine Electronics Association (NMEA): www.nmea.org/
- Bluetooth Special Interest Group: www.bluetooth.com

Summary

This concludes the two chapters on using NetStumbler and MiniStumbler. As you have seen, both programs allow you to gather a lot of information about wireless networks using standard "off the shelf" hardware. The information collected is broad enough to be of interest from network security professionals to RF technicians to hobbyists.

Solutions Fast Track

Operational Details

☑ NDIS 5.1 Drivers, Wireless cards, and NetStumbler

☑ Detailed information on all the data collected in the Right Pane columns

☑ IP Address Look Up will run WHOIS searches on ARIN, RIPE, and APNIC databases

Option Settings

☑ To get the optimum use from NetStumbler, many of the functions must be set up correctly. Many of those options are located in the Network Stumbler Options dialog box under **View | Options**. It has four main tabs and multiple suboptions.

☑ The General tab controls the scanning speeds and automatic adjustment, starting scans when opening a new document, the automatic reconfiguration of a wireless card, querying an AP for names; and saving files automatically.

☑ The Display tab controls the manner that the Longitude and Latitude are shown.

☑ The GPS tab controls the port and communications settings for obtaining GPS data.

☑ The Scripting tab controls the running of external script programs that may interface with NetStumbler.

☑ The MIDI tab controls the playing of MIDI musical notes.

☑ NetStumbler comes with ten sound files, which are installed by default. Each sound is associated within the program with a specific action. The standard sounds can be replaced with new sounds of your liking.

Disabling Network Protocols

☑ Disable network protocols to avoid any possible illegal actions.

☑ Disable TCP/IP via the command line on Windows 95, Windows 98/98SE, Windows ME, Windows 2000, and Windows XP using IPCONFIG.EXE.

☑ Alternately, disable TCP/IP via the graphical interface on Windows 95, Windows 98/98SE, and Windows ME using WINIPCFG.EXE.

☑ Disable TCP/IP on a PocketPC by manually entering an IP address of 0.0.0.0 and a subnet mask of 0.0.0.0.

Additional RF Equipment: Antennae and Cables

☑ An antenna in the 3dBi to 8dBi range is a good choice for WarDriving.

☑ A Magnetic Mount makes placing and using the antenna on a vehicle very convenient.

☑ A pigtail is needed to connect the wireless card to the antenna in most cases.

Using a GPS Receiver with NetStumbler and MiniStumbler

☑ GPS receivers calculate your position using triangulation from satellite signals.

☑ NetStumbler uses the GPS information to log the user's location when a WLAN is detected.

☑ Both NetStumbler and the GPS must be configured to communicate with each other.

☑ The GPS must be set up and properly initialized before being used with NetStumbler.

Putting It All Together: The Complete "Stumbling Setup"

☑ A typical NetStumbler setup includes: Laptop, Wireless Card, Antenna Pigtail, Antenna, GPS, and GPS Serial cable

☑ A typical MiniStumbler setup includes: iPAQ PocketPC, expansion pack, wireless card, antenna pigtail, antenna, GPS, GPS serial cable, serial synchronization cable for iPAQ, DB9 Gender Adapter, and Null Modem Adapter.

☑ A minimal MiniStumbler setup includes: iPAQ PocketPC, expansion pack, wireless card, "Puck"- or "Mouse"-style GPS, and GPS serial cable.

☑ Additional accessories that are helpful: a mobile power supply for the laptop or PocketPC, multiple-socket cigarette lighter adapter, and a DC-AC power inverter.

Exporting NetStumbler Data

☑ NetStumbler includes three options for exporting the collected data as text.

☑ Some of the exported data is encoded in hexadecimal form, requiring some knowledge of hex arithmetic for further analysis.

Additional Resources

☑ NetStumbler Web site: www.netstumbler.com

☑ NetStumbler Forums Web site: http://forums.nestumber.com

☑ Marius Milner's Web site: www.stumbler.net

☑ NetStumbler listserv: www.michiganwireless.org/lists.html

☑ NetStumbler listserv archive: www.michiganwireless.org/archive/maillist.html

☑ National Marine Electronics Association (NMEA): www.nmea.org/

Frequently Asked Questions

The following Frequently Asked Questions, answered by the authors of this book, are designed to both measure your understanding of the concepts presented in this chapter and to assist you with real-life implementation of these concepts. To have your questions about this chapter answered by the author, browse to **www.syngress.com/solutions** and click on the **"Ask the Author"** form. You will also gain access to thousands of other FAQs at ITFAQnet.com.

Q: Is a GPS satellite receiver required to use NetStumbler or MiniStumbler?

A: No. Either program functions very well without using a GPS receiver. Using the applications without a GPS receiver just means that you will not be able to log the locations of any APs you might find.

Q: My GPS doesn't seem to work on the serial port of my PocketPC. The GPS receiver's serial communications settings are correct. So why does MiniStumbler say "config error" instead of the GPS coordinates?

A: Disable any other drivers before attempting to use the GPS. Many times the culprit is an external keyboard driver that uses the serial port.

Q: My iPAQ expansion unit has two PCMCIA slots. Can I run a wireless card and a GPS PC card in adjoining slots?

A: Unfortunately, this is going to be difficult at best and may not work at all. The problem is a physical size limitation rather than anything imposed by the MiniStumbler program. Due to the size of the antenna bulge on most wireless Ethernet cards and the antenna portion of most GSP cards, there is just not enough room to physically place both cards in the space provided. You could probably do this with a card that uses an external as opposed to an internal antenna, but you'd be losing the "all in one" package that most people desire. One user on the NetStumbler forums has used an ORiNOCO card, a Haicom 303E CompactFlash GPS, and a PCMCIA/CompactFlash converter. The Haicom 303E has a hinge between the CompactFlash section and the antenna section, allowing clearance between the GPS and ORiNOCO antennae. This is probably as close as you can get to a single package setup.

Q: My AP is using WPA encryption, but it shows up as "WEP" in the Encryption column. Why is this?

A: NetStumbler detects encryption based on whether it sees the 0010 (Privacy) Flag in the response that it receives to the Beacon Request. NS doesn't particularly know (or care) what the actual encryption method is, only that 0010 is set in the Flags. This is reported as "WEP" in NetStumbler since WEP was the only available encryption level when NS was first created.

Q: Should I use NetStumbler while connected to my network?

A: No. NetStumbler is designed to detect networks; it is not intended to be run while actually using a network connection. Because of the way that it functions, NetStumbler may repeatedly disconnect you (for instance, every time it reconfigures the wireless network card). Obviously, this will interrupt normal network operations and is something to be avoided.

Q: I keep finding the SSID "SST-PR-1" for an ad-hoc network almost everywhere I run NetStumbler or MiniStumbler. It has shown up in the city and the countryside, in different cities and states, and even on highways in the middle of nowhere. Is this some government conspiracy? Are the "Men In Black" using WiFi? What is it?

A: Conspiracy theorists can relax, or at least find a different subject to worry about. "SST-PR-1" is the SSID used by the Sears Home Service van fleet across North America. Sears' technicians use a handheld computer that works in an ad-hoc peer-to-peer network with a computer in the service van. It allows the technicians to do any number of things from tracking parts inventory to getting directions to a customer's home.

## Chapter 4

Installing Kismet in Slackware Linux 9.1

Solutions in this Chapter:

- **Preparing Your System for Installation with an ORiNOCO Gold (Hermes Chipset) Card**

- **Preparing Your System for Installation with a Prism 2 Chipset Card**

- **Installing Kismet**

☑ **Summary**

☑ **Solutions Fast Track**

☑ **Frequently Asked Questions**

Introduction

Kismet is the most popular WarDriving application for Linux users. Unlike NetStumbler, Kismet is a passive wireless scanner. A passive scanner does not broadcast, it simply "listens" for any traffic on the 802.11 bands. To accomplish this, the wireless card must be put into monitor mode. Contrary to popular belief, monitor mode and promiscuous mode are not the same thing. Monitor mode allows the card to capture packets without associating with a specific network. Promiscuous mode allows the card to capture any packets transmitted on the network that the card is associated with. Kismet requires monitor mode because it can be configured to channel hop. Channel hopping is configuring the card to listen on a channel for a specified time frame and then change or "hop" to another channel. Channel hopping allows Kismet to discover wireless networks that are broadcasting on any of the 802.11 specified channel frequencies. Getting a card into monitor mode has generally been the stumbling block for new WarDrivers that want to use Kismet. Enabling monitor mode on many cards can be a frustrating, if not difficult, process. This chapter details the process of enabling monitor mode on two of the most common chipsets: Hermes and Prism 2.

In addition to its other features, Kismet doesn't rely on the Service Set Identifier (SSID) broadcast beacon to determine the existence of a wireless access point. Therefore, more access points can often be discovered. This is useful while WarDriving and when attempting to find rogue access points that a user may have attached to your corporate network.

However, one problem that Linux users face when attempting to install Kismet is the diversity offered among different distributions. Fedora Linux has a different file structure than SuSE Linux, while both of these differ from Slackware Linux. These are only a few of the many distributions to choose from. However, as Fedora Linux and Slackware Linux are two of the most popular Linux distributions for WarDrivers, we will focus on these. This chapter details how to prepare your Slackware Linux 9.1 installation for use with Kismet. While, in the next chapter, the steps you need to take for Fedora Linux are presented.

In older versions of Slackware Linux, a kernel upgrade or modification was often required to use Kismet. That is no longer the case. The stock kernel that ships with Slackware 9.1 is version 2.4.22. This kernel does not need to be upgraded or modified to use Kismet. The kernel used in this walkthrough is the 2.4.23 kernel. The stock kernel was upgraded to address a Linux kernel vulnerability related to the do_brk() function that could lead to a root level compromise.

I recommend upgrading your kernel to version 2.4.23 or later. Slackware has provided kernel upgrade packages at:

- ftp://ftp.slackware.com/pub/slackware/slackware-9.1/patches/packages/kernel-ide-2.4.23-i486-1.tgz

- ftp://ftp.slackware.com/pub/slackware/slackware-9.1/patches/packages/kernel-modules-2.4.23-i486-1.tgz

- ftp://ftp.slackware.com/pub/slackware/slackware-9.1/patches/packages/kernel-source-2.4.23-noarch-2.tgz

Tools & Traps…

Upgrading the Kernel to 2.4.23

Upgrading the 2.4.22 kernel to 2.4.23 using the Slackware packages also requires that the ALSA sound packages be upgraded. Slackware has provided these packages at:

- ftp://ftp.slackware.com/pub/slackware/slackware-9.1/patches/packages/alsa-driver-0.9.8-i486-1.tgz

- ftp://ftp.slackware.com/pub/slackware/slackware-9.1/patches/packages/alsa-lib-0.9.8-i486-1.tgz

- ftp://ftp.slackware.com/pub/slackware/slackware-9.1/patches/packages/alsa-oss-0.9.8-i486-1.tgz

- ftp://ftp.slackware.com/pub/slackware/slackware-9.1/patches/packages/alsa-utils-0.9.8-i486-1.tgz

Depending on your configuration, additional package upgrades may also be required. For more information on this vulnerability and upgrading your kernel packages, refer to the Slackware security advisory at: www.slackware.com/security/viewer.php?l=slackware-security&y=2003&m=slackware-security.718266.

Kismet is a robust program. For many WarDrivers, the allure of finding access points that are not broadcasting SSID alone makes Kismet their choice. For others, the ability to WarDrive while using their favorite Linux distribution is the key. Either way, Kismet offers Linux WarDrivers an alternative to NetStumbler.

Preparing Your System for Installation with an ORiNOCO Gold (Hermes Chipset) Card

Many Kismet users begin their WarDriving experience using NetStumbler in Windows. Because NetStumbler was designed to use Hermes-based cards such as the ORiNOCO Gold card, many users have this card and want to use the same card with Kismet. Unfortunately, the stock drivers for this card do not allow the card to enter monitor mode. This requires patching the ORiNOCO drivers and the pcmcia-cs drivers. A kernel upgrade may not be required, but the source code for the Linux Kernel must be on the system.

Getting pcmcia-cs Patched and Working

In order to set your ORiNOCO card into monitor mode, you need to patch the pcmcia-cs and the ORiNOCO drivers. Patching both of these has, traditionally, been a poorly documented process, though it is relatively straightforward. In as much, this process is detailed in the following sections of this chapter.

Installing pcmcia-cs

The first thing you need to do is obtain a version of pcmcia-cs that has a monitor mode patch available. The current version with a patch, at the time of this writing, is pcmcia-cs-3.2.3. The Shmoo group provides updated information on the pcmcia-cs patches on their Web site (http://airsnort.shmoo.com/orinocoinfo.html). Because Slackware 9.1 ships with pcmcia-cs-3.2.5 you will actually need to downgrade to pcmcia-cs-3.2.3. When a patch for pcmcia-cs-3.2.5 becomes available, this will no longer be necessary and you will be able to patch the installed version of pcmcia-cs. In order to install the pcmcia-cs modules, you must have root privileges, and so you will need to use the **su** command to switch to root if you have not already done so. See Figure 4.1.

Figure 4.1 Using the **su** Command to Switch the User to root

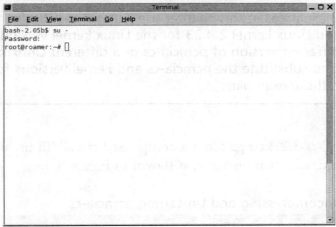

First, download the pcmcia-cs. You can download any version from: http://prdownloads.sourceforge.net/pcmcia-cs, or download the 3.2.3 directly from: http://prdownloads.sourceforge.net/pcmcia-cs/pcmcia-cs-3.2.3.tar.gz. Next, save or copy pcmcia-cs-3.2.3 to /usr/src, as shown in Figure 4.2. If you did not install the kernel source package when installing Slackware 9.1, you need to install that package from the Slackware CD-ROM.

Figure 4.2 Copying pcmcia-cs to /usr/src

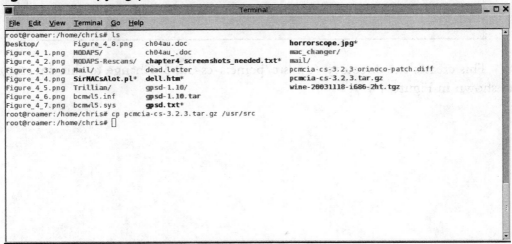

> **NOTE**
>
> All of the examples in this chapter use pcmcia-cs-3.2.3 for the pcmcia-cs version and Linux kernel 2.4.23 for the Linux kernel version. If you are using a different version of pcmcia-cs or a different Linux kernel version you need to substitute the pcmcia-cs and kernel versions for those shown in these examples.

The pcmcia-cs–3.2.3.tar.gz file is a compressed tarball. To install it, you need to uncompress it, and then un-tar it, as shown in Figure 4.3.

Figure 4.3 Uncompressing and Un-tarring pcmcia-cs

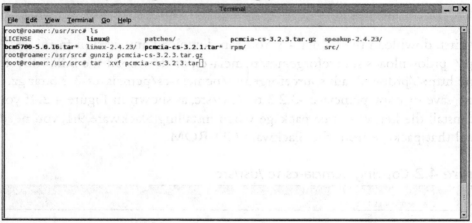

This creates the directory /usr/src/pcmcia-cs–3.2.3. Change to this directory, as shown in Figure 4.4.

Figure 4.4 Change to the /usr/src/pcmcia-cs-3.2.3 Directory

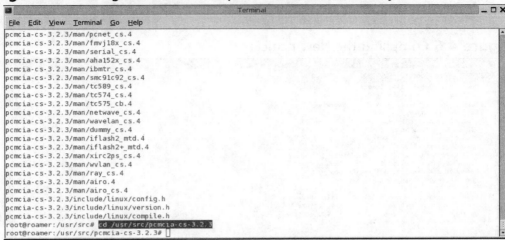

Next, you need to build the new pcmcia-cs modules. This is accomplished in three steps:

1. Type **make config** to configure the pcmcia-cs module for compilation.

2. Enter **make all** to compile the pcmcia-cs module.

3. Type **make install** to install the new pcmcia-cs module.

These three steps are demonstrated in Figures 4.5, 4.6, and 4.7.

Figure 4.5 Configuring the New pcmcia-cs

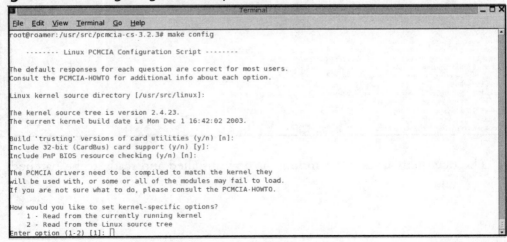

Unless you have made any changes to the default paths, you can choose the default for each of the questions asked during the **make config** phase.

Figure 4.6 Compiling the New pcmcia-cs

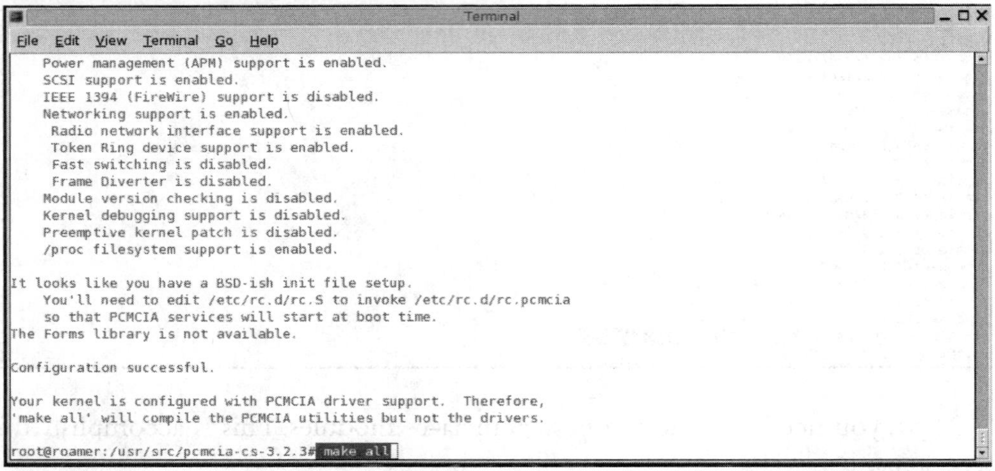
Terminal
File Edit View Terminal Go Help
Power management (APM) support is enabled.
SCSI support is enabled.
IEEE 1394 (FireWire) support is disabled.
Networking support is enabled.
Radio network interface support is enabled.
Token Ring device support is enabled.
Fast switching is disabled.
Frame Diverter is disabled.
Module version checking is disabled.
Kernel debugging support is disabled.
Preemptive kernel patch is disabled.
/proc filesystem support is enabled.
It looks like you have a BSD-ish init file setup.
You'll need to edit /etc/rc.d/rc.S to invoke /etc/rc.d/rc.pcmcia
so that PCMCIA services will start at boot time.
The Forms library is not available.
Configuration successful.
Your kernel is configured with PCMCIA driver support. Therefore,
'make all' will compile the PCMCIA utilities but not the drivers.
root@roamer:/usr/src/pcmcia-cs-3.2.3# make all

Figure 4.7 Installing the New pcmcia-cs

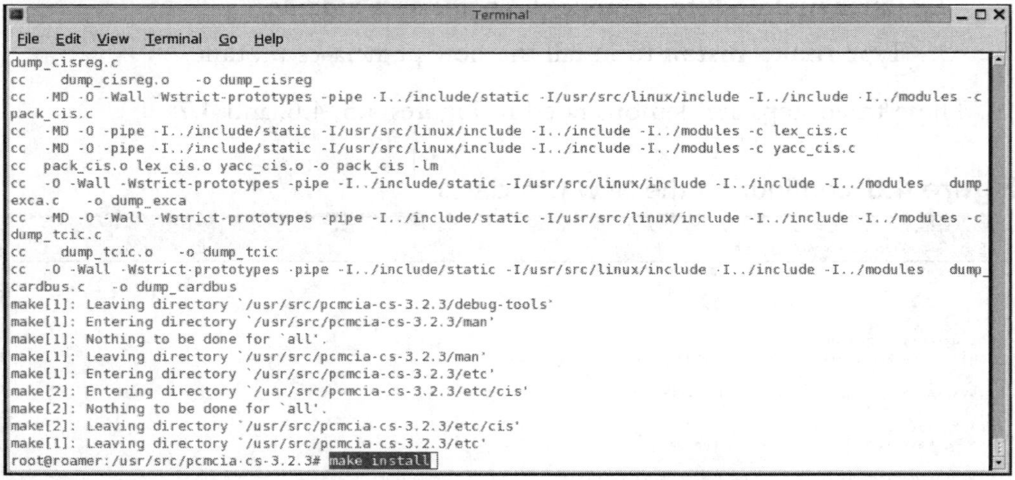
Terminal
File Edit View Terminal Go Help
dump_cisreg.c
cc dump_cisreg.o -o dump_cisreg
cc -MD -O -Wall -Wstrict-prototypes -pipe -I../include/static -I/usr/src/linux/include -I../include -I../modules -c
pack_cis.c
cc -MD -O -pipe -I../include/static -I/usr/src/linux/include -I../include -I../modules -c lex_cis.c
cc -MD -O -pipe -I../include/static -I/usr/src/linux/include -I../include -I../modules -c yacc_cis.c
cc pack_cis.o lex_cis.o yacc_cis.o -o pack_cis -lm
cc -O -Wall -Wstrict-prototypes -pipe -I../include/static -I/usr/src/linux/include -I../include -I../modules dump_
exca.c -o dump_exca
cc -MD -O -Wall -Wstrict-prototypes -pipe -I../include/static -I/usr/src/linux/include -I../include -I../modules -c
dump_tcic.c
cc dump_tcic.o -o dump_tcic
cc -O -Wall -Wstrict-prototypes -pipe -I../include/static -I/usr/src/linux/include -I../include -I../modules dump_
cardbus.c -o dump_cardbus
make[1]: Leaving directory `/usr/src/pcmcia-cs-3.2.3/debug-tools'
make[1]: Entering directory `/usr/src/pcmcia-cs-3.2.3/man'
make[1]: Nothing to be done for `all'.
make[1]: Leaving directory `/usr/src/pcmcia-cs-3.2.3/man'
make[1]: Entering directory `/usr/src/pcmcia-cs-3.2.3/etc'
make[2]: Entering directory `/usr/src/pcmcia-cs-3.2.3/etc/cis'
make[2]: Nothing to be done for `all'.
make[2]: Leaving directory `/usr/src/pcmcia-cs-3.2.3/etc/cis'
make[1]: Leaving directory `/usr/src/pcmcia-cs-3.2.3/etc'
root@roamer:/usr/src/pcmcia-cs-3.2.3# make install

The new pcmcia-cs-3.2.3 module is now installed and ready to be patched.

Patching the ORiNOCO Drivers

Now that you have installed pcmcia-cs-3.2.3, or another pcmcia-cs module that can be patched, you need to apply the ORiNOCO Monitor Mode Patch for your pcmcia-cs version. A listing of all the pcmcia-cs patches available for download is maintained at http://airsnort.shmoo.com/orinocoinfo.html. Because we have installed pcmcia-cs-3.2.3, we need the pcmcia-cs-3.2.3-orinoco-patch.diff (http://airsnort.shmoo.com/pcmcia-cs-3.2.3-orinoco-patch.diff). Save or copy pcmcia-cs-3.2.3-orinoco-patch.diff into the /usr/src/pcmcia-3.2.3 directory as shown in Figure 4.8.

Figure 4.8 Save or Copy the Patch to the /usr/src/pcmcia-cs-3.2.3 Directory

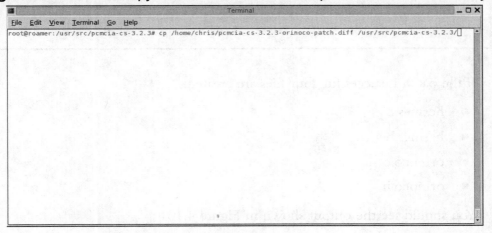

Using the **patch** command, patch the pcmcia-cs module, as shown in Figure 4.9.

Figure 4.9 Patching the pcmcia-cs Module

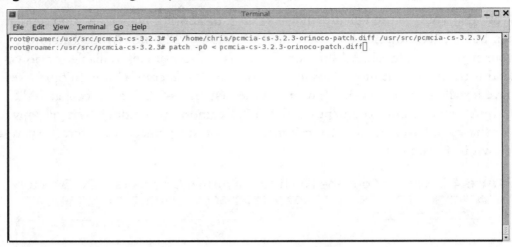

If the patch is successful, four files are created:

- hermes.c
- hermes.h
- orinoco.c
- orinoco.h

You should see the output shown in Figure 4.10

Figure 4.10 Successful Output of the Orinoco Monitor Mode Patch

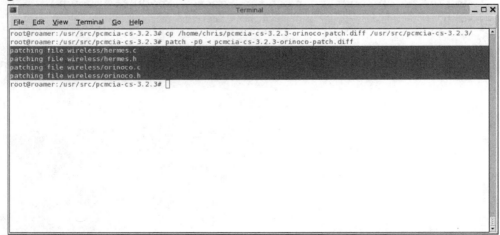

If you do not see the output shown in Figure 4.10, you have likely missed a step or made a typographical error. Try running the **patch** command again to remedy the problem, ensuring that the command used is:

```
patch -p0 < pcmcia-cs-3.2.3-orinoco-patch.diff
```

Next, change to the /usr/src/pcmcia-3.2.3/wireless directory, as shown in Figure 4.11.

Figure 4.11 Changing Directories to /usr/src/pcmcia-cs-3.2.3/wireless

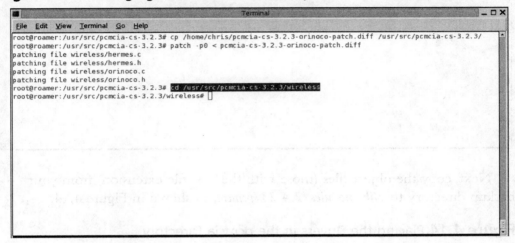

In order to work properly, the files you just patched need to be rebuilt. Use the **make all** command, as shown in Figure 4.12.

Figure 4.12 Rebuilding the Patched Files

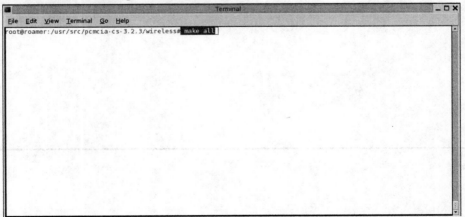

Finally, create a backup directory to store your newly patched pcmcia files, as shown in Figure 4.13.

Figure 4.13 Creating a Backup Directory and Copying Your Files

Next, copy the object files (those with the ".o" file extension) from your backup directory to */lib/modules/2.4.23/pcmcia,* as shown in Figure 4.14.

Figure 4.14 Placing the Drivers in the pcmcia Directory

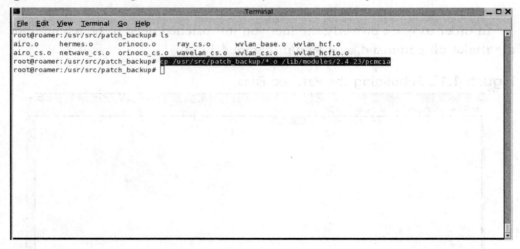

Then, copy the object files (those with the ".o" file extension) from your backup directory to */lib/modules/2.4.23/kernel/drivers/net/wireless,* as shown in Figure 4.15.

Figure 4.15 Placing the Drivers in the Modules Directory

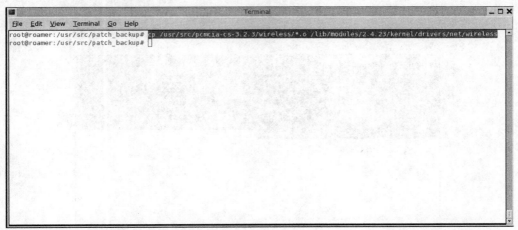

A backup directory is created to store the files because any kernel upgrades or changes you make will, in all likelihood, overwrite your patched drivers in the /lib/modules tree. By creating a backup directory to store the patched drivers, you can copy them from the backup into the new or modified /lib/modules/<kernel version> tree.

Verifying that It All Works

After you have upgraded your pcmcia-cs version and patched the ORiNOCO driver modules, you should verify that it is all working properly before installing Kismet.

In order for Kismet to function correctly, two things need to be working properly:

- The ORiNOCO card
- Monitor mode

If you performed the pcmcia-cs upgrade properly, your ORiNOCO card will work correctly. To verify this, insert your card into your PCMCIA slot and boot up. If you have already started your system, insert the ORiNOCO card and restart the PCMCIA services using the command:

`/etc/rc.d/rc.pcmcia restart`

You should hear two short "beeps" if the card was properly detected. Next, using the **ifconfig** *<interface>* command, where *<interface>* is the device name of your ORiNOCO card, verify that the card is present.

Figure 4.16 Verifying the Presence of the ORiNOCO Card

If information about your ORiNOCO card is not displayed, try bringing the card "up" using the **ifconfig** command. For instance, if your ORiNOCO card is the eth0 device, type: **ifconfig eth0 up** and then **ifconfig eth0**. You should now see information on your card similar to Figure 4.16.

NOTE

Depending on your laptop configuration, you will likely need to type **eth0, eth1, eth2**, and so on.

Next, verify that the patch worked correctly using the **iwpriv** *<interface>* command. If you correctly patched the ORiNOCO driver modules, you will see *monitor* listed in the output, as shown in Figure 4.17.

Figure 4.17 Verifying the ORiNOCO Patch Allows Monitor Mode

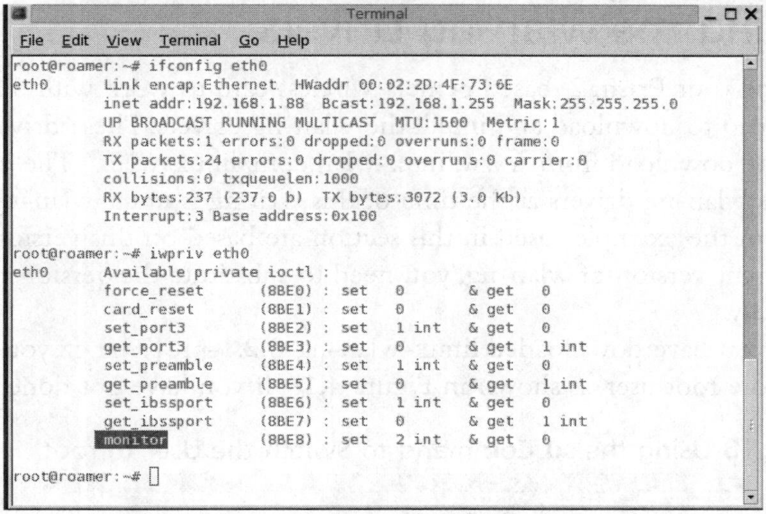

If **monitor** is listed as shown in Figure 4.17, you are ready to move on to installing Kismet.

Preparing Your System for Installation with a Prism 2 Chipset Card

Wireless cards based on the Prism 2 chipset are very popular with Kismet users. One reason for this is their availability. Many manufacturers make cards using the Prism 2 chipset, including the original Linksys cards, Netgear, SMC, and Cisco. Another reason for their popularity among Kismet users is their ease of installation. Unlike Hermes-based cards, Prism 2 cards do not require a driver patch in order to be placed into monitor mode.

Using a Prism 2–based card with Kismet only requires verifying that the pcmcia-cs version is 3.1.33 or later, and that the wlan-ng drivers are installed.

Upgrading pcmcia-cs

In order to get most Prism 2–based cards into monitor mode, you need to have pcmcia-cs version 3.1.33 or later. Slackware 9.1 installs pcmcia-cs-3.2.5 so an upgrade is not necessary in order to use your Prism 2–based wireless card with Kismet.

Downloading and Installing the wlan-ng Drivers

In order for your Prism 2–based pcmcia wireless card to work with Slackware 9.1, you need to download and install the wlan-ng drivers. These drivers are available for download from www.linux-wlan.com/linux-wlan/. The current version of the wlan-ng drivers at the time of this writing is linux-wlan-ng-0.2.1-pre17. All of the examples used in this section are based on this version. If you use a different version of wlan-ng, you need to substitute the version information appropriately.

Once you have downloaded linux-wlan-ng-0.2.1-pre17.tar.gz you need to switch to the root user, as shown in Figure 4.18, if you have not done so already.

Figure 4.18 Using the **su** Command to Switch the User to root

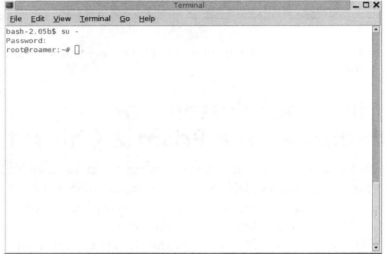

Next, uncompress and untar the linux-wlan-ng-0.2.1-pre17.tar.gz file, as shown in Figure 4.19.

Figure 4.19 Uncompressing and Untarring the Drivers

This creates a directory called linux–wlan–ng–0.2.1–pre17 with several subdi-rectories. Change to thelinux–wlan–ng–0.2.1–pre17 directory, as shown in Figure 4.20.

Figure 4.20 Changing to the Newly Created Directory

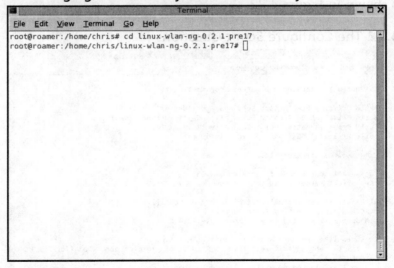

Building the linux-wlan-ng-0.2.1-pre17 drivers is a relatively simple process. First, issue the **make config** command, as shown in Figure 4.21.

Figure 4.21 Building the Drivers

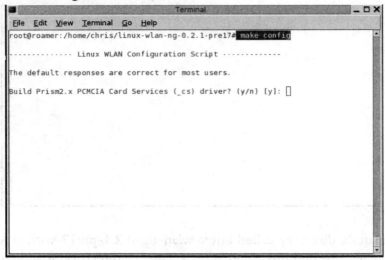

You will be prompted to answer several questions. In most cases, the configure script is able to determine the correct answer, and then prompts it as the default, as shown in Figure 4.22.

Figure 4.22 The Configure Script Questions

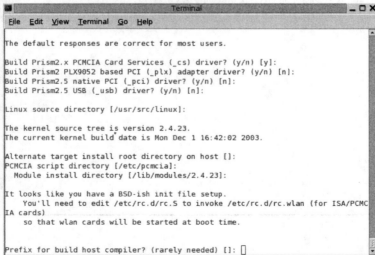

If the default answer is not correct, particularly in regard to paths, enter the correct answer.

If your answers were correct, you will see a message stating that the configuration was successful after the configure script completes. A successful configuration is shown in Figure 4.23.

Figure 4.23 The Configuration Was Successful

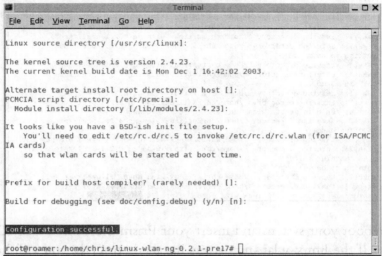

Next, issue the **make all** command, as shown in Figure 4.24. The **make all** command compiles the wlan-ng drivers.

Figure 4.24 Issuing the make all Command

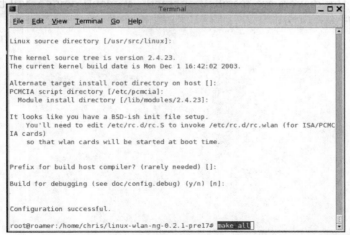

Finally, issue the **make install** command to install the drivers in the appropriate directory, as shown in Figure 4.25.

Figure 4.25 Installing the New wlan-ng Drivers

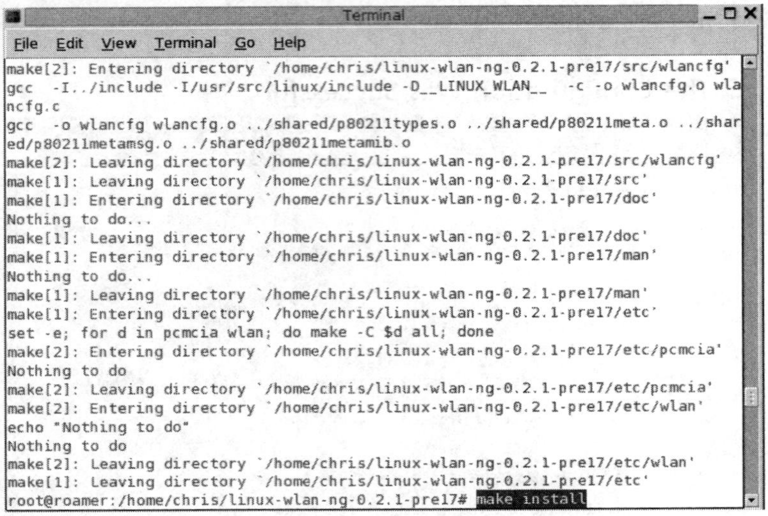

Next, reboot your system and insert your Prism 2 card in a PCMCIA slot during post. If the linux–wlan–ng drivers installed correctly, you will here two short beeps during startup.

Verifying that It All Works

Verifying that the drivers installed successfully is very simple. Issue an **ifconfig –a** command. If the drivers are installed correctly, a wlan0 device will be displayed, as shown in Figure 4.26.

Figure 4.26 A Successful Installation

Installing Kismet

After you have ensured that you have a wireless card that can be placed in monitor mode, installation of Kismet is a very straightforward process. This section
details where to get the software, and how to install it on your Slackware 9.1
installation.

Obtaining the Kismet Software

The latest version of Kismet is available for download from the Kismet Web site
at www.kismetwireless.net/download.shtml. The current stable version of Kismet
at the time of this writing is 4.0.1. If you do not want to download the most
recent version, or if you would prefer to download the development version, you
can browse all available versions at http://kismetwireless.net/code/.

NOTE

All of the examples and instructions in this Chapter use Kismet 4.0.1. If
you are using a different version of Kismet, you need to change the version information in these examples as appropriate.

After you have downloaded kismet–feb.04.01.tar.gz, uncompress and untar the package, as shown in Figure 4.27.

Figure 4.27 Uncompressing and Untarring the Kismet Files

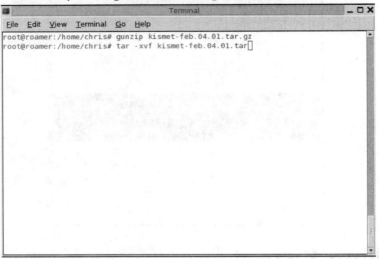

This creates the kismet–feb.04.01 directory. Change the directory to kismet–feb.04.01, as shown in Figure 4.28.

Figure 4.28 Changing to the Kismet Directory

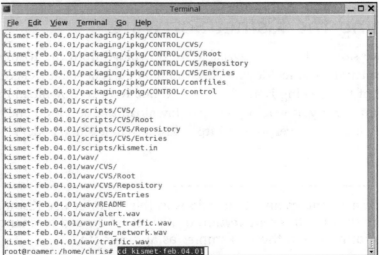

Now you are ready to begin configuring and installing Kismet.

Configuring the Kismet Software for Installation

Preparing to compile and install Kismet is a two-step process.

1. Configuring the installation script

2. Generating dependencies

First, you need to configure the installation script. From the kismet-feb.04.01 directory, run the configure script, as shown in Figure 4.29.

Figure 4.29 Configuring the Installation Script

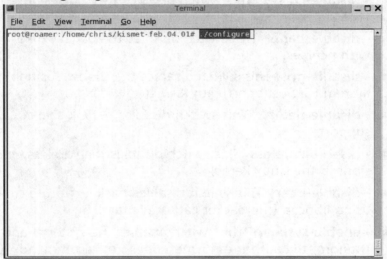

The proper way to run this is with the "./" in front of configure. This indicates that the script to run is the configure script in the current, or "./" directory. Alternately, the same results could be achieved by issuing the command with the full path to configure.

Tools & Traps...

The Kismet Configuration Options

Not every laptop is configured the same way. The packages installed and the hardware configurations can vary in a virtually infinite number of combinations. Kismet takes these differences into account and offers you the ability to tailor Kismet to your specific environment using special switches with the configure script.

These are the configuration switches and what they accomplish when invoked:

- **--disable-curses** This switch disables the "curses" user interface.
- **--disable-panel** This switch disables the panel extensions with ncurses.
- **--disable-gps** This switch disables the Global Positioning System (GPS) support with Kismet.
- **--disable-netlink** This switch disables netlink socket capture support.
- **--disable-wireless** This switch disables the wireless extensions in the Linux kernel.
- **--disable-pcap** This switch disables packet capture support using libpcap (the packet capture library).
- **--enable-syspcap** This switch enables the system libpcap. Dragorn, the author of Kismet, does not recommend the use of this switch.
- **--disable-setuid** This switch disables the suid cabability of Kismet. Dragorn, the author of Kismet, does not recommend the use of this switch.
- **--enable-wsp100** This switch enables the use of a WSP 100 remote sensor.
- **--enable-zaurus** This switch enables extra features used by the Sharp Zaurus Personal Digital Assistant (PDA).

Continued

- **--enable-local-dumper** This switch forces kismet to use a dump format other than Ethereal, even if Ethereal is installed on the system.

- **--with-ethereal=DIR** This switch adds support for Ethereal wiretap logs. DIR should be replaced with the path to ethereal.

- **--without-ethereal** This switch disables support for Ethereal wiretap logs.

- **--enable-acpi** This switch enables Advanced Configuration and Power Interface (ACPI) support for Kismet.

To use these switches, append them to configure when it is invoked. For example, to configure Kismet without the curses interface, issue the following command: **root@roamer:/home/chris/kismet-feb.04.01# ./configure –disable-curses**

NOTE

Advanced Configuration and Power Interface (ACPI) must be enabled in the Linux kernel for this switch to work.

Next, you need to generate dependencies using the **make dep** command, as shown in Figure 4.30.

Figure 4.30 Generating Dependencies

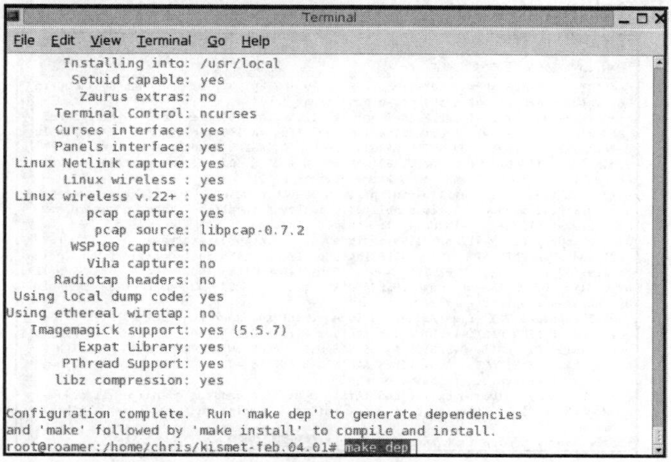

```
                                    Terminal                           _ □ ×
File  Edit  View  Terminal  Go  Help
         Installing into: /usr/local
          Setuid capable: yes
           Zaurus extras: no
         Terminal Control: ncurses
        Curses interface: yes
         Panels interface: yes
Linux Netlink capture: yes
        Linux wireless : yes
Linux wireless v.22+ : yes
           pcap capture: yes
            pcap source: libpcap-0.7.2
         WSP100 capture: no
           Viha capture: no
        Radiotap headers: no
Using local dump code: yes
Using ethereal wiretap: no
     Imagemagick support: yes (5.5.7)
           Expat Library: yes
         PThread Support: yes
        libz compression: yes

Configuration complete.  Run 'make dep' to generate dependencies
and 'make' followed by 'make install' to compile and install.
root@roamer:/home/chris/kismet-feb.04.01# make dep
```

You are now ready to compile Kismet.

Compiling the Kismet Software

Once the dependencies have been generated, issuing the **make** command compiles Kismet using the GNU C Compiler, gcc, as shown in Figure 4.31.

Figure 4.31 Compiling Kismet

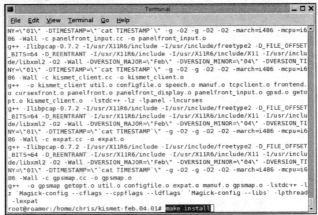

Installing the Kismet Software

Finally, issue the **make install** command, as shown in Figure 4.32, to install your Kismet installation in the appropriate directories.

Figure 4.32 Installing Kismet

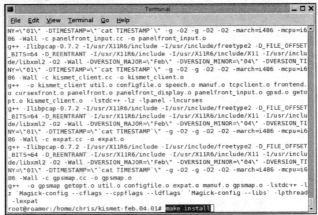

Unless you have an installation error, you should have an output similar to that shown in Figure 4.33.

Figure 4.33 Success!

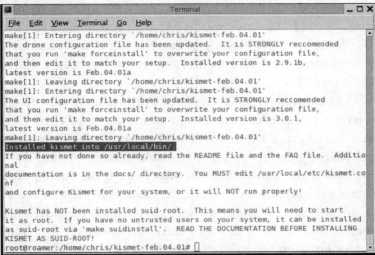

Kismet is now installed on your computer. Before you can use Kismet you need to edit the Kismet Configuration file, kismet.conf. The configuration options are detailed in Chapter 6 of this book.

Summary

In the eyes of many WarDrivers, Kismet is the application of choice because of its capability to detect both access points that are broadcasting their SSID as well as those in stealth mode. In order to achieve this functionality, Kismet needs to place the wireless card in monitor mode. Monitor mode has been both a blessing and a curse for WarDrivers. A blessing because it can detect cloaked access points, a curse because getting the card into monitor mode has been a difficult process for many WarDrivers.

Hermes-based cards like the ORiNOCO, can be used with Kismet, however you need to have a compatible pcmcia-cs module and a patched ORiNOCO driver. Prism 2–based cards are much easier to place in monitor mode through the use of the wlan-ng drivers and a compatible pcmcia-cs module.

Once you have a compatible version of pcmcia-cs and the appropriate drivers for your wireless card installed, the actual installation of Kismet is a very simple process. Like many Linux packages, a configure script is provided that attempts to create a Makefile with the proper configuration options for your system. After you run the configuration script, you need to run a dependency check to ensure that all of the proper dependencies are present and/or created. Finally, the **make install** command compiles Kismet for your system and places the binaries in the proper directories.

Once Kismet is compiled, the configuration files must be edited to reflect your specific system. Information on these configuration options is provided in Chapter 6.

Solutions Fast Track

Preparing Your System for Installation with an ORiNOCO Gold (Hermes Chipset) Card

☑ The pcmcia-cs module that Slackware 9.1 installs by default is version 3.2.5. To use a Hermes chipset–based wireless card, you need a patched version of pcmcia-cs. Currently, there is no patch available for pcmcia-cs 3.2.5 so you need to downgrade to pcmcia-cs–3.2.3 so you can patch it.

☑ The pcmcia-cs modules can be downloaded from: http://prdownloads.sourceforge.net/pcmcia-cs.

☑ The ORiNOCO and Hermes drivers need to be patched as well to enable monitor mode so that Kismet will work.

☑ The ORiNOCO patches are available from the Shmoo Web site at http://airsnort.shmoo.com/orinocoinfo.html.

☑ If everything was patched correctly, the **iwpriv <interface>** command will display that the *monitor* option is available.

Preparing Your System for Installation with a Prism 2 Chipset Card

☑ A pcmcia-cs version later than 3.1.33 is required for a Prism 2 chipset card to work with Kismet. Slackware 9.1 installs version 3.2.5 by default so an upgrade to pcmcia-cs is not necessary.

☑ The Linux wlan-ng drivers are designed to allow Prism 2–based cards to enter monitor mode. These drivers are available from www.linux-wlan.com/linux-wlan/.

☑ Once the Linux wlan-ng drivers are installed, your Prism 2–based card will work with Kismet.

Installing Kismet

☑ The current, stable version of Kismet is 4.0.1.

☑ Kismet can be downloaded from www.kismetwireless.net/download.shtml.

☑ Installation of Kismet is a very straightforward process involving only three steps:

- ./configure
- make dep
- make install

☑ After Kismet is installed, the configuration files must be edited to include your systems configuration information before Kismet can be used.

Frequently Asked Questions

The following Frequently Asked Questions, answered by the authors of this book, are designed to both measure your understanding of the concepts presented in this chapter and to assist you with real-life implementation of these concepts. To have your questions about this chapter answered by the author, browse to **www.syngress.com/solutions** and click on the **"Ask the Author"** form. You will also gain access to thousands of other FAQs at ITFAQnet.com.

Q: What wireless cards will work with Kismet?

A: According to the Kismet Web site (www.kismetwireless.net), the following cards and chipsets are supported:

- Cisco

    Aironet 340

    Aironet 350

- Prism 2

    Linksys

    D-Link

    Zoom

    Demarctech

    Microsoft

    Many others

- ORiNOCO

    Lucent ORiNOCO-based cards such as the WaveLAN

    Airport

- AIRPORT

    Airport cards under Mac OS X using the Viha drivers

- ACX100

    Dlink 650+

Q: Will Kismet work on a Macintosh?

A: Yes. Kismet will work on Linux, BSD-based systems, Mac OS X, as well as on Windows systems using Cygwin.

Q: I like to use Stumbverter to map my WarDrives. Is there a way to convert my Kismet logs to a format that I can feed into Stumbverter?

A: Yes. Using WarGlue (www.lostboxen.net/warglue/), you can convert your Kismet logs to NetStumbler format and then export them to Summary for use with Stumbverter.

Q: I like WarDriving with my Personal Digital Assistant instead of a laptop. Will Kismet work with my PDA?

A: Hewlett Packard or Compaq iPAQs that have been set up to dual boot Linux can run Kismet. Also, the Sharp Zaurus runs a modified Linux kernel and there are Kismet packages available that will work with it.

Q: If people don't broadcast their SSID, isn't that a clue that they don't want their access points to be found? Why would I want to use a product like Kismet that seems to violate that?

A: There are several answers to this question. First, in order to gain a true statistical analysis of wireless networks that are currently deployed, you need to find all of them, not just those that are broadcasting SSID. Second, many security professionals or network administrators can use Kismet to detect rogue access points that have been placed on their network in stealth mode. If they relied on NetStumbler or other active scanners only, they wouldn't be aware of these rogue access points that could provide an unauthorized entry point into their network.

Q: What is the difference between an active scanner and a passive scanner?

A: At its most basic level, an active scanner sends out a request beacon "asking" if there are any wireless networks in range. If an access point is configured to respond to these beacons, the access point is discovered. A passive scanner doesn't transmit any traffic. It simply "listens" for any traffic that is being broadcast. If this traffic is present, a passive scanner has discovered the access point.

Q: Kismet doesn't appear to work with any 802.11g cards. Why is this?

A: Kismet is primarily a Linux program. Currently, very few 802.11g card manufacturers provide Linux drivers for their cards. Without a driver, and the ability to place the card in monitor mode, Kismet will not work.

Q: Is there someplace I can go to discuss Kismet with other Kismet users?

A: Yes, the Kismet Forums (www.kismetwireless.net/forum.php) are a collection of discussion areas for Kismet users. You can also subscribe to the Kismet mailing list by sending an e-mail to wireless-subscribe@kismetwireless.net. There is also a lot of Kismet discussion on the WarDriving mailing list. To subscribe, go to: http://mailsrv.dis.org/mailman/listinfo/wardriving.

## Chapter 5

Installing Kismet in Fedora Core 1

Solutions in this Chapter:

- **Preparing Your System for Installation with an ORiNOCO Gold (Hermes Chipset) Card**

- **Preparing Your System for Installation with a Prism 2 Chipset Card**

- **Installing Kismet**

☑ **Summary**

☑ **Solutions Fast Track**

☑ **Frequently Asked Questions**

Introduction

Similar to the discussion in Chapter 4, the key to WarDriving using Kismet is being able to put the wireless card into monitor mode. Enabling monitor mode on many cards can be a frustrating, if not difficult, process. This chapter details the process of enabling monitor mode on two of the most common chipsets; Hermes and Prism 2 under the Fedora Core 1 operating system, also known as Yarrow. Both the Hermes and Prism 2 chipsets work by default under the Fedora Yarrow version. This chapter assumes that you already have at least the basic wireless networking operational under Fedora with either a Hermes chipset or Prism 2 chipset.

Because Kismet doesn't rely on the Service Set Identifier (SSID) broadcast beacon to determine the existence of a wireless access point, more access points can often be discovered. This is useful when WarDriving and when attempting to find rogue access points that a user may have attached to your corporate network.

The stock kernel that ships with Fedora Yarrow is version 2.4.22 and does not need to be upgraded or modified by the user in order to use Kismet. The kernel used in this walkthrough is the 2.4.22 kernel.

Kismet is a robust program. For many WarDrivers, the allure of finding access points that are not broadcasting SSID alone makes Kismet their choice. For others, the ability to WarDrive while using their favorite Linux distribution is the key. Yet another group of users prefer a Kismet/Linux configuration because it allows them more flexibility with scripting and data manipulation. The key point here is that Kismet offers Linux WarDrivers an excellent alternative to NetStumbler and Microsoft Windows.

Preparing Your System for Installation with an ORiNOCO Gold (Hermes Chipset) Card

It can probably safely be said that many of today's WarDrivers started the hobby using NetStumbler under Microsoft Windows. The reasons are simple, the combination of this operating system and the easy to use Graphical User Interface (GUI) of NetStumbler provide a fertile platform for learning many of the nuances of wireless networking without having to get into many of the technical details. Because NetStumbler was designed to use Hermes-based cards such as the ORiNOCO Gold card, many users have this card and want to use the same card with Kismet. Unfortunately, the stock drivers for this card do not allow the card to enter monitor mode. This requires patching the ORiNOCO drivers under Fedora. A kernel upgrade may not be required, but the source code for the Linux Kernel must be on the system. At the time of this writing, Fedora shipped with the 2.4.22–1.2115 version of kernel.

Getting the ORiNOCO Drivers Patched and Working

The default drivers that ship with most Linux distributions were written by David Gibson and are typically very reliable. The downside to this is that the Gibson drivers don't, by themselves, allow the interface to be put into monitor mode. Because of this, the ORiNOCO drivers require a patch from the Shmoo Group. The patch comes in the form of a .diff file and is relatively simple to install. You can obtain the file from: http://airsnort.shmoo.com/orinocoinfo.html.

Tools & Traps…

Does Your Card Have Monitor Mode?

There is a quick and easy way to check to see if your wireless card has the ability to go into monitor mode with the current configuration of drivers. There is a command under most Linux distributions called *iwpriv*. By utilizing this command, we can locate any potential options that a wireless card is allowed to take. These options are defined by the drivers used by your wireless card, which are loaded when your computer boots up. You must be logged in to the system as the root user in order to use this command. Looking at the command shown in Figure 5.1, you can see that the monitor option is not listed. This is a sign that you need the Shmoo Group patch on your wireless drivers.

Continued

Figure 5.1 Checking for Monitor Mode

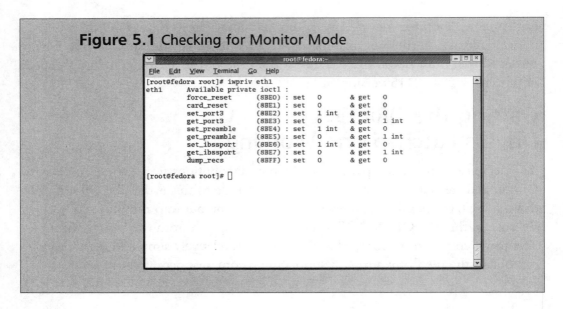

The first step in getting your drivers patched is to log in as the root user on the machine in question. The root user has complete control over all aspects of the laptop. Any mistakes you make during this process could potentially cause you great pain and suffering. Consider backing up any critical data you may have on the drive before beginning the processes outlined in this chapter. The process for logging in as the root user are shown in Figure 5.2. Make sure you know your own root password because in the following figure we've hidden it from view.

Figure 5.2 Using the *su* Command to Switch User to root

Upgrading and Patching the ORiNOCO Drivers

Upgrading the ORiNOCO drivers is a fairly simple process and will be done at the same time you patch the drivers. You'll want to download the latest stable drivers from Dave Gibson's Web site at ozlabs.org/people/dgibson/dldwd/. At the time of this writing, the latest stable version of the drivers is orinoco-0.13e.tar.gz. You'll need to download this file and place it into a subdirectory under your /root directory.

When you have the new drivers downloaded and untarred, you need to download the matching ORiNOCO patch file from the Shmoo Group Web site. You'll want to download the ORiNOCO-013e-patch.diff file from their Web site at airsnort.shmoo.com/orinocoinfo.html. Save the file in the same directory containing your new ORiNOCO driver files. The directory listing should look similar to that in Figure 5.3.

Figure 5.3 Directory Listing of Appropriate Driver Files

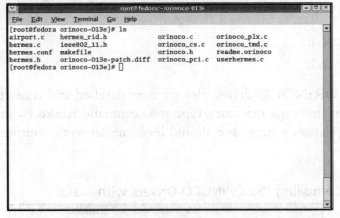

Using the **patch** command, we want to patch the ORiNOCO driver files with the Shmoo Group .diff file, as shown in Figure 5.4.

Figure 5.4 Patching the ORiNOCO Drivers

If the patch is successful, four files are created:

- hermes.c
- hermes.h
- orinoco.c
- orinoco.h

The new ORiNOCO driver files are now patched and ready to be compiled. While in the same directory, type the command **make** by itself. This will start the compilation process and should look similar to the output shown in Figure 5.5.

Figure 5.5 Compiling the ORiNOCO Drivers with *make*

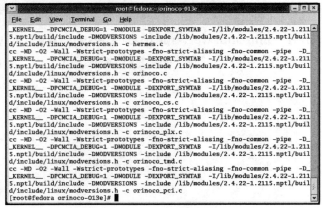

If you do not see the output shown in Figure 5.5, you have likely missed a step or made a typographical error. Try typing in the **patch** command again to remedy the problem, ensuring that the command used is the following:

```
patch -p0 < orinoco-013e-patch.diff
```

Assuming that everything has worked up to this point, you will now have all the files necessary to install your new ORiNOCO drivers. This is done using the **make install** command. Type the command **make install** by itself on the command line, while still in the same directory. This causes the operating system to install the compiled drivers into the appropriate place. The output of the **make install** command should look similar to the output in Figure 5.6.

Figure 5.6 Installing the ORiNOCO Drivers with *make install*

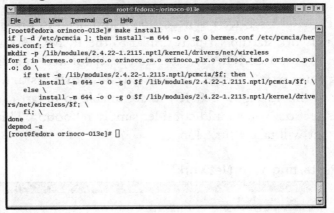

If there were no errors, the new ORiNOCO drivers are now installed properly on your Fedora system. If you had problems, try starting over from the beginning of this chapter. These steps work fine on new Fedora systems with the GNU C compiler (GCC) and the correct kernel source files installed.

Now you need to restart the PCMCIA card service and restart your network. To restart the PCMCIA service, type **/etc/rc3.d/S24pcmcia restart**. This command should produce the output seen in Figure 5.7.

Figure 5.7 Restarting the PCMCIA Service in Fedora

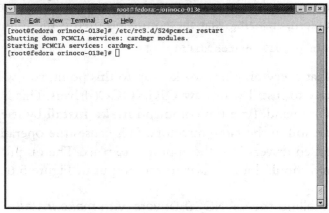

With the PCMCIA service restarted, you'll also need to restart your networking. The network startup script is similar to the PCMCIA startup script you just used to restart the PCMCIA service, except it's located in a different directory. To restart your network, type **/etc/init.d/network restart**. You should get output similar to that in Figure 5.8. If you are unable to restart the services as detailed in this section, you should consider simply rebooting. This will serve the same purpose but will take a little longer.

Figure 5.8 Restarting Your Network

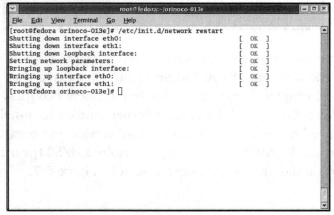

You can now verify that the ORiNOCO drivers are working properly by running the **iwpriv** command, as you did earlier in this process. If you'll recall from Figure 5.1, the option for monitor mode was not originally set for the

ORiNOCO card. However, running the command again should show *monitor* as one of the options for the card. Your results should look like those shown in Figure 5.9.

Figure 5.9 Verifying Monitor Mode on the ORiNOCO Card

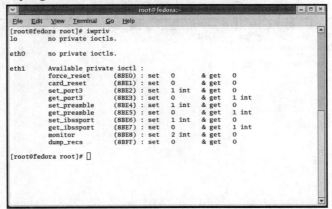

Preparing Your System for Installation with a Prism 2 Chipset Card

Wireless cards based on the Prism 2 chipset are very popular with Kismet users. One reason for this is their availability. Many manufacturers make cards using the Prism 2 chipset, including the original Linksys cards, Netgear, SMC, and Cisco. Another reason for their popularity among Kismet users is the ease of installation. Unlike Hermes-based cards, Prism 2 cards do not require a driver patch in order to be placed into monitor mode.

Using a Prism 2–based card with Kismet only requires installing the wlan-ng drivers and fixing a known bug in Fedora that causes the wlan-ng installation to break the PCMCIA services.

Downloading and Installing the wlan-ng Drivers

In order for your Prism 2–based PCMCIA wireless card to work with Fedora, you need to download and install the wlan-ng drivers. These drivers are available for download from www.linux-wlan.com/linux-wlan/. At the time of this writing, the version of the wlan-ng drivers was linux-wlan-ng-0.2.1-pre17. All of the examples used in this section are based on this version. If you use a different version of wlan-ng, you need to substitute the version information appropriately.

Once you have downloaded linux-wlan-ng-0.2.1-pre17.tar.gz, you need to switch to the root user, as shown in Figure 5.10, if you have not done so already.

Figure 5.10 Using the *su* Command to Switch User to root

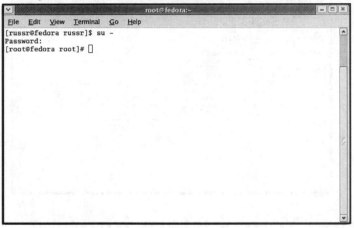

Next, uncompress and untar the linux-wlan-ng-021-pre17.tar.gz file, as shown in Figure 5.11.

Figure 5.11 Uncompressing and Untarring the Drivers

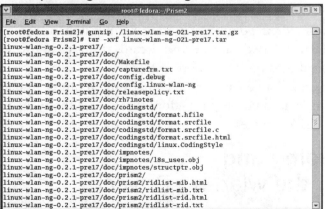

This creates a directory called linux-wlan-ng-0.2.1-pre17 with several subdirectories. Change to the linux-wlan-ng-0.2.1-pre17 directory as shown in Figure 5.12

Figure 5.12 Changing to the Newly Created Directory

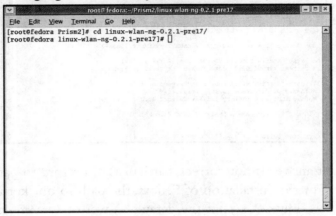

Building the linux-wlan-ng-0.2.1-pre17 drivers is a relatively simple process. First, issue the **make config** command, as shown in Figure 5.13.

Figure 5.13 Building the Drivers

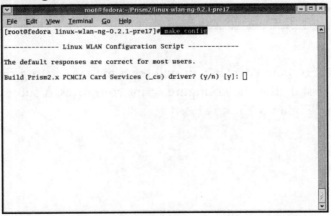

You will be prompted to answer several questions. In most cases, the configure script is able to determine the correct answer and prompts it as the default, as shown in Figure 5.14.

Figure 5.14 The Configure Script Questions

If the default answer is not correct, particularly in regard to paths, enter the correct answer. For this installation of Fedora, the path to our kernel source code is actually /usr/src/linux-2.4/, not the default answer of /usr/src/linux/.

> **NOTE**
>
> If you installed Fedora with the Full Install option, the source code files for the kernel may actually be installed in /usr/src/linux. You can check this for sure by running the command *ls –ls /usr/src*.

If your answers were correct, you will see a message stating that the configuration was successful after the configure script completes. A successful configuration is shown in Figure 5.15.

Figure 5.15 The Configuration Was Successful

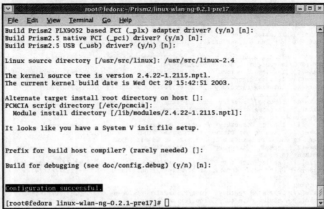

Next, issue the **make all** command, as shown in Figure 5.16. The **make all** command compiles the wlan-ng drivers.

Figure 5.16 Issuing the *make all* Command

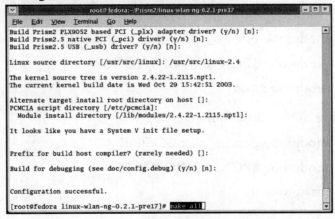

Finally, issue the **make install** command to install the drivers in the appropriate directory, as shown in Figure 5.17.

Figure 5.17 Installing the New wlan-ng Drivers

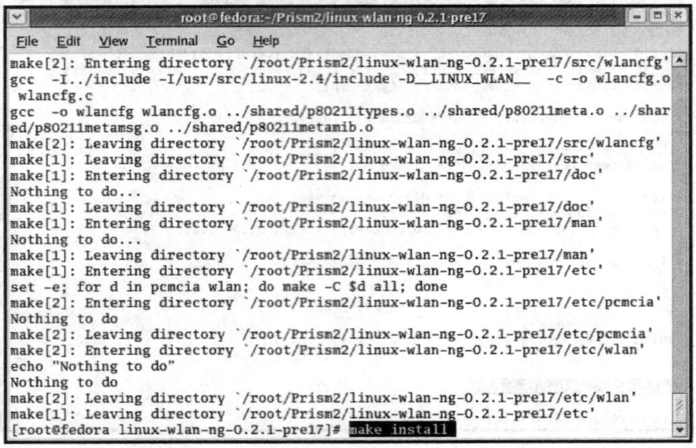

```
root@fedora:~/Prism2/linux-wlan-ng-0.2.1-pre17
File  Edit  View  Terminal  Go  Help
make[2]: Entering directory `/root/Prism2/linux-wlan-ng-0.2.1-pre17/src/wlancfg'
gcc  -I../include -I/usr/src/linux-2.4/include -D__LINUX_WLAN__  -c -o wlancfg.o
 wlancfg.c
gcc  -o wlancfg wlancfg.o ../shared/p80211types.o ../shared/p80211meta.o ../shar
ed/p80211metamsg.o ../shared/p80211metamib.o
make[2]: Leaving directory `/root/Prism2/linux-wlan-ng-0.2.1-pre17/src/wlancfg'
make[1]: Leaving directory `/root/Prism2/linux-wlan-ng-0.2.1-pre17/src'
make[1]: Entering directory `/root/Prism2/linux-wlan-ng-0.2.1-pre17/doc'
Nothing to do...
make[1]: Leaving directory `/root/Prism2/linux-wlan-ng-0.2.1-pre17/doc'
make[1]: Entering directory `/root/Prism2/linux-wlan-ng-0.2.1-pre17/man'
Nothing to do...
make[1]: Leaving directory `/root/Prism2/linux-wlan-ng-0.2.1-pre17/man'
make[1]: Entering directory `/root/Prism2/linux-wlan-ng-0.2.1-pre17/etc'
set -e; for d in pcmcia wlan; do make -C $d all; done
make[2]: Entering directory `/root/Prism2/linux-wlan-ng-0.2.1-pre17/etc/pcmcia'
Nothing to do
make[2]: Leaving directory `/root/Prism2/linux-wlan-ng-0.2.1-pre17/etc/pcmcia'
make[2]: Entering directory `/root/Prism2/linux-wlan-ng-0.2.1-pre17/etc/wlan'
echo "Nothing to do"
Nothing to do
make[2]: Leaving directory `/root/Prism2/linux-wlan-ng-0.2.1-pre17/etc/wlan'
make[1]: Leaving directory `/root/Prism2/linux-wlan-ng-0.2.1-pre17/etc'
[root@fedora linux-wlan-ng-0.2.1-pre17]# make install
```

wlan-ng Issues with Fedora

The installation of the wlan-ng drivers will normally break the Fedora installation of PCMCIA. You'll need to edit the /etc/init.d/pcmcia and remove the .o from the following lines in the files (see also Figure 5.18):

- /sbin/modprobe pcmcia_core.o $CORE_OPTS

- /sbin/modprobe $PCIC.o $PCIC_OPTS

- /sbin/modprobe ds.o

The resulting lines should look like this:

- /sbin/modprobe pcmcia_core $CORE_OPTS

- /sbin/modprobe $PCIC $PCIC_OPTS

- /sbin/modprobe ds

Figure 5.18 Fedora Installation of PCMCIA

When the changes have been made, you will need to restart the PCMCIA services. This is done by typing in the command **/etc/rc3.d/S24pcmcia restart**. See Figure 5.19 for an example.

Figure 5.19 Restarting the PCMCIA Services

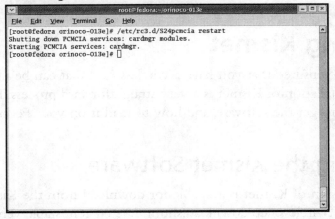

Next, reboot your system and insert your Prism 2 card in a PCMCIA slot during post. If the linux-wlan-ng drivers installed correctly, you will hear two short beeps during startup.

Verifying that It All Works

Verifying that the drivers installed successfully is very simple. Issue an **ifconfig –a** command. If the drivers installed correctly, a wlan0 device will be displayed, as shown in Figure 5.20.

Figure 5.20 A Successful Installation

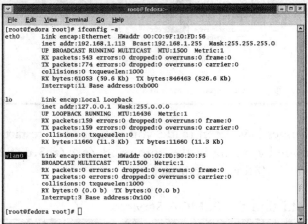

Installing Kismet

After you have ensured that you have a wireless card that can be placed in monitor mode, installation of Kismet is a very straightforward process. This section details where to get the software, and how to load it on your Fedora Linux installation.

Obtaining the Kismet Software

The latest version of Kismet is available for download from the Kismet Web site at www.kismetwireless.net/download.shtml. The current stable version of Kismet at the time of this writing is 4.0.1. If you do not want to download the most recent version, or if you would prefer to download the development version, you can browse all available versions at http://kismetwireless.net/code/.

NOTE

All of the examples and instructions in this Chapter use Kismet 4.0.1. If you are using a different version of Kismet, you need to change the version information in these examples as appropriate.

After you have downloaded kismet-feb0401.tar.gz, uncompress and untar the package as shown in Figure 5.21.

Figure 5.21 Uncompressing and Untarring the Kismet Files

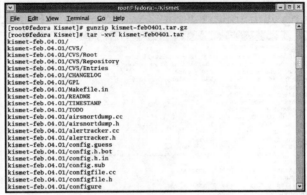

This creates the kismet-feb.04.01 directory. Using the **cd** command, change the directory to **kismet-feb.04.01,** as shown in Figure 5.22.

Figure 5.22 Changing to the Kismet Directory

There are some issues with installing Kismet under Fedora. Depending on the installation type you chose when you installed Fedora, you may or may not have all the requisite packages installed on your laptop. For instance, if you've installed just the workstation load, you will be missing some vital components for the installation of Kismet.

To remedy this situation, you'll want to use the command-line package retrieval software, *yum*. Yum allows you to specify packages you need to install and if you have a current Internet connection, it will connect to a server, find all relevant dependencies, and install them all. See the examples in Figures 5.23 and 5.24 for samples of how to use the *yum* command.

Figure 5.23 Using *yum* to Install the flex and ncurses Packages

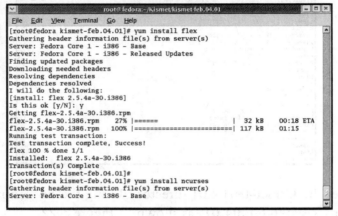

Figure 5.24 Using *yum* to Install the gcc-c++ Package

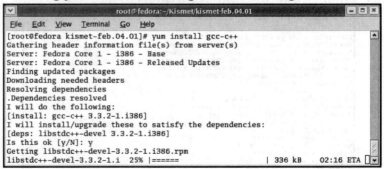

Once you have all the required packages installed for your Kismet needs, you are ready to begin configuring and installing Kismet.

Configuring the Kismet Software for Installation

Preparing to compile and install Kismet is a two-step process.

1. Configuring the installation script
2. Generating dependencies

First, you need to configure the installation script. From the kismet-feb.04.01 directory, run the configure script, as shown in Figure 5.25.

Figure 5.25 Configuring the Installation Script

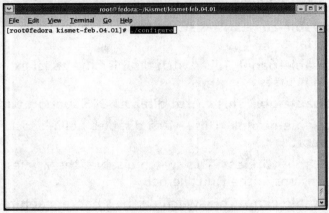

The proper way to run this is with the "./" in front of configure. This indicates that the script to run is the configure script in the current, or "./" directory. Alternately, the same results could be achieved by issuing the command with the full path to configure.

Tools & Traps…

The Kismet Configuration Options

Not every laptop is configured the same way. The packages installed and the hardware configurations can vary in a virtually infinite number of combinations. Kismet takes these differences into account and offers you the ability to tailor Kismet to your specific environment using special switches with the configure script.

These are the configuration switches, also shown in Chapter 4, and what they accomplish when invoked:

- **--disable-curses** This switch disables the "curses" user interface.

- **--disable-panel** This switch disables the panel extensions with ncurses.

- **--disable-gps** This switch disables GPS support with Kismet.

- **--disable-netlink** This switch disables netlink socket capture support.

- **--disable-wireless** This switch disables the wireless extensions in the Linux kernel.

- **--disable-pcap** This switch disables packet capture support using libpcap (the packet capture library).

- **--enable-syspcap** This switch enables the system libpcap. Dragorn, the author of Kismet, does not recommend the use of this switch.

- **--disable-setuid** This switch disables the suid cabability of Kismet. Again, Dragorn does not recommend the use of this switch.

- **--enable-wsp100 enable WSP100 remote sensor capture device** This switch enables the use of a WSP 100 remote sensor.

- **--enable-zaurus** This switch enables extra features used by the Sharp Zaurus Personal Digital Assistant (PDA).

Continued

- **--enable-local-dumper** This switch forces kismet to use a dump format other than Ethereal, even if Ethereal is installed on the system.
- **--with-ethereal=DIR** This switch adds support for Ethereal wiretap logs. DIR should be replaced with the path to ethereal.
- **--without-ethereal** This switch disables support for Ethereal wiretap logs.
- **--enable-acpi Enable linux-kernel ACPI support** This switch enables Advanced Configuration and Power Interface (ACPI) support for Kismet.

ACPI must be enabled in the Linux kernel for this switch to work.

NOTE

To use these switches, append them to configure when it is invoked. For example, to configure Kismet without the curses interface, issue the following command:

```
root@fedora  root/kismet-4.0.1/# ./configure –disable-curses
```

Next, you need to generate dependencies using the **make dep** command, as shown in Figure 5.26.

Figure 5.26 Generating Dependencies

You are now ready to install Kismet.

Installing the Kismet Software

Before Kismet can be used, it needs to be compiled and installed. One command accomplishes both of these tasks: *make install*. Issue the **make install** command (as shown in Figure 5.27) to compile and install your Kismet installation.

Figure 5.27 Installing Kismet

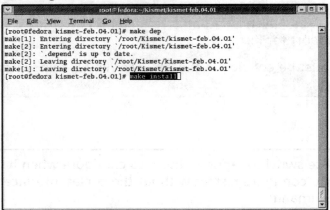

Unless you have an installation error, your output should be similar to that shown in Figure 5.28.

Figure 5.28 Success!

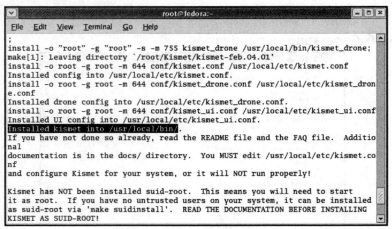

Kismet is now installed on your computer. Before you can use Kismet though, you need to edit the Kismet Configuration file, kismet.conf. The configuration options are detailed in Chapter 6 of this book, "Configuring and Using Kismet."

Summary

In the eyes of many WarDrivers, Kismet is the application of choice because of its ability to detect both access points that are broadcasting their SSID as well as those in stealth mode. In order to achieve this functionality, Kismet needs to place the wireless card in monitor mode. Monitor mode has been both a blessing and a curse for WarDrivers. A blessing because it can detect cloaked access points, a curse because getting the card into monitor mode has been a difficult process for many WarDrivers.

Hermes-based cards, like the ORiNOCO, can be used with Kismet; however, you need to have a compatible pcmcia-cs module and a patched ORiNOCO driver. Prism 2–based cards are much easier to place in monitor mode. The wlan-ng drivers and a compatible pcmcia-cs module allow Prism 2 cards to enter monitor mode.

Once you have a compatible version of pcmcia-cs and the appropriate drivers for your wireless card installed, the actual installation of Kismet is a very simple process. Like many Linux packages, a configure script is provided that attempts to create a Makefile with the proper configuration options for your system. After you run the configuration script, you need to run a dependency check to ensure that all of the proper dependencies are present and/or created. Finally, the **make install** command compiles Kismet for your system and places the binaries in the proper directories.

Once Kismet is compiled, the configuration files must be edited to reflect your specific system. Information on these configuration options is provided in Chapter 6, "Configuring and Using Kismet."

Solutions Fast Track

Preparing Your System for Installation with an ORiNOCO Gold (Hermes Chipset) Card

☑ The PCMCIA services do not need to be upgraded within the Fedora operating system in order to load the new ORiNOCO drivers.

☑ The ORiNOCO and Hermes drivers need to be patched to enable monitor mode so that Kismet will work.

☑ The ORiNOCO patches are available from the Shmoo Web site at http://airsnort.shmoo.com/orinocoinfo.html.

☑ If everything was patched correctly, the **iwpriv <interface>** command will display that the monitor option is available.

Preparing Your System for Installation with a Prism 2 Chipset Card

☑ The Linux wlan-ng drivers are designed to allow Prism 2–based cards to enter monitor mode. These drivers are available from www.linux-wlan.com/linux-wlan/.

☑ A flaw in Fedora causes the installation of the wlan-ng drivers to effectively break the PCMCIA service. Therefore, you'll need to edit the /etc/init.d/pcmcia file.

☑ Once the Linux wlan-ng drivers are installed, your Prism 2–based card will work with Kismet.

Installing Kismet

☑ The current, stable version of Kismet is 4.0.1.

☑ Kismet can be downloaded from www.kismetwireless.net/download.shtml.

☑ The installation of Kismet is a very straightforward process involving only three steps:

- ./configure

- make dep

- make install

☑ After Kismet is installed, the configuration files must be edited to include your system's configuration information before Kismet can be used.

Frequently Asked Questions

The following Frequently Asked Questions, answered by the authors of this book, are designed to both measure your understanding of the concepts presented in this chapter and to assist you with real-life implementation of these concepts. To have your questions about this chapter answered by the author, browse to **www.syngress.com/solutions** and click on the **"Ask the Author"** form. You will also gain access to thousands of other FAQs at ITFAQnet.com.

Q: What wireless cards will work with Kismet?

A: According to the Kismet Web site (www.kismetwireless.net), the following cards and chipsets are supported:

Cisco

1. Aironet 340

2. Aironet 350

Prism 2

1. Linksys

2. D–Link

3. Zoom

4. Demarctech

5. Microsoft

6. Many others

ORiNOCO

1. Lucent ORiNOCO–based cards such as the WaveLAN

2. Airport

AIRPORT

■ Airport cards under Mac OS X using the Viha drivers

ACX100

■ Dlink 650+

Q: Will Kismet work on a Macintosh?

A: Yes. Kismet will work on Linux, BSD-based systems, Mac OS X, and can even be used on Windows systems using Cygwin.

Q: I like to use Stumbverter to map my WarDrives. Is there a way to convert my Kismet logs to a format that I can feed into Stumbverter?

A: Yes. Using WarGlue (www.lostboxen.net/warglue/), you can convert your Kismet logs to NetStumbler format and then export it to Summary for use with Stumbverter.

Q: I like WarDriving with my Personal Digital Assistant instead of a laptop. Will Kismet work with my PDA?

A: Hewlett Packard or Compaq iPAQs that have been set up to dual boot Linux can run Kismet. Also, the Sharp Zaurus runs a modified Linux kernel and there are Kismet packages available that will work with it.

Q: If people don't broadcast their SSID, isn't that a clue that they don't want their access points to be found? Why would I want to use a product like Kismet that seems to violate that?

A: There are several answers to this question. First, in order to gain a true statistical analysis of wireless networks that are currently deployed, you need to find all of them, not just those that are broadcasting SSID. Second, many security professionals or network administrators can use Kismet to detect rogue access points that have been placed on their network in stealth mode. If they only relied on NetStumbler or other active scanners, they wouldn't be aware of these rogue access points that could provide an unauthorized entry point into their network.

Q: What is the difference between an active scanner and a passive scanner?

A: At its most basic, an active scanner sends out a request beacon "asking" if there are any wireless networks in range. If an access point is configured to respond to these beacons, the access point is discovered. A passive scanner doesn't transmit any traffic. It simply "listens" for any traffic that is being broadcast. If this traffic is present, a passive scanner has discovered the access point.

Q: Kismet doesn't appear to work with any 802.11g cards. Why is this?

A: Kismet is primarily a Linux program. Currently, very few 802.11g card manufacturers provide Linux drivers for their cards. Without a driver, and the ability to place the card in monitor mode, Kismet will not work.

Q: Is Fedora any more difficult to use than other distributions for WarDriving?

A: Actually, no it's not. The key is knowing how to get the computer loaded and configured correctly from the start. If you've been using another distribution of Linux up to this point, you may run into the normal problems associated with changing your operating system.

Q: What is the most common issue with using Fedora for WarDriving?

A: The biggest issue is the installation process of the operating system itself. Fedora gives you multiple options for installing the operating system. We recommend that, unless you're a veteran user of Fedora, you do a full installation so that all the right components are in place. This will save you a lot of hassle when you're installing the wireless network drivers and Kismet.

Q: Is there someplace I can go to discuss Kismet with other Kismet users?

A: Yes, the Kismet Forums (www.kismetwireless.net/forum.php) are a collection of discussion areas for Kismet users. You can also subscribe to the Kismet mailing list by sending an e-mail to wireless-subscribe@kismetwireless.net. There is also a lot of Kismet discussion on the WarDriving mailing list. To subscribe, go to http://mailsrv.dis.org/mailman/listinfo/wardriving.

## Chapter 6

Configuring and Using Kismet

Solutions in this Chapter:

- Using the Global Positioning System Daemon (GPSD) with Kismet

- Configuring Kismet

- Starting Kismet

- WarDriving Using Kismet

☑ Summary

☑ Solutions Fast Track

☑ Frequently Asked Questions

Introduction

Now that you have installed Kismet, you are ready to begin configuring and using it on your Linux distribution of choice. Unlike NetStumbler, which is basically ready to use once it is installed, Kismet requires some post-installation configuration in order to be functional. This chapter will detail that post-installation configuration.

First, we'll take a look at installing and configuring the Global Positioning System Daemon (GPSD) for use with Kismet.

Using the Global Positioning System Daemon (GPSD) with Kismet

In order to map the WarDrive results garnered with Kismet, you need to install and configure GPSD. GPSD is a Linux add-on daemon written by Russ Nelson and is available for download at: www.pygps.org/gpsd/downloads/. The current version of GPSD is gspd-1.10. This section details the installation and usage of GPSD with Kismet.

> **NOTE**
>
> GPSD is not required in order to successfully use Kismet. If you do not intend to map your results, you can skip this section.

Installing GPSD

Installing GPSD is a very straightforward process. First, download gpsd-1.10.tar.gz from www.pygps.org/gpsd/downloads/gpsd-1.10.tar.gz, as shown in Figure 6.1.

Figure 6.1 Downloading GPSD

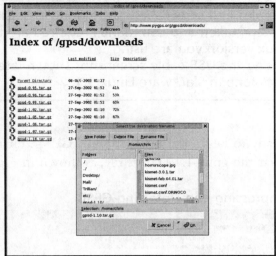

Next, you need to make sure that you have changed to the root user, as shown in Figure 6.2, if you have not done so already.

Figure 6.2 Becoming the Root User

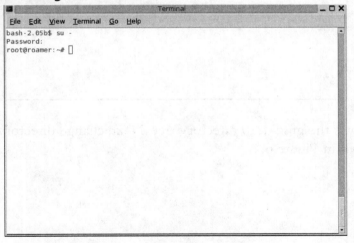

NOTE

All of the examples and screenshots were done in Slackware Linux 9.1; however, the steps taken and commands required are the same regardless of the Linux version you are using.

Ck3k provided the USB cable screenshot shown later in Figure 6.12, which was also done in Slackware Linux 9.1.

Now you are ready to begin the installation of GPSD. First, you need to uncompress and untar the gpsd–1.10.tar.gz file, as shown in Figure 6.3.

Figure 6.3 Uncompressing and Untarring GPSD

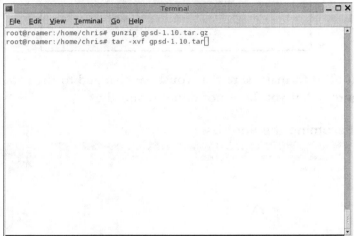

This creates the gpsd–1.10 directory tree. Next, change directory to gpsd–1.10, as shown in Figure 6.4.

Figure 6.4 Changing to the gpsd-1.10 Directory

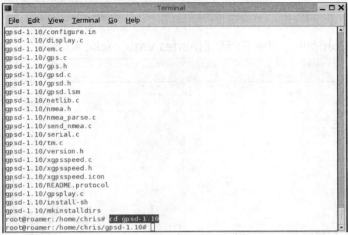

Once the GPSD installation scripts are uncompressed and untarred, the installation of GPSD is a simple three-step process:

1. Execute the configure script.
2. Compile the GPSD binaries.
3. Copy the GPSD binaries to your desired location.

First, you need to execute the configure script. Like most Unix-style configure scripts, this is accomplished by issuing the **./configure** command, as shown in Figure 6.5. The './' in front of configure indicates that the configure file in the current, or "./", directory should be executed.

Figure 6.5 Executing the Configure Script

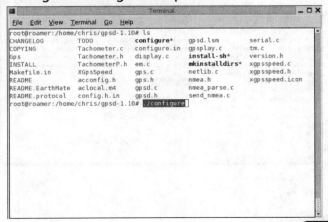

Next, issue the **make** command, as shown in Figure 6.6, to compile the GPSD binaries.

Figure 6.6 Compiling the GPSD Binaries with *make*

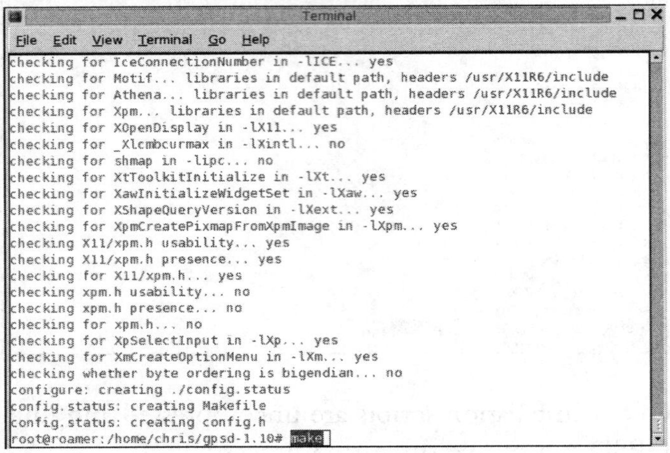

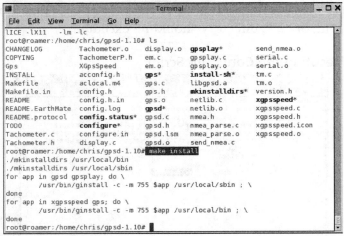

Next, the GPSD binaries (gps and gpsd) need to be copied to the locations from which they can be executed. The app-defaults file also needs to be copied to the appropriate directory. Issuing the **make install** command, as shown in Figure 6.7, accomplishes this.

Figure 6.7 Issuing the *make install* Command

Now you have successfully installed GPSD and are ready to start the daemon and use it with Kismet. You can verify that the gps and gpsd binaries were successfully copied to the appropriate directories by issuing the **which** command for each, as shown in Figure 6.8. The output of *which* displays the full path to the command that it was issued against.

Figure 6.8 Verifying the Installation of GPS and GPSD

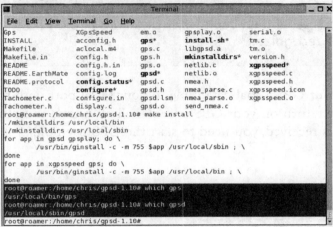

Starting GPSD

There are two ways to use GPSD with Kismet:

- Serial Data Cable
- USB Data Cable

In the following two sections, you will be shown the commands required to start GPSD with each.

Starting GPSD with Serial Data Cable

The most common way to use GPSD is with a serial data cable.

Notes from the Underground...

Connecting the GPS Serial Data Cable

Because of the nature of serial ports, it is a good idea to connect your GPS' serial data cable prior to booting your Linux distribution. If you connect your serial data cable after Linux has already booted, it may or may not be recognized.

Connect your GPS' serial data cable to your serial port with the computer turned off. Next, turn on your GPS unit and allow it time to acquire a signal. Once a signal is received, you need to start the GPS daemon, as shown in Figure 6.9.

Figure 6.9 Starting GPSD with a Serial Data Cable

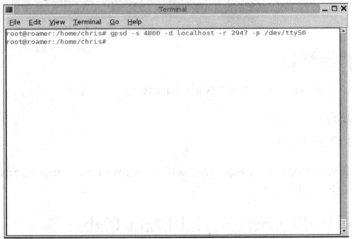

NOTE

You must have root privileges to start the GPSD.

This starts GPSD listening on port 2947. You can verify that GPSD is listening on this port by opening a Telnet session to it, as shown in Figure 6.10. You can also verify that the process started using the *ps -ef* command, as shown in Figure 6.11.

Figure 6.10 Establishing a Telnet Session with GPSD

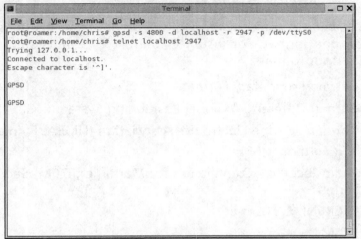

Figure 6.11 Viewing the GPSD Process

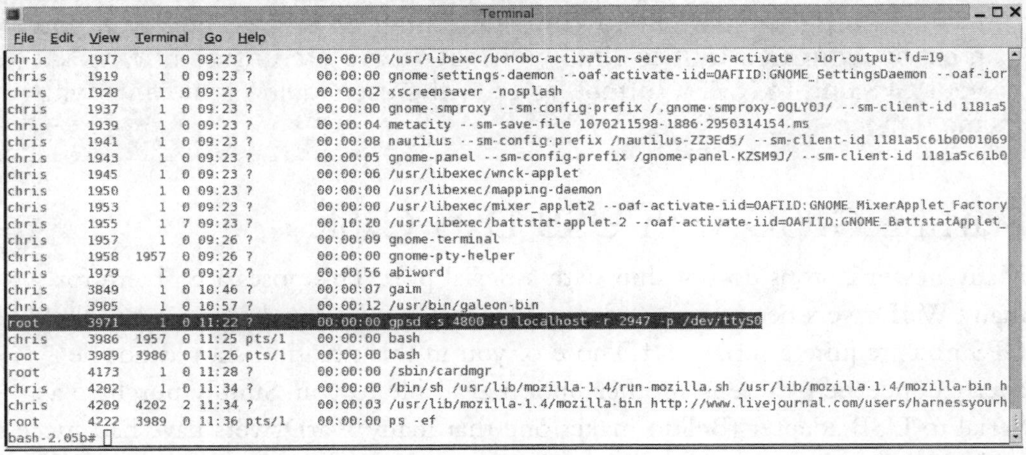

Tools & Traps…

GPS Data Formats

It is very important to use the correct data format on your GPS unit in order for Kismet to correctly receive GPS data. Many GPS units support more than one format. For instance, Garmin GPS units support seven different output formats:

1. Garmin Proprietary Format
2. Garmin Differential Global Positioning System (DGPS) Format
3. National Marine Electronics Association (NMEA) Format
4. Text Format
5. Radio Technical Commission for Maritime (RTCM) Services Format
6. RTCM/NMEA Format
7. RTCM/Text Format

Some WarDriving applications, like NetStumbler, support multiple formats. NetStumbler supports both NMEA and Garmin proprietary formats. In order for Kismet to correctly gather GPS data, however, you must set your GPS Unit to NMEA Format. If you are unsure how to set your GPS unit to NMEA format, refer to the users guide that came with the unit.

Starting GPSD with USB Data Cable

Many newer laptops do not ship with a Serial port. This poses a problem for many WarDrivers because most data cables that can be purchased for handheld GPS units require a serial port. Those of you in this situation should not be overly concerned; there is another option available to you. Simply purchase a Serial to USB adapter (Belkin makes one that many WarDrivers have had success with) and connect your data cable to it. Then, issue the command shown in Figure 6.12 to start GPSD.

Figure 6.12 Starting GPSD with a USB Data Cable

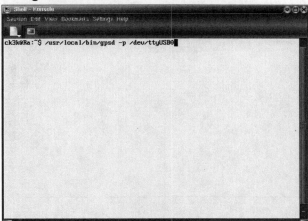

> **NOTE**
>
> You must have root privileges to start the GPSD.

Configuring Kismet

Now that you have installed Kismet and GPSD, you are ready to modify the
Kismet configuration files so that Kismet will work on your system. Unlike many
Windows programs (such as NetStumbler) that will work as soon as they are
installed, Kismet must be tailored to your specific system.

Modifying the kismet.conf File

Before Kismet will work on your system, you need to customize the kismet.conf
file (found in /usr/local/etc/) to your environment. Using your favorite text
editor (vi, pico, emacs, and so on) open /usr/local/etc/kismet.conf for editing, as
shown in Figure 6.13.

Figure 6.13 Editing the /usr/local/kismet.conf File

You must have root privileges to edit the kismet.conf file.

Figure 6.14 shows the kismet.conf file open for editing.

Figure 6.14 Preparing to Edit the kismet.conf file

Setting an *suiduser*

Unless you compiled Kismet with the "suid-root" option, which is an extremely insecure way to use Kismet, you first need to set an suiduser in the kismet.conf file, as shown in Figure 6.15. This is the user that Kismet will run as and should be a normal user account.

Figure 6.15 Setting the *suiduser* Variable

Enabling Support for Hermes Cards

By default, the kismet.conf file is configured for use with Cisco cards. In order to use Kismet with your ORiNOCO, or other Hermes chipset–based card, you must edit the kismet.conf file to recognize and use your ORiNOCO card. First, comment out the line for the Cisco card by placing a "#" in front of the line. Then, remove the "#" in front of the ORiNOCO line, as shown in Figure 6.16.

Figure 6.16 Editing the kismet.conf File to Use Your ORiNOCO Card

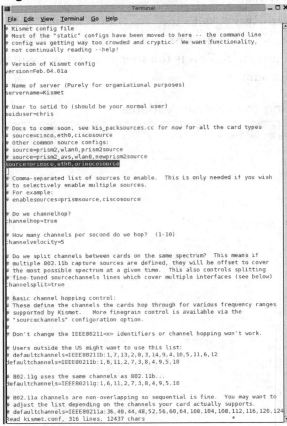

Next, you may need to change the device to be used by Kismet. By default, the ORiNOCO line is set to use eth0 as your capture device. If your system uses eth1, eth2, or a different device, this needs to be edited appropriately. Figure 6.16 shows the proper configuration for an ORiNOCO card configured as eth0.

Enabling Support for Prism 2 Cards

If you are using a Prism 2–based card, you also need to edit the kismet.conf file appropriately. First, comment out the line for the Cisco card by placing a "#" in front of the line. Then, remove the "#" in front of the Prism2 line, as shown in Figure 6.17.

Figure 6.17 Editing the kismet.conf File to Use Your Prism 2 Card

Next, you need to change the device to be used by Kismet. By default, the Prism2 line is set to use wlan0 as your capture device. If your system uses wlan1, wlan2, or a different device, this needs to be edited appropriately. Figure 6.17 shows the proper configuration for a Prism 2–card configured as wlan0.

Setting the Channel-Hopping Intervals

Next, you need to set the channel-hopping interval. This is the number of times that Kismet will force the card to monitor a different channel per second. By default, this value is set to five. To monitor more channels per second you need to increase this value. To monitor fewer channels per second, this value needs to be decreased. Figure 6.18 shows a kismet.conf file that has been configured to change channels, or "hop," seven times per second.

Figure 6.18 Kismet is Configured to Hop Seven Channels Per Second

If you wanted to monitor only one specific channel, you should set the *chan-nelhop* value to "false", as shown in Figure 6.19.

Figure 6.19 Disabling Channel Hopping

Enabling GPS Support

The last setting you need to configure in the kismet.conf file is the GPS support. If you intend to use GPSD, as shown earlier in this chapter, then the default settings in the kismet.conf file are acceptable. As Figure 6.20 shows, by default, Kismet is configured to use a GPS device and listen on port 2947.

Figure 6.20 Kismet Is Configured to Use a GPS

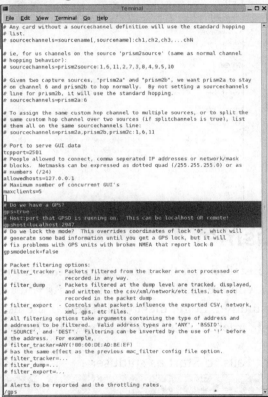

If you don't intend to use a GPS, then the "gps" value should be changed to false, as shown in Figure 6.21.

Figure 6.21 Kismet Is Configured for Use without a GPS

Starting Kismet

Now that Kismet is installed and the configuration file, kismet.conf, has been tailored to your system, you are ready to start Kismet. As you recall, we set a normal user account as the suiduser. Logic dictates that this is the user we should be logged in as to start Kismet. As Figure 6.22 shows, this is not the case.

Figure 6.22 Kismet Fails to Start as suiduser

Using the suiduser account, does not work because the normal user does not have write permission to set the process identification number file (kismet_server.pid) in the /var/run/ directory tree. This is easily overcome. Change to the root user using the **su** command. Normally, when we do this, we use the *su -* command (shown in Figure 6.23).

Figure 6.23 Changing to root Using *su -*

As you can see in Figure 6.24, however, this doesn't work either.

Figure 6.24 Kismet Fails to Start as root

```
Terminal                                                    _ □ ×
 File  Edit  View  Terminal  Go  Help
Source 0 (orinocosource): Opening orinoco source interface eth0...
Spawned channelc control process 2082
Dropped privs to chris (1000) gid 100
Allowing clients to fetch WEP keys.
Logging networks to Kismet-Feb-16-2004-1.network
Logging networks in CSV format to Kismet-Feb-16-2004-1.csv
Logging networks in XML format to Kismet-Feb-16-2004-1.xml
Logging cryptographically weak packets to Kismet-Feb-16-2004-1.weak
Logging cisco product information to Kismet-Feb-16-2004-1.cisco
Logging gps coordinates to Kismet-Feb-16-2004-1.gps
Logging data to Kismet-Feb-16-2004-1.dump
Writing data files to disk every 300 seconds.
Mangling encrypted and fuzzy data packets.
Tracking probe responses and associating probe networks.
Reading AP manufacturer data and defaults from /usr/local/etc/ap_manuf
Reading client manufacturer data and defaults from /usr/local/etc/client_manuf
FATAL: Dump file error: Unable to open dump file Kismet-Feb-16-2004-1.dump (Permission denied)
Sending termination request to channel control child 2082...
Waiting for channel control child 2082 to exit...
WARNING: Sometimes cards don't always come out of monitor mode
         cleanly.  If your card is not fully working, you may need to
         restart or reconfigure it for normal operation.
Kismet exiting.
root@roamer:~# []
```

This time, permission is denied when Kismet attempts to write the dump file. How can this be? The root account has permission to write to any directory so it should be able to write the dump file. While this is true, as you can see in Figure 6.25, Kismet already dropped our privileges to the suiduser (in this case "chris") and our working directory is /root, which is owned by the root user.

Figure 6.25 Privileges Are Dropped to the suiduser

If you can't start Kismet as a normal user, and you can't start Kismet as root, how can you start Kismet? You need to have root privileges without the root environment. The *su -* command changes to the root user in the root environment. If you just issue the *su* command (as your normal user) without the "-" appended, you gain root privileges, but maintain your normal user environment. The difference is shown in Figure 6.26.

Figure 6.26 The Difference between *su -* and *su*

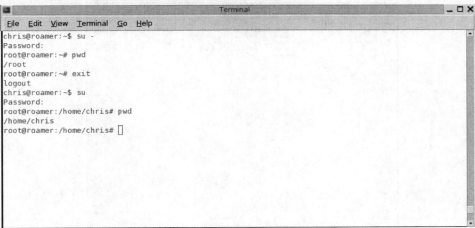

As you can see, you now have root privileges, but have maintained your normal user environment. Now Kismet can be started successfully, as shown in Figure 6.27.

Figure 6.27 Kismet Starting

Once Kismet has run through its startup procedure, it begins to identify access points, as shown in Figure 6.28.

Figure 6.28 Kismet Running

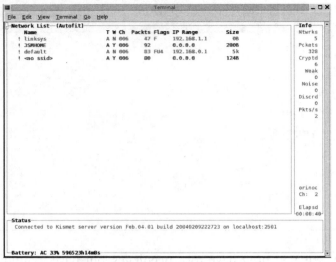

Now that you have successfully started Kismet, you are ready to WarDrive. In the next section, we'll look at the Kismet interface and how to successfully navigate it.

WarDriving Using Kismet

In order to successfully utilize Kismet, you need to understand the user interface. This section explains the information displayed on the Kismet user interface, and the keyboard commands used to successfully navigate Kismet.

The Kismet User Interface

The Kismet user interface, as shown in Figure 6.29, is divided into three frames:

Figure 6.29 The Initial Kismet User Interface

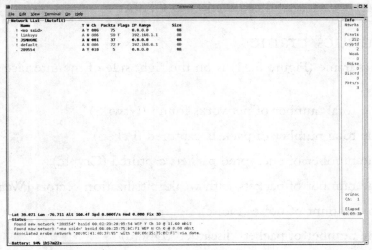

1. The Network Display
2. The Statistics Frame
3. The Status Frame

The Network Display

The Network Display (Figure 6.30) lists the Service Set Identifiers (SSIDs) of any found wireless networks. This frame covers most of the Kismet user interface.

Figure 6.30 The Network Display

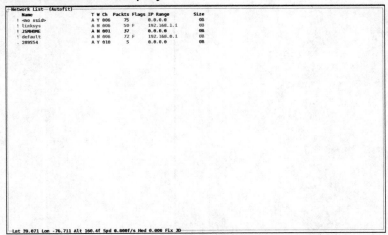

The lower left-hand corner of the Network Display shows the GPS information if you have a successful connection to GPSD.

The Statistics Frame

The Statistics frame (Figure 6.31) is on the right side of the interface and lists the following:

- The total number of networks found (Ntwrks)
- The total number of packets captured (Pckets)
- The number of encrypted packets captured (Cryptd)
- The number of packets with weak initialization vectors (Weak)
- The amount of noise (Noise)
- The number of packets discarded (Discrd)
- The number of packets captured per second (Pkts/s)
- The type of card used (orinoc, prism, and so on)
- The Channel currently being sniffed (Ch:)
- The Time Kismet has been running (Elapsd)

Figure 6.31 The Statistics Frame

The Status Frame

The Status frame (see Figure 6.32) maintains a scrolling display of all networks found and, if applicable, the Battery status.

Figure 6.32 The Status Frame

```
Status
 Found new network "289554" bssid 00:02:2D:28:95:54 WEP Y Ch 10 @ 11.00 mbit
 Found new network "<no ssid>" bssid 00:06:25:75:BC:F1 WEP N Ch 0 @ 0.00 mbit
 Associated probe network "00:0C:41:40:37:95" with "00:06:25:75:BC:F1" via data.

Battery: 94% 1h57m22s
```

Keyboard Commands

To get help in Kismet, simply type the letter **h** while the Kismet display is in the active window. This brings up the Help display, as shown in Figures 6.33 and 6.34.

Figure 6.33 The Help Display Begins

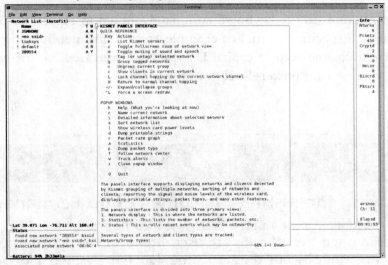

Figure 6.34 The Help Display Continues

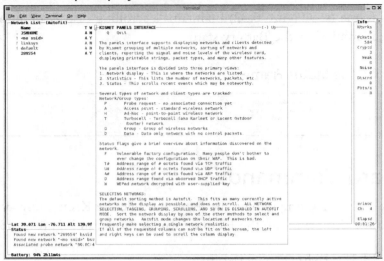

Kismet responds to the keyboard commands shown in Figures 6.33and 6.34 by performing a specific action. For example, to stop channel hopping and stay on the current channel, type a capital **L**. Typing a lowercase **l**, on the other hand, opens the wireless card power–level popup window.

Tools & Traps…

Removing the Kismet Welcome Popup Permanently

When you start Kismet 4.0.1, a Welcome message (shown in Figure 6.35) is superimposed over the Kismet user interface. Pressing the spacebar closes this window, but the next time you start Kismet, the Welcome message is back.

Continued

Figure 6.35 The Initial Kismet Popup

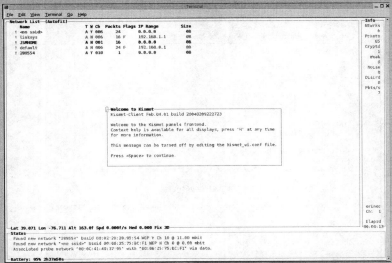

First, using the **su** command, change to the root user. Next, change to the **/usr/local/etc** directory, as shown in Figure 6.36.

Figure 6.36 Changing to the /usr/local/etc Directory

Using your favorite editor, open the **kismet_ui.conf** file, as shown in Figure 6.37.

Continued

Figure 6.37 Editing the kismet_ui.conf File

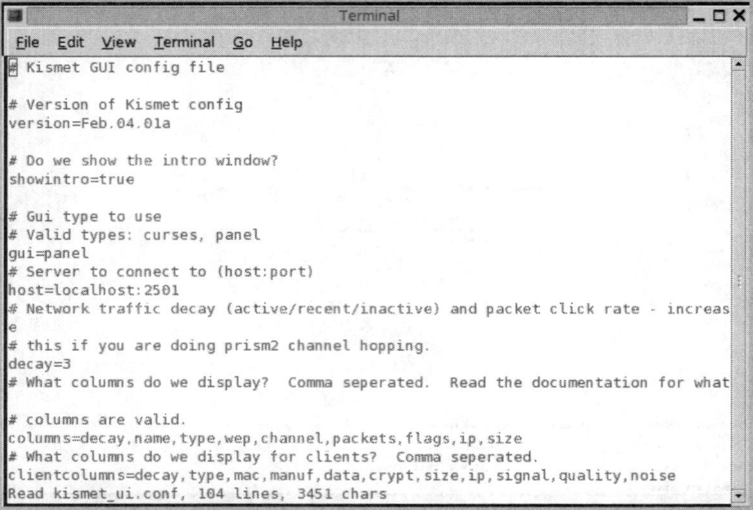

Change the value of the *showintro* variable from true to false, as shown in Figure 6.38.

Figure 6.38 Changing the *showintro* Value

Continued

Now, save the changes you made to **kismet_ui.conf** and restart Kismet. The Welcome message is no longer displayed on startup (see Figure 6.39).

Figure 6.39 The Welcome Message No Longer Appears

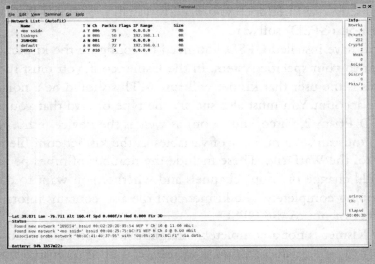

While Kismet is running, Kismet data is automatically saved. When you have finished WarDriving, simply type a capital **Q** to quit Kismet and close the application. Since your card was in monitor mode, you need to either restart the PCMCIA services or reboot your system to resume normal wireless network usage.

Summary

Kismet is a very powerful tool for WarDrivers that prefer to use Linux. Unlike some other WarDriving programs, some configuration is required so that Kismet will work with your system. First, if you want to log the coordinates of the access points you discover with Kismet, you need to install the Global Positioning System Daemon (GPSD) software.

After you have installed GPSD, you need to configure the kismet.conf file to tailor Kismet to your specific system. In the kismet.conf, you must specify an suiduser. This is the user that kismet will run as. This should be a normal user, not the root account. You must also specify the type of card that you are using (ORiNOCO, Prism 2, Cisco, and so on) as well as the device (eth0, eth1, wlan0, or another). You can set a number of variables in the kismet.conf file that allows you to control the WarDrive. These include the number of times per second Kismet should change or "hop" channels and whether you want to disable channel hopping completely. The kismet.conf file also contains information about whether or not to use GPSD.

Starting Kismet is not a completely straightforward process because of the suiduser. Since Kismet runs as a non-root user, you need to ensure that you have that user's environment variables and permissions, but still have the root privileges needed to start Kismet. The easiest way to do this is to use the *su* command rather than the *su –* command prior to starting Kismet.

To successfully WarDrive using Kismet, you need to understand the Kismet user interface. The Kismet user interface is divided into three main parts: the Networks Display, the Statistics Frame, and the Status Frame. The Networks Display lists all of the wireless networks that Kismet has discovered and the current GPS position information. The Statistics Frame displays information about the type of traffic Kismet has captured. The Status Frame scrolls information about the networks Kismet discovers as well as the battery status.

A typical WarDrive using Kismet is accomplished with three main steps:

1. Change to root using the *su* command from the suiduser account noted in kismet.conf.

2. Start GPSD listening on the port noted in kismet.conf. By default, GPSD listens on port 2947.

3. Start Kismet.

Once Kismet is started, verify that you are receiving GPS coordinates by looking for the GPS position information on the Networks Display of the Kismet user interface. If you are, you can begin WarDriving using Kismet.

Solutions Fast Track

Using the Global Positioning System Daemon (GPSD) with Kismet

- ☑ In order to use a GPS unit with Kismet, you need to install GPSD.

- ☑ Download GPSD from www.pygps.org/gpsd/.

- ☑ Uncompress and untar GPSD.

- ☑ Execute the configure script, then run **make** and **make install**.

- ☑ Start GPSD before starting Kismet so that GPS coordinates are logged for found networks.

Configuring Kismet

- ☑ Before you can use Kismet, you must edit the kismet.conf file located in /usr/local/etc.

- ☑ You must set a normal (non-root) user as suiduser.

- ☑ Set the *source* variable to the appropriate type of card and interface of your system.

- ☑ Set the *channelhop* and *channelvelocity* variables. If you want to enable channel hopping, set the *channelhop* variable to "true." If you want Kismet to monitor only a single channel, set this variable to "false." The *channelvelocity* variable indicates the number of times the Kismet channel hopper changes channels each second.

- ☑ Set the *gps* and *gpshost* variables. If you intend to use a GPS unit with Kismet, set the *gps* variable to true. If you do not intend to use a GPS, set this value to false. If you are using a GPS and have set the *gps* variable to true, set the port that GPSD on which GPSD is listening in the *gpshost* variable. By default, GPSD listens on port 2947.

Starting Kismet

☑ In order to start Kismet, you need to have root privileges, but must maintain the ability for the user set as "suiduser" in kismet.conf to write the log files.

☑ This is accomplished by logging in as the suiduser and then using the *su* command without a "-" appended to change to the root user.

☑ Next, simply issue the *kismet* command and Kismet starts and begins identifying wireless networks.

WarDriving Using Kismet

☑ The Kismet user interface is divided into three main sections, or frames.

☑ The Networks Display shows all of the wireless networks that Kismet has identified. The Networks Display also shows the current GPS data if you are using a GPS unit.

☑ The Statistics Frame displays information such as the total number of networks identified, the number of packets captured, and the type of packets captured.

☑ The Status Frame displays a scrolling list of all networks found, as they are found, and the battery life of your system if you have it configured to do so.

☑ Pressing the "h" key while Kismet is running displays the Kismet keyboard help. There are a number of display options that can be used to manipulate the Kismet user interface.

☑ Kismet automatically saves data while it is running. When you are finished WarDriving, simply type a capital "Q" to quit and close the application.

Frequently Asked Questions

The following Frequently Asked Questions, answered by the authors of this book, are designed to both measure your understanding of the concepts presented in this chapter and to assist you with real-life implementation of these concepts. To have your questions about this chapter answered by the author, browse to **www.syngress.com/solutions** and click on the **"Ask the Author"** form. You will also gain access to thousands of other FAQs at ITFAQnet.com.

Q: Can I change the user interface colors that Kismet uses by default?

A: Yes. The kismet_ui.conf file found in /usr/local/etc allows you to change the default colors and many other options that are specific to the kismet user interface. The following variables determine the colors used by Kismet:

- **backgroundcolor** The color of the background on the user interface.

- **textcolor** The text color used by the Kismet user interface for all text except access points found.

- **bordercolor** The color of the borders separating the three main frames of the user interface.

- **titlescolor** The color for titles on the user interface.

- **monitorcolor** The color used on the user interface for GPS and battery information.

- **wepcolor** The color Kismet uses to display access points with Wired Equivalent Privacy (WEP) enabled.

- **factorycolor** The color Kismet uses to show access points with default settings.

- **opencolor** The color Kismet uses to show access points that are not using WEP but do not have default settings.

- **cloakcolor** The color Kismet uses to show cloaked networks that have been discovered.

Q: What colors can I use on the Kismet user interface?

A: You can use black, red, yellow, green, blue, magenta, cyan, and white. If you want the text to be bolded, prepend the word "hi-" to the color. For example, to use bolded red to denote your GPS and battery information, set the *monitorcolor* variable to "hi-red" in the kismet_ui.conf file.

Q: Kismet saves Weak Initialization Vectors (IVs). Does this mean that I can use Kismet to crack WEP?

A: No. Kismet simply saves the Weak IVs so they can be fed into another program such as WEPCrack for cracking. Kismet it not designed to crack WEP keys.

Q: How does Kismet determine if an access point it has discovered is using a default SSID?

A: The ap_manuf file located in /usr/local/etc is a flat text file that has the different Media Access Control (MAC) addresses used by different manufacturers and their default SSIDs. If the MAC address and SSID are listed in this file, Kismet considers the SSID to be the default.

Q: How many different log files does Kismet generate, and what are their differences?

A: Kismet generates the following log files:

- **dump** A raw packet dump.
- **network** A plaintext log of detected networks.
- **csv** A plaintext log of detected networks in Comma Separated Value (CSV) format.
- **xml** An Extensible Markup Language (XML) formatted log of networks.
- **weak** The weak packets detected and stored in AirSnort format.
- **cisco** A log of Cisco equipment discovered in Cisco Discovery Protocol (CDP) format.
- **gps** A log of the Global Positioning System coordinates.

By default, Kismet generates all seven of these logs. You can change this by editing the *logtypes* variable in the kismet.conf file.

Q: Can I change the sound that Kismet plays when it finds a new access point?

A: Yes. Kismet plays the .wav file indicated in the *sound_alert* variable field of the kismet_ui.conf. You can change this to any .wav file that you want as long as you provide the full path to the .wav file.

Q: How do I get Kismet to display my battery status?

A: The *apm* variable of the kismet_ui.conf file must be set to "true" in order for your battery status to be displayed in the Kismet user interface. You must also have Advanced Power Management (APM) enabled in your Linux kernel.

## Chapter 7

Mapping WarDrives Using StumbVerter

Solutions in this Chapter:

- **Mapping the Wireless World**
- **Mapping WarDrives Using StumbVerter**
- **Mapping WarDrives Using DiGLE from WiGLE**

- ☑ **Summary**
- ☑ **Solutions Fast Track**
- ☑ **Frequently Asked Questions**

Introduction

You have gone for a WarDrive. You now have a set of logged access points with their coordinates and other relevant data, and you think, "How am I going to make some use of this? How will I be able to see patterns in the geographical distribution of access points?" Mapping your data sets may be the answer.

There are several ways to map data. StumbVerter is a tool that's designed to take advantage of the automation capabilities of Microsoft MapPoint. MapPoint is commercially available mapping software that covers North America and Europe. StumbVerter processes data captured with NetStumbler and generates maps that you can easily view and manipulate. You can also access online mapping engines that create maps for you free of charge. In this chapter we discuss the process of installing, configuring, and using StumbVerter to map your WarDriving results as well as using the Delphi Geographic Logging Engine (DiGLE). By the end of the chapter, you will know how to create colorful and informative access point distribution maps.

Mapping the Wireless World

When we go for a WarDrive, we gain real-time information about the wireless access points we find along a route. But what happens when we finish and go home to process the results?

One way of representing the wireless world in our local area is to map the results of our WarDrives and extract our conclusions from the resulting maps. Here are some examples of information we can gather once the data is mapped:

- Increasing use of wireless in certain areas
- Monitoring the increase or decrease of wireless installations
- Checking on the security awareness of wireless users

As we will see in this chapter, many mapping solutions can be used to accomplish these tasks. Some solutions are very expensive and cumbersome; others are more light and malleable.

Basic Mapping Concepts

When plotting your WarDriving data on a map, it is important to understand what you are seeing. In other words, it is important to understand what a map represents. Maps provide a visual representation of a specific area. By understanding the basic concepts of mapping, you are better able to interpret the data represented on the maps you generate. This section provides the background information necessary to understand and interpret your maps.

What Is a Map?

This may sound like an odd question, but some people do not have a clear understanding of the exact definition of a map. Let's clear it up. A map is a representation of real-world geographical features, onto which additional data (crop distribution, animal populations, or the like) can be overlaid, and which allows us to quickly and easily refer to these real-world features without actually being there. This representation can take many forms, such as aerial photographs, paper road maps, satellite imagery, digital maps, and more. Each of these forms is used for a particular job and process—for example, a satellite image is of little use for navigating an unknown city in a car, but it may provide vital information to an intelligence analyst.

From here on, we delve into the topic of maps and *cartography*, the science of map making, but we will stay within the most basic facts and knowledge. For the rest of this explanation of basic mapping concepts, we assume that the maps we'll talk about are paper-based.

Map Projections

A basic feature of a map is the *projection*. The projection of a map is simply the way that the real-world geographical features (rivers, roads, and so on) have been drawn on the paper. A great source of further information about map projections is Peter H. Dana's page at www.colorado.edu/geography/gcraft/notes/mapproj/mapproj_f.html. Since map projections are a complex subject, outside the scope of this book, we won't go into more detail here.

Scales and Map Size

Each map has a *scale*, which is a relative measure of the units of distance on the paper that map onto the real-world environment.

For example, if a map has a scale of 1:5000, this means that 1 unit of distance on the map corresponds to 5,000 of the same distance units in the ground covered by the map. Thus, we can measure distances between map features accurately—for example, 2 inches on the map would equal 10,000 inches, or approximately 833 feet, in the real world.

Coordinates and Units

A *coordinate* is a pair of numbers that identify a position in a two-dimensional plane (for example, the Earth's surface) with respect to a fixed datum.

The most commonly used coordinate system uses *latitude* and *longitude*, which are expressed as angles (usually in degrees, but they can be expressed in radians or other angular units, too). In this coordinate system, the Earth is divided from the North Pole to the South Pole by lines called *meridians* and from east to west by lines called *parallels*. To set a fixed reference point that corresponds to 0 degrees of latitude and longitude, the Greenwich, England, meridian was chosen as the longitude reference (which measures the angle east or west), and the Equator was chosen as the latitude reference (which measures the angle north or south).

An example of a coordinate in this system is 41 degrees 53 minutes north, 2 degrees 32 minutes west. Each degree has 60 minutes of arc in it, and each minute of arc has 60 seconds of arc, enabling us to define a coordinate with a resolution of meters or centimeters.

Raster or Scanned Maps

One way to introduce and use real-world geographical information in a computer system is to optically scan a paper map of the area and scale we are interested in and save it on a computer as a standard graphics file. This file will be made up of pixels, the size of which will correspond to so many degrees, minutes, or seconds of latitude and longitude in the real world, according to the scale of the map and the resolution at which we scan it.

This solution has advantages and disadvantages. For starters, any mapping software used to process this scanned map must be capable of recognizing the relationship between the image's pixels and the real-world coordinates, which requires calibration. To calibrate a scanned map, the usual technique is to give the mapping software a few pixel positions of which we know the exact real-world coordinates. From there the program can interpolate the coordinates of any pixel in the image. For a large number of maps, this process is very time consuming and expensive in the long run. Also, the map image loses visual quality as we zoom in closer to see more detail, and we cannot hide features such as labels or roads to make the map more clear. We are limited to a What You See Is What You Get (WYSIWYG) interface.

Vector Maps

The other common map format is called a *vector map*. As the name implies, the map is a file that contains the coordinates of different features and information enabling a viewer that supports the file format to display these features, including roads, points of interest, labels, and more. In essence, a road in a vector map consists of a series of points with known coordinates, joined by a graphical feature (a colored line) that we see as the road. In a scanned map, the road is made up of the hundreds or thousands of individual pixels that draw the road outline.

We can easily see that a vector map will take up considerably less disk space than a scanned map that displays the same features and detail level, since only a few connected points are required to draw roads or other features.

Mapping WarDrives with StumbVerter

Now that we understand the basic concepts of mapping, we are ready to move on to mapping our WarDrives. The first tool we'll investigate is StumbVerter, a program written by Michael Puchol (also known as Mother) that takes input data from NetStumbler and plots the access points found on Microsoft MapPoint maps.

NOTE

StumbVerter is a freeware product, but it requires Microsoft MapPoint to function. MapPoint is a commercial product available for between $250 and $300.

The current version of StumbVerter, available for download from www.sonar-security.com, is StumbVerter 1.5 and requires Microsoft MapPoint 2004. If you have an older version of MapPoint, you will need to download StumbVerter 1.0 Beta 5 from www.michiganwireless.org/tools/Stumbverter/.

NOTE

The examples shown in this chapter utilize Microsoft MapPoint 2002 and StumbVerter 1.0 Beta 5. The processes for installing and using StumbVerter 1.5 with Microsoft MapPoint 2004 are the same as those presented in this chapter.

Installing StumbVerter

After you have installed Microsoft MapPoint and downloaded the appropriate version of StumbVerter, you need to install StumbVerter. First, extract the StumbVerter setup files contained in the zip archive that you downloaded. You can unzip the files to an existing directory or create a new directory for the setup files, as shown in Figure 7.1.

Figure 7.1 Unzipping the StumbVerter Files to a New Directory

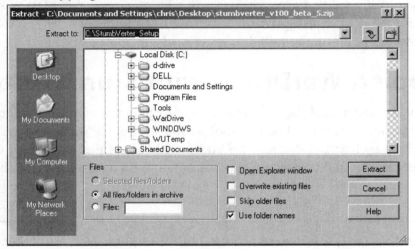

Next, navigate to the directory you extracted the files to. Four files should have been extracted, as shown in Figure 7.2.

Figure 7.2 The StumbVerter Setup Files

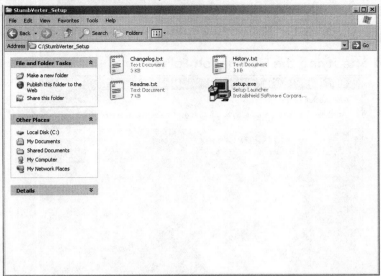

Double-click **setup.exe** to begin the StumbVerter installation (see Figure 7.3).

Figure 7.3 Installation Begins

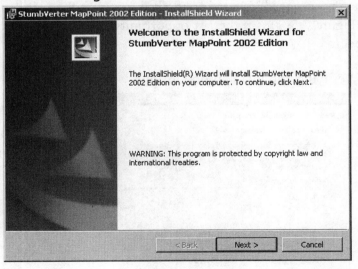

Next, you are asked to specify a destination folder, as shown in Figure 7.4. This is the folder where the StumbVerter setup program installs the StumbVerter software. You can safely use the default option on this screen.

Figure 7.4 Specifying the Destination Folder

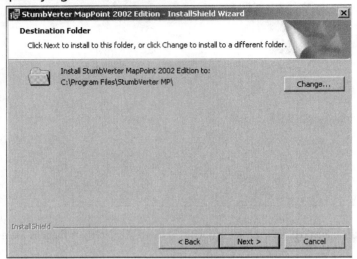

Click **Next** to proceed. You are now asked to verify the installation options, as shown in Figure 7.5. This is the last opportunity to make changes before installation begins.

Figure 7.5 Verifying the Installation Options

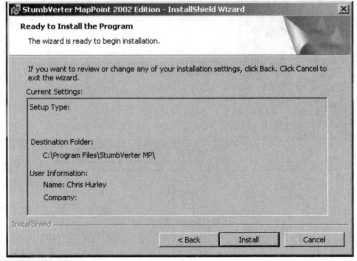

Click **Install** to install StumbVerter on your system. If your installation is successful, you will see the dialog box shown in Figure 7.6.

Figure 7.6 Installation Complete

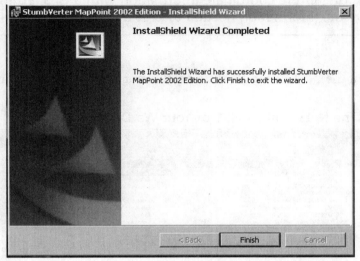

Click **Finish** and you are ready to begin mapping your WarDrives with StumbVerter.

Generating a Map With StumbVerter

Now that you have installed Microsoft MapPoint and StumbVerter, you are ready to map your WarDrive. To use StumbVerter, you must first export your NetStumbler NS1 file and then import it to MapPoint.

Exporting NetStumbler Files for Use With StumbVerter

To map your WarDrive with StumbVerter, you need to export your NetStumbler NS1 file to Summary format.

NOTE

You must have used a global positioning system (GPS) unit to capture coordinates on your WarDrive in order to map it with StumbVerter. If you do not capture coordinate information with a GPS, StumbVerter will not have the information needed to plot the access points.

First, open the NS1 of the WarDrive you want to map, as shown in Figure 7.7.

Figure 7.7 The NetStumbler NS1 of Your WarDrive

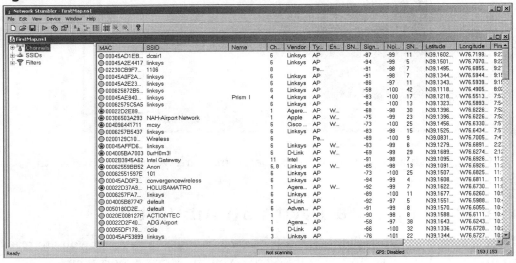

Next, choose **File | Export | Summary**, as shown in Figure 7.8.

Figure 7.8 Preparing to Export the NS1 File

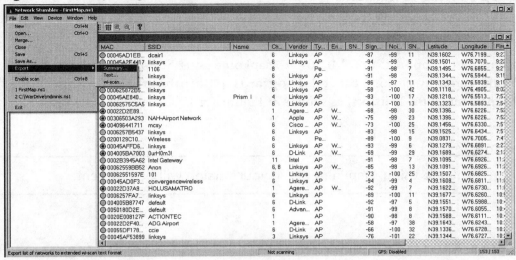

Choose a name and location for the Summary file, as shown in Figure 7.9.

Figure 7.9 Exporting to Summary

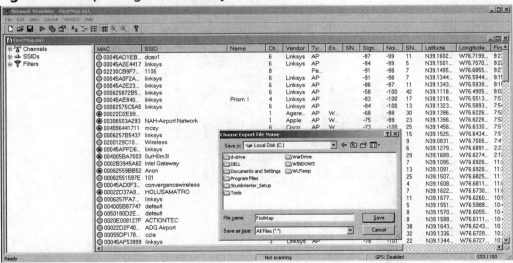

Click **Save** to export the Summary file. Now you are ready to import the Summary to MapPoint using StumbVerter.

Importing Summary Files to MapPoint With StumbVerter

Once you have exported your NetStumbler NS1 file to Summary format, you are ready to import it into Microsoft MapPoint using StumbVerter. First, start StumbVerter by clicking **Start | Programs | StumbVerter | StumbVerter MapPoint 2002 Edition,** as shown in Figure 7.10.

NOTE

If you are using MapPoint 2004, your version will be different.

Figure 7.10 Starting StumbVerter

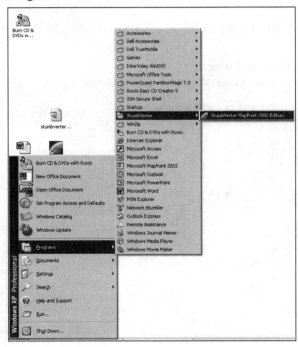

Next, you need to open a new map. Click **Map | Create new North America** (or **Create new Europe**), as shown in Figure 7.11.

Figure 7.11 Using StumbVerter to Open the Map

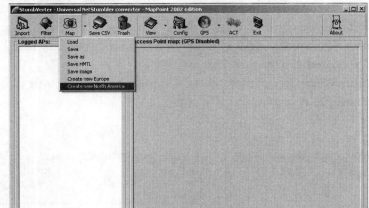

Now you need to import the Summary file you exported from NetStumbler. Click the **Import** icon to open the Open dialog box. Navigate to the location of the Summary file you want to import and select it, as shown in Figure 7.12.

Figure 7.12 Choosing the Summary File to Import

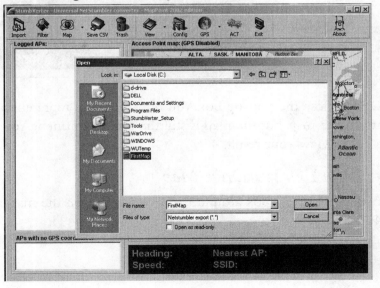

Click **Open**, and StumbVerter will begin importing your Summary file. A list of the Service Set Identifiers (SSIDs) for each of the access points with GPS coordinates is displayed in the **Logged APs:** window. The SSIDs of any access points without GPS coordinates, which will not be mapped, are listed in the **APs with no GPS coordinates:** window.

When StumbVerter has completed the import, a text box will indicate that the import is complete, as shown in Figure 7.13.

Figure 7.13 Import Complete

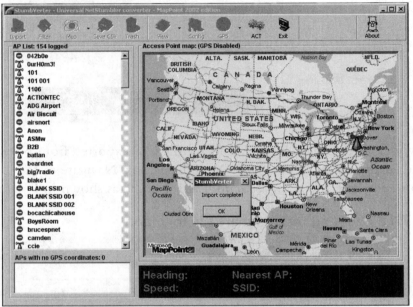

Click **OK** to close the pop-up box. You now see icons representing your access points on the map, but the map is still the entire continent. You need to zoom in to better view your results.

Zooming in On Your WarDrive Map

Using your mouse, create a box around the access points on the map, as shown in Figure 7.14.

Figure 7.14 Determining an Area to Zoom in On

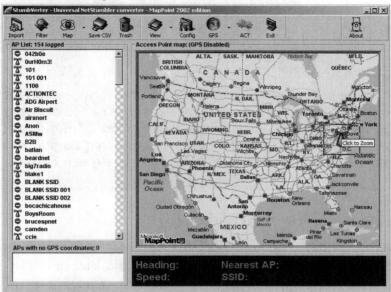

Using your mouse, click inside the box to zoom in on the selected area. Continue creating the boxes and zooming in until you have a map that represents your WarDrive, as shown in Figure 7.15.

Figure 7.15 Your First Map

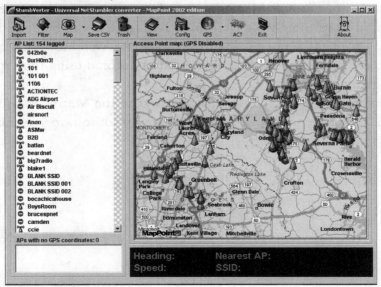

What Do the Icons Mean?

Each access point on a map created with StumbVerter is represented by a "radio tower" icon. The default icons have either a red base or a green base. The icons with the red base indicate an access point that has Wired Equivalent Privacy (WEP) enabled. Access points that do not require the use of WEP are represented by the icons with the green base.

Saving Maps with StumbVerter

Now that you have imported your WarDrive into MapPoint with StumbVerter, you need to save it so that you can either view it again later or display it somewhere (such as a Web page). StumbVerter offers three different formats to save your map:

- Microsoft MapPoint .ptm
- Hypertext Markup Language (HTML)
- Bitmap image

Maps saved in Microsoft MapPoint .ptm format can only be opened later with Microsoft MapPoint. Maps saved in HTML format can be uploaded "as is" to a Web server or can be opened with your favorite Web browser. Maps saved as bitmap images can be manipulated, converted, and stored using most graphic editing programs.

To save your map, click the down arrow next to the **Map** icon, as shown in Figure 7.16, and choose the format in which you want to save your map.

Figure 7.16 Saving Your Map

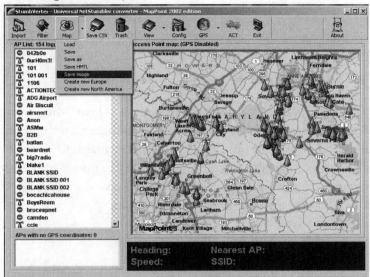

You are prompted for the filename for your saved map. Enter a name in the **File name:** text box, and click **Save** to save your map, as shown in Figure 7.17.

Figure 7.17 Choosing a Filename for Your Map

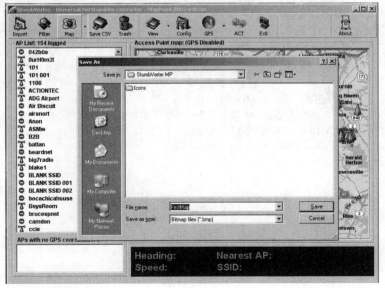

After you have saved your map, you are ready to go back out and WarDrive some more.

Mapping WarDrives with DiGLE from WiGLE.net

Not every WarDriver is in a position to shell out $300 for Microsoft MapPoint to use with StumbVerter. Luckily, you can access online mapping engines that allow you to upload your data sets and generate free maps. One such mapping engine is the Delphi Imaging Geographic Lookup Engine (DiGLE) from the Wireless Geographic Logging Engine, or WiGLE (www.wigle.net). Using data sets generated with your favorite WarDriving software, you can create a map that represents your WarDrive with DiGLE.

Notes from the Underground...

Uploading Statistics to WiGLE

One way to add some enjoyment to your WarDriving experience is to compare the number of access points you have discovered to the results from other WarDrivers. You can do this by uploading your results to the WiGLE database. To upload your results to WiGLE and have your statistics counted, you first need to register with the site. Registration is free and takes only a few seconds. You can register at www.wigle.net/gps/gps/Register/main/, as shown in Figure 7.18, by simply entering your name and e-mail address and choosing a password. You must also accept the end-user license agreement (EULA).

Continued

Figure 7.18 The WiGLE Registration Page

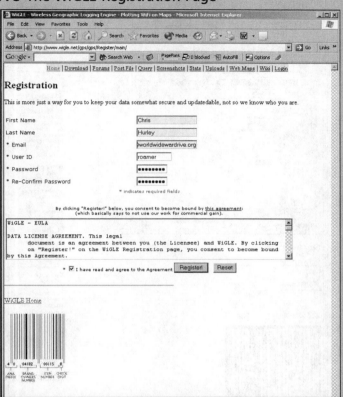

After you have registered, you need to log in to the WiGLE server each time you want to upload data and create a map.

You can upload data from any of the following sources and formats to WiGLE:

- NetStumbler .ns1, text, wiscan, and summary exports
- Dstumbler text output
- Kismet .csv, .xml, .gps, and CWGD output files
- MacStumbler plist, .xml, and wiscan formats
- Pocket Warrior text output

To upload your data set, point your Web browser to www.wigle.net/gps/gps/GPSDB/postfile/ and click the **Browse** button. A

Continued

window will open that allows you to navigate to the location where your data set is stored, as shown in Figure 7.19.

Figure 7.19 Browsing to Your Data Set

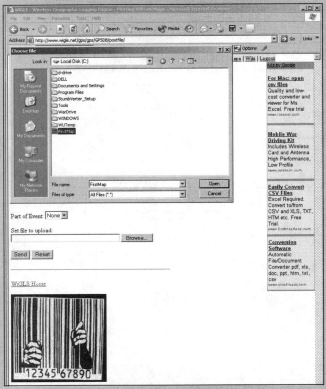

Once you have located and selected your data set, click **Open** to close this window.

Next, click **Send** to upload your data set. Your statistics are now in the WiGLE database. You can check your statistics and those of others who upload to WiGLE at www.wigle.net/gps/gps/GPSDB/stats/.

DiGLE for Windows is available for download from www.wigle.net/gps/gps/GPSDB/dl/. Once you have unzipped the DiGLE client, navigate to the directory where you stored it. For instance, if you unzipped the client in C:, you would change to C:\DiGLE, as shown in Figure 7.20.

Figure 7.20 Changing to the DiGLE Directory

Next, double-click **DiGLE.exe** to start the DiGLE client, shown in Figure 7.21.

Figure 7.21 The DiGLE Client

To successfully map your WarDrive with DiGLE, you need the MapPack for the area you covered. By default, DiGLE comes with the MapPack for Chicago, Illinois. If your WarDrive was not of Chicago, you need to get a MapPack for the area you drove. You can generate and/or download MapPacks from www.wigle.net/gps/gps/GPSDB/mappacks/. Download the appropriate MapPack and unzip the contents into your DiGLE directory, as shown in Figure 7.22. WiGLE has map packs available for every county in the United States and most major metropolitan cities.

Figure 7.22 Unzipping the New MapPack

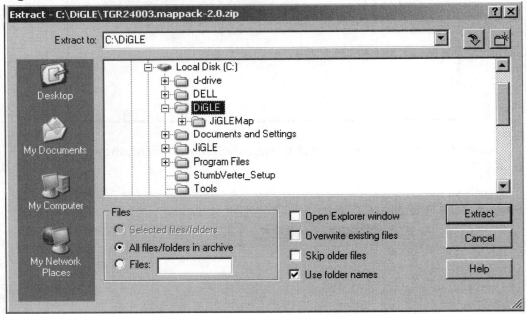

Restart DiGLE. The new MapPack is available, as shown in Figure 7.23.

Figure 7.23 The New MapPack Is Available

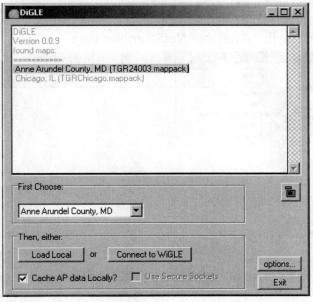

Next, click the **Load Local** button to display the **Open** window, as shown in Figure 7.24.

Figure 7.24 Preparing to Open Your WarDrive Log

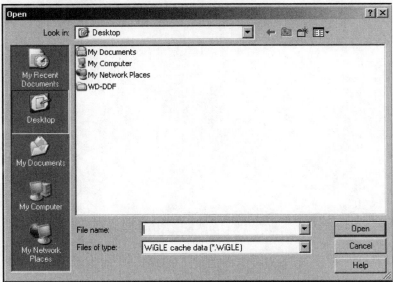

Select **NetStumbler stumble file (*.ns1)** from the **Files of type** drop-down list, as shown in Figure 7.25.

Figure 7.25 Displaying Available NetStumbler Logs

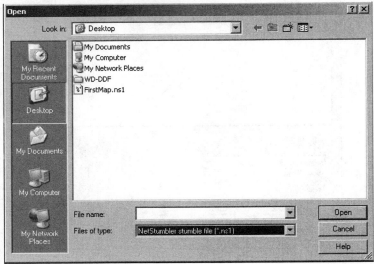

Select the NetStumbler log for the WarDrive you want to map. DiGLE plots the access points discovered during your WarDrive and displays them on the map, as shown in Figure 7.26.

Figure 7.26 The DiGLE Map Is Generated

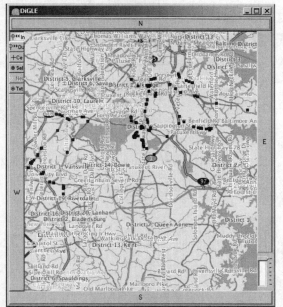

Tools & Traps…

Displaying More Information with DiGLE

DiGLE allows you to display information about the access points that you have discovered on your map. By selecting the Options button on the DiGLE interface, you can choose to display only access points with a specific SSID, only those with DHCP enabled, and the access points that only you have discovered when using the online option.

Clicking the map area causes it to zoom in, as shown in Figure 7.27.

Continued

Figure 7.27 Zooming In

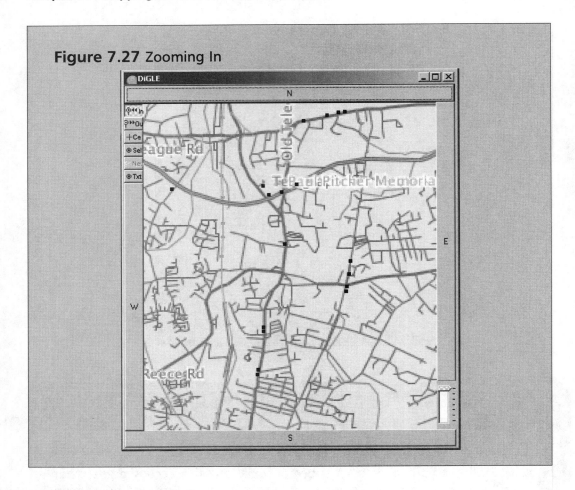

Summary

Mapping your WarDriving data is a good way to analyze data for a specific area to determine its overall wireless security posture. If you want to analyze only your specific data, StumbVerter is the best option for you. StumbVerter allows you to import NetStumbler data into Microsoft MapPoint and generate a map of your WarDrive.

Although StumbVerter is a freeware program, it relies on Microsoft MapPoint, which is a commercial program that costs between $250 and $300. Many WarDrivers don't want to invest this amount of money on mapping software. DiGLE from WiGLE.net allows you to download MapPacks for the area of your WarDrive and generate free maps.

By mapping your WarDrive, you are better able to visualize the security posture of wireless networks in an area. You can easily compare your results with those of other WarDrivers or chart the differences over time for one specific area.

Solutions Fast Track

Mapping the Wireless World

☑ A map is a representation of real-world geographical features onto which additional data can be overlaid.

☑ A basic feature of a map is the projection—the way geographical features have been drawn on the paper.

☑ A map's scale is the relative measure of the units of distance on the paper that map to the real-world environment.

☑ Coordinates are a pair of numbers that identify a position in a two-dimensional plane with respect to a fixed datum. The most commonly used coordinate system consists of *latitude* and *longitude.*

Mapping WarDrives Using StumbVerter

☑ StumbVerter, a free program available for download from www.michiganwireless.org/tools/Stumbverter/, allows you to import your NetStumbler data sets into Microsoft MapPoint and generate maps.

☑ StumbVerter is easy to install, requiring no additional setup beyond executing the setup program.

☑ Before you can import your NetStumbler data into MapPoint with StumbVerter, you must export it to the NetStumbler Summary file format.

Mapping WarDrives Using DiGLE from WiGLE

☑ The Delphi Geographic Logging Engine (DiGLE) is available for download from the Wireless Geographic Logging Engine (WiGLE) Web site at www.wigle.net/gps/gps/GPSDB/dl/.

☑ DiGLE does not require the purchase of a commercial mapping program. However, you must download the WiGLE MapPack of the area you want to map from www.wigle.net/gps/gps/GPSDB/mappacks.

Frequently Asked Questions

The following Frequently Asked Questions, answered by the authors of this book, are designed to both measure your understanding of the concepts presented in this chapter and to assist you with real-life implementation of these concepts. To have your questions about this chapter answered by the author, browse to **www.syngress.com/solutions** and click on the **"Ask the Author"** form. You will also gain access to thousands of other FAQs at ITFAQnet.com.

Q: Why should I map my WarDrives?

A: Mapping your WarDrives provides you with a visual representation of the data that you collected. You can use these maps to easily determine the security posture of access points that have been deployed in the area you surveyed.

Q: Are there any online mapping engines other than WiGLE?

A: Yes, WiFi Maps (www.wifimaps.com) is another online mapping engine that allows you to upload your data and generate free maps.

Q: Are there any mapping programs available for Linux?

A: You can use the Java Geographic Logging Engine (JiGLE) available from WiGLE (www.wigle.net) in Linux, and many other UNIX-based operating systems. You can also use GPSMap, which is installed with Kismet.

Q: Why should I upload my data to WiGLE, since it doesn't generate a custom map?

A: The WiGLE database currently holds information on over 700,000 unique access points. This data can be queried to get a realistic overview of the security posture of the wireless networks deployed worldwide. By uploading your data to WiGLE, you help ensure that this database is as complete as possible.

## Chapter 8

Organizing WarDrives

Solutions in this Chapter:

- The Origin of Organized WarDriving
- The WorldWide WarDrive Is Born
- What the Results of the WorldWide WarDrive Mean
- The Future of the WorldWide WarDrive

☑ Summary

☑ Solutions Fast Track

☑ Frequently Asked Questions

Introduction

I wish that I could take credit for coming up with the idea of organized WarDriving, but that would be oversimplifying the true history of organized WarDriving and would be insincere. The truth is that the idea of organized WarDriving evolved over the course of a year or so from a vague idea that was discussed amongst WarDrivers online into a few specific events.

This chapter provides some background on those early conversations and how they evolved into the DefCon 10 WarDriving Contest. The lessons learned from the DefCon 10 WarDriving contest and what steps were taken to avoid repeating the errors of the past are presented. We look at the origin of the contest, including the behind-the-scenes planning and how the contest came into existence. More importantly, this chapter covers the organization of the contest itself and what rules were used and why. The scoring script that was used is also presented. These include scoring problems as well as data formatting problems. The source code for converting data from Kismet logs to wi-scan format is also provided along with a discussion of the problems encountered in converting the data.

We take a look at how the DefCon 10 WarDriving Contest led to the idea of a small WarDrive to completely cover one city and how that small WarDrive evolved over the past two years into the WorldWide WarDrive, a global event involving hundreds of participants. This chapter covers the mistakes that were made along the way and how they were addressed. I provide an analysis of the results of the WorldWide WarDrives (WWWDs), and the direction that organized WarDriving, particularly the WWWD, will take in the immediate future.

Detailed information on each of the five largest organized WarDrives (DefCon 10 WarDriving Contest, DefCon 11 WarDriving Contest, and all three WorldWide WarDrives) is presented in the chronological order that they took place, along with some tips and tricks on organizing WarDrives in your area. The techniques presented here will help you organize a successful WarDrive whether it is for a large event like the WorldWide WarDrive, or a small WarDrive with a few friends in your area.

The Origin of Organized WarDriving

Human beings are social creatures. Anytime there is more than one person participating in any activity we tend to seek out others that also participate. This gives us insight into how others are doing things, allows us to interact with them, and often results in a meeting of some sort. A good example of this is computer gamers. As broadband Internet became a reality for home users a few years ago, gamers were able to play in online communities with virtually no lag time. There was no longer a need to congregate for LAN parties to play games. But, to this day, gamers will pack up their full-sized desktop computers, monitors, and equipment to get together for LAN parties and play. The exact same thing could be accomplished online with the exception of one aspect—the social aspect. It is fun to be in a room with your friends doing something that everyone enjoys, together.

WarDriving is no different. People began getting together to WarDrive from day one. Why drive around a neighborhood by yourself, when you could e-mail your friend and have him bring his equipment and ride shotgun? Online communities such as the NetStumbler Forums (http://forums.netstumbler.com) and the Kismet Forums (www.kismetwireless.net/forum.php) quickly sprung up. In addition to providing information on setup and configuration of the tools, this gave WarDrivers the ability to talk online with other people that had similar interests. The NetStumbler Forums even started an "Other Stumblers" forum (http://forums.netstumbler.com/forumdisplay.php?s=&forumid=13). This is a place where WarDrivers can post their location and find other WarDrivers in their area. Internet Relay Chat (IRC) channels like #netstumbler on EF Net provide a place for WarDrivers to discuss WarDriving online with others. The natural extension of these online communities is organized WarDriving.

The DefCon 10 WarDriving Contest

In 2002, WarDriving was still a relatively new idea in the hacking and security communities. As is always the case, there was discussion amongst the DefCon staff on how to improve the show. One way that has consistently worked has been to add contests. Contests such as Capture the Flag and Hacker Jeopardy have become mainstays and are two of the most anticipated (and discussed) events at DefCon. I and several other people had talked in the DefCon Forum's IRC channel (#dc-forums on EF Net) about getting together and WarDriving the entire city of Las Vegas while we were there for DefCon. blackwave immediately ran with the idea and posted information about a coordinated WarDrive of Las Vegas on the DefCon Forums (http://forum.defcon.org).

How the Idea Came About

blackwave wasn't aware that I had mentioned this to the other DefCon organizers as an idea for a potential new contest. blackwave had already started a thread on the DefCon forums that was soliciting interest in WarDriving all of Las Vegas, and several people had posted that they were interested in participating. Once the idea was approved as something that we wanted to add to DefCon as a contest, a general call went out to the DefCon staff asking for a volunteer to run it. Because WarDriving and wireless security in general were areas of personal interest to me, I immediately volunteered to organize and run the contest.

Choosing the Staff

Once the contest was approved, I contacted blackwave by e-mail to let him know that the DefCon staff had decided to do a WarDriving Contest rather than proceed with an unofficial WarDrive of the city. Because blackwave had taken the initiative to begin putting the WarDrive of Las Vegas together, I asked him to help out with organizing the contest, and he agreed.

All of this was taking place about six weeks before DefCon so we were under some serious time constraints to get things planned and organized before DefCon started. The first thing we needed to do was assemble a staff. We immediately brought Russ Rogers on board to help us coordinate with the DefCon organizers. This was an easy choice as Russ had been a member of the DefCon staff for several years longer than I had and was more likely to get timely responses to issues the contest staff might run into. Next, we brought on FAWCR and FReCKLeS to work the sign-up booth. Sign-ups would be done on site in the Vendor Area at DefCon.

The last piece of the puzzle was scoring. We were about a month away from DefCon and still hadn't determined the rules for the contest. We decided it would be a good idea to bring a person on to exclusively handle the scoring for the contest. Pete Shipley volunteered to write a script for scoring as well as generate all of the maps that would be needed.

Determining the Rules

Now that we had a staff in place, we needed to determine the rules of the contest. It was imperative that the contest be a WarDriving contest, and not a free for all where people would attempt to gain unauthorized access to wireless networks that were deployed throughout Las Vegas. In order to accomplish this, we needed to state clearly the goals of the contest. We decided to award one point for every access point that each team found. If more than one person on a team found the same access point, it would only be counted once. An additional two points would be awarded for access points that had both a default Service Set Identifier

(SSID) and did not have Wired Equivalent Protocol (WEP) encryption enabled. Finally, five more points would be awarded for each access point that was only discovered by one team and no other. This made it possible to get up to eight points for a single access point. Pete quickly wrote the following PERL script, which has become the basis for several other programs (as discussed later in this chapter), to automate the scoring process for the contest:

```perl
#!/usr/bin/perl -w


# Sun Jul 28 18:55:00 PDT 2002
#
#
# this could have been done in one pass with half lines (and run 50%
faster)
# but I wanted it to be readable, so people can't complain about their
# scores.
#
#           -Pete Shipley <shipley@dis.org>
#            http://www.dis.org/shipley
#
#
# score = #_of_APs + ( #_of_open_APs * 2 ) + ( #_unique_APs * 5)
#
# Input:
#
# From Netstumbler:
#     Menu -> File -> Export -> Summary
#
# N 37.8627800\tW 122.2762283\t( linksys )\tBBS\t( 00:04:5a:26:ee:dd
)\t03:21:36 (GMT)\t[ 14 66 52 ]\t# (   )\t0001\t0040\t100
#
# the Lat & Lon can be signed or have N/W designations.
#
#
# To run:
#
```

```perl
#       ./score.pl teamA.txt teamB.txt teamC.txt teamD.txt ...
#
# Teamnames can be the chars a-z0-9 and "-"
#



#change this to starting/base location
local $home_lat = 37.8645117;
local $home_lon = -122.2802733;


# a hash of teamnames
local %teams;
local %ssids;


# a hash array of found APs for scoring unique APs
local %allaps;


# list of default SSIDs
local $default_list = "^101\$".
                      "|^WLAN\$".
                      "|^Default SSID\$".
                      "|^Wavelan\$".
                      "|^tsunami\$".
                      "|^WaveLAN Network".
                      "|^Apple Network [0-9a-f]+".
                      "|^Air[Pp]ort Network [0-9a-f]+".
                      "|^default\$".
                      "|^ANY\$".
                      "|^any\$".
                      "|^linksys\$".
                      "|^Wireless\$".
                      "|^2\$".
                      "|^BRIDGE\$".
                      "|^Compaq\$".
                      "|^xlan\$".
                      "|^intel\$".
```

```perl
                              "|^comcomcom\$";

sub main {
    my $total;


    foreach $i ( @ARGV )  {
     my $teamname;
     my %teamdata;
     my $score;


     $i =~ /([\w\d-]*)\.txt/;
     $teamname = $1;


     $teams{$teamname}->{score} = 0;
     $teams{$teamname}->{apcount} = 0;
     $teams{$teamname}->{unique_ap} = 0;
     $teams{$teamname}->{open_ap} = 0;
     $teams{$teamname}->{score} = 0;
     $teams{$teamname}->{distance} = 0;
     $teams{$teamname}->{withwep} = 0;
     $teams{$teamname}->{default_ssid} = 0;


     # read in the teams data as an array and save it
     # ignoring comments, 0 lat&lon, and invalid lines
     &read_team_data($teamname);



     # test stuff;
     #print "$teamname:  $teams{$teamname}->{score}  APs\n";
     #$ha = $teams{$teamname}{data};
     #$score =  keys %$ha;
     #print "Score = $score\n";


    }
```

```perl
   # work out unique AP   bonuses
   # and store them in the team hash
   &calc_team_scores;

   # print out the results for each team
   foreach $k ( keys %teams ) {
    my $j;
    my $ha = $teams{$k}{data};

    print  "\n$k :\n";
    print  "\t $teams{$k}{apcount}\tAPs located\n";

    next if $teams{$k}{apcount} == 0;

    print  "\t $teams{$k}{unique_ap}\tUnique APs, ";
    printf "%3.1f%%\n",
            ( ($teams{$k}{unique_ap} / $teams{$k}{apcount}) * 100.0);
    print  "\t $teams{$k}{open_ap}\tOpen/Default APs\n";

    # some extra stats
    printf "\t\t%3.1f%% WEP, %3.1f%% Default SSID, %3.1f%% noWEP & Default
    SSID\n",
         ( ($teams{$k}{withwep} / $teams{$k}{apcount}) * 100.0),
         ( ($teams{$k}{default_ssid} / $teams{$k}{apcount}) * 100.0),
         ( ($teams{$k}{open_ap} / $teams{$k}{apcount}) * 100.0);

    printf "\t\t%2.3f\tMost distant AP (Miles)\n", $teams{$k}{distance};

    print  "\t $teams{$k}{score}\tTotal Score\n";
    print  "\n\n";

    # test stuff;
#     print " withwep $teams{$k}{withwep}".
#          " default_ssid $teams{$k}{default_ssid}\n";

   }
```

```
    # some more extra stats
    $total = keys %allaps;
    print "Total APs found $total\n";

    $total = keys %ssids;
    print "Total SSIDs found $total\n";

    return;
}



# it would be faster and cleaner to do all the math here but then
# people may complain about their scores if they can't see the number add
up
# in front of them
#

sub calc_team_scores {
    my $team;
    my $mac;

    foreach $team ( keys %teams ) {
     my $aplist = $teams{$team}{data};

        # first we have to work out the number of unique APs located
        foreach $mac ( keys %$aplist ) {
            $teams{$team}->{unique_ap}++      if ( $allaps{$mac} == 1);
        }

        # then do the math
        $teams{$team}->{score} =
                $teams{$team}->{apcount} +
            ( $teams{$team}->{unique_ap} * 5) +
            ( $teams{$team}->{open_ap}   * 2);
```

```
        }


     return;

}



# Approximate distance in miles is simply:  sqrt(x * x + y * y)
#
#     where x = 69.1 * (lat2 - lat1)
#     and y = 69.1 * (lon2 - lon1) * cos(lat1/57.3)
#
sub distance_in_miles {
     my ($lat, $lon) = @_;
     my ($x, $y);

     return 0 if ($lat == 0.0);

     $x = 69.1 * ($home_lat - $lat);
     $y = 69.1 * ($home_lon - $lon) * cos($lat/57.3);

     return( sqrt($x * $x + $y * $y));
}



# read in the log, count wep, and ssid stuff..
sub read_team_data {
     local ($team) = @_;
     local %known_macs;
     local $j = 0;
     local $dist;
     local $distance = 0;
     local $total_default_ssid = 0;
     local $total_wep = 0;
     local $total_open = 0;

     unless (open STUMBLE_LOG, $i) {
```

```perl
 warn "Failed to open $i: $!\n";
 return ;
}

while (<STUMBLE_LOG>) {
 my @junk;
 local ($lat, $lon, $ssid, $mac, $flag) = 0;
 local $has_wep = 0;
 local $has_default_ssid = 0;

 chomp;

 my $line = $_;
 next if /^$/;  # skip blank lines
 next if /^#/;  # skip comment lines

 @junk = split(/\t/);

 next if $#junk < 9; # skip short lines

 # extract lat & lon
 $lat = $junk[0];
 $lon = $junk[1];


 #extract MAC address
    $junk[4] =~ m/([0-9a-f][0-9a-f]:[0-9a-f][0-9a-f]:[0-9a-f][0-9a-
    f]:[09a-f][0-9a-f]:[0-9a-f][0-9a-f]:[0-9a-f][0-9a-f])/;
 $mac = $1;
 next unless defined $mac;     # skip bad mac lines
 $mac =~ tr/a-z/A-Z/;

 # extract SSID
 $junk[2] =~ /\(\s+(.*)\s+\)/;
 $ssid = $1;
 $has_default_ssid = 1 if ($ssid =~ /$default_list/);
```

```perl
# extract flag for testing for WEP usage.
if ( defined $junk[8]) {
    $flag = hex $junk[8];
} else {
    $flag = 0;
}
$has_wep = 1 if ($flag & 0x0010);

# convert lat and lon to signed decimal
if ($lon =~ /^[EW]/i ) {
    @junk=split(/\s/,$lon);
    $lon=$junk[1];
    $lon *= -1 if $junk[0] =~ /W/i;

    @junk=split(/\s/,$lat);
    $lat=$junk[1];
    $lat *= -1 if $junk[0] =~ /S/i;
}
# skip AP with out a location (lat = 0)
next unless ($lat != 0.0);

# record each MAC once...
unless (defined $known_macs{$mac}) {
    $known_macs{$mac} = $line ;
    $allaps{$mac}++;
    $j++;

    $ssids{$ssid}++;

    # calc distance and record greatest distance
    # this can be useful for close ties and runner-ups
    $dist = distance_in_miles($lat, $lon);
    $distance = $dist if ($distance < $dist);

    $total_wep++ if $has_wep;
```

```
        $total_default_ssid++ if $has_default_ssid;
        $total_open++ if ( $has_default_ssid == 1 && $has_wep == 0);
    }

  next;
}


close(STUMBLE_LOG);

# count test.
#print "j = $j\n";

$teams{$team}->{apcount} = $j;
$teams{$team}->{data} = \%known_macs;
$teams{$team}->{distance} = $distance;
$teams{$team}->{open_ap} = $total_open;
$teams{$team}->{withwep} = $total_wep;
$teams{$team}->{default_ssid} = $total_default_ssid;


    return;
}


&main;
```

Initially, we had considered allowing the contestants to drive at any time for as long as they wanted, but this idea was quickly discarded because it would be completely unmanageable. After a lot of discussion amongst the contest staff, we decided it would be best to have everyone WarDriving at the same time. We also decided to limit it to a two-hour time frame and that a maximum of four people could participate on a team. This included the driver(s) and any direct participants. In order to further standardize the results, all data that was turned in to the contest staff for scoring had to be in wi-scan format with extensions.

NOTE

One theme of the DefCon WarDriving Contest that still holds true to this day is the loose wording of the rules. We have always maintained the position that if it isn't specifically forbidden, it is allowed. We have taken some criticism for this stance, but because it is a hacker conference, we always want to see what new and innovative ideas people will come up with to meet the letter of the law while skirting the spirit of it. This has led to some interesting results, as you will see in the Lessons Learned sections later in this chapter.

Running the Contest

A couple of weeks before the contest, bks from NetStumbler (www.netstumbler.com) contacted me and asked if NetStumbler.com could sponsor the contest. He offered a 5-dBi omni-directional antenna, ten ORiNOCO pigtails, and ten t-shirts as prizes. I was excited at the prospect of associating the contest with NetStumbler and this was the first time that I had considered not paying for the prizes out of my own pocket. This is a good thing, since the winners would probably have just gotten a t-shirt if I had been forced to pay for the prizes. As soon as I posted the rules at the Security Tribe Web site, I started getting e-mails from other people that wanted to donate prizes to the contest. We ended up with several t-shirts, beer steins, 802.11b wireless cards, stickers, a laptop computer, and more. We had enough prizes to give the top five teams some sort of prize; this far exceeded our expectations.

To sign up for the contest, anyone who was interested was required to sign up at the WarDriving contest table in the Vendor area at DefCon. We expected that about 20–25 people would be interested in competing and were prepared for that type of response. On Friday when the vendor area opened, we put FAWCR and FReCKLeS at the sign-up table and both blackwave and I spent some time there as well. Contestants were required to sign up with a team name, and the names or handles of their team members. We had a piece of regular lined paper for people to sign up on, and no sign to alert people of the sign-up location at all. blackwave drew an extremely cheesy-looking "Sign Up for WarDrive Here" sign on a couple of sheets of printer paper and taped it to the wall to tell potential contestants where to sign up. Since a good portion of DefCon attendees either don't have a car or couldn't put a complete team together, we took it upon ourselves to assemble teams for those that wanted to compete, but were lacking transportation, a complete team, or both.

To our complete surprise, over 100 contestants on twenty-six teams signed up for the contest. Of those twenty-six teams, about half were teams that signed up together, the other half were teams that we put together on site. This contest would take place throughout the city of Las Vegas as opposed to on the grounds of the Alexis Park Hotel. Because of this, and the overwhelming response to the contest, the organizers started to get nervous. The DefCon lawyer came to me and told me that in order to participate in the contest, each contestant would have to sign a "hold harmless" legal disclaimer (see Figure 8.1).

Figure 8.1 The DefCon 10 WarDriving Contest Legal Disclaimer

Hold Harmless and Disclaimer Re: War Driving Contest:
   Any/All contestants who:
   Improperly or illegally access a network or enter access points non-encrypted or otherwise by any means, with or without intent, are subject to the following conditions:

     1) Are not protected from any/all civil or criminal liabilities by the DefCon Conference, DefCon Communications Inc., or the Alexis Park Hotel and;

     2) Will be considered by the above listed entities as on an Independent Adventure, and subject to their own civil/criminal consequences and will hold the above cited entities harmless from any of the above listed consequences they incur.

We had reserved a room at DefCon to meet and kick off the contest. All of the people that had signed up needed to be in the room an hour prior to the start of the contest. Anyone that needed to be assigned to a team received their team assignments at this time. This is also when we passed the disclaimer forms out for signature. We let the contestants know that if they did not sign the disclaimer, they could not participate. Each result that was uploaded would be cross-referenced with the disclaimer to ensure that we had one on file before their results would count. Many DefCon attendees were very privacy- and anonymity-conscious and the disclaimer did not sit well with some of them, especially since it was never mentioned before they were required to sign it. About 20 people on five teams refused to sign the disclaimer and dropped out of the contest. This left us with about 80 contestants on 21 teams.

We immediately experienced two problems. First, it took more than an hour to get the teams assigned and all of the disclaimers signed. Second, because we had about 80 participants, all of whom were scheduled to leave the same place simultaneously, it was no longer feasible to do it this way. With 80 people driving the same area simultaneously, this was the largest coordinated WarDrive that had ever been undertaken (at the time). If we had done a "gentlemen start your engines" type of start, there would have been a massive traffic jam just getting out of the parking lot of the Alexis Park. Since we had limited the contestants to only two hours of drive time, we were afraid that some contestants would spend a good portion of that time just trying to get out of the Alexis Park parking lot. I coordinated with Pete Shipley and we decided that we would modify the rules slightly and start scoring each person's data at the timestamp of the first access point found rather than at a specific time. Any access points that they found in the next two hours would count. That way people wouldn't have to worry about getting stuck in a traffic jam and wouldn't take unnecessary risks while driving.

Once everyone had taken to the streets blackwave, FAWCR, and I organized the disclaimers and turned them over to the lawyer. Pete spent the next hour and a half doing interviews and preparing to score the data. After all of the disclaimers were turned over, blackwave and I began preparation for the data dump. Our intent was for Pete to have an anonymous FTP server on the DefCon wireless LAN. We had a room reserved for the data dump so that if people had any problems uploading their data, we would be there to help out.

The WarDrive itself went off without any incidents. No one had broken any laws, no one warchalked any of the found access points, no one was arrested or detained for traffic violations. About two hours after the start of the WarDrive, teams started to file into the data dump area to upload their results for scoring. We thought that the hard part was over at this point… we were very much mistaken.

The one lesson that any DefCon staff member should always remember is that DefCon is a hacker conference. Nothing ever goes as planned and the data dump was no exception. As people started filing in, we announced, verbally, the IP address of the data dump FTP server. Word spread like wildfire throughout the conference and within a few minutes there were at least 20 fake data dump FTP servers put online. We had to defend against man-in-the-middle attacks, ARP spoofing, data sniffing, and other assaults. The number of attacks we were fending off was staggering, but in the end caused a Denial of Service against our FTP server.

About one third of the contestants actually got their data up to the FTP server without issue. Another third uploaded their data with some assistance from us. Pete and I were furiously tracking down the bogus dump servers that had gone online and got as many as possible shut down. This helped people in getting to the legitimate server, but the ARP spoofing continued throughout the evening. Finally, after about two hours we told the remaining third of the contestants that hadn't been able to get their data to us that we would allow them to give us their data on floppy disk, CD, or USB drive. We finally had all the data and could begin scoring.

Both Converge and Tim McGuffin had written scripts that would convert Kismet logs into wi-scan format with extensions. These had been put on the contest Web page so that people didn't have to write their own conversion script. A lot of the contestants seemed to have a hard time using them correctly, however, and many of the data sets were not formatted correctly. Pete and I discussed how to handle this. We wanted as many "scored" results as possible, especially since this was the first contest of its sort and we wanted a good showing. We wanted to make sure all the contestants enjoyed themselves. Not scoring their data would have frustrated a lot of them. Also, a good deal of press interest had been generated in the contest and we wanted a good showing for any stories that were written. Pete decided that he would manually fix the bad data sets so that he could score them. I am sure that he thought this was going to be a short process—probably an hour or two. It ended up taking Pete nearly ten hours to get all of the data sets that were incorrectly formatted into a state where they could be scored.

Once all of the data had been converted into a usable format, scoring itself went relatively smoothly. A total of 1804 unique access points were discovered in and around Las Vegas. Of the 21 teams that submitted data, four had data sets that we were unable to correctly format, so they received scores of zero. The other 17 teams had their data scored. Team WirelessCon won with a total score of 1893. They detected 550 access points, 42 percent of which (231) were unique to their team. One team had either converted their data badly or attempted to cheat (we believe their data conversion script was bad) and all of their access points were in the middle of the Pacific Ocean. We gave them a score of zero. The complete results of the DefCon 10 WarDriving Contest can be found at www.defcon.org/html/defcon-10/dc-10-post/defcon-10-wardrive-post.html.

Lessons Learned

We learned several lessons during the inaugural year of the DefCon WarDriving Contest. One of the biggest hurdles that we ran into was the problem of getting the Kismet data properly converted into wi-scan format with extensions. We knew that we had to address this issue before we could have a truly successful contest and started working on a remedy (which is discussed later in this chapter) about one month after DefCon 10 ended.

The prize situation also needed to be addressed. NetStumbler came through with exactly what they promised and those were some of the most popular prizes. DefCon provided each member of the first place team with a black DefCon badge. This badge entitled the winner to free admission to DefCon 11 and is only given to contest winners. Because there is no way to get the black badge other than winning, it is one of the most coveted pieces of DefCon memorabilia. Unfortunately, some of the prizes donated did not live up to their billing. The best example of this is the laptop computer. It was donated in non-working order with no power supply and a dead battery. This prize was awarded to the second place team who never got it in working order. There were several similar instances with the prizes. Again, we determined that prizes would need to be addressed early in the planning process for the next year. The "bragging rights" of winning a DefCon contest are important, but a tangible prize is also important.

We learned a serious lesson about the DefCon wireless network; don't rely on it! Because of the nature of the conference, people are going to interfere with the DefCon wireless network. We decided before DefCon 10 ended that we would place the contest data server on the wired network for future contests. As is noted later in this chapter, we still had more lessons to learn in this regard at DefCon 11.

Our sign was sad. We certainly learned that we needed to plan well in advance and get a professional looking sign printed up to let people know where the registration area was located. blackwave did the best he could and even put the)(Open Node warchalking symbol on the sign he drew up. That didn't change the fact that while Capture The Flag unveiled their most elaborate set up to date, complete with a live scoreboard on a giant screen, we had a hand-drawn sign on blank printer paper. This would be remedied for the next contest.

The idea of loosely defining the rules definitely worked. In the true spirit of following the letter of the law but not the spirit one team, the Shmoo group, attempted an extremely innovative maneuver. They approached a local television news station and offered up a "ride along" on the contest for a news crew. There was one catch to the offer. The news crew had to provide the transportation, their traffic helicopter. They would be able to cover the entire city and more in the two hours allotted with plenty of time to spare. I got wind of this a few hours before the contest started, and was thrilled with the idea. This was the type of idea that would generate buzz about the contest and would be talked about for years to come. Unfortunately, the news crew didn't show up at the appointed meeting place so the contestants had to resort to more conventional means. Also, because it had now been tried, I implemented "The Shmoo Rule" for future contests: Ground transportation only.

Finally, we learned that the sign-up process we had in place was completely unmanageable. We had virtually no idea how many contestants to expect, and only planned for about one quarter of the actual number of participants. We hadn't automated many aspects of sign-up and team assignment because we really thought it would be simple to do it once we were at DefCon. We knew that we had to have an online sign-up process in place prior to DefCon 11 in order to know how many people were going to participate, plan for them, and make the contest run more smoothly.

Post DefCon 10 Discussion

Once I got home from DefCon, I monitored the DefCon Forums and the NetStumbler Forums to try to get a feel for the contestants' opinions of the contest. For the most part, the response was good. The problems that we already knew about were pointed out. Still, the people who participated almost all said that they had a good time and would participate the next year. That was our primary goal, so we considered the contest a success despite the problems we had run into. I found out on the NetStumbler Forums that The Watcher, one of the members of Team WirelessCon, lived very close to me. I contacted him about an idea I had to do a WarDrive of the entire city of Baltimore and asked him if he would be interested in working on this with me. He was interested. I didn't realize it at the time, but a new phase of organized WarDriving had just begun.

The WorldWide WarDrive Is Born

Since The Watcher and I had decided to WarDrive Baltimore together, I thought it would be fun to see if anyone else might be interested in driving with us. There were several people on the NetStumbler Forums that were interested in coming along. Renderman decided to try to do a drive of Red Deer, Canada on the same day. He and I discussed the idea of a "World Stumbling Day" in which people all over the world would WarDrive their areas on the same day.

WorldWide WarDrive 1

I posted this "World Stumbling Day" idea in the DefCon Forums to see if there might be any interest from the members; there was. By this time, there were several people that wanted to WarDrive their area. We chose August 31, 2002 for our WarDrive date. I didn't care for the term World Stumbling Day and decided that WorldWide WarDrive had a better sound. I posted information about the WorldWide WarDrive on my Web site, Security Tribe (www.securitytribe.com). We needed some way to let people know what areas were involved, and how many people were planning to participate. I put up a guestbook-type message board for people to use for signing up and coordinating. Throughout the next week, I received several e-mails from people that were interested but didn't want to post their e-mail addresses or locations on a public message board. I decided to move all of the coordination to the WarDriving mailing list (http://mailsrv.dis.org/ mailman/listinfo/wardriving) where people could make arrangements in a more private forum.

Organization

At this point, I knew that I needed to put some sort of page up with general information about the event. Word had started to circulate and a general buzz was growing about the event, particularly in the computer underground. I posted a page that had each of the areas that were being coordinated and the coordinator's contact information. There were only about six or seven coordinators on this page when it was first posted. That number grew to ten by the day of the event.

I had done absolutely no promotion for the first WorldWide WarDrive other than a general announcement on the WarDriving mailing list and the existing posts on the NetStumbler and DefCon Forums. The idea was spreading by word of mouth through the underground. One thing people should understand about the WorldWide WarDrive is that I intentionally leave organization of the individual areas up to the local organizers. I don't have a "press kit" or anything with a prefabricated press release for people to use. For the first WorldWide WarDrive, I only offered up basic guidance on local organization. That was primarily based around making sure that people didn't attach to any networks that were discovered. I also let each local organizer know that he was responsible for getting a merged data set to me. Organizers were asked to send me either a merged

NetStumbler .ns1 file or a wi-scan dump with extensions. I would then collate the data and manually generate the statistical analysis.

The organizers from Canada, Renderman and JJKaczor, thought it would be a good idea to send a press release out to the Canadian press. This was an idea that I completely disagreed with. I am not a person that enjoys doing interviews or any kind of self-promotion. This is not from some sense of modesty. There are three primary reasons for my standoffishness with the press.

1. I don't like taking credit for other people's accomplishments. The WorldWide WarDrive is collaboration. I can't do it by myself. A lot of people work very hard to ensure that the event goes off without a hitch (or at least as few hitches as possible). The press tends to like using words such as "founder" and "organizer." This gives me a lot more credit than I deserve.

2. The press has a tendency to point out primarily the negative aspects of any so-called "underground" event.

3. I have become gun-shy when it comes to the press after watching the way they have twisted quotes from me and other collaborators in past interviews regarding DefCon.

I pointed these issues out to Renderman and JJKaczor and strongly cautioned them against issuing a general press release. They felt that it was important to send something out though, and did. This was a decision they would later come to regret as you will see in the Lessons Learned section.

The Canadian press release did have an impact on the participation in the WorldWide WarDrive. After a few Canadian papers and news Web sites picked the story up, there was even more notice taken of the event in the United States. American papers and Web sites were quoting and mirroring the Canadian stories and interest in the event picked up dramatically. One of the most important things that came from the Canadian press release was that the Chicago, Illinois group Deadtech (www.deadtech.net) became aware of the event and volunteered to organize Chicago. These guys really knew how to organize. Unlike other organizers in other cities (including me), these guys didn't just choose a meeting place and time. Deadtech put together a complete class on how to WarDrive, encouraged people who didn't understand WarDriving to come and learn what it was all about and even tag along with more experienced people. They also planned a big post-WarDrive party for everyone to get together afterwards. They have done this for every WorldWide WarDrive and that probably explains why they have consistently had one of the best turnouts.

As August 31ˢᵗ approached, I was paying attention to the weather forecasts and noticed that thunderstorms were expected in Baltimore. Driving in the rain is not fun; let alone WarDriving in the rain. I contacted a few of the people that were planning to attend and asked them what they thought about postponing our drive until the following Saturday. The general consensus was that no one wanted to drive in the rain, so the announcement was made that the Baltimore drive would be one week after most of the other areas. Although at the time this was a decision based solely on the weather, it turned out to be a major decision in how the WorldWide WarDrive would be organized from that point forward. Since we were now extending the WorldWide WarDrive over an entire week, people started e-mailing me to ask if they could submit data for each day as opposed to only on the 31ˢᵗ. I decided that the WorldWide WarDrive would be the entire week. Each subsequent WorldWide WarDrive has been a week-long event.

On the evening of the 31ˢᵗ, the organizers began e-mailing me their results. I continued to receive results from them for the next few days. On September 4ᵗʰ, 2002, the WorldWide WarDrive would change forever. I was in Washington, D.C. doing some work when my cell phone rang. I was in a meeting so I turned it off. About an hour later, I left the meeting and turned the phone back on to find that I had missed fourteen calls, most of them from Russ. I called him back before I checked my voicemail to try to find out what the emergency was. He told me that the Security Tribe Web server was being hit with a Distributed Denial-of-Service (DDoS) attack. I told him to log in and shut the Web server down and that I would check on it when I got home. As it turned out, it wasn't a DDoS per se. It was what I have come to call an "Industry-Induced Denial-of-Service Attack."

Unbeknownst to me, Slashdot had run a story about the WorldWide WarDrive (http://slashdot.org/articles/02/09/04/1238219.shtml). Because Security Tribe is a medium-traffic Web site even during the busiest times, I had set the concurrent connections threshold to 100. Slashdot has a very large readership, and many of its patrons clicked the link that was provided to the Security Tribe Web site. This caused the server to be overloaded. Later that evening, I tried turning the Web server back on, but the connections immediately hit 100. Again, because Security Tribe is a hobby server, I didn't have the type of service plan that would allow many more connections than that and I didn't feel comfortable increasing the threshold. I ended up leaving the server offline for about a day and a half, long enough for the story to be replaced on the Slashdot front page.

For the most part, the Slashdotting was a frustration, but not a major issue. My mail server still worked and I could access the box remotely. It did generate a lot of awareness for the event though, and I began to receive e-mails from WarDrivers asking if they could submit their data from that week even if they hadn't participated in an organized area drive. I decided that any data that was collected during the week of the WorldWide WarDrive could be submitted even if an organized drive wasn't attended. This is a policy that has been maintained throughout the history of the WorldWide WarDrive.

Lessons Learned

The first WorldWide WarDrive was an eyeopener in many ways. I had no idea that the event would generate the amount of interest from the WarDriving community and the press that it did. I quickly realized that if I wanted to do future WorldWide WarDrives, it would need its own identity. Most of the reaction from the WarDriving community was positive and people seemed to be interested in doing it again. I purchased the domain www.worldwidewardrive.org so that I could move information about the WorldWide WarDrive off of Security Tribe, which was not a wireless security site but rather a general security site and repository for whitepapers I had written, as well as presentations I had given in the past.

Many of the drives were organized simply by taking a city map and cutting it into sections; giving each driver a piece of the map. This is a completely ineffective way to plan a WarDrive. Many drivers that participated found themselves in areas that were unsavory to say the least. Low income, urban areas were dangerous to drive in. Also, when people are struggling to pay for their food, it is highly unlikely that they are spending money to deploy wireless networks. I knew that before we did this again, steps had to be taken to maximize the effectiveness of the drives.

What completely surprised me was the reaction from the Information Security community. The SANS Institute, in their weekly *News Bites*, negatively portrayed the event. Their September 9, 2002 edition carried the following story "Wardriving Reveals Lack of LAN Security."

> "A week-long worldwide wardrive revealed that many wireless LANs (local area networks) don't employ even basic security. A New Jersey–based company is selling complete wardriving kits. A consultant for the company observed that wardriving is legal and has legitimate uses. [Editor's Note (Murray): it is legal to look in your neighbor's open window but nice people do not do it. There is no

more corrupting idea than the current one that that which is legal is, ipso facto, ethical.]"

www.computerworld.com/mobiletopics/
mobile/story/0,10801,74103,00.html
www.computerworld.com/mobiletopics/
mobile/story/0,10801,74102,00.html

Another surprise was the reaction of the Canadian Security Intelligence Service (CSIS). After hearing of the WorldWide WarDrive from the press release issued by Renderman and JJKaczor, the CSIS opened an investigation into the two of them and the WorldWide WarDrive. Their investigation discovered no malicious intent or actions and was quickly closed. The lesson was learned that if a press release is going to be issued, statements such as participants will be "converging on" an area should be avoided.

This brings me to the main lesson learned from the first WorldWide WarDrive. If you are going to engineer an event such as this that has the potential to be controversial, it is important to state the goals up-front. I had not done this with the first WorldWide WarDrive. It was put together relatively quickly, and spawned from a small group of friends getting together to drive one city. I didn't realize that it would be perceived in a negative way by anyone. This was addressed with the second WorldWide WarDrive.

Statistics from WorldWide WarDrive 1

When all was said and done, over a hundred WarDrivers participated in the first WorldWide WarDrive. Twenty-two areas were represented in six countries on two continents (North America and Europe). There were eight categories of statistics generated. I compiled and generated all of the statistics by hand, as shown in Table 8.1.

Table 8.1 The Statistics from the First WorldWide WarDrive

CATEGORY	TOTAL	PERCENT
TOTAL APs FOUND	9374	100
WEP Enabled	2825	30.13
No WEP Enabled	6549	69.86
Default SSID	2768	29.53
Default SSID and No WEP	2497	26.64

Continued

Table 8.1 The Statistics from the First WorldWide WarDrive

CATEGORY	TOTAL	PERCENT
Unique SSIDs	3672	39.17
Most Common SSID	1778	18.97
Second Most Common SSID	623	6.65

WorldWide WarDrive 2

Almost immediately after the first WorldWide WarDrive, I started getting e-mails from people wanting to know when the next one would take place. Most of these were from people that heard about the first one from media stories after it had ended and wanted to participate in future drives. Renderman contacted me and asked if it would be possible to have another WorldWide WarDrive before the weather got too bad in Canada and parts of the U.S. I decided that it would be worthwhile to have another WorldWide WarDrive before the end of the year to capitalize on the interest that had been generated from the first one while it was still fresh in people's minds.

Organization

After checking the calendar, I chose October 26th through November 2nd, 2002 for the dates of the second WorldWide WarDrive (WWWD2). Before announcing the dates for the WWWD2, I knew that I could avoid some of the problems of the first one by clearly stating the goals of the event up-front. I decided that the easiest way to do this would be to put a Frequently Asked Questions (FAQ) section up on the WorldWide WarDrive Web site (www.worldwidewardrive.org/faq.html). I ended up putting the FAQ on the front page of the Web site, right under the announcement of the WWWD2 dates, until after the WWWD2 was over.

The FAQ was a good idea. It allowed me to address many of the issues that people didn't understand. The first two FAQ items address what the WWWD is and what the goals are.

- **What is the WorldWide WarDrive?** The WorldWide WarDrive is an effort by security professionals and hobbyists to generate awareness of the need by individual users and companies to secure their access points.

The goal of the WorldWide WarDrive (or WWWD) is to provide a statistical analysis of the many access points that are currently deployed.

- **What do you hope to accomplish?** We feel that many end users are not aware that the factory or "default" settings on access points do not take any security measures into account. By providing these statistics, we hope that end users will become aware of the need to take simple measures to secure their access points.

Notes from the Underground…

Stumbler Code of Ethics

Even though the FAQ addressed most of the things I wanted people to know about the WWWD, I thought it was important to create a general set of guidelines to address the ethical behavior that should be adhered to by WarDrivers. These guidelines apply not only during the WorldWide WarDrive but anytime they go out WarDriving. I asked Renderman if he would be willing to assemble this for inclusion on the WorldWide WarDrive page. He agreed and the Stumbler Code of Ethics was born.

These are by no means rules that must be followed, but they are a collection of suggestions for safe, ethical, and legal stumbling. I encourage you to follow them.

1. Obey traffic laws. It's your community, too. Traffic laws are there for everyone's safety—besides, doing doughnuts at 3 A.M. are rewarded with unwanted attention from the authorities.

2. Obey private property and no-trespassing signs. Don't trespass in order to scan an area—that's what the directional antenna is for. You wouldn't want people trespassing on *your* property, would you?

3. Don't connect. The vast majority of APs out there were not intended by their owners to be accessed by you, even if they configured it so you could access it if you wanted to. There is much legal question as to the trouble you can get into for accessing a network through a misconfigured AP. Also, it's a matter of respect—you wouldn't want people rooting

Continued

through *your* computers just because *you* happened to make a mistake, so don't do it to them.

4. Don't use your data for personal gain. Share the data with like-minded people, show it to people who can change things for the better, but don't try and make any money or status off your data. It's just wrong to expect these people to reward you for pointing out their own stupidity.

5. Don't warchalk other people's networks. Only chalk your own if you want to indicate your willingness to share access. If you chalk some stranger's network, it dilutes the use of the symbols to indicate free access. If you're a business and you have both a public AP and a non-public one, indicate which is the open one, but also indicate the closed one with the closed symbol, differentiating them so people know the difference.

6. Observe that old hiker motto "Take only pictures, leave only footprints" and adapt it as your own. Thus, stumblers should "Take only SSIDs, leave only tire marks." Leaving tire marks by not loitering and moving on is better than leaving a log entry by doing something stupid.

As soon as the dates were announced on the Web site and the FAQ had been put up, I e-mailed the announcement to the WarDriving and Kismet mailing lists. Then I posted the announcement on the NetStumbler Forums, the Kismet Forums, and the DefCon Forums. That was the extent of the "promotion" done for the WWWD2. There was no general press release sent out, as I wanted to avoid any inaccurate and sensationalist stories being released.

I sent a general e-mail out to the organizers letting them know that I would accept their data from October 26th until November 9th, 2002 but that only data sets containing data collected between October 26th and November 2nd would be counted. This gave organizers a week to combine the data from their areas before sending it to me. Again, the organizers would need to send me their combined data by e-mail so that I could combine it into the master file for statistical analysis. I also sent this information to the mailing lists and posted it on the FAQ. This was so that people who did not participate in an organized drive but still wanted to submit their data would have the opportunity to do so.

Once the dates were announced and people started planning their drives, I needed to address the issue of maximizing the results of the WarDrive. I decided that rather than drive Baltimore again, I would organize Annapolis, the state capitol of Maryland. I got in touch with ffrf, one of the participants from the first WWWD in Baltimore and asked for his help with this problem. He developed a program that would take income data from the latest census and generate color-coded maps to note the income levels for a specific area using MapBlast (www.ffrf.net/maps/annapolis-small-mb-overlay-labels.png).

Tools & Traps…

Converting the Data

Since not all of the WarDrivers were using NetStumbler (which makes it very easy to convert data to wi-scan format with extensions), we needed to get the organizers a standardized way to convert Kismet data to the proper format. Tim McGuffin and ffrf had combined their efforts and developed a conversion program that would allow the organizers to convert data. I provided this program to the organizers so that they could easily convert the data before they sent it to me.

```perl
#!/usr/bin/perl


## Medic's kismet to extended wi-scan converter
## Current as of: August 26, 2002


$csvfilename = $ARGV[0];


$cwgdfilename = $ARGV[1];



if (!defined $csvfilename) {print "USAGE:./convert.pl CSVFILE
CWGDFILE\nYou are missing the CSV File\n"; exit}


if (!defined $cwgdfilename) {die "USAGE:./convert.pl CSVFILENAME
```

Continued

```
CWGDFILE\nYou are missing the CWGD File\n";exit}

open(CSVFILE,$csvfilename) or die "Can't open CSV file";

while (<CSVFILE>) {

  chomp;

  next if /^$/;

  next if /^#/;

  @temp = split(";");

#  for $x (0 .. 20){

#    $csvarray[$csvcount][$x] = $temp[$x];

#  }

#HASH

   $temp[3] = lc($temp[3]);

   $ssidhash{$temp[3]} = $temp[2];

   $networktypehash{$temp[3]} = $temp[1];

   $channelhash{$temp[3]} = $temp[5];

   $wephash{$temp[3]} = $temp[7];

#/HASH
```

Continued

```
      $csvcount++

}

print "# \$Creator: Kismet to wi-scan 0.6 by Medic\n";

print "# \$Format: wi-scan\n";

print "# Latitude\tLongitude\t( SSID )\tType\t( BSSID )\tTime
(GMT)\t[SNR Sig Noise ]\t# ( Name
)\tFlags\tChannelbits\tBcnIntvl\n";

print "# \$DateGMT:\n";

open(CWGDFILE,$cwgdfilename) or die "Can't open CWGD file";

while (<CWGDFILE>) {

  chomp;

  next if /^$/;

  next if /^#/;

  @cwgdarray = split(/\t/);

  if ($cwgdarray[0] ne "00:00:00:00:00:00") {

    $bssid =lc($cwgdarray[0]);

    $latitude = $cwgdarray[2];
```

Continued

```
    $longitude = $cwgdarray[3];


    $findtime = $cwgdarray[10];


    $signal = $cwgdarray[8];


    $noise = $cwgdarray[9];


    $snr = $signal - $noise;


    $bcnintvl = 100;



    GetInfo($bssid);


    FixChannel();


    FixNetwork();


    FixDate();


    FixFlags();


    FixCoords();


    print "$latitude\t$longitude\t( $ssid )\t$networktype\t( $bssid
)\t$findtime (GMT)\t[ $snr $signal $noise ]\t# (
)\t$flags\t$channelbits\t$bcnintvl\n";


  }


}
```

Continued

```perl
sub FixCoords{

  if ($latitude =~ /^\-/i){

    @templat = split(/\-/i,$latitude);

    $latitude = @templat[1];

    $latitude = "S " . $latitude;

    } else {

    $latitude = "N " . $latitude;

  }

  if ($longitude =~ /^\-/i){

    @templon = split(/\-/i,$longitude);

    $longitude = @templon[1];

    $longitude = "W " . $longitude;

    } else {

    $longitude = "E " .$longitude;

  }

}

sub FixFlags{
```

Continued

```
    $wepbit = "0";


    $ntypebit = "0";


    if ($wep eq "Yes") {$wepbit = "1"}


    if ($networktype eq "BBS") {$ntypebit = "1"} else {$ntypebit =
"2"}


    $flags =  "00" . $wepbit . $ntypebit;


}


sub FixDate{


    @junk = split(" ",$findtime);


    $findtime = $junk[3];


}


sub FixNetwork{


    if ($networktype eq "infrastructure" or $networktype eq "probe")
{$networktype = "BBS"} else {$networktype = "Ad-hoc"}


}


sub FixChannel{


    $channelbits = "0000";
```

Continued

```
      if ($channel eq "00") {$channelbits = "0001"}

      if ($channel eq "01") {$channelbits = "0002"}

      if ($channel eq "02") {$channelbits = "0004"}

      if ($channel eq "03") {$channelbits = "0008"}

      if ($channel eq "04") {$channelbits = "0010"}

      if ($channel eq "05") {$channelbits = "0020"}

      if ($channel eq "06") {$channelbits = "0040"}

      if ($channel eq "07") {$channelbits = "0080"}

      if ($channel eq "08") {$channelbits = "0100"}

      if ($channel eq "09") {$channelbits = "0200"}

      if ($channel eq "10") {$channelbits = "0400"}

      if ($channel eq "11") {$channelbits = "0800"}

}

sub GetInfo($bssid) {

#   $y = 0;

#   for $y (0 .. $#csvarray){

#   if ($bssid eq lc($csvarray[$y][3])) {
```

Continued

```
#      $ssid = $csvarray[$y][2];

#      $networktype = $csvarray[$y][1];

#      $channel = $csvarray[$y][5];

#      $wep = $csvarray[$y][7];

#  }

#  $y++;

#  }

#HASH

   $ssid = $ssidhash{$bssid};

   $networktype = $networktypehash{$bssid};

   $channel = $channelhash{$bssid};

   $wep = $wephash{$bssid};

#/HASH

}
```

Lessons Learned

The second WorldWide WarDrive was probably the most trying of all of them. Attempting to put a second WorldWide WarDrive together so quickly after the first was a mistake. I still had not developed an automated way to generate the statistics and getting the results together was difficult. The initial press reaction was also quite negative. The amount of press that was generated for the WWWD2 was quite a bit larger than the first. By the time the results were released, the number of positive stories and negative stories had evened out quite a bit. That was encouraging, but I still felt that the press did not understand my goal with the project and realized that something would have to be done to address that before another WWWD could take place.

There were a lot of people interested in organizing their areas and if anyone contacted me with an e-mail address or Web page stating that they wanted to do some organizing, I posted their information. There were some cases where I didn't check their contact page before posting it on the organizer site (www.worldwidewardrive.org/wwwd2/organizers.html). Two problems resulted from this:

1. Some people volunteered to organize but because I didn't query them at all, I didn't realize that they were not trustworthy. There were several people that signed up as area organizers for the WWWD2 that never submitted their data. In fact, most of these people ignored my repeated e-mails asking for their data so I don't know if people participated but their data was never submitted, or if the organizer never got together with other drivers.

2. More disturbing, one wireless security company tried to generate business by using their corporate Web page as the organizer site. Their page had only been listed on the organizer site for two days before I checked it out and removed it. I knew that I would have to specifically address this issue before another WorldWide WarDrive could take place.

Statistics from the WorldWide WarDrive 2

Despite the problems, I still consider the WWWD2 a success. Over 200 people participated (twice as many as the first WWWD) in 32 areas, representing seven countries on four continents. I dropped the statistic for Unique SSIDs from the analysis for two reasons. First, because I was still generating the statistics manually and there were so many more access points found than the first WWWD, it was just not feasible. Second, I had received feedback that the Unique SSID statistic wasn't very useful. Table 8.2 reflects this.

Table 8.2 The Statistics from the Second WorldWide WarDrive

CATEGORY	TOTAL	PERCENT
TOTAL APs FOUND	24958	100
WEP Enabled	6970	27.92
No WEP Enabled	17988	72.07
Default SSID	8802	35.27
Default SSID and No WEP	7847	31.44
Most Common SSID	531	21.28
Second Most Common SSID	2048	8.21

WorldWide WarDrive 3

Almost immediately after WWWD2, I started getting e-mails asking about the next WorldWide WarDrive. I still hadn't recovered from the second at this point and wasn't even sure if there would even be a third. I either ignored these e-mails or replied letting people know that when the dates for the next one were decided they would be announced on the WarDriving and Kismet mailing lists, and on the NetStumbler, DefCon, and Kismet forums. I decided to take a few months and not think about the WWWD. By the time 2003 had rolled around, I had received enough inquiries that I realized the event had to go on. I am glad that it did, because the third WorldWide WarDrive (WWWD3) was, without a doubt, the most successful.

Organization

The first two WorldWide WarDrives had showed me a lot about how not to do things. Before I announced the WWWD3, I wanted to address some of these problems rather than just repeat them. Most of the problems with the first WWWD were addressed in some way during the organization of the WWWD2, but the WWWD2 revealed a whole new set of issues that needed to be taken care of; most of these were more serious than those from the first WWWD. With the WWWD3, I undertook the greatest planning, preparation, and organization of any WWWD to date. I wanted the event to both run smoothly and get the message out to the right people at the right time.

　　The first thing I needed to do was standardize the data upload process. I contacted ffrf again and asked if he would be willing to write a Web-based application that would allow for automated upload of the data from either individuals or the coordinators. I needed something that would accept only NetStumbler .ns1 files. I also wanted the data quarantined so that uploaded data would not be accessible by the public. I didn't want someone to be able to access and download the .ns1 files from the server. This is because it has never been my objective to post or make public individual .ns1's or data on individual access points but rather give a snapshot of the wireless networks deployed at the time of the event. Since this was a relatively easy application to write, fffrf agreed and provided me with the following PHP script:

```
<html>
<head>
<?


//////////////////////////////////////////
//////////////////////////////////////////
//CONFIGURATION

$upload_dir = "/usr/home/chris/wwwd3/";
$admin_email_addy = "roamer@worldwidewardrive.org";



//////////////////////////////////////////
//////////////////////////////////////////



function isValidEmail($address, $checkMX = false)
  {
        $valid_tlds = array("arpa", "biz", "com", "edu", "gov", "int", "mil",
        "net", "org", "ad", "ae", "af", "ag", "ai", "al", "am", "an", "ao",
        "aq", "ar", "as", "at", "au", "aw", "az", "ba", "bb", "bd", "be",
        "bf", "bg", "bh", "bi", "bj", "bm", "bn", "bo", "br", "bs", "bt",
        "bv", "bw", "by", "bz", "ca", "cc", "cf", "cd", "cg", "ch", "ci",
        "ck", "cl", "cm", "cn", "co", "cr", "cs", "cu", "cv", "cx", "cy",
        "cz", "de", "dj", "dk", "dm", "do", "dz", "ec", "ee", "eg", "eh",
        "er", "es", "et", "fi", "fj", "fk", "fm", "fo", "fr", "fx", "ga",
        "gb", "gd", "ge", "gf", "gh", "gi", "gl", "gm", "gn", "gp", "gq",
        "gr", "gs", "gt", "gu", "gw", "gy", "hk", "hm", "hn", "hr", "ht",
```

```
"hu", "id", "ie", "il", "in", "io", "iq", "ir", "is", "it", "jm",
"jo", "jp", "ke", "kg", "kh", "ki", "km", "kn", "kp", "kr", "kw",
"ky", "kz", "la", "lb", "lc", "li", "lk", "lr", "ls", "lt", "lu",
"lv", "ly", "ma", "mc", "md", "mg", "mh", "mk", "ml", "mm", "mn",
"mo", "mp", "mq", "mr", "ms", "mt", "mu", "mv", "mw", "mx", "my",
"mz", "na", "nc", "ne", "nf", "ng", "ni", "nl", "no", "np", "nr",
"nt", "nu", "nz", "om", "pa", "pe", "pf", "pg", "ph", "pk", "pl",
"pm", "pn", "pr", "pt", "pw", "py", "qa", "re", "ro", "ru", "rw",
"sa", "sb", "sc", "sd", "se", "sg", "sh", "si", "sj", "sk", "sl",
"sm", "sn", "so", "sr", "st", "su", "sv", "sy", "sz", "tc", "td",
"tf", "tg", "th", "tj", "tk", "tm", "tn", "to", "tp", "tr", "tt",
"tv", "tw", "tz", "ua", "ug", "uk", "um", "us", "uy", "uz", "va",
"vc", "ve", "vg", "vi", "vn", "vu", "wf", "ws", "ye", "yt", "yu",
"za", "zm", "zr", "zw");

// Rough email address validation using POSIX-style regular expressions
if (!eregi("^[a-z0-9_]+@[a-z0-9\-]{2,}\.[a-z0-9\-\.]{2,}$", $address))
  return false;
else
  $address = strtolower($address);

// Explode the address on name and domain parts
$name_domain = explode("@", $address);

// There can be only one ;-) I mean... the "@" symbol
if (count($name_domain) != 2)
  return false;

// Check the domain parts
$domain_parts = explode(".", $name_domain[1]);
if (count($domain_parts) < 2)
  return false;

// Check the TLD ($domain_parts[count($domain_parts) - 1])
if (!in_array($domain_parts[count($domain_parts) - 1], $valid_tlds))
  return false;
```

```
    // Searche DNS for MX records corresponding to the hostname
($name_domain[0])
    if ($checkMX && !getmxrr($name_domain[0], $mxhosts))
      return false;

    return true;
  }


function make_clean($value) {
//  if ( preg_match( '/[^a-zA-Z0-9\/_.-]/', $page_param ) ) {
  $legal_chars = "%[^0-9a-zA-Z ]%"; //allow letters, numbers & space
  $new_value = preg_replace($legal_chars,"",$value); //replace with ""
  return $new_value;
}


function make_clean_email($value) {
//  $legal_chars = "%[^0-9a-zA-Z ]%"; //allow letters, numbers & space
//  $new_value = preg_replace($legal_chars,"",$value); //replace with ""
  $new_value = str_replace('@', '-', $value);
  return $new_value;
}


if (($_FILES['img1'] != "") && ($_POST['handle'] != "") &&
(isValidEmail($_POST['email']))) {

    $today = date("y.m.d.G.i.s");   //Year.Month.Day.Hour.Minute.Second
    $user_handle = make_clean($_POST['handle']);
    $user_email = $_POST['email'];
    $user_conf = $_POST['conf'];
    $user_addr = $_SERVER['REMOTE_ADDR'];
    $user_filesize = $_FILES['img1']['size'];
    $friendlyemail = make_clean_email($_POST['email']);
```

```
    $prettyfilename = $today."_".$user_handle."_".$friendlyemail.".ns1";
    $finalfilename =
$upload_dir.$today."_".$user_handle."_".$friendlyemail.".ns1";



?>
<title>WWWD 3 :: Upload Form</title>
<body>
<? echo $user_filesize;?> bytes received..<p>
<?

    //5374654e
    $handle = fopen ($_FILES['img1']['tmp_name'], "rb");
    $contents = fread ($handle, 4);
    fclose ($handle);
    if (bin2hex($contents) == "4e657453") {
?>
Valid .NS1 file detected..<p>
<p>
<?

    copy($_FILES['img1']['tmp_name'], $finalfilename)
            or die("Couldn't copy the file!");


    $newdate = date ("F dS Y h:i:s A");


        if ($user_conf) {
                ?>Sending email confirmation..<p><?
            $subject = "WWWD3 submission confirmation";
                $emailbody = "This email confirms that we have received
                your WWWD3 data:\n\n    Name: $user_handle\n    Email:
                $user_email\n    File Size: $user_filesize\n    Time:
                $newdate\n\n";
                    mail($user_email, $subject, $emailbody, "From:
                    roamer@worldwidewardrive.org\r\n");
        } else {
```

```
            ?>Email confirmation not selected.. skipping<p><?
        }


    $subject = "WWWD3 SUBMIT: $user_handle from $user_addr";
    $emailbody = "A new submission has been received:\n\n    Name:
$user_handle\n    Email: $user_email\n    Sent confirmation email:
$user_conf\n    From IP: $user_addr\n    File Name: $prettyfilename    \n
File Size: $user_filesize\n    Time: $newdate\n\n";


    //Send email to admin
      mail($admin_email_addy, $subject, $emailbody, "From:
      roamer@worldwidewardrive.org\r\n");


    ?>
<b>Thanks for participating in the third WorldWide Wardrive!</b>
    <?


    } else {


?>
<b>Invalid .NS1 file detected.  Please go back and check that the file that
you are uploading is a NetStumbler .NS1 file.</b>
<p>
<?


    }




//var_dump($_POST);
//var_dump($_FILES);




} else {


    die("Form is missing information.  Please go back and enter a name,
valid email address, and file.");
```

```
}


?>



</body>
</html>
```

   With the upload script generated, I no longer needed to be concerned with getting hundreds of attachment filled e-mails from the individuals and organizers that participated. Now I needed to make sure that there was a standardized way to get the data into NetStumbler .ns1 format. In the past, I had just taken the wi-scan dumps and imported them into NetStumbler, then saved them off to .ns1. Since I now wanted all data in .ns1 format from the start, I needed an easier way for participants to get this done. Luckily, the Church of WiFi (CoWF), had been working on a project to do just this. The project, called WarGlue, was a cross platform suite of WarDriving tools designed to give WarDrivers several different utilities to manipulate their logs.

   blackwave, Converge, and ffrf were the primary authors of these tools. I contacted them and let them know what I was planning for WWWD3 and asked when they would have the WarGlue suite ready. They essentially asked me when I would need it. I still had one piece of the puzzle to take care of before I could announce the dates, but I told them I was shooting for March 31st for the WWWD3 announcement and that I hoped to do a joint announcement with them to announce the WWWD3 and release WarGlue to the world. We decided this would work and I began work on the final piece.

   Because the security community and the press had unfortunately not understood the goals of the first two WorldWide WarDrives, I wanted to try to explain it to them in a more effective way. I decided the best way to accomplish this would be to hold a presentation at a security conference, and intended to present the information at DefCon 11. Unfortunately, the Call for Papers (CFP) for DefCon 11 had not opened yet. I contacted The Dark Tangent, the primary organizer and founder of DefCon, directly and pitched my idea. I wanted to give a presentation entitled "The WorldWide WarDrive: The Myths, the Misconceptions, the Truth, the Future" at DefCon 11. This presentation would detail all of the goals of the project, the history of the project, the issues and problems I had run into to date. I would also reveal the complete statistical analysis and results of the WWWD3 for the first time. The Dark Tangent was impressed with the idea and agreed to give me a speaker slot at DefCon. I truly appreciated him doing this long before the official CFP went out. With the major pieces of the organization puzzle in place, I could go forward with the announcement on March 31st, 2003.

I chose June 28th through July 5th, 2003 for the dates of the WWWD3. This gave me time to generate the statistics and add them into the presentation before DefCon 11, which took place August 1st through 3rd, 2003. With the dates decided, I got back in touch with the CoWF and asked them to write up their portion of the announcement, to be jointly released on March 31st, 2003.

With our target dates decided, we needed to move forward with getting the programs generated. The CoWF needed to get WarGlue ready for release. The primary component of WarGlue that would be needed for the WorldWide WarDrive was WarKizniz. WarKizniz is a program that would take Kismet data and convert it into NetStumbler .ns1 format. As promised, the CoWF delivered WarGlue on time. The entire suite is available for download at www.michigan-wireless.org/tools/. WarKizniz allowed participants to do the data conversion on their end and upload it using the automated upload script.

Before I could release the announcement, I needed to address the issue of organizers. I did not want organizers that didn't agree with the goals of the project. I also didn't want companies that would use the guise of the WWWD to attempt to generate business for their company. I created the following statement that I required anyone who wanted to organize an area to read and accept prior to being listed on the organizers page, as shown in Figure 8.2.

Figure 8.2 The WorldWide WarDrive Organizer Agreement

If you are interested in organizing a local drive for the Third WorldWide WarDrive, please read this:

I don't want organizers to be folks that are trying to use this as a springboard to generate business for their company or turn it into a money-making opportunity (that is, I will secure these for you for $$). If you just believe in the goals of the project, which are detailed in the WWWD FAQ, and want to help out in your area, then continue reading.

If you are still interested in coordinating your area, and are cool with the above, then all I need is the e-mail address you want listed on the organizers page, the name or handle you want listed, and a Web site for your local event (if you have one). While a Web site is not required, it makes coordination much easier and you will probably get more interest because you can put the info out there (for instance, meeting times/places) for them without proposed participants having to contact

Continued

Figure 8.2 The WorldWide WarDrive Organizer Agreement

you via e-mail first. This allows people to maintain their anonymity, which many consider very important.

If after reading the above you still want to coordinate your area, send an e-mail to roamer@worldwidewardrive.org.

Once the dates were announced, organizers started getting their areas lined up. I realized right away that this was going to be a bigger event than the two previous WorldWide WarDrives. I knew that I had to address the statistical generation issue. It had taken me nearly 12 hours to compile the statistics and generate the maps from the WWWD2. If it turned out this one was bigger, as I expected, I knew that I would not be able to generate the statistics by hand. I had to create the statistical generation program. Because I had the code from the DefCon 10 WarDriving contest, which actually provided a lot of the functionality for parsing the data sets that I would need, I used it as a guide and created the statistical generation program. I wrote the main command-line interface and blackwave updated it to allow for some additional functionality.

```perl
#!/usr/bin/perl
####################################
##9:33 PM 8/30/2003
#CoWFSG - Church of WiFi Stat Generator
# cowfsg-cli.pl written and maintained by
#roamer@worldwidewardrive.org
## can be downloaded from
#http://www.michiganwireless.org/tools//statgen/
####################################
# 9:34 PM 8/30/2003
# parameters updated: blackwave
####################################
my $ioflag = -1;
if ($#ARGV==-1)
{
 die "usage: cowfsg-cli.pl [-file | -screen | -both] input(wiscan)
output(ascii)\n";
}
elsif ($#ARGV==0)
{
```

```perl
  $ioflag = $#ARGV;
}
elsif ($#ARGV==1)
{
  $ioflag = $#ARGV;
}
elsif ($#ARGV==2)
{
  $ioflag = $#ARGV;
}
else
{
  die "usage: cowfsg-cli.pl [-file | -screen | -both] input(wiscan)
output(ascii)\n";
}

my $outflag = 3; #default
if ($ARGV[0] eq '-screen')
{
  $outflag = 0;
}
elsif ($ARGV[0] eq '-file')
{
  $outflag = 1;
}
elsif ($ARGV[0] eq '-both')
{
  $outflag = 2;
}


if (($outflag != 3) && ($ioflag < 1))
{
  die "error: check usage: not enough arguments... \n";
}


if (($outflag >1) && ($ioflag < 2))
```

```
{
 die "error: check usage: not enough arguments... \n";
}


$indexStart=0;
if ($ioflag >=1)
{
 $indexStart=1;
}


# list of default SSIDs, this list differs from netstumbler's
local $default_list =     "^101\$".
                          "|^WLAN\$".
                          "|^Default SSID\$".
                          "|^Wavelan\$".
                          "|^tsunami\$".
                          "|^WaveLAN Network".
                          "|^Apple Network [0-9a-f]+".
                          "|^Air[Pp]ort Network [0-9a-f]+".
                          "|^default\$".
                          "|^ANY\$".
                          "|^any\$".
                          "|^linksys\$".
                          "|^Wireless\$".
                          "|^2\$".
                          "|^BRIDGE\$".
                          "|^Compaq\$".
                          "|^xlan\$".
                          "|^intel\$".
                          "|^comcomcom\$";


# get the input and output from command line
get_data($ARGV[$indexStart]);


if (($outflag == 1) || ($outflag == 2))
{
```

```perl
 write_file($ARGV[$indexStart+1]);
}

if (($outflag ==0) || ($outflag ==2))
{
 write_screen();
}

#process the input file
sub get_data {
$infile=$ARGV[$indexStart];
chomp $infile;


open (SUMMARY, $infile) || (die "unable to open input file $infile\n");

while (<SUMMARY>) {
        my @data;
        local ($lat, $lon, $ssid, $mac, $flag) = 0;
        local $has_wep = 0;
        local $has_default_ssid = 0;

        chomp;

        my $line = $_;
        next if /^$/;  # skip blank lines
        next if /^#/;  # skip comment lines

        @data = split(/\t/);

        next if $#data < 9; # skip short lines

        # extract lat &amp; lon
        $lat = $data[0];
        $lon = $data[1];
```

```perl
#extract MAC address
$data[4] =~ m/([0-9a-f][0-9a-f]:[0-9a-f][0-9a-f]:[0-9a-f][0-9a-
f]:[0-9a-f][0-9a-f]:[0-9a-f][0-9a-f]:[0-9a-f][0-9a-f])/;
$mac = $1;
next unless defined $mac;         # skip bad mac lines
$mac =~ tr/a-z/A-Z/;

# extract SSID
$data[2] =~ /\(\s+(.*)\s+\)/;
$ssid = $1;
$has_default_ssid = 1 if ($ssid =~ /$default_list/);

# extract flag for testing for WEP usage.
if ( defined $data[8]) {
    $flag = hex $data[8];
} else {
    $flag = 0;
}
$has_wep = 1 if ($flag &0x0010);

# convert lat and lon to signed decimal
if ($lon =~ /^[EW]/i ) {
    @data=split(/\s/,$lon);
    $lon=$data[1];
    $lon *= -1 if $data[0] =~ /W/i;


    @data=split(/\s/,$lat);
    $lat=$data[1];
    $lat *= -1 if $data[0] =~ /S/i;
}
# skip AP with out a location (lat = 0)
next unless ($lat != 0.0);

# record each MAC once...
unless (defined $known_macs{$mac}) {
```

```perl
        $known_macs{$mac} = $line ;
        $allaps{$mac}++;
        $aps++;


        $ssids{$ssid}++;


        $total_wep++ if $has_wep;
        $total_default_ssid++ if $has_default_ssid;
        $total_open++ if ( $has_default_ssid == 1 && $has_wep == 0);
       $total_no_wep=$aps-$total_wep;
      $total_percent=100;
       $wep_percent=$total_wep/$aps*100;
       $no_wep_percent=$total_no_wep/$aps*100;
       $def_ssid_percent=$total_default_ssid/$aps*100;
      $open_percent=$total_open/$aps*100;
}


     next;
   }


   close(SUMMARY);


#process the output file
sub write_file
{
$outfile=$ARGV[$indexStart+1];
chomp $outfile;
open (STATS, ">$outfile") || die ("unable to open output file $outfile");


# print the results to the output file
print STATS "Total APs found=                    $aps $total_percent% \n";
print STATS "APs with WEP enabled=                  $total_wep ";
printf STATS ("%.2f",$wep_percent);
print STATS "% \n";
print STATS "APs without WEP enabled=                $total_no_wep ";
```

```
printf STATS ("%.2f",$no_wep_percent);
print STATS "% \n";
print STATS "APs with a Default SSID=                    $total_default_ssid ";
printf STATS ("%.2f",$def_ssid_percent);
print STATS "% \n";
print STATS "APs with a Default SSID and no WEP enabled=    $total_open ";
printf STATS ("%.2f",$open_percent);
print STATS "%\n";
close (STATS);
}


#process the output
sub write_screen
{
# print the results to the output file
print STDOUT "Total APs found=                    $aps $total_percent% \n";
print STDOUT "APs with WEP enabled=                  $total_wep ";
printf STDOUT ("%.2f",$wep_percent);
print STDOUT "% \n";
print STDOUT "APs without WEP enabled=                 $total_no_wep ";
printf STDOUT ("%.2f",$no_wep_percent);
print STDOUT "% \n";
print STDOUT "APs with a Default SSID=                $total_default_ssid ";
printf STDOUT ("%.2f",$def_ssid_percent);
print STDOUT "% \n";
print STDOUT "APs with a Default SSID and no WEP enabled=   $total_open ";
printf STDOUT ("%.2f",$open_percent);
print STDOUT "%\n";
}


}
```

Additionally we thought it would be good to have a graphical user interface (GUI) for people that wanted to use one. blackwave created the GUI and both programs were released on the Church of WiFi Web site (www.churchofwifi.org/statgen).

```perl
#!/usr/bin/perl -w
#####################################
##5:53 PM 8/30/2003
#CoWFSG - Church of WiFi Stat Generator
# cowfsg-gui.pl v 1.0
## filename: cowfsg-gui.pl
#created and maintained by
#blackwave@hushmail.com
## using perl/Tk
#for use with
#cowfsg-cli.pl written and maintained by
#roamer@worldwidewardrive.org
## both can be downloaded from
#http://www.michiganwireless.org/tools//statgen/
#####################################
use Tk;
use File::Copy;
my $mw = new MainWindow(-title => 'CoWFSG - Church of WiFi Stat
Generator');
$mw->geometry('500x400');
my $mb = $mw->Menu(-type => 'menubar');
$mw->configure(-menu => $mb);
my $fm = $mb->cascade(-label => '~File',
                           -tearoff => 0);
$fm->command(-label => 'Open ...',
               -command => sub {&bfd($mw)});
$fm->command(-label => 'Save As ...',
               -command => sub {&sad($mw)});
$fm->command(-label => 'Exit ...',
               -command => sub {exit});
my $am = $mb->cascade( -label => '~About',
                             -tearoff => 0);
```

```perl
$am->command(-label => 'About ...',
              -command => sub {&ad($mw)});
my $image = $mw->Photo(-file => "CoWF-logo.gif");
$mw->Button(-text => 'Exit', -command => sub {&bfd($mw)},
              -image => $image)->pack;
ad();
my $rtd = $mw->Scrolled("Text")->pack();
$rtd->insert('end',"Hint: You need to open a file - click Something");
rmtmpf();
MainLoop;

sub bfd
{
my $w = $_[0];
my $types;
my $wsf;
my $rsout='cowfsg_gui_output_asc';
my @types =(["wi-scan files", [qw/.*/]],);
$wsf = $w->getOpenFile(-filetypes => \@types);
if ($wsf ne "")
{
my $rstr = qx(perl cowfsg-cli.pl -file $wsf $rsout);
system($rstr);
#my $rtd = $mw->Scrolled("Text")->pack();
$rtd->delete("1.0", "end");
open(FH, $rsout) || die "Could not open file $rsout";
while (<FH>)
{
 $rtd->insert('end', $_);
}
close(FH);
}
}
#save as drop down
sub sad
{
```

```
my $w = $_[0];

my $types;

my $wsvf;

my $rsout='cowfsg_gui_output_asc';

my $rsav= `cowfsg-default-saved.txt';

my @types =(["wi-scan files", [qw/.*/]],);

$wsvf = $w->getSaveFile(-filetypes => \@types,
                              -initialfile => $rsav);

copy("$rsout","$wsvf");

rmtmpf();

}

# about drop down

sub ad

{

my $atr='CoWFSG - Church of WiFi Stat Generator written and maintained by
blackwave@hushmail.com http://www.michiganwireless.org/tools//statgen/';

$mw->Label(-textvariable => \$atr, -relief => 'ridge', -wraplength => 500)-
>pack(-side => 'bottom', -fill => 'x');

}

#clean up if required

sub rmtmpf

{

my $rsout='cowfsg_gui_output_asc';

unlink $rsout;

}

# NMEA!

# End of File.
```

At this point, the work had been done. I set up an e-mail alias (media@world-widewardrive.org) designed specifically to handle requests from the media. Although I was slightly more accessible to the media, I still didn't do a lot of interviews. This is because most of the media requests came in between the end of the WWWD3 and DefCon 11. Most of the media requests wanted the results and I had promised that they would be released to the world for the first time at DefCon 11 during my presentation. I kept my promise and not even the primary organizers, blackwave, Converge, ffrf, and Renderman were given access to the results. I did reserve a front row seat for them at my presentation though and made sure to point out all of the hard work that they had put into the WWWD from its inception to the present.

Lessons Learned

Overall, I was very happy with the WWWD3. I was amazed by both the level of participation and the commitment that others have to this project. Agent Green, in addition to coordinating the WWWD3 for the entire state of Massachusetts, contacted me about selling WWWD3 t-shirts. He was willing to foot the bill for the shirts and would sell them from his Web site. I told him to go ahead with it. One thing that some people didn't seem to understand about the WWWD3 t-shirt was that when you have a small run of shirts like this, it is very cost ineffective. Agent Green sold them for $20, including shipping. People immediately started complaining that we were trying to make money off of sales from the shirts. This was simply not true. Agent Green covered the costs to make the shirts. He received all proceeds from the sales, but also lost quite a bit of money on the shirts. I should have put this information on the Web page when I first announced that the shirts were for sale, but I didn't. I think this led to some of the confusion about the potential profit from the shirts. Amazingly, even though he lost money, Agent Green still plans to make shirts for the WWWD4 and offer them for sale.

On that same note, Maui, the organizer from Korea, contacted me and asked if I would mind if he had some WorldWide WarDrive coins made. These are the same type of commemorative coins that United States Military units present to unit members to show their appreciation (see Figure 8.3). Once again, Maui wanted to pay for these out of his own pocket and provide them to me for distribution. I told him to go ahead with it. I am not sure what the production of the coins cost, but I am sure they were very expensive and they look great. We agreed that these coins would never be sold and would only be available to those individuals that had contributed to the WorldWide WarDrive in a major way. These individuals would be given a coin to show appreciation for their hard work.

Figure 8.3 The WorldWide WarDrive Coin

Since so much time had passed between the second and third WorldWide WarDrives, I had the opportunity to sit back and see how the event was perceived. More importantly, I had the opportunity to realize how much more effective this event is if the time is taken to organize it properly and plan the event several months in advance. There had been talk of doing the WWWD once every three months. Because of the success of the WWWD3, this idea was completely scrapped. Once a year is the right frequency for the WWWD.

Statistics from the WorldWide WarDrive 3

There is no doubt that the third WorldWide WarDrive was the most successful. Over 300 people participated in 52 areas, representing 11 countries on four continents Additionally, data was submitted from Australia without GPS coordinates and wasn't included in the statistics. The Most Common SSID and Second Most Common SSID were not calculated this time around. This is because for the third straight time the most common was Linksys and the second most common was Default. This statistic wasn't providing any real, valuable information. See Table 8.3.

Table 8.3 The Statistics from the Third WorldWide WarDrive

CATEGORY	TOTAL	PERCENT
TOTAL APs FOUND	88122	100
WEP Enabled	28427	27.92
No WEP Enabled	59695	72.07
Default SSID	24525	35.27
Default SSID and No WEP	21822	31.44

The DefCon 11 WarDriving Contest

The last organized WarDrive that I will discuss is the DefCon 11 WarDriving Contest. The DefCon 10 contest was a complete success. Even with the problems that we encountered, the majority of the contestants said they had a good time and wanted to do it again. The DefCon 11 contest was in many ways more successful than its predecessor, but in many ways more trying. Unlike the previous year, where the entire contest was planned in a few weeks, we began planning early in the year. Some basic brainstorming actually began in late 2002, with the bulk of the planning being done in early 2003. We decided to have the contest planned out and ready to go by April, 2003. This would give us three to four months to deal with any issues that popped up between the contest announcement, and the actual start of DefCon.

The staff for the DefCon 11 contest was very similar to the staff from the previous year. Only one change was made. Rather than have Pete Shipley score the contest, we asked Converge to be the official scorer, and Pete would handle the press inquiries that the contest generated.

Incorporating the Lessons Learned from the DefCon 10 WarDriving Contest

We knew that the prize situation from the previous year was not acceptable. I approached Black Beetle and The Dark Tangent in March and requested that DefCon kick in prizes for the contest. I wanted the DefCon leather jackets that Capture the Flag and Hacker Jeopardy winners get. Because this was only the second year of the contest, they decided that was too big a prize. They did, however, agree to provide the coveted black badge again as well as a limited edition DefCon hooded fleece that was not available for purchase by general contest attendees. We also decided that only the contest winners would receive a prize as opposed to the DefCon 10 contest where the top five teams received prizes. We wanted the winners to be more exclusive than the previous year.

Because of the problems experienced at DefCon 10 with the wireless network, I decided that the data server had to be on the wired network. My thought was that with the data server on the wired network, each contestant could use a wired Ethernet port and upload their data. As you will see later, this didn't work out exactly as I had planned, but the server was placed on the wired network.

I was embarrassed by our contest sign from DefCon 10. In early May, I contacted Black Beetle and asked if we could get a sign with the contest logo printed up that matched the glossy speaker area signs that DefCon prints up. Black Beetle was great about making sure our sign was prepared. By the time the contest had rolled around, the contest logo (see Figure 8.4) was very familiar to the contestants and the sign was easy for them to spot so they would know where to check in and complete the contest registration forms.

Figure 8.4 The DefCon 11 WarDriving Contest Logo

I loved the way we allowed the rules to be loosely interpreted. This was an element of the contest that I wanted to make sure we kept in place. The rest of the contest staff agreed with me and the only new rule that was added was the "Shmoo Rule" stating that only ground transportation could be used for the contest.

We spent most of our time addressing the sign-up process, and found ourselves completely overwhelmed at DefCon 10 trying to get the teams together. To make things easier, we decided to start the sign-up process at the end of March, 2003 and have an online only sign-up process.

Keeping It New and Different

We knew that it would not be fun to just go out and WarDrive Las Vegas again. In order for the contest to be successful a second year, there had to be a new element to it. To accomplish this, Russ came up with the idea of a tournament-style contest. This time, the contest would encompass two WarDriving days instead of just one. There would be a total of 12 teams, with a maximum of five contestants allowed to participate in each. Based on the results of the first day of WarDriving, only the top six teams would be allowed to advance to the final round and compete for the championship.

We also contacted some selected sponsors and asked them to contribute money to the event. Since the prizes were only going to the overall winning team, we wanted all of the contestants to have a souvenir from the contest. For the first time, we asked the contestants to pay a five-dollar entry fee. We supplemented this entry fee with the money from the sponsors and gave every participant three things that only WarDriving contestants could get. The first was a bumper sticker with the contest logo on it. They also received a dog tag with the contest logo on one side and the DefCon logo on the other, along with a dog tag silencer. They also got a long-sleeve t-shirt with the contest logo on the front, the DefCon logo on the back, and the "WarDriving is not a crime" logo down one sleeve. The contestants were more than happy to pay the five-dollar entry fee and the contest items were a big hit.

Running the Contest

Once we started allowing people to sign up for the contest, the slots on all 12 teams quickly began to fill up. In order to complete their registration for the contest, they needed to do two things. First, I would e-mail them the liability disclaimer (this was the same disclaimer that we had them physically sign the year before; see Figure 8.1). They were required to reply to that stating that they accepted the terms of the disclaimer. Then, once on site, each contestant was required to check in with the contest staff and pay their five-dollar entry fee. At that time, we would give them their shirt, dog tag (see Figure 8.5), and bumper sticker. The 12 teams were full by the end of May, and we opened up a standby list. This was a list of people that would fill slots that were not claimed by someone who had signed up online.

Figure 8.5 The DefCon 11 WarDriving Contest Dog Tag

The contest was two days of driving. The first day, Friday, was a two-hour drive. When contestants checked in with the contest staff, we gave them their username/password combination so that they could upload their data when they were finished driving. We also notified them of the geographical boundaries for the first stage of the contest. This was different from the previous year when we used anonymous FTP for the data upload. For the first day, all 12 teams would participate. Only access points found on Paradise Road in Las Vegas and east of Paradise would be counted. The top six teams would qualify for round two, a three-hour drive on Saturday that would take place on Paradise Road and west.

The first day's drive went smoothly, but once again we ran into problems with the data uploads. Although the data server was on the wired network as promised, DefCon did not offer any wired connections for attendees at DefCon 11. All network access was wireless. Because of this, we ran into many of the same problems from the year before. Contestants had a hard time getting a connection because of the number of rogue access points that were in range posing as DefCon access points. At one point, I ran NetStumbler and there were over a hundred rogue access points in range of the Alexis Park Hotel. We quickly got the word out to contestants that they could provide us their data on floppy, CD-ROM, or USB disk drive. About half of the contestants were able to successfully log in and upload their data. The others were forced to physically give us their data.

On the morning of the first drive, we discovered a bug in the conversion program that contestants needed to convert their kismet data to wi-scan with extensions. The bug was essentially that if an access point had an SSID that started with parentheses, the conversion script would crash. Since we were unable to get the updated script to the contestants quickly enough, we allowed them to upload their unconverted data from the drive so that Converge could do the conversion with the patched script. We repeated this for day two just so things would be consistent for the contestants.

After the first drive, members of The Lords of Wireless team contacted me and asked what exactly I meant by "Paradise Road and west." I told them that it meant exactly that. Anything west of Paradise Road would be counted. They explained that they wanted to send one of their team members to Los Angeles, California and have him start his drive there. I told them that if they provided me with proof such as gas receipts, restaurant receipts, and so forth that showed he had left Las Vegas on Saturday morning and drove during the allotted three hours only, I would accept their data. They agreed and sent one of their team members to Los Angeles the next morning. This was an excellent strategy because all of the access points he found in Los Angeles would have been "unique." This means that each of the access points found there would have been worth a minimum of six points; one for an access point and five more because it was unique. He did provide me with the proof that I had asked for, unfortunately, he didn't get the data to us in a readable format, and so those results didn't get counted.

In the end, it didn't matter since The Lords of Wireless won the contest even without the Los Angeles data. They barely edged out last year's champion, Team WirelessCon, as shown in Table 8.4.

Table 8.4 Partial Results from the DefCon 11 WarDriving Contest

Place	Team	AP	WEP	SSID	Unique	Total
1	Lords of Wireless	2219	612	748	1264	7883
2	Team WirelessCon	1983	625	604	737	6048

The complete results of the DefCon 11 WarDriving Contest are available at www.defcon.org/html/defcon-11/defcon-11-postcon.html.

Lessons Learned

Despite our best efforts, the DefCon 11 WarDriving Contest still had some problems that need to be addressed for future contests. First, this was the last year that a simple WarDrive of Las Vegas could be done. Even though there are more wireless networks being deployed every day, driving the same city over and over again is not going to be enjoyable for the contestants. This has to be addressed for the DefCon 12 WarDriving Contest.

The loose interpretation of the rules has been successful in that it is always fun to see the ideas people will come up with to meet the letter of the law while violating the spirit. Even though the Lords of Wireless data from Los Angeles was not counted because of formatting problems, a lot of the contestants did not feel that it was fair to allow this data. These contestants were very vocal about this and it put a damper on the contest for some of the organizers. In addition to the "Shmoo Rule" from DefCon 10, future contests will have the "WiGLE Rule." The WiGLE rule states that only data from the state of Nevada will be counted. It is named the WiGLE Rule because the Lords of Wireless team was comprised of several members of the WiGLE mapping Web site (www.wigle.net).

The data dump continued to be an issue. Once again, many contestants had a hard time connecting to the data server. The DefCon WarDriving contest staff has come up with a plan to address this issue. For future contests, an area will be set aside for the data dump to take place. Each contestant will need to connect to a switch that we will provide via a wired connection. In addition, each contestant will be required to upload their data to this server. The data server will also be con-nected directly to this switch, thus bypassing the DefCon network completely.

Finally, the data format issue was once again a problem. The bug that was dis-covered in the WarGlue software the morning of the contest threw the data dump into disarray. This is the second year in a row that the wi-scan with exten-sions format has caused problems for Kismet users. Future contests will not rely on this format. Contestants will be required to submit their data in NetStumbler .ns1 format. They will be able to use the WarKizniz conversion script to convert any Kismet logs to NetStumbler .ns1 format. Requiring contestants to use this format opens up several options to the scoring staff. NetStumbler makes it easy to convert the data to a flat text dump, wi-scan format, or wi-scan with exten-sions. Using the NetStumbler format was also very successful for the WorldWide WarDrive 3, so now this format has a proven track record of success.

What the Results of the WorldWide WarDrive Mean

The results of the WorldWide WarDrives provide a snapshot of the wireless net-works currently deployed throughout the world. In this section, we look at the results from the first three WorldWide WarDrives and how they have changed from one to the next. The progression of five areas are discussed: the total number of access points discovered, the percentage of those that have WEP enabled, the percentage that do not have WEP enabled, the percentage of access points with default SSIDs, and the percentage of access points with default SSIDs that do not have WEP enabled. We also look at what these results say about the state of wireless security.

Analysis of the Results

When the statistics for the first WorldWide WarDrive were generated, several categories of statistics were tabulated that were not particularly relevant to the security community. As the WWWD has progressed, the statistics have been honed down to a relevant set that gives an accurate view of the security posture of wireless networks that are deployed worldwide.

A total of 9374 access points were found during the first WorldWide WarDrive. Of those, 30.13 percent had WEP enabled. The second WWWD discovered 24,958 access points. The percentage of access points deployed with WEP enabled dropped 2.21 percent to 27.92 percent. The percentage of access points without WEP enabled went from 69.86 percent to 72.07 percent. The percentage of access points with default SSID increased from 28.53 percent to 35.27 percent, while the percentage of access points with default SSID that did not have WEP enabled went from 26.64 percent to 31.44 percent. These last two, at first glance, are the most disturbing. They represent the number of access points that were deployed with absolutely no changes made to the default configuration. This would allow anyone to connect to these access points without having to make any changes on their systems.

I was initially very disappointed with the results of the second WWWD. My first thought was that the message was not getting out and that the project was not worthwhile. A closer look indicates that this is not necessarily the case. The number of access points discovered for the first WWWD was extremely small in comparison to the number of access points that were actually deployed. It is likely that the results from the first WWWD were not truly representative of the overall wireless access points that have been deployed. The second WWWD, on the other hand, provided a much more realistic view of the true statistics. A larger statistical sampling will always provide a more accurate view. The primary differences between the first and second WWWDs, which took place only a few weeks apart, were the number of areas covered and the number of access points found (more than twice as many).

The changes from the second to third WWWD were more encouraging. A total of 88,122 access points were discovered during the third WWWD. This is more than triple the number found during the second WWWD. The results from the third WWWD provide the most accurate overview of the state of wireless networks deployed worldwide. The percentage of access points that had WEP enabled increased 4.34 percent from 27.92 percent to 32.26 percent. The percentage of access points that did not enable WEP dropped from 72.07 percent to 67.74 percent. Access points with a default SSID dropped from 35.27 percent to 27.83 percent while the percentage of those that also did not enable WEP went from 31.44 percent to 24.76 percent. This represents a 6.44 percent decrease in the percentage of access points deployed with "out of the box" configurations.

Implications of the Results in Regard to Wireless Security

The results of the last two WorldWide WarDrives give reason to be optimistic. Even with the largest statistical sampling, all of the statistical indicators were better from the third WWWD than the second. There is still a long way to go. End users are becoming more aware of the need to enable security features on their access points, but 67.74 percent of the users out there still aren't using the most basic encryption on their wireless networks. Some of this can be attributed to users (mostly commercial) that allow access to their wireless networks only through a virtual private network (VPN) tunnel. The VPN tunnel is encrypted and, therefore, these networks do not use WEP. There is no way to determine the number of networks that fall into this category. Because the majority of the access points found during the third WWWD were discovered in residential areas, this is likely not a statistically significant amount.

The more disturbing statistic is the number of default or "out of the box" installations that are currently deployed. Nearly one of every four access points currently deployed has had no modifications made to the configuration. These access points can be accessed by anyone who discovers the signal. The message is getting out, but there are still a large number of people who are enjoying the benefits of wireless networking without eliminating the risk of their systems being compromised, or their network resources being utilized by unauthorized users. A complete step-by-step guide to locking wireless networks down is included in Chapter 10: Basic Wireless Security.

The Future of the WorldWide WarDrive

Had the results of the third WorldWide WarDrive continued to show a decrease in the number of access points that were being deployed securely, or if the message was not effectively being communicated to the general public, I had planned to end the project. Thankfully, this was not the case. The results from the third WWWD were encouraging enough for the project to continue forward.

Some exciting changes are on the horizon for the WorldWide WarDrive. The success of the automated upload procedure inspired me to continue to automate the WWWD processes. In addition to the upload form, the data will be analyzed in real-time and the statistics updated as the results come in. This change will become effective with the fourth WWWD, which will take place in the summer of 2004. By the fifth WorldWide WarDrive, the maps will be generated in real-time as well. This will complete the automation process and provide participants in the WWWD with instant feedback.

The WWWD will continue to be an annual event until either there is no longer interest from the WarDriving and security communities, or the state of wireless security significantly improves. Once the WWWD is no longer relevant, it will end.

Summary

Organized WarDriving has progressed significantly over the course of the past two years. What started as an ad-hoc, very unorganized effort by a few people to get together and WarDrive one city has evolved into user communities and worldwide events. The DefCon WarDriving contests initially provided a competitive environment for WarDrivers to display their skills and strategies. These contests gave way to the WorldWide WarDrive.

The WorldWide WarDrive provides a constructive, organized way for WarDrivers to help get the word out to the general public that wireless networks are not secure using out-of-the-box configurations. The press coverage that these events have generated has helped to relay the message to end users. By providing the public with information about both the state of wireless security worldwide, as well as information on how to secure access points, the WWWD has helped to improve the overall state of wireless security over the course of the past two years.

While the goal of improving wireless security is a noble one, it is not the only goal of organized WarDriving. Getting together with other people that share your interests is fun. To increase the effectiveness and enjoyment of the WarDrive, it's important for the organizer to plan out the area that will be driven. It is also a good idea to have some type of social event associated with the WarDrive. A class for people that are new to the hobby prior to the actual WarDrive is a great way to do this. While after the WarDrive, organizing a get together (a cookout, meeting at a local restaurant, and so on) is a great way for people to talk about the hobby as well. The Chicago WorldWide WarDrive organizers have perfected this.

In addition to the social aspect of organized WarDriving, people who participate in organized WarDrives get the opportunity to share their experiences and discuss improvements in the technology. They also get to share tips and tricks they have learned with each other. As this information is shared and more people become aware of technological advances, the wireless community can't help but benefit.

Solutions Fast Track

The Origin of Organized WarDriving

☑ The idea of organized WarDriving has probably been around as long as the idea of WarDriving itself. People enjoy getting together with others that share similar interests to socialize and exchange ideas.

☑ The DefCon 10 WarDriving Contest was the first publicized and organized WarDrive that took place on a large scale.

☑ Once they returned home from DefCon, participants in the DefCon 10 WarDriving Contest that lived near each other wanted to get together to WarDrive in their hometowns.

The WorldWide WarDrive Is Born

☑ A small WarDrive of Baltimore, Maryland was publicized on the Internet.

☑ People from other areas expressed interest in WarDriving their areas at the same time, and the idea of a World Stumbling Day was discussed.

☑ The World Stumbling Day became the WorldWide WarDrive, an organized effort by security professionals and hobbyists to provide a statistical analysis of the security posture of currently deployed wireless networks.

What the Results of the WorldWide WarDrive Mean

☑ The results of the first WorldWide WarDrive are probably statistically invalid because too small of a sample was collected.

☑ The second WorldWide WarDrive took place a few weeks after the first and provided a much more realistic snapshot of the state of wireless security. This is primarily because the statistical sample was much larger. Many more areas were also represented. Unfortunately, the statistics showed that a large number of wireless networks were deployed with little or no security measures enabled.

☑ The third WorldWide WarDrive was the most successful WorldWide WarDrive to date. More than three times the number of access points were discovered.

☑ Many more areas were covered for the third WorldWide WarDrive. This also provided a more realistic view of the security of wireless networks worldwide than its predecessors did.

☑ About one of every four access points currently deployed still uses the out-of-the-box configuration; however, this number has decreased during the course of the WorldWide WarDrives.

☑ Only about one third of wireless networks deployed are using the built-in encryption that is available. This number has also increased throughout the history of the WorldWide WarDrive. This indicates that the message is getting out to the end users.

The Future of the WorldWide WarDrive

☑ The WorldWide WarDrive will continue as an annual event as long as it is relevant.

☑ The WorldWide WarDrive will continue to improve the way that participants can upload their data and get instant feedback on the results.

Frequently Asked Questions

The following Frequently Asked Questions, answered by the authors of this book, are designed to both measure your understanding of the concepts presented in this chapter and to assist you with real-life implementation of these concepts. To have your questions about this chapter answered by the author, browse to **www.syngress.com/solutions** and click on the **"Ask the Author"** form. You will also gain access to thousands of other FAQs at ITFAQnet.com.

Q: Where can I find more information about the WorldWide WarDrive?

A: Information about the WorldWide WarDrive can be found at the official WorldWide WarDrive Web site: www.worldwidewardrive.org.

Q: Why doesn't the WorldWide WarDrive make the data sets (Kismet dumps and NetStumbler .ns1's) that are turned in available to the general public?

A: The goal of the WorldWide WarDrive is not to provide information about specific access points. The goal is to provide a general statistical overview of the access points that are currently deployed worldwide. Making the data found by participants would in no way further that goal.

Q: Is the WorldWide WarDrive the only organized WarDriving event?

A: People get together to WarDrive every day. This is organized WarDriving in its most pure form. The WorldWide WarDrive is, however, the only event that allows WarDrivers to organize a WarDrive to cover entire areas and then commingle their data with that of other WarDrivers around the world to provide an analysis of wireless networks worldwide.

Q: How can I organize my area for the WorldWide WarDrive?

A: Information on signing up to organize an area for the WorldWide WarDrive is available at www.worldwidewardrive.org. Organizers need to be individuals who are interested in promoting wireless security by providing free information. Companies or consultants that are looking for a way to turn the WorldWide WarDrive into a money-making venture are not allowed to be area organizers.

## Chapter 9

Attacking Wireless Networks

Solutions in this Chapter:

- **The Direct Approach**
- **Defeating MAC Address Filtering**
- **Finding Cloaked Access Points**
- **Man-in-the-Middle Attacks on Wireless Networks**
- **Attacking Encrypted Networks**

Introduction

Wireless networks are vulnerable to attackers. This statement should not come as a big surprise because *all* networks are vulnerable to attackers. Wireless network security is discussed in detail in Chapters 10 ("Basic Wireless Network Security") and 11 (Advanced Wireless Network Security), but before we look at ways to defend your wireless network, you need to understand what you are defending it from.

This chapter provides you with an understanding of how attackers compromise wireless networks, as well as the common approaches that are used. The level of security on these networks ranges from none at all to commercial-grade secondary security mechanisms. The approaches and techniques are presented to help wireless network administrators understand what they must defend against and should not be used to gain unauthorized access to wireless networks. These techniques are also valuable for performing wireless penetration tests and testing the security of your own wireless network.

It is important to note that the attacks presented in this chapter can be used to gain unauthorized access to wireless networks. You should never attempt these attacks without authorization from the owner of the wireless network. Accessing networks of any kind (wired or wireless) without authorization is a crime and can result in prosecution and possibly jail time. It should also be noted that unauthorized attacks are not WarDriving. In fact, WarDriving has nothing to do with attacking wireless networks. This is a distinction that many media outlets have misunderstood and has led to some of the misinformation about WarDriving.

The Direct Approach

According to statistics from the third World Wide WarDrive, approximately one of every four access points currently deployed is in a *default configuration*. The *default configuration* means that there is no encryption enabled and the Service Set Identifier (SSID) has not been changed from the factory settings. The "direct approach" can be used to gain access to wireless networks in the default configuration. In short, the direct approach, in a nutshell, refers to "requesting" a connection to the access point. This is an extremely simple process in both Windows and Linux.

Accessing Wireless Networks Using the Direct Approach in Windows

In order to access a wireless network with a default configuration from a Windows machine, all that you need is a *wireless client manager*. The wireless client manager is the configuration software that either ships with the wireless card, or is built into the operating system (as is the case with Windows XP). This section details how to accomplish this with Windows XP's built-in wireless connection manager, as well as using the ORiNOCO client manager in Windows 2000.

Windows XP

Windows XP is designed to make connecting to wireless networks achievable through a simple, four-step process:

1. Verify that the Wireless Zero Configuration Service is running.

2. Insert a wireless card.

3. Open the connection manager.

4. Choose a network to attach to.

The Wireless Zero Configuration Service starts by default in Windows XP; however, installing some programs can cause this service to be disabled or set to manual. To verify that the Wireless Zero Configuration Service is started, go to **Start | Settings | Control Panel** and then double-click **Administrative Tools**. This will open the Administrative Tools window (see Figure 9.1).

Figure 9.1 The Administrative Tools Window

Double-click the **Services** icon to open the Services window (Figure 9.2).

Figure 9.2 The Services Window

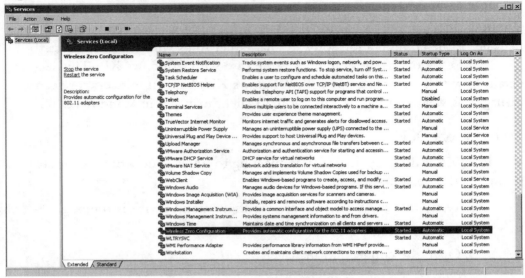

Verify that the Wireless Zero Configuration Service is started and set to Automatic, as shown in Figure 9.3.

Figure 9.3 The Wireless Zero Configuration Service

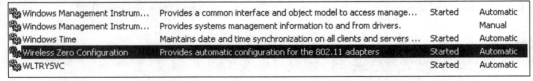

If the Wireless Zero Configuration Service does not show as "Started" and "Automatic," right-click the service and choose **Properties** (see Figure 9.4). Set the Startup Type to **Automatic**, **and** then click the **Start** button to start the service.

Figure 9.4 The Wireless Zero Configuration Properties Window

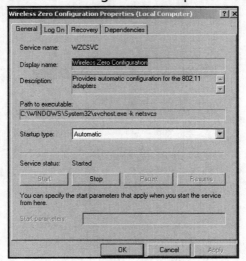

Once the Wireless Zero Configuration Service is running, insert your wireless card. Windows XP will attempt to automatically determine the type of card and install the appropriate driver for it. You should have your driver available in case Windows XP cannot determine the correct driver for your card.

After Windows XP detects your card and installs the driver, Windows XP will inform you if there are available wireless networks in range (see Figure 9.5). Click this dialogue and the Wireless Network Connection properties dialogue will open. This window displays any wireless networks that are available (see Figure 9.6).

Figure 9.5 Networks Detected

Figure 9.6 Available Wireless Networks

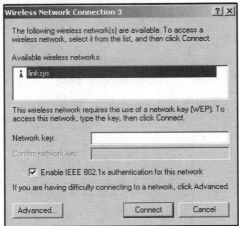

Simply choose the network that you want to connect to and click **Connect**. Windows XP will inform you that the network doesn't have encryption enabled and will ask if you still would like to connect (see Figure 9.7). Choose **Yes** and you have gained access to the network. Many networks will have a Dynamic Host Configuration Protocol (DHCP) server enabled that will configure your connection for use on the network/Internet. This will work with any network that has default settings. Additionally, if a network has had the SSID changed, but no other security measures have been taken, these steps will work in Windows XP.

Figure 9.7 A Final Warning

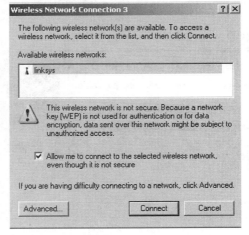

Some Networks May Appear to Be Accessible Using the Direct Approach

Some networks may appear to be in a default configuration and accessible using the direct approach. This may not be the case. The Linksys access point shown in Figure 9.6 is an example of this situation. Although it has a default SSIS (Linksys) it also has Wired Equivalent Privacy (WEP) enabled. If the windows XP Wireless Network Connection window prompts for a "**Network key**," then a WEP key is required.

Not all wireless networks that appear as "Available" are actually accessible using the direct approach. The steps needed to gain access to these networks are provided in the "Attacking Encrypted Networks" section later in this chapter.

Windows 2000

The direct approach in Windows 2000 is in many ways easier than using Windows XP. One difference is that a third-party client manager is required. Accessing a wireless network with default settings in Windows 2000 is a simple, three-step process.

1. Installing a client manager

2. Inserting the wireless NIC

3. Configuring the client manager for use on default networks

The first step is installing a wireless client manager. This usually comes on the CD-ROM that came with your card. For this example, we will use the ORiNOCO client manager. The client manager that comes with your card may look slightly different, but the steps are basically the same.

Once the client manager is installed, insert your wireless network interface card (NIC) into an open Personal Computer Memory Card International Association (PCMCIA) slot on your laptop. Next, double-click the client manager icon on the bottom right of your Windows taskbar. This will open the client manager program (see Figure 9.8).

Figure 9.8 The Wireless Client Manager

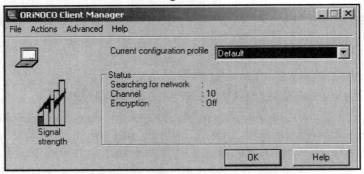

From the menu, select **Actions | Add/Edit Configuration Profile**. This opens the Add/Edit Configuration Profile window (see Figure 9.9).

Figure 9.9 The Add/Edit Configuration Profile Window

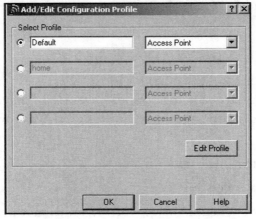

Select the radio button next to the "Default" profile and click **Edit Profile**. This opens the options for editing the Default configuration profile. Make sure that the **Network Name** field is blank, as shown in Figure 9.10, and then click **OK**.

Figure 9.10 The Basic Configuration Tab

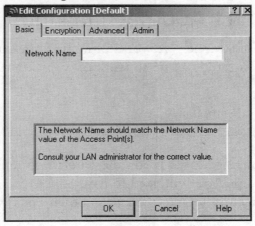

Continue to click **OK** to close each open window.

Using this configuration profile automatically connects to any wireless network with default settings, as shown in Figure 9.11.

Figure 9.11 A Connection Is Made

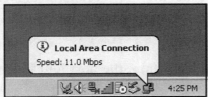

It really is as simple as that. If your network settings are configured to request a DHCP address (as they are, by default, with a new adapter) and the network you have connected to is providing DHCP addresses (as they are, by default), you now have access. Depending on the configuration of the wireless network, you can use the Internet or browse Windows shares on the network, for example. You have the same level of access as any authorized user of the wireless network.

Accessing Wireless Networks Using the Direct Approach in Linux

Gaining access to default wireless networks in Linux is an extremely simple process. After your wireless card is set up to work on your Linux distribution, there are only two steps.

1. Edit the wireless.opts file.

2. Reboot.

The first thing you need to do is edit the wireless options file located at /etc/pcmcia/wireless.opts. You will need to have Super User (root) privileges to do so. Change the directory to /etc/pcmcia and then open wireless.opts for writing.

```
root@roamer:/home/roamer# cd /etc/pcmcia
root@roamer:/etc/pcmcia# vi wireless.opts
```

Scroll down and comment out any setting that you may have for your own network. To comment out a line in most Linux configuration files, simply place a pound sign (#) in front of the line you want ignored. Next, locate the line that reads:

```
# NOTE : Remove the following four lines to activate the samples below …
```

Remove the pound sign (#) from the next four lines so that it looks like Figure 9.12.

Figure 9.12 Commenting Lines in wireless.opts

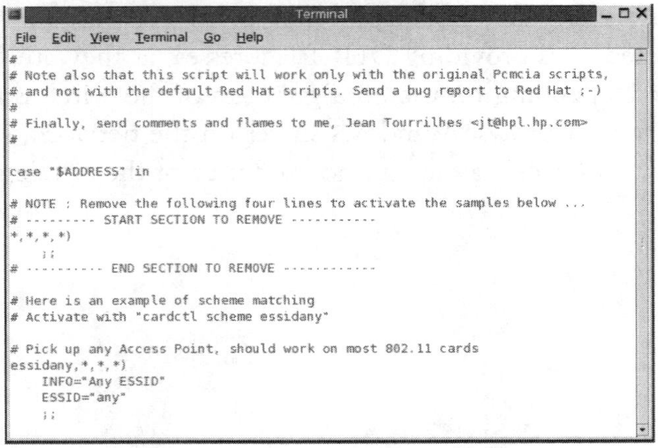

```
#
# Note also that this script will work only with the original Pcmcia scripts,
# and not with the default Red Hat scripts. Send a bug report to Red Hat ;-)
#
# Finally, send comments and flames to me, Jean Tourrilhes <jt@hpl.hp.com>
#

case "$ADDRESS" in

# NOTE : Remove the following four lines to activate the samples below ...
# --------- START SECTION TO REMOVE ----------
*,*,*,*)
    ;;
# ---------- END SECTION TO REMOVE ----------

# Here is an example of scheme matching
# Activate with "cardctl scheme essidany"

# Pick up any Access Point, should work on most 802.11 cards
essidany,*,*,*)
    INFO="Any ESSID"
    ESSID="any"
    ;;
```

Save your changes and then restart the PCMCIA services or reboot.

```
root@roamer:/etc/pcmcia# shutdown -r now
```

When the PCMCIA services start after the reboot, two short beeps will sound. If there is a default network in range, your system will gain access and connect to it.

Variation on the Direct Approach in Linux

Many default networks have a DHCP server set up automatically and will assign addresses in the 192.168.1.1–100 range. In rare cases, a wireless network is configured with default settings, but DHCP has been disabled. In order to access these networks, you will need to set your IP address manually. In Windows, this is accomplished by changing the **Properties** in the TCP/IP Settings. In Linux, this is done by using the *ifconfig* command.

```
root@roamer:/root# ifconfig eth0 192.168.1.69 netmask 255.255.255.0
root@roamer/root# route add default gw 192.168.1.1
```

> **NOTE**
>
> eth0 should be replaced with your card's interface designation (for example: eth1, wlan0, and so on).

In some cases, users have changed the IP range utilized by their wireless network. In these instances, you may have to experiment with the IP address and router settings until you find the correct one. For example, try setting your IP address to 192.168.2.222, 192.168.3.222, or something similar. It is a good idea to avoid addresses between 100 and 199 in the last octet (for example, 192.168.4.101) because these are more likely to already be in use. If you conflict with an address that is already in use, your access to the network is more likely to be noticed.

Linux users may have an advantage when trying to determine the IP address range in use. As Kismet (see Chapters 4–6 for more information on Kismet) monitors traffic, it will often detect the IP address range in use. Kismet usually needs time and several packets in order to determine the range, but it could take less time than trying to figure it out by guessing.

Defeating MAC Address Filtering

One security measure that many wireless network administrators put in place is *filtering by MAC address*. Enabling MAC address filtering is discussed in greater detail in Chapter 11, "Basic Wireless Security," but, essentially, this implementation allows only network cards with certain MAC addresses to connect to your network. However, as with any security measure, a determined, knowledgeable attacker can usually find a way around such an obstacle.

Most commercial- and consumer-grade wireless networking equipment sends the MAC address clear text even if WEP is enabled. This means that if you passively sniff the traffic on a wireless network using a freeware tool such as Ethereal (www.ethereal.com), you can determine one or more MAC addresses that are allowed to connect to the network. If MAC address filtering is the only security measure in place, you just need to change your MAC address to one that is allowed access. In this section, we look at how to do this in Windows XP, Windows 2000, and Linux.

Defeating MAC Address Filtering in Windows

Changing your MAC address in Windows is not a difficult process. The steps that you need to take vary slightly between Windows XP and Windows 2000. We will also take a look at automated tools that are freely available to facilitate this process.

Manually Changing the MAC Address in Windows XP and 2000

Changing your MAC address in Windows XP or 2000 is done by modifying the Windows Registry.

NOTE

Modifying the Registry can be dangerous and can cause the system to become unstable if it is done incorrectly.

Go to **Start | Run** and type in **regedit**. This will start the Registry Editor (see Figure 9.13).

Figure 9.13 The Windows Registry Editor

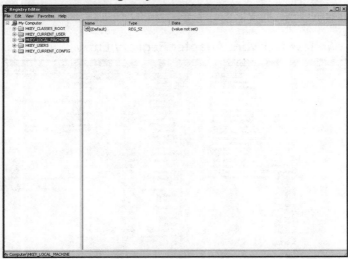

Expand the **HKEY_LOCAL_MACHINE | System | CurrentControlSet | Control** folders (see Figure 9.14).

Figure 9.14 Expanding the Registry

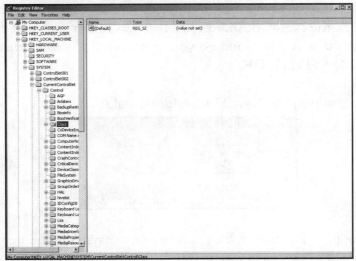

Scroll down to the **Class** folder and expand it. Next, scroll down to the **{4D36E972-E325-11CE-BFC1-08002bE10318}** folder and expand it. This folder contains the Windows XP Registry information regarding network adapters installed on your system. Scroll through each folder until you find your wireless network adapter, as shown in Figure 9.15.

Figure 9.15 Wireless Network Adapter Registry Entry

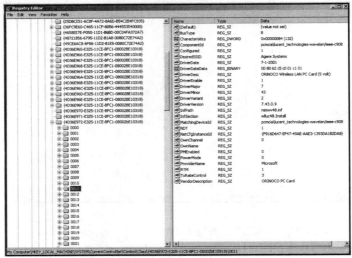

From the Registry Editor menu, choose **Edit | New | String Value**. This creates a new REG_SZ string and prompts for a value. Type **NetworkAddress**. Now, right-click the NetworkAddress key that was just created and choose **Modify**. Enter the new MAC address you want to use in the **Value Data** field (see Figure 9.16) and click **OK**.

Figure 9.16 Entering the New MAC Address Value

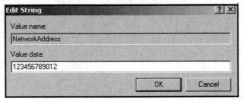

Simply close the Registry Editor and reboot the system. The new MAC address is assigned as the system starts. Verify this by typing **ipconfig /all**.

To return the MAC address to its original, hardware-assigned value, delete the key that you just created and reboot the system.

> **NOTE**
>
> Changing the MAC address to a random address *may* cause the adapter not to bind correctly and prompt the card to become unresponsive to the network. This is because some cards require that the first six bits of the MAC address conform to the IANA Number Assignments Database (www.iana.org/assignments/ethernet-numbers) in order to function correctly. The latest MAC address Organization Unique Identifier (OUI) listing is available at http://standards.ieee.org/regauth/oui/oui.txt.

Changing the MAC Address in Windows XP and 2000 Using Automated Tools

blackwave has developed a program called BWMACHAK, that changes the MAC address of an ORiNOCO card, and is available at www.irvineunderground.org/blackwave/bwmachak.zip. BWMACHAK is an easy-to-use command-line program that requires only three steps.

1. Remove the card.

2. Run BWMACHAK.

3. Reinsert the card.

After removing your ORiNOCO card from your PCMCIA slot, run BWMACHAK from the command line.

```
C:\>BWMACHAK.EXE 00022D123456
```

Now reinsert the ORiNOCO card and type **ipconfig /all** to verify the new MAC address.

To return the card to its original MAC address, run BWMACHAK with the remove string.

```
C:\>BWMACHAK.EXE <removembwmachak>
```

> **NOTE**
>
> Changing the MAC address to a random address in Windows XP and 2000 using automated tools will have the same effect as changing the address manually.

Defeating MAC Address Filtering in Linux

Similar to Windows, defeating MAC address filtering when using a Linux operating system is accomplished by changing the MAC address assigned to your wireless card. This is an extremely simple process in Linux that can be accomplished from the command line, or by using automated tools.

Manually Changing the MAC Address in Linux

Changing the MAC address that your wireless interface uses in Linux requires only three simple steps.

1. Bringing the interface down.

2. Configuring the new MAC address.

3. Bringing the interface back up.

Before making changes to the interface configuration, you should disable or bring the card down. This is accomplished using the *ifconfig* command.

```
root@roamer:/root# ifconfig eth0 down
```

> **NOTE**
>
> eth0 should be replaced with your card's interface designation (for example: eth1, wlan0, and so on).

Next, configure the interface to use a MAC address that is allowed to access the wireless network. For example, if you had discovered that the MAC address 00022D123456 was allowed to connect to the network, you could assign that MAC address to your card using the *ifconfig* command.

```
root@roamer:/root# ifconfig eth0 hw ether 00:02:2D:12:34:56
```

Now, simply bring the interface back up, once again using the *ifconfig* command.

```
root@roamer:/root# ifconfig eth0 up
```

The card is now configured and using the MAC address 00022D123456. You can verify this by viewing the configuration of the card. The first six bits (00:02:2D) are called the Organization Unique Identifier (OUI). In this case, the OUI is consistent with an ORiNOCO card. It is always a good idea to use the proper first bits for your card. The latest MAC address OUI listing is available at http://standards.ieee.org/regauth/oui/oui.txt.

```
root@roamer:/root# ifconfig eth0
eth0      Link encap:Ethernet    HWAddr 00:02:2D:12:34:56
```

Changing the MAC Address in Linux Using Automated Tools

The Church Of Wifi has developed a tool to automate MAC address changing for Linux operating systems; SirMACsAlot (www.michiganwireless.org/tools/). SirMACsAlot can be run three different ways.

- From the command line with prompts
- From the command line with arguments
- Using the GUI interface

If no command-line arguments are supplied, SirMACsAlot prompts for the interface you would like to change the MAC address on. SirMACsAlot then prompts for the new MAC address you want to assign to that interface.

SirMACsAlot can also be run directly from the command line by providing two arguments: the interface and the MAC address.

```
root@roamer:/root# ./SirMACsAlot.pl eth0 00022D123456
```

SirMACsAlot can also be run from the graphical user interface (GUI) by entering the network interface and MAC address values into the relevant textboxes.

Once you have run SirMACsAlot, you can verify that the MAC was set correctly by viewing the configuration of the card.

```
root@roamer:/root# ifconfig eth0
```

```
eth0    Link encap:Ethernet    HWAddr 00:02:2D:12:34:56
```

If MAC address filtering is the only security measure that the wireless network employs, you can now access the network by following the steps outlined earlier in Accessing Wireless Networks Using the Direct Approach in Linux.

Finding Cloaked Access Points

Many wireless network administrators "cloak" their access points by putting them in "stealth" mode. This is accomplished by disabling the SSID broadcast. However, active scanners like NetStumbler do not detect cloaked access points. These access points can be found using passive scanners like Kismet or AirSnort.

Finding Cloaked Access Points with Kismet

One of the biggest benefits that passive scanners like Kismet have to offer is the ability to detect access points that are not broadcasting their SSID. Discovering cloaked access points with Kismet is accomplished by placing your wireless card in monitor mode. Older versions of Kismet required that Kismet be placed in monitor mode manually using the *kismet_monitor* command.

```
root@roamer:/root# kismet_monitor
root@roamer:/root# kismet
```

The current version of Kismet calls *kismet_monitor* when Kismet is started. See Figure 9.17.

Figure 9.17 Kismet Running

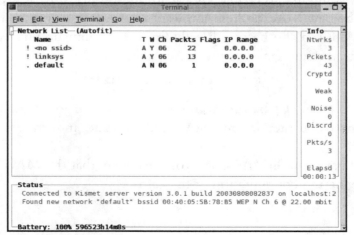

When Kismet discovers a cloaked access point, it will initially list it as having no SSID, as shown in Figure 9.6. As Kismet collects more packets, it will be able to determine the SSID.

More information on installing, configuring, and running Kismet is provided in Chapters 4–6 of this book.

Finding Cloaked Access Points with AirSnort

AirSnort is a passive wireless scanner developed by the Shmoo Group (http://airsnort.shmoo.com). Like Kismet, AirSnort will automatically activate your card in monitor mode when it is started. Any cloaked access points that AirSnort initially finds will project a blank SSID, but after enough packets are collected, AirSnort is able to determine the SSID of the cloaked network. Unlike Kismet, AirSnort has additional functionality that is extremely valuable to an attacker. This functionality, along with a more detailed discussion of AirSnort is presented in the Attacking Wired Equivalent Privacy (WEP) Encrypted Networks section of this chapter. See Figure 9.18.

Figure 9.18 AirSnort Running

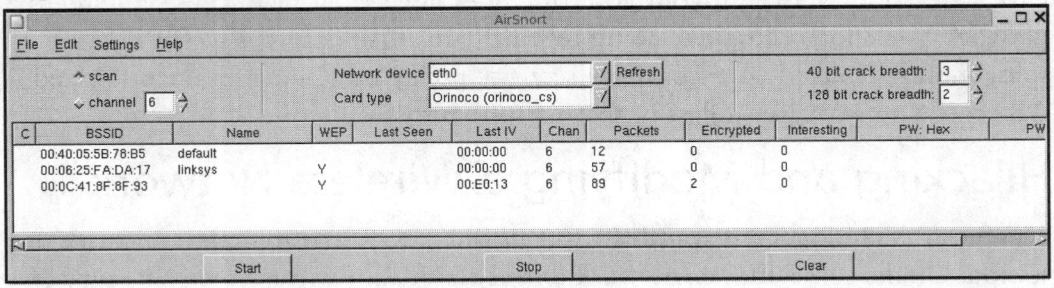

Man-in-the-Middle Attacks on Wireless Networks

Placing a rogue AP (an unauthorized access point placed on a network by an individual) within range of wireless stations is a wireless-specific variation of a *man-in-the-middle attack*. If the attacker knows the SSID the network uses (which, as we have seen, is easily discoverable) and the rogue AP has enough strength, wireless users have no way of knowing that they are connecting to an unauthorized AP.

Using a rogue AP, an attacker can gain valuable information about the wireless network, such as authentication requests, the secret key that is in use, and so on. Often, the attacker will set up a laptop with two wireless adapters, in which the rogue AP uses one card and the other is used to forward requests through a wireless bridge to the legitimate AP. With a sufficiently strong antenna, the rogue AP does not have to be located in close proximity to the legitimate AP.

For example, the attacker can run the rogue AP from a car or van parked some distance away from the building containing the network. However, it is also common to set up hidden rogue APs (under desks, in closets, and so on) close to, and within, the same physical area as the legitimate AP. Due to their virtually undetectable nature, the only defense against rogue APs is vigilance through frequent site surveys (using tools such as AirMagnet, NetStumbler, and AiroPeek) and physical security.

Frequent site surveys also have the advantage of uncovering the unauthorized APs that company staff members might have set up in their own work areas, thereby compromising the entire network and completely undoing the hard work that went into securing the network in the first place. These unauthorized APs are usually set up with no malicious intent but rather were created for the convenience of the user, who might want to be able to connect to the network via his or her laptop in meeting rooms, break rooms, or other areas that do not have wired outlets. Even if your company does not use, or plan to use, a wireless network, you should consider doing regular wireless site surveys to see if someone has violated your company security policy by placing an unauthorized AP on the network, regardless of that person's intent.

Hijacking and Modifying a Wireless Network

Numerous techniques are available for an attacker to *hijack* a wireless network or session. Unlike some attacks, network and security administrators may be unable to distinguish between the hijacker and a legitimate passenger.

Many tools are available to the network hijacker. These tools are based on basic implementation issues within almost every network device available today. As TCP/IP packets go through switches, routers, and APs, each device looks at the destination IP address and compares it with the IP addresses it knows to be local. If the address is not in the table, the device hands the packet off to its default gateway.

This table is used to coordinate the IP address with the MAC addresses that are known to be local to the device. In many situations, this list is a dynamic one that is built up from traffic passing through the device and through Address Resolution Protocol (ARP) notifications from new devices joining the network.

There is no authentication or verification that the request the device received is valid. Thus, a malicious user is able to send messages to routing devices and APs stating that his MAC address is associated with a known IP address. From then on, all traffic that goes through that router destined for the hijacked IP address will be handed off to the hacker's machine.

If the attacker spoofs as the default gateway or a specific host on the network, all machines trying to get to the network or the spoofed machine will connect to the attacker's machine instead of their intended target. If the attacker is clever, he will only use this information to identify passwords and other necessary information and route the rest of the traffic to the intended recipients. If he does this, the end users will have no idea that this *man in the middle* has intercepted their communications and compromised their passwords and information.

Another clever attack can be accomplished through the use of rogue APs. If the attacker is able to put together an AP with enough strength, the end users might not be able to tell which AP is the authorized one that they should be using. In fact, most will not even know that another AP is available. Using this technique, the attacker is able to receive authentication requests and information from the end workstation regarding the secret key and where users are attempting to connect.

These rogue APs can also be used to attempt to break into more tightly configured wireless APs. Utilizing tools such as AirSnort and WEPCrack requires a large amount of data to be able to decrypt the secret key. An intruder sitting in a car in front of your house or office is noticeable and thus will generally not have time to finish acquiring enough information to break the key. However, if the attacker installs a tiny, easily hidden machine in an inconspicuous location, this machine could sit there long enough to break the key and possibly act as an external AP into the wireless network it has hacked.

Once an attacker has identified a network for attack and spoofed his MAC address to become a valid member of the network, the attacker can gain further information that is not available through simple sniffing. If the network being attacked is using SSH to access the hosts, just stealing a password might be easier than attempting to break into the host using an available exploit.

By simply ARP-spoofing the connection with the AP, the attacker can appear to be the host from which the attacker wants to steal passwords. The attacker can then cause all wireless users who are attempting to SSH into the host to connect to the rogue machine instead. When these users attempt to sign on with their passwords, the attacker is then able to, first, receive their passwords, and, second, pass on the connection to the real end destination. If the attacker does not perform the second step, it increases the likelihood that the attack will be noticed because users will begin to complain that they are unable to connect to the host.

Attacking Encrypted Networks

One of the most common ways that administrators attempt to protect their wireless networks is with encryption. Unfortunately, the two primary means of protection, Wired Equivalent Protection (WEP) and WiFi Protected Access (WPA), have flaws that allow them to be exploited. This section discusses how to attack networks that are protected by WEP and WPA.

Attacking Wired Equivalent Protection (WEP) Encrypted Networks

The most commonly used form of encryption protecting wireless networks is WEP. WEP is a flawed implementation of the Rivest Cipher 4 (RC4) encryption standard. Scott Fluhrer of Cisco Systems, Itsik Mantin, and Adi Shamir of the Weizmann Institute detailed the flaws in WEP in their joint paper *Weaknesses of the Key Scheduling Algorithm of RC4* (www.drizzle.com/~aboba/IEEE/ rc4_ksaproc.pdf).

In short, WEP utilizes a fixed secret key. Weak initialization vectors are sometimes generated to encrypt WEP packets. When enough weak initialization vectors are captured, the secret key can be cracked. There are a number of tools available on the Internet that can be used to crack WEP encryption. This section details how to use AirSnort on Linux and WEPCrack on Windows to crack WEP.

Attacking WEP with AirSnort on Linux

When enough weak initialization vectors are identified, AirSnort begins attempting to crack the WEP key. There are about sixteen million possible initialization vectors generated by wireless networks using WEP. Approximately nine thousand of these are weak. AirSnort considers these nine thousand weak initialization vectors as "interesting." According to The Shmoo Group, most WEP keys can be guessed after collecting approximately two thousand weak initialization vectors.

Tools & Traps…

Installing and Configuring AirSnort

AirSnort is a valuable tool that can be used by WarDrivers to locate wireless networks. It can also be used by attackers to crack WEP encryption on wireless networks.

Installing AirSnort is a relatively straightforward process. First, download the current version from Sourceforge (http://sourceforge.net/project/showfiles.php?group_id=33358). Then uncompress and untar the source. Afterward, change into the AirSnort directory that is created:

```
root@roamer:/root# gunzip airsnort-0.2.2b.tar.gz

root@roamer:/root# tar -xvf airsnort-0.2.2b.tar

root@roamer:/root# cd airsnort-0.2.2b
```

For most systems, compiling and installing AirSnort requires only three steps:

```
root@roamer:/root/airsnort-0.2.2b# ./autogen.sh

root@roamer:/root/airsnort-0.2.2b # make

root@roamer:/root/airsnort-0.2.2b # make install
```

This compiles AirSnort and places the AirSnort binaries in the /usr/local/bin/ directory.

To start AirSnort, open a terminal window inside your X-Windows environment and issue the *airsnort* command. This opens the AirSnort program (see Figure 9.19).

```
root@roamer:/root/airsnort-0.2.2b # airsnort
```

Continued

Figure 9.19 AirSnort Opens

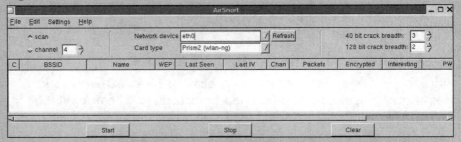

First, you need to select the network device to put into monitor mode. In order for monitor mode to work, you must follow the instructions provided in Chapters 4 and 5 of this book. Using the drop-down menu, select your wireless card (for example, Eth0, eth1, or wlan0).

Next, choose your Card type, as shown in Figure 9.20.

Figure 9.20 Choosing the Card Type

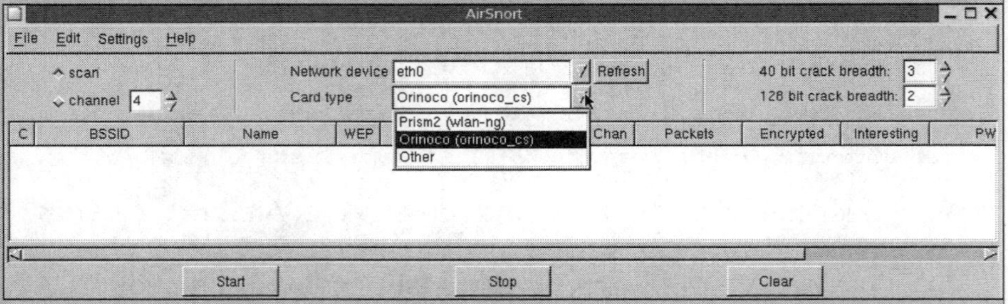

If you know the channel a specific access point is broadcasting on, you can choose to only monitor that channel. If not, or if you just want to discover any wireless networks in the area, choose "scan" to hop channels searching for wireless networks.

After all the settings have been set appropriately, click Start. AirSnort will place your card in monitor mode and begin collecting information. See Figure 9.21.

Continued

Figure 9.21 AirSnort Starts Monitoring

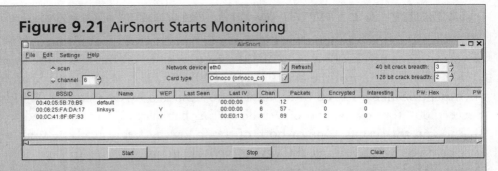

After some weak initialization vectors have been collected, AirSnort will begin attempting to crack the WEP key. A vast majority (approximately 95 percent) of weak initialization vectors provide no usable information about the WEP key. One way you can try to decrease the amount of time it takes to crack the key is by increasing the crack breadth in AirSnort. According to the Shmoo group's Frequently Asked Questions site for AirSnort (http://airsnort.shmoo.com/faq.html) this will increase the number of key possibilities examined when AirSnort attempts to crack the WEP key. See Figure 9.22.

Figure 9.22 Increasing the Crack Breadth

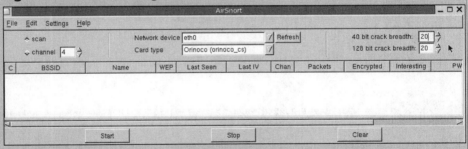

The most difficult part of attacking wireless networks deployed with WEP encryption enabled is the amount of time it takes. It usually requires a minimum of 1200 weak initialization vectors to crack the WEP key. It can take days or even weeks to capture this many weak initialization vectors.

Attacking WEP with WEPCrack on Windows

WEPCrack (http://wepcrack.sourceforge.net) is a set of Open Source PERL
scripts intended to break 802.11 WEP secret keys. It was the first publicly available implementation of the attack described by Fluhrer, Mantin, and Shamir in
their paper. Since a PERL interpreter is not installed by default with Windows
Server 2003 (or any version of Windows, for that matter), you will need to install
one to run the scripts. One or both of the following freely available solutions
will give you what you need: Cygwin (www.cygwin.com) or ActiveState
ActivePerl (www.activestate.com/Products/ActivePerl).

The more robust option is to install Cygwin. Cygwin is a Linux-like environment for Windows that consists of a DLL (cygwin1.dll) to provide Linux
emulation functionality and a seemingly exhaustive collection of tools, which
provide the Linux look and feel. The full suite of PERL development tools and
libraries are available; however, the PERL interpreter is all that is required to run
the WEPCrack scripts, as shown in Figure 9.23.

Figure 9.23 Executing WEPCrack.pl in Cygwin

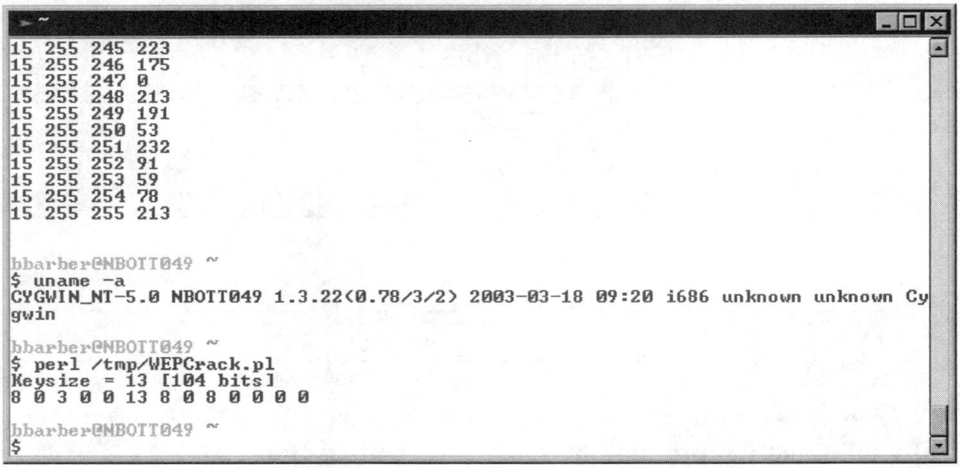

```
15 255 245 223
15 255 246 175
15 255 247 0
15 255 248 213
15 255 249 191
15 255 250 53
15 255 251 232
15 255 252 91
15 255 253 59
15 255 254 78
15 255 255 213


bbarber@NBOTT049 ~
$ uname -a
CYGWIN_NT-5.0 NBOTT049 1.3.22(0.78/3/2) 2003-03-18 09:20 i686 unknown unknown Cy
gwin

bbarber@NBOTT049 ~
$ perl /tmp/WEPCrack.pl
Keysize = 13 [104 bits]
8 0 3 0 0 13 8 0 8 0 0 0

bbarber@NBOTT049 ~
$
```

The other option, using a Windows-based PERL interpreter, may be desir-
able if you have no need for Linux emulation functionality on your workstation
or server. ActiveState ActivePerl, available by free download from the ActiveState
Web site (www.activestate.com), provides a robust PERL development environment that is native to Windows. WEPCrack was written so that it could be
ported to any platform that has a PERL interpreter without needing to modify

the code. Figure 9.24 demonstrates the WEPCrack.pl script running natively in Windows without modification from a Windows command prompt.

Figure 9.24 Executing WEPCrack.pl at the Windows Command Prompt

Using the Cracked Key in Windows XP

Once you have cracked the WEP key, you must configure your client to access the network. In Windows XP, this requires the following four steps:

1. Open the Wireless Network Properties.

2. Add a Preferred Network.

3. Enter the SSID.

4. Enter the WEP key.

First, double-click the Wireless Network Connection icon on the Windows taskbar. This will open the Wireless Network Connection status window. Select the **Wireless Networks** tab. See Figure 9.25.

Figure 9.25 The Wireless Network Properties

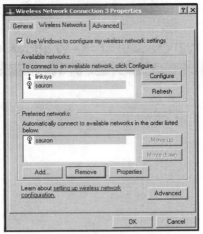

Click the **Add...** button to open the Wireless Network Properties window. Enter the SSID of the network that you want to access. Next, uncheck the **This key is provided for me automatically** checkbox. This will make the **Network Key** and **Confirm Network Key** text boxes available. See Figure 9.26.

Figure 9.26 Preparing to Enter the Captured Key

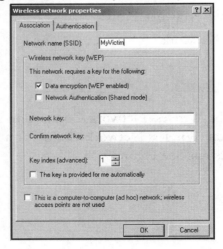

Enter the WEP key that you obtained in the **Network Key** and **Confirm Network Key** textboxes and then click **OK**. You have now accessed a WEP-protected network. See Figure 9.27.

Figure 9.27 Accessing the Network

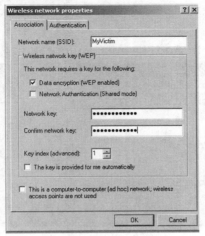

Using the Cracked Key in Windows 2000

To access a wireless network that you have cracked the WEP key for from Windows 2000, follow these four steps:

1. Open the Client Manager.

2. Create a new Profile.

3. Enter the SSID of the target network.

4. Enter the captured WEP key.

The first thing you need to do is open your client manager. Double-click the client manager icon on the Windows taskbar. This will bring up the Client Manager window, as shown in Figure 9.28.

Figure 9.28 The ORiNOCO Client Manager

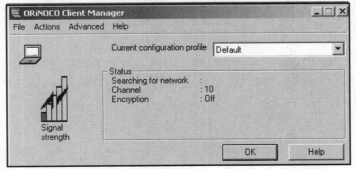

Navigate to **Actions | Add/Edit Configuration Profile** to create a new configuration profile for the network you want to associate with. See Figure 9.29.

Figure 9.29 Preparing to Add a New Configuration Profile

This opens the Add/Edit Configuration Profile window. Select the radio button beside an empty configuration profile and add a name for the target network. See Figure 9.30.

Figure 9.30 Naming the Target

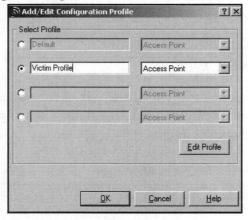

Click on **Edit Profile** to open the Edit Configuration window. In the Network Name textbox, enter the SSID of the network you want to associate with. See Figure 9.31.

Figure 9.31 The Edit Configuration Window

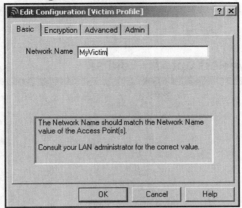

Next, click the **Encryption** tab and enter the WEP key that you cracked, and then click **OK**. You have now accessed a WEP-protected network. See Figure 9.32.

Figure 9.32 Entering the Cracked WEP Key

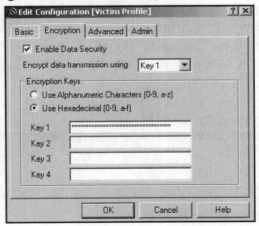

Using the Cracked Key in Linux

Accessing a wireless network that you have cracked the WEP key for from Linux requires only two steps.

1. Edit the wireless.opts file.
2. Restart PCMCIA services.

The first thing you will need to do is edit the /etc/pcmcia/wireless.conf file to include the SSID of the target network and the WEP key that you cracked. See Figure 9.33.

Figure 9.33 Open wireless.opts for Editing

Make sure that you have commented out the appropriate lines in the /etc/pcmcia/wireless.opts file, as shown in Figure 9.34. Then find the appropriate section for your wireless card and enter the SSID in the "ESSID" field. Next, change the Mode to "Ad-Hoc" and the Key to the WEP key that you cracked, as shown in Figure 9.35.

Figure 9.34 Configuring the wireless.opts File

Figure 9.35 More Configurations for the wirless.opts File

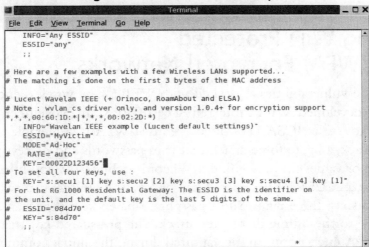

The last thing you need to do is restart PCMCIA services so that the changes you have made will take effect. In Slackware Linux, this is accomplished by issuing the restart option to the /etc/rc.d/rc.pcmcia startup script, as shown in Figure 9.36. The method of restarting PCMCIA services varies from distribution to distribution, but when necessary, you can reboot the system. Any changes you have made will take effect when PCMCIA services are started at boot time.

Figure 9.36 Restarting PCMCIA Services

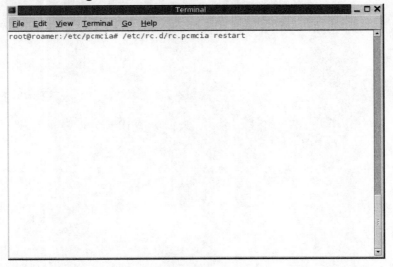

Once PCMCIA services restart, you are associated with the target access point.

Attacking WiFi Protected Access (WPA) Encrypted Networks

Because of the vulnerabilities associated with WEP, a new wireless encryption standard was developed, WiFI Protected Access (WPA). In November, 2003, Robert Moskowitz of ICSA Labs discovered that WPA is vulnerable to an offline dictionary attack, a brute force attack that tries passwords and or keys from a pre-compiled list of values (http://wifinetnews.com/archives/002452.html).

WPA utilizes a 256-bit pre-shared key or a passphrase that can vary in length from eight to sixty-three bytes. Short passphrase-based keys (less than 20 bytes) are vulnerable to the offline dictionary attack. The pre-shared key that is used to set up the WPA encryption can be captured during the initial communication between the access point and the client card. Once you have captured the pre-shared key, you can use that to essentially "guess" the WPA key using the same concepts that are used in any password dictionary attack. In theory, this type of dictionary attack takes less time and effort than attacking WEP.

While there are currently no tools available to automate cracking WPA, it is only a matter of time before they are available.

Summary

Wireless networks can be attacked in a number of different ways. Because so many wireless networks are deployed with default configurations, it is possible to access them simply by being in range with a properly configured client. This is accomplished by setting up a default configuration profile in the wireless settings of your operating system. The exact steps taken to do this vary between operating systems, but the concept is the same. If an access point is deployed with a default configuration, an attacker will only need to set up a default configuration profile and the wireless network will be compromised.

In some cases, it is necessary to go slightly beyond the default configuration. Because some network administrators have disabled the DCHP server on their wireless network, it is occasionally necessary to manually set the IP address on the attacking client card. Most wireless networks are deployed using an IP address in the 192.168.1.0 Class C space. Manually setting the client to an IP address in this range is often all that is needed to gain access to the resources available to the target network. If that range doesn't work, it is sometimes necessary to try a few different Class C ranges to find the right one. Kismet can also determine the IP range in use if enough packets have been captured.

Some network administrators allow only specific wireless cards to access their network. This is accomplished by MAC address filtering. However, this can also be defeated. Windows systems can be configured to send a spoofed MAC address by modifying the Registry or by using automated tools like BWMACHAK. The same can be accomplished on Linux systems by using the *ifconfig* command or tools like SirMACsAlot.

Another security measure that must be overcome in order to access some wireless networks is cloaked access points. A cloaked access point refers to one that has been set up not to broadcast its beacon. However, tools like Kismet and AirSnort can find these access points. Such tools operate in *monitor mode,* passively sniffing all wireless traffic. After enough traffic has been captured, Kismet and AirSnort can determine the SSID that the access point is using, after which the client can be configured to use that SSID and access the network.

The encryption standards that are utilized by wireless networks are flawed and can be defeated. Using tools like AirSnort and WEPCrack, an attacker can crack the WEP key used on a wireless network and configure a client with the captured WEP key. This will allow the attacker to access the wireless network. WPA is also flawed and in some cases is vulnerable to a dictionary attack.

Finally, at times, a combination of one or all of the attacks outlined in this chapter is required. For example, if a network administrator has disabled SSID broadcast, enabled WEP, and filtered access by MAC address, an attacker needs to follow the steps for each of the attacks designed to defeat those security mechanisms. However, this can be a tedious and time-consuming process.

Solutions Fast Track

The Direct Approach

☑ Many wireless networks can be accessed by an attacker with little or no modifications to their client software. This is because access points with default or "out-of-the-box" configurations allow anyone to connect to them.

☑ Windows XP will "find" any wireless networks within range that are broadcasting the SSID. Connecting to these only requires that you accept the security warning letting you know there is no data encryption enabled on the access point.

☑ Windows 2000 can be configured to use a default profile that will associate with any access point with a default configuration

☑ Linux systems can be configured to associate with wireless networks that have default configurations by editing the /etc/pcmcia/wireless.opts file.

☑ If the wireless network you are trying to access doesn't have a DHCP server enabled, you need to manually set your IP address. If you aren't able to determine the IP range in use on the wireless network, you can guess using some common IP ranges.

Defeating MAC Address Filtering

☑ Networks that are configured to filter access by MAC address can be accessed by spoofing the MAC address of your wireless card. This can be done in Windows and LinuxX

☑ Modifications can be made to the Registry in both Windows 2000 and Windows XP that allow you to change the MAC address of your wireless card.

☑ There are programs such as BWMACHAK available that can change the MAC address of your wireless card.

☑ The *ifconfig* command can be used on Linux systems to change the MAC address of the wireless card.

☑ Programs such as SirMACsAlot are available to automate MAC address spoofing on Linux systems.

Finding Cloaked Access Points

☑ Cloaked access points are access points that have been configured to not broadcast their SSID beacon.

☑ Active scanners such as NetStumbler do not detect cloaked access points.

☑ Passive scanners like Kismet and AirSnort can detect cloaked access points.

☑ Once a cloaked access point is discovered by a passive scanner, the SSID can be discovered after enough traffic has been captured.

Man-in-the-Middle Attacks on Wireless Networks

☑ Wireless networks are vulnerable to man-in-the-middle attacks. This is when a rogue, or unauthorized, access point is placed in proximity to a legitimate wireless network. Users will connect to the rogue access point.

☑ Once users have connected to the rogue access point, the traffic that they send can be sniffed by an attacker.

☑ Attackers can glean login information, passwords, and other important information from the traffic they sniff.

Attacking Encrypted Networks

☑ The two primary types of encryption used on wireless networks are Wired Equivalent Protection (WEP) and WiFi Protected Access (WPA). Both WEP and WPA are vulnerable to attacks.

☑ Linux users can passively sniff wireless traffic using AirSnort. When enough weak initialization vectors have been discovered by AirSnort, it can crack the WEP key.

☑ Windows users can use WEPCrack to crack WEP keys of a target network.

☑ Once the WEP key has been cracked, the attacker can configure his machine, regardless of the operating system he is using, to use the cracked key and associate with the network.

☑ WPA is vulnerable to dictionary attacks if the pre-shared key is less than 20 characters.

Frequently Asked Questions

The following Frequently Asked Questions, answered by the authors of this book, are designed to both measure your understanding of the concepts presented in this chapter and to assist you with real-life implementation of these concepts. To have your questions about this chapter answered by the author, browse to **www.syngress.com/solutions** and click on the **"Ask the Author"** form. You will also gain access to thousands of other FAQs at ITFAQnet.com.

Q: Is there a list of tools that can be used to scan and attack wireless networks?

A: A fairly comprehensive list of wireless discovery and attack tools can be found at www.networkintrusion.co.uk/wireless.htm

Q: Is it illegal to access a wireless network even if it has a default configuration and no security measures enabled?

A: Yes. At a minimum, it is theft of service to access any network, wired or wireless, that you have not received authorization from the owner to access.

Q: How long does it take to crack a WEP key?

A: This depends on the amount of traffic on the wireless network. For every one million packets transmitted, approximately 120 interesting packets will be captured. It takes at least 1200 interesting packets to crack the key. Assuming you capture one million packets a day, it would take a minimum of 10 days to crack the key. If the key is changed frequently (say once a week) you might never crack the WEP key.

Q: If a wireless network uses a secondary authentication scheme such as Cisco's Lightweight Extensible Authentication Protocol (LEAP), can it still be compromised?

A: Yes. In August of 2003, Cisco acknowledged that LEAP is vulnerable to a dictionary attack. In October of 2003, Joshua Wright (http://home.jwu.edu/jwright/) released the "Asleep" tool that can exploit this vulnerability.

Chapter 10

Basic Wireless Network Security

Solutions in this Chapter:

- Enabling Security Features on a Linksys WAP11 802.11b Access Point

- Enabling Security Features on a Linksys BEFW11SR 802.11b Access Point/Router

- Enabling Security Features on a Linksys WRT54G 802.11b/g Access Point/Router

- Enabling Security Features on a D-Link DI-624 AirPlus 2.4GHz Xtreme G Wireless Router with 4-Port Switch

- Configuring Security Features on Wireless Clients

☑ Summary

☑ Solutions Fast Track

☑ Frequently Asked Questions

Introduction

In Chapter 9, "Attacking Wireless Networks," we looked at valid methods that an attacker can use to gain access to wireless networks. In this chapter, we will discuss ways that wireless networks can be configured to reduce the risk of a successful attack.

A knowledgeable attacker, who is determined to compromise your system specifically, will probably be successful. In a home environment, it is unlikely that you will face this type of attacker, but for preventive measures, the steps presented in this chapter are designed to reduce your risk of becoming a target of convenience. A good analogy is *The Club* that many motorists place on their steering wheels when they lock their cars. A knowledgeable car thief that is looking to steal a particular car can easily pick the lock on The Club in a matter of seconds. You may ask, "then what is the point of even putting The Club on my car?" The point is that the car thief has a parking lot full of cars, many without The Club. Why would he bother to waste the extra time picking the lock on The Club, when he can simply choose a different car?

Wireless security is similar. Because there are so many wireless networks that are still configured with out of the box settings, an attacker that is looking for a target of convenience (for example, a network, but not necessarily your network) will likely choose one of the more vulnerable networks. This chapter looks at how to configure the basic security settings on the four most popular access points currently deployed (Linksys WAP11, BEFW11SR, and WRT54G, and the D-Link DI-624).

There are four very simple steps that are sufficient for most home users:

1. Use a unique Service Set Identifier (SSID).
2. Disable SSID broadcast.
3. Enable Wired Equivalent Privacy (WEP) encryption.
4. Filter access by Media Access Control (MAC) address.

Enabling Security Features on a Linksys WAP11 802.11b Access Point

The Linksys Wireless Access Point (WAP) 11 802.11b access point was one of the first access points deployed by a large number of people. The WAP11 was the wireless access point many users purchased that already had a home network with a router set up. The WAP11 requires a separate router in order to allow access to any non-wireless devices, to include Internet access. This section details the minimum steps you should take to configure the WAP11 securely. All of the steps outlined in this section should be done from a computer that is connected to your wired network. This is because as you make changes the access point will need to reset. When the access point resets, you will likely lose your wireless connection momentarily.

Setting a Unique SSID

The first step you need to take is to set a unique SSID for your access point. When you log in to your access point, by default there is no username assigned to the WAP11 and the password is *admin*. This brings up the initial setup screen (Figure 10.1).

Figure 10.1 The Linksys WAP11 Initial Setup Screen

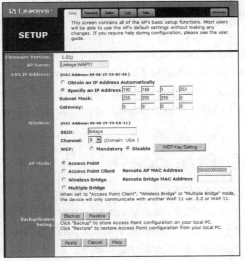

In the **AP Name** field, choose a name for your access point. This is NOT the SSID, but it is prudent to set this to a unique name. Many access points are named after the address of the owner or the company name, making them easier for an attacker to target. Next, replace "Linksys" with a unique SSID. This can be anything that you want, though it is not a good idea to use your address, phone number, social security number, or any other information that identifies you specifically. Figure 10.2 depicts the setup screen after a unique AP Name and SSID have been chosen.

Figure 10.2 A Unique AP Name and SSID Are Set

Once these are set, click **Apply** and your changes are stored. Setting a unique SSID is a good first step for practicing security, but without taking additional steps it is relatively useless. A unique SSID will contain a combination of upper- and lowercase letters, numbers, and special characters. Additionally, using non-printable characters will cause some WarDriving applications to crash or identify the SSID incorrectly.

Disabling SSID Broadcast

After you have set a unique SSID on your access point, the next step is to disable the SSID broadcast. By default, access points transmit a beacon to let wireless users know that they are there. Active scanners such as NetStumbler rely on this beacon to find access points. By disabling the SSID broadcast, you have effectively placed your access point in *stealth,* also known as *cloaked,* mode.

To disable the SSID broadcast, first click the **Advanced** tab on the initial setup screen. This will take you to the screen shown in Figure 10.3.

Figure 10.3 The Advanced Settings

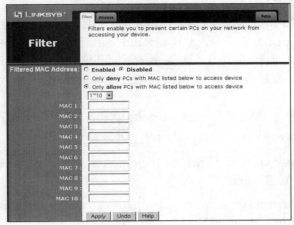

Next, click the **Wireless** tab to bring up the advanced wireless settings, as shown in Figure 10.4.

Figure 10.4 The Advanced Wireless Settings

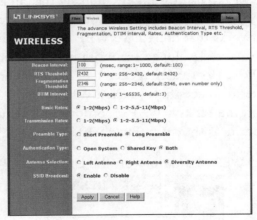

Select the **Disable** radio button, and then click **Apply** to save your settings. Passive scanners, such as Kismet and AirSnort, have the ability to detect cloaked access points, but disabling SSID broadcast is one more step toward an effective overall security posture.

Enabling WEP

After you have set a unique SSID and disabled SSID broadcast, the next step is to enable WEP encryption. The flaws associated with WEP have been widely publicized and discussed. Inasmuch, because it is possible to crack WEP keys, you should not rely on WEP alone, but use WEP as a part of your overall security posture.

Although WEP is flawed, actually cracking the WEP key is not a simple process on a home network, for two primary reasons.

1. The amount of traffic that must be generated in order to successfully crack the WEP key.

2. Vendors have taken steps to eliminate or reduce the number of Weak Initialization Vectors (IVs) that are transmitted.

In Chapter 9, "Attacking Wireless Networks," we learned that it usually requires at least 1200 Weak IVs be collected before a WEP key is cracked. On a home network it can take days, weeks, or even months to generate enough traffic to capture that many Weak IVs. It is highly unlikely that an attacker will invest that amount of time into attacking a simple home network; especially when there are so many networks that don't have WEP enabled.

Many vendors have also developed firmware upgrades that reduce or eliminate the number of Weak IVs that are generated. This further increases the amount of time it takes to successfully crack a WEP key.

To enable WEP on the Linksys WAP11, on the main setup screen select the **Mandatory** radio button, as shown in Figure 10.5.

Figure 10.5 Making WEP Mandatory on the Linksys WAP11

Next, click **WEP Key Setting** to open the WEP Key Setting window, as shown in Figure 10.6.

Figure 10.6 The WEP Key Setting Window

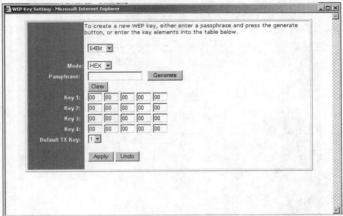

In the **WEP Key Setting** window, change **64Bit** to **128Bit** in the drop-down box (as shown in Figure 10.7) to require 128-bit WEP keys. As the number of bits implies, 128-bit WEP provides a stronger, harder to crack key than 64-bit.

Figure 10.7 Select 128-Bit WEP

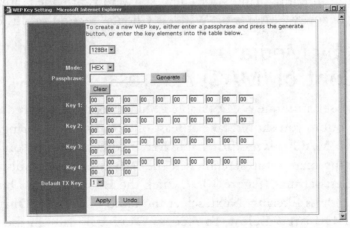

Leave the Mode set to HEX and choose a strong passphrase to generate your keys. A strong passphrase consists of a combination of upper- and lowercase letters, numbers, and special characters. Once chosen, enter your passphrase in the **Passphrase** text box and click **Generate**. This will create four WEP keys. See Figure 10.8.

Figure 10.8 Generating WEP Keys

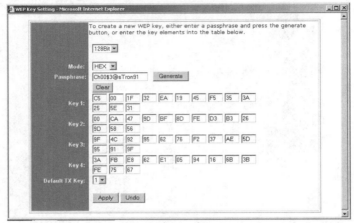

Since four keys are generated, you need to decide which one your client should use. Set the **Default TX Key** to the number (1–4) that you want to use on your network. Once you have generated your WEP keys and chosen the key to transmit, click **Apply** to save your settings.

Information on configuring your client software is provided later in the "Configuring Security Features on Wireless Clients" section of this chapter.

Filtering by Media Access Control (MAC) Address

Once you have set a unique SSID, disabled SSID broadcast, and required the use of WEP encryption, you should take at least one more step: filtering by Media Access Control (MAC) address. To enable MAC address filtering on the Linksys WAP11, from the main setup screen click the **Advanced** tab to display the advanced wireless settings (Figure 10.9). Click the **Enabled** radio button to enable MAC address filtering. Next, select the radio button for **Only Allow PCs With MAC Listed Below To Access Device**. Finally, in the text boxes labeled **MAC 1** thru **MAC 10**, list the MAC addresses of any wireless clients that are allowed to access your wireless network. Click **Apply** to save and enable your settings. Instructions for finding the MAC address of your card are provided in the "Tools & Traps" sidebar in this chapter.

Figure 10.9 Enable MAC Address Filtering

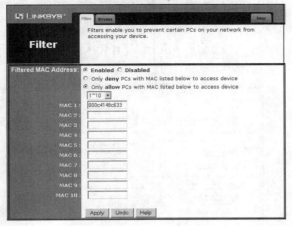

Finding the Media Access Control (MAC) Address of Wireless Cards

Finding the Media Access Control (MAC) address of your wireless card is a simple process. The easiest way is to look at the back of the card itself, as every wireless card has a label on the back that provides information like: the FCC ID, the encryption standard that is supported, and the MAC address. Figure 10.10 shows this label.

Figure 10.10 Finding the MAC Address on the Card Label

Continued

Windows 2000 and XP users can find the MAC address using the *ipconfig /all* command.

Figure 10.11 Using *ipconfig /all* in Windows to Determine the MAC Address

The Physical Address highlighted in Figure 10.11 is the MAC address for the wireless card. Linux users can determine the MAC address of their card using the *ifconfig <interface>* command.

The highlighted HWaddr shown in Figure 10.12 is the MAC address of the wireless card.

Figure 10.12 Using *ifconfig* to Determine the MAC Address in Linux

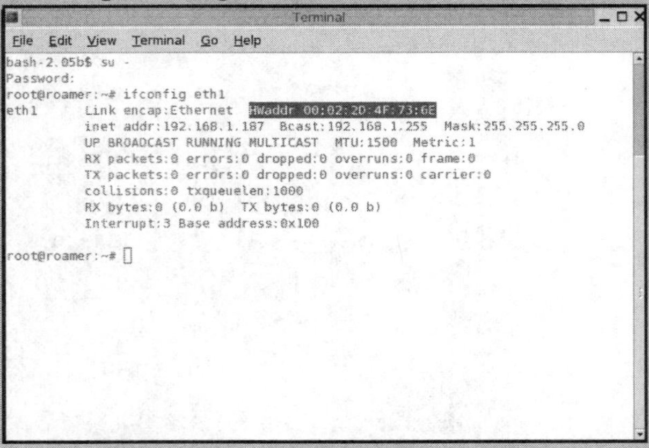

Enabling Security Features on a Linksys BEFW11SR 802.11b Access Point/Router

The most popular 802.11b access point currently deployed is the Linksys BEFW11SR Access Point/Router. The BEFW11SR gained popularity because it combined both a wireless access point and a wired router into one device. This section details the minimum steps you should take to configure the BEFW11SR securely. All of the steps outlined in this section should be done from a computer that is connected to your wired network. This is because, as you make changes, the access point will need to reset. When the access point resets, you will likely lose your wireless connection momentarily.

Setting a Unique SSID

The first step you need to take is to assign a unique SSID to your access point. When you log in, you'll find, by default, that BEFW11SR has no username and the password is *admin*. This brings up the initial setup screen (see Figure 10.13).

Figure 10.13 The Linksys BEFW11SR Initial Setup Screen

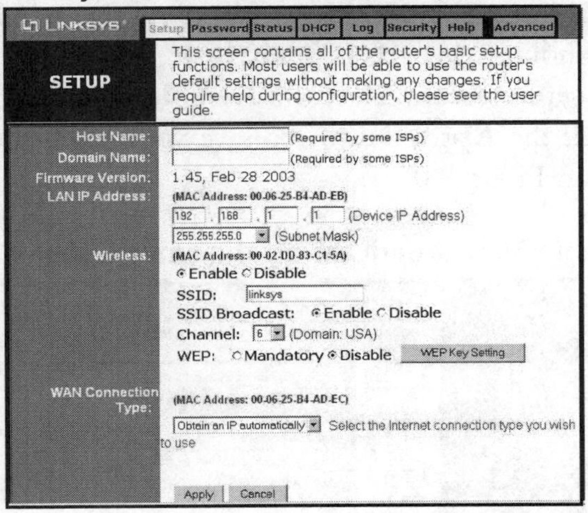

Next, enter a unique SSID in the **SSID** textbox, as shown in Figure 10.14.

Figure 10.14 Entering a Unique SSID

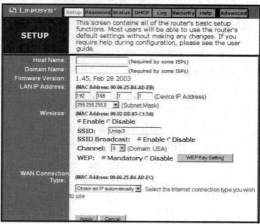

Finally, click the **Apply** button to save your new SSID.

Disabling SSID Broadcast

After you have assigned a unique SSID to your BEFW11SR, you should disable SSID broadcast. Disabling SSID broadcast prevents active wireless scanners like NetStumbler from finding your access point.

From the initial setup screen, select the **Disable** radio button next to SSID Broadcast. Next, click the **Apply** button to save your settings and disable SSID broadcast, as shown in Figure 10.15.

Figure 10.15 Disable SSID Broadcast on the Linksys BEFW11SR

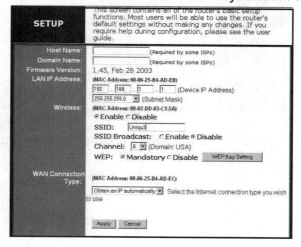

Enabling WEP

Once you have set a unique SSID and disabled SSID broadcast, the next security measure you should enable is WEP encryption. On the initial setup screen, select the **Mandatory** radio button next to WEP, as shown in Figure 10.16.

Figure 10.16 Select the Mandatory Radio Button

Next, click the WEP Key Setting button to open the WEP Key Setting window. Enter a strong passphrase in the **Passphrase** textbox and click the **Generate** button. This generates a WEP key for your network, as shown in Figure 10.17.

Figure 10.17 Generate a WEP Key

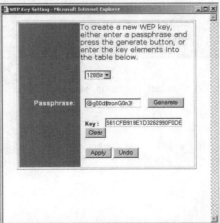

Next, click the **Apply** button to save your settings. You also need to configure any wireless clients that use the BEFW11SR with the same WEP key. Instructions for setting up wireless clients are presented in the Configuring Security Features on Wireless Clients section later in this chapter.

Filtering by Media Access Control (MAC) Address

After you have set a unique SSID, disabled SSID broadcast, and enabled WEP, your next step is to filter by Media Access Control (MAC) address. Filtering by MAC address allows only wireless clients with pre-determined MAC addresses to connect to the access point.

From the initial setup screen, click the **Advanced** tab. This brings up the advanced settings window. Next, click the **Wireless** tab to open the advanced wireless settings window, as shown in Figure 10.18.

Figure 10.18 The Advanced Wireless Settings Window

Select the **Enable** radio button next to Station MAC Filter, as shown in Figure 10.19.

Figure 10.19 Enable Station MAC Filter

Then, click the **Edit MAC Filter Setting** button to open the **Wireless Group MAC Table** window, shown in Figure 10.20.

Figure 10.20 The Wireless Group MAC Table Window

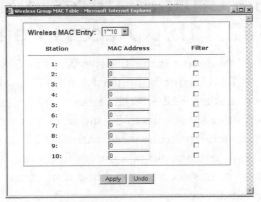

Next, enter the MAC addresses of the clients that are allowed to access your wireless network in the **MAC Address** textboxes and select the **Filter** checkbox next to each of them, as shown in Figure 10.21.

Figure 10.21 Enter Allowed MAC Addresses

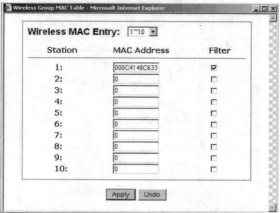

Finally, click the **Apply** button on the **Wireless Group MAC Table** window, the **Advanced Wireless Settings** window, and the initial setup screen to save your settings.

Enabling Security Features on a Linksys WRT54G 802.11b/g Access Point/Router

The most popular 802.11g device is the Linksys WRT54G 802.11b/g Access Point/Router. The WRT54G gained popularity in 2003 as 802.11g devices became more common and affordable. 802.11g devices operate on the 2.4 GHz band, like 802.11b, but offer speeds up to 54 megabits per second (Mbps). Additionally, 802.11g devices are compatible with 802.11b cards. This section details the minimum steps you should take to configure the WRT54G securely. All of the steps outlined in this section should be done from a computer that is connected to your wired network.

Setting a Unique SSID

The first security measure you should enable on the Linksys WRT54G is setting a Unique SSID. When you log in to the WRT54G, by default, there is no username required and the password is *admin*. This brings up the initial setup screen (see Figure 10.22).

Figure 10.22 The Linksys WRT54G Initial Setup Screen

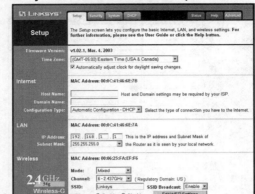

In the **SSID** textbox, enter a unique SSID, as shown in Figure 10.23.

Figure 10.23 Setting a Unique SSID on the WRT54G

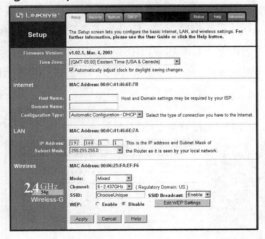

Then, click the **Apply** button to save your settings.

Disabling SSID Broadcast

After you have set a unique SSID, disable the SSID broadcast. From the initial setup screen, select **Disable** from the **SSID Broadcast** drop-down box, as shown in Figure 10.24.

Figure 10.24 Disable SSID Broadcast

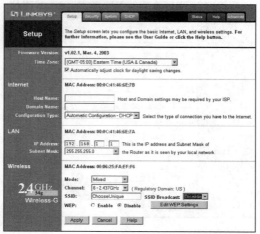

Then, click the **Apply** button to save your settings and disable SSID broadcast.

Enabling WEP

Once you have set a unique SSID and disabled SSID broadcast, you need to require the use of 128-bit WEP encryption. From the initial setup screen, choose the **Enable** radio button next to WEP to require WEP encryption, as shown in Figure 10.25.

Figure 10.25 Enable WEP on the WRT54G

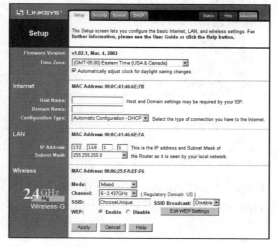

Next, click the **Edit WEP Settings** button, opening the **WEP Keys** window. Select **128 bits 26 hex digits** from the **WEP Encryption** drop-down box to require 128-bit WEP. Type a strong passphrase in the **Passphrase** textbox. This is the passphrase that will be used as the basis for generating WEP keys. Click the **Generate** button to generate four WEP keys, as shown in Figure 10.26.

Figure 10.26 The WEP Keys Window

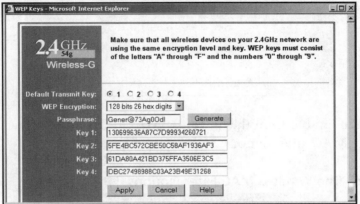

Next, select the key (1–4) that you will initially use by choosing the appropriate radio button next to **Default Transmit Key**. Finally, click **Apply** on both the **WEP Keys** window and the initial setup screen to save your settings.

Filtering by Media Access Control (MAC) Address

After you have set a unique SSID, disabled SSID broadcast, and enabled WEP encryption, you need to filter access to the WRT54G by MAC address.

First, from the initial setup screen click the **Advanced** tab to display the **Advanced Wireless** screen (see Figure 10.27).

Figure 10.27 The Advanced Wireless Screen

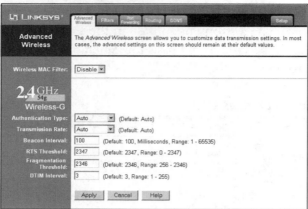

Next, select **Enable** from the **Wireless MAC Filter** drop-down box. This will reveal the MAC filter options, as shown in Figure 10.28.

Figure 10.28 The Wireless MAC Filter Options

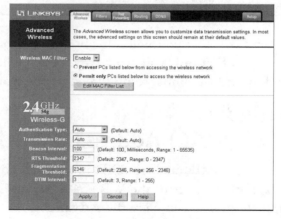

Choose the **Permit Only PCs Listed Below To Access The Wireless Network** radio button, and click the **Edit MAC Filter List** button to display the **MAC Address Filter List** window (see Figure 10.29).

Figure 10.29 The MAC Address Filter List Window

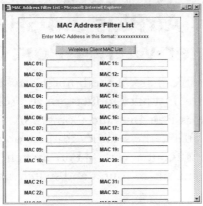

Enter the MAC addresses of wireless clients that are allowed to access your wireless network in the provided textboxes and then click **Apply**, as shown in Figure 10.30.

Figure 10.30 Enter Allowed MAC Addresses

Finally, click **Apply** in the **Advanced Wireless** window to save your settings and enable filtering by MAC address.

Enabling Security Features on a D-Link DI-624 AirPlus 2.4GHz Xtreme G Wireless Router with 4-Port Switch

Although Linksys has a sizable share of the home access point market, D-Link also has a large market share. D-Link products are also sold at most big computer and electronics stores such as Best Buy and CompUSA. This section details the steps you need to take to enable the security features on the D-Link 624 AirPlus 2.4GHz Xtreme G Wireless Router with 4-Port Switch. The DI-624 is an 802.11g access point with a built-in router and switch similar in function to the Linksys WRT54G.

Setting a Unique SSID

The first security measure to enable on the D-Link DI-624 is setting a unique SSID.

First, you need to log into the access point. Point your browser to 192.168.0.1. Use the username **admin** with a blank password to access the initial setup screen (see Figure 10.31).

Figure 10.31 The D-Link DI-624 Initial Setup Screen

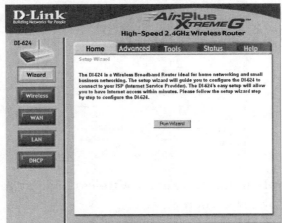

Next, click the **Wireless** button on the left side of the screen to bring up the **Wireless Settings** screen, as shown in Figure 10.32.

Figure 10.32 The Wireless Settings Screen

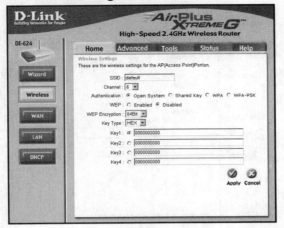

In the **SSID** textbox, enter a unique SSID, as shown in Figure 10.33, and click **Apply** to save and enable the new SSID.

Figure 10.33 Set a Unique SSID

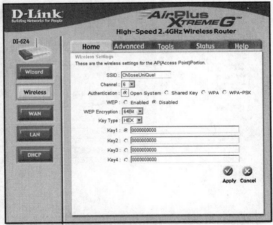

Enabling Wired Equivalent Privacy

After you have set a unique SSID, you will need to enable 128-bit WEP encryption.

First, choose the **Enabled** radio button next to WEP, as shown in Figure 10.34.

Figure 10.34 Enable WEP

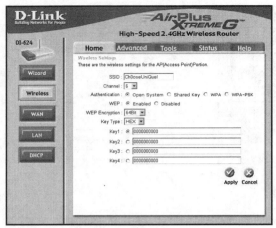

Next, choose **128Bit** from the **WEP Encryption** drop-down box, as shown in Figure 10.35.

Figure 10.35 Require 128-Bit WEP Encryption

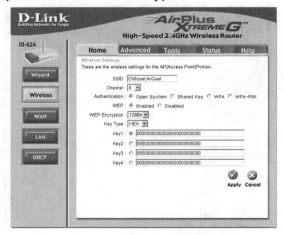

Then, you will need to assign a 26-character hexadecimal number to at least Key1 (see Figure 10.36). A 26-digit hexadecimal number can contain the letters A–F and the numbers 0–9.

Figure 10.36 Assign WEP Keys

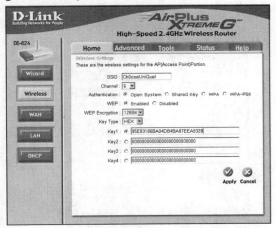

Finally, after you have assigned your WEP keys, click **Apply** to save your settings. Any wireless clients that connect to the DI-624 must be configured to use this WEP key.

Filtering by Media
Access Control (MAC) Address

After you have set a unique SSID and enabled 128-bit WEP encryption, you should filter access to the wireless network by MAC address.

First, click the **Advanced** tab, as shown in Figure 10.37.

Figure 10.37 The Advanced Options Screen

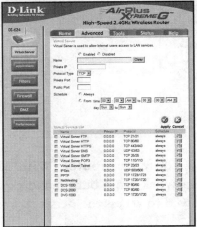

Next, click the **Filters** button on the left side of the screen, as shown in Figure 10.38.

Figure 10.38 The Advanced Filters Options

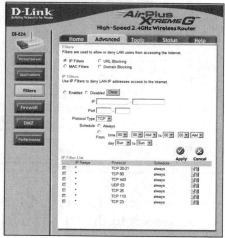

Then choose the **MAC Filters** radio button. This makes the MAC Filtering options visible, as shown in Figure 10.39.

Figure 10.39 The MAC Filtering Options

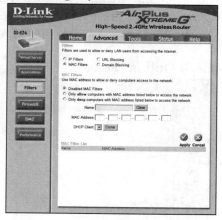

Finally, select the **Only Allow Computers With MAC Address Listed Below To Access The Network** radio button and enter the MAC address of each client card that is allowed to access the network. You must also enter a descriptive name, of your choice, for each client in the **Name** textbox (see Figure 10.40). Note that you must click **Apply** after each MAC address entered.

Figure 10.40 Filter by MAC Address

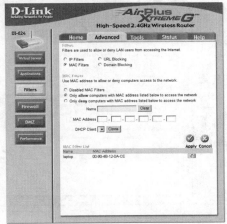

Disabling SSID Broadcast

After you have set a unique SSID, enabled 128-bit WEP, and filtered access by MAC address, you need to disable SSID broadcast.

From the **Advanced Features** screen, click the **Performance** button, as shown in Figure 10.41.

Figure 10.41 The Advanced Performance Options

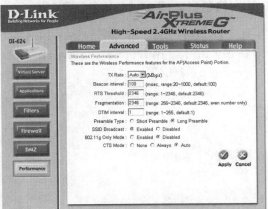

Select the **Disabled** radio button next to SSID Broadcast and click **Apply** to save your settings, as shown in Figure 10.42.

Figure 10.42 Disabling SSID Broadcast

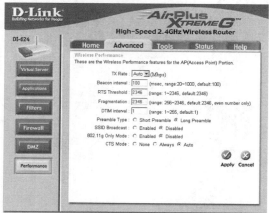

Configuring Security Features on Wireless Clients

After you have configured your access points to utilize security features, you will then need to configure each wireless client to work with your access points. This means that each wireless client needs to be configured with the correct SSID and have the appropriate WEP key entered and selected.

Configuring Windows XP Clients

For Windows XP Clients, double-click the **Wireless Network Connections** icon on the taskbar to bring up the **Wireless Network Connection Properties** window (see Figure 10.43).

Figure 10.43 The Windows XP Wireless Network Connection Properties Window

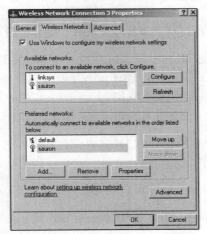

Next, click the **Add** button to add a new preferred network. Enter the SSID of your network in the **SSID** textbox, and un-check **The Key Is Provided For Me Automatically**. Then, enter the WEP key for your wireless network in the **Network Key** and **Confirm Network Key** textboxes, as shown in Figure 10.44.

Figure 10.44 Configuring Windows XP Clients for Use

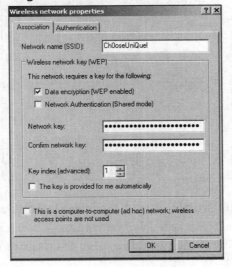

Finally, choose the appropriate key index (1–4) and click **OK**. If your settings are correct, you will be connected to your access point.

Configuring Windows 2000 Clients

Unlike Windows XP, with Windows 2000 you will need to configure the wireless client software that came with your wireless card. The examples shown in this section are for the ORiNOCO client manager. The exact steps for other client managers may differ, but the basic idea is the same.

1. Create a wireless profile for your access point.
2. Enter the SSID of your access point.
3. Enter the WEP key for your wireless network.

To create a wireless profile for your access point, double-click the **client manager** icon on the taskbar to open the Client Manager. Choose **Actions | Add/Edit Configuration Profile** to open the **Add/Edit Configuration Profile** window, as shown in Figure 10.45. Select the radio button next to a blank profile and enter the name of the profile.

Figure 10.45 The Configuration Profiles

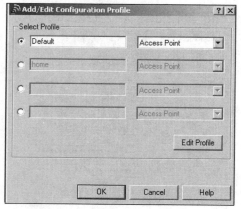

Next, click the **Edit Profile** button. On the **Basic** screen, enter the SSID of your access point in the **Network Name** textbox. Then, click the **Encryption** tab, as shown in Figure 10.46. Choose the **Use Hexadecimal** radio button and enter your WEP keys (1–4).

Figure 10.46 Entering the WEP Key

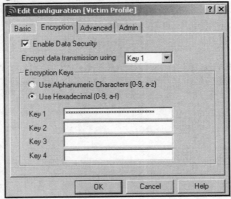

Finally, click **OK** to save your settings. Your wireless client is now configured for use with your access point.

Configuring Linux Clients

Configuring wireless clients for use with your network after security features have been enabled is a simple two-step process.

1. Edit the /etc/pcmcia/wirless.opts.

2. Restart PCMCIA services or reboot.

First, you need to edit the /etc/pcmcia/wireless.opts file (see Figure 10.47).

Figure 10.47 Editing the wireless.opts File

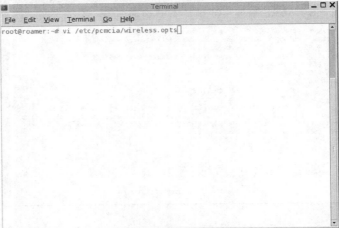

Ensure that the four lines starting with the line that reads **START SECTION TO REMOVE** have been commented out by placing a pound sign (#) in front of each, as shown in Figure 10.48.

Figure 10.48 Commenting Lines Out of the wireless.opts File

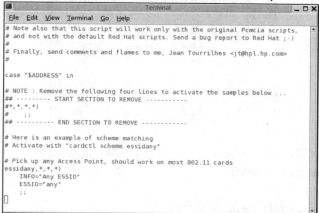

Next, find the appropriate section for your wireless card. Enter the SSID your access point uses in the **ESSID** section. Then, enter the WEP key for your wireless network in the **KEY** section, as shown in Figure 10.49, and save your changes.

Figure 10.49 Entering the SSID and WEP Key

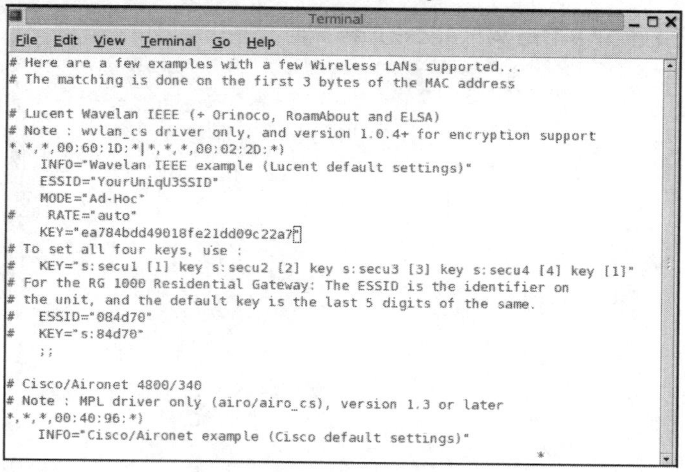

Before your settings take effect, you need to restart the Personal Computer Memory Card International Association (PCMCIA) services. The method for restarting PCMCIA services varies and depends on the Linux distribution you are using. In Slackware, Linux PCMCIA services are restarted by issuing the following command:

```
root@roamer: ~# /etc/rc.d/rc/pcmcia restart
```

If you are unsure how to restart PCMCIA services on your distribution, you can reboot. When the system restarts, your settings will take effect.

Notes from the Underground…

Enabling Security Features on the Xbox

Many Xbox owners like to take advantage of the Xbox Live feature. Xbox Live allows gamers to connect their Xbox to the Internet and play selected games against online opponents. Since the Xbox is often connected to a TV that isn't necessarily in the same room with most of the household computer equipment, wireless networking is a natural choice for this connection.

There are several wireless bridges (like the Linksys WET 11 Wireless Ethernet Bridge) available that will connect the Xbox to a home network. These devices must be configured to use the wireless network's security features.

First, log in to the WET 11. By default, the WET 11 is configured to use the IP address 192.168.1.251 (see Figure 10.50).

Continued

Figure 10.50 The Linksys WET 11 Initial Setup Screen

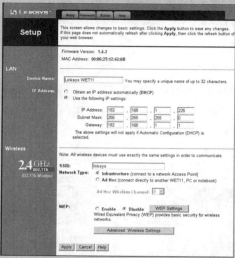

Enter the SSID for your wireless network in the SSID textbox, and then select the Enable radio button next to WEP (see Figure 10.51).

Figure 10.51 Set the SSID and Enable WEP

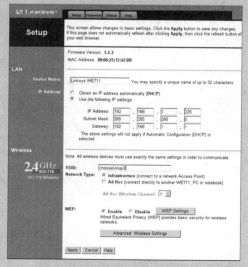

Continued

Click the WEP Settings button to open the Shared Keys window (see Figure 10.52). Select 128 bit 26 hex digits from the drop-down box and then enter the WEP keys that your wireless network uses. The WEP keys can be entered in either of two ways:

- Generate the keys using the same passphrase used to generate the keys on your access point.

- Manually enter the WEP keys that your access point uses.

Figure 10.52 Enter the WEP Keys

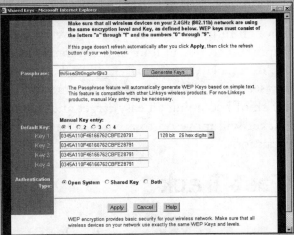

Next, click the Apply button on the Shared Keys window and the initial setup screen to save your settings. Finally, add the MAC address of your WET 11 to your allowed MAC address list on your access point.

Summary

Regardless of the particular brand or model of access point that you choose for your home network, by default it is set up very insecurely. At a minimum, four basic security measures should be enabled:

1. Change the default Service Set Identifier (SSID).
2. Disable the SSID broadcast.
3. Enable 128-Bit Wired Equivalent Privacy (WEP) encryption.
4. Filter by Media Access Control (MAC) address.

These steps are enough in most cases to protect low-traffic wireless networks used at home. It is important to use all four of these measures in order to deploy your wireless network using a layered security approach. While it is true that no network is completely secure, enabling these security measures on your wireless network reduces the risk of becoming an easy target and increases the likelihood that a prospective attacker will move on to a wireless network that does not employ the same precautions.

Solutions Fast Track

Enabling Security Features on a Linksys WAP11 802.11b AP, Linksys BEFW11SR 802.11b AP/Router, WRT54G 802.11b/g AP/Router, and D-Link DI-624 AirPlus 2.4GHz Xtreme G Wireless Router with 4-Port Switch

These have been consolidated because they are the recommendations for securing any AP/router and are not specific to a particular hardware.

☑ Assigning a unique SSID to your wireless network is the first security measure that you should take. Any attacker with a "default" configuration profile is able to associate with an access point that has a default SSID. While assigning a unique SSID in and of itself doesn't offer much protection, it is one layer in your wireless defense.

☑ Many attackers use active wireless scanners to discover target wireless networks. Active scanners rely on the access point beacon to locate it. This beacon broadcasts the SSID to any device that requests it. Disabling SSID broadcast makes your access point "invisible" to active scanners. Because your access point can still be discovered by passive wireless scanners, this step should be used in conjunction with other security measures.

☑ Wired Equivalent Privacy (WEP) encryption, at a minimum, should be used on your home wireless network. Although there are tools available that make it possible to crack WEP, the amount of traffic that needs to be generated make it unlikely an attacker will take the time to do so on a home, or low-traffic, network. Adequate security for these networks is provided by 128-bit WEP.

☑ Filtering by Media Access Control (MAC) address allows only wireless cards that you specifically designate to access your wireless network. Again, it is possible to spoof MAC addresses, therefore you shouldn't rely on MAC address filtering exclusively. It should be part of your overall security posture.

☑ Each of the four security steps presented in this chapter can be defeated. Fortunately, for most home users they do provide adequate security for a wireless network. By enacting a four-layer security posture on your wireless network, you have made it more difficult for an attacker to gain access to your network. Because the likelihood of a strong "return" on the attacker's time investment would be low, he is likely to move on to an easier target. Don't allow your wireless network to be a target of convenience.

Configuring Security Features on Wireless Clients

☑ Windows XP clients are configured using the Wireless Connection Properties and the Windows XP Wireless Client Manager. To associate with your access point once the security features have been enabled, your access point must be added as a Preferred Network. You need to enter the SSID and the WEP key during the configuration process.

☑ Windows 2000 does not have a built-in wireless client manager like Windows XP. You need to enter the SSID and WEP key into a profile in the client manager software that shipped with your wireless card.

☑ Linux users need to configure the /etc/pcmcia/wireless.opts file in order to access a wireless network with the security features enabled. The SSID and WEP key need to be entered in the appropriate section of the /etc/pcmcia/wireless.opts file. Restarting PCMCIA services or rebooting allows these settings to take effect.

Frequently Asked Questions

The following Frequently Asked Questions, answered by the authors of this book, are designed to both measure your understanding of the concepts presented in this chapter and to assist you with real-life implementation of these concepts. To have your questions about this chapter answered by the author, browse to **www.syngress.com/solutions** and click on the **"Ask the Author"** form. You will also gain access to thousands of other FAQs at ITFAQnet.com.

Q: Why should I bother using Wired Equivalent Privacy (WEP) encryption if it can be cracked?

A: Due to the low amount of wireless network traffic that is usually generated on a home wireless network, it would take an attacker an extremely long time to capture enough packets to successfully crack the WEP key of your network. An attacker is unlikely to devote the required time and effort to cracking the WEP key on a home network when there are so many home networks that have no security measures enabled.

Q: What are the different transmission keys used for?

A: With many access points, you can generate four WEP keys at once. You can switch between these keys by configuring the access point to use a different transmission key (1–4). You must then configure your wireless client to use the same WEP key (1–4) as the access point.

Q: How often should I change my WEP key?

A: This depends on the amount of traffic on your wireless network. The more traffic you generate, the easier it is to crack your WEP key. However, by frequently changing your WEP key, every month at least, you can essentially render the packets an attacker has captured useless. You can change your WEP key as often as you like, even every day if so desired.

Q: Aside from setting a default SSID, disabling SSID broadcast, enabling 128-bit WEP, and filtering by MAC address, are there other security measures I can take?

A: Of course there are. Some other easy security measures you can implement are to disable the Dynamic Host Configuration Protocol (DHCP) server on your router, use a non-default IP address range, do not allow configuration changes to be made from a wireless, and keep your firmware up-to-date. Some of these topics are covered in Chapter 11, "Advanced Wireless Security," of this book.

Advanced Wireless Network Security

Solutions in this Chapter:

- Implementing WiFi Protected Access (WPA)
- Implementing a Wireless Gateway with Reef Edge Dolphin
- Implementing a VPN on a Linksys WRV54G VPN Broadband Router
- Implementing RADIUS with Cisco LEAP
- Understanding and Configuring 802.1X RADIUS Authentication

☑ Summary

☑ Solutions Fast Track

☑ Frequently Asked Questions

Introduction

The security measures discussed in Chapter 10, Basic Wireless Network Security are, as a general rule, sufficient for most home wireless users. Corporate users, however, should not rely on basic security measures alone to protect their wireless networks. In this chapter, we discuss some of the more advanced ways you can reduce the risk of your wireless network being compromised. By implementing some (or all) of the security mechanisms in this chapter, you have done all that you can feasibly do to reduce the risk of your wireless network being compromised.

In this chapter, you will also learn about different methods of secondary authentication such as Virtual Private Networks (VPNs) and Remote Authentication and Dial-In User Service (RADIUS). A secondary authentication mechanism requires that, in addition to association with a wireless access point, a user must authenticate (that is, log in) using some other means. But, first, we will look at the replacement for Wired Equivalent Privacy (WEP): WiFi Protected Access (WPA).

Implementing WiFi Protected Access (WPA)

WiFi Protected Access (WPA) is designed to provide wireless users with an encryption mechanism that is not susceptible to the vulnerabilities of Wired Equivalent Privacy (WEP). Most 802.11g access points either ship with the option to use WPA or a firmware upgrade can be downloaded from the access point manufacturer.

Before enabling WPA, you should ensure that your wireless card has WPA drivers. As with access points, you often need to update the card's drivers, firmware, or both in order to take advantage of WPA. This section details how to set up WPA encryption on two access points: the D-Link DI-624 and the Linksys WRV54G. You will also learn how to configure your wireless client to use WPA.

Configuring the D-Link DI-624 AirPlus 2.4GHz Xtreme G Wireless Router with 4-Port Switch

The D-Link DI-624 ships with WPA capability. This means that no firmware upgrade is necessary and you can start using WPA as soon as the DI-624 comes out of the box. First, you need to log into the DI-624 from a wired connection. Then, point your browser to 192.168.0.1 and supply the username **admin** with a blank password when prompted. This opens the initial configuration screen, as seen in Figure 11.1.

Figure 11.1 The DI-624 Initial Configuration Screen

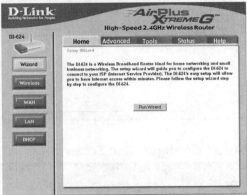

Next, click the **Wireless** button on the left to open the wireless configuration options window, as shown in Figure 11.2.

Figure 11.2 The Wireless Configuration Options Window

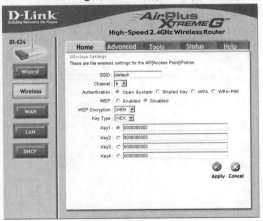

Next, choose either the **WPA** or **WPA-PSK** Authentication options. The WPA option requires a RADIUS server, whereas WPA-PSK (Pre Shared Key) sets a passphrase that must also be entered in the client WPA configuration settings. See Figures 11.3 and 11.4.

Figure 11.3 The WPA Configuration Screen

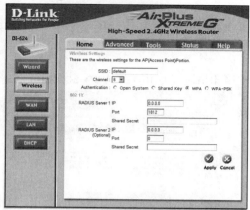

Figure 11.4 The WPA-PSK Configuration Screen

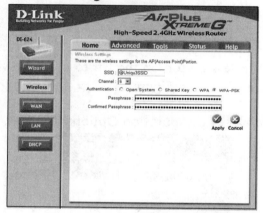

Damage & Defense...

Known WPA-PSK Vulnerability

WPA-PSK utilizes a 256-bit pre-shared key or a passphrase that can vary in length from 8 to 63 bytes. Short passphrase-based keys (less than 20 bytes) are vulnerable to the offline dictionary attack. The pre-shared key that is used to set up the WPA encryption can be captured during the initial communication between the access point and the client card. Once an attacker has captured the pre-shared key, he can use that to essentially "guess" the WPA key using the same concepts used in any password dictionary attack. In theory, this type of dictionary attack takes less time and effort than attacking WEP. Choosing a passphrase that is more than 20 bytes mitigates this vulnerability.

Enter either your RADIUS server information and Shared Secret for WPA or a strong passphrase that is more than 20 bytes long, and then click **Apply** to save your settings and enable WPA.

Configuring the Linksys WRV54G VPN Broadband Router

The Linksys WRV54G VPN–Broadband Router may require a firmware upgrade to allow WPA capability. Firmware version 2.10 or later is required for WPA functionality on the WRV54G. To enable WPA, you need to log in to the WRV54G, as shown in Figure 11.5. Point your browser to the IP address of the WRV54G. By default, this is 192.168.1.1. There is no username required and the default password is **admin**.

Figure 11.5 The Linksys WRV54G Initial Configuration Screen

Next, click the **Wireless** tab to display the Wireless Network Settings, as seen in Figure 11.6.

Figure 11.6 The Wireless Networks Settings Screen

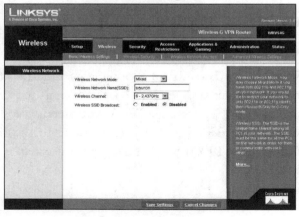

Then, choose the **Wireless Security** option to display the Wireless Security settings, as seen in Figure 11.7.

Figure 11.7 The Wireless Security Settings

The **Security Mode** drop-down box displays the four modes of security available on the WRV54G:

- WPA Pre-Shared Key
- WPA Radius
- RADIUS
- WEP

WPA RADIUS requires a RADIUS server, as shown in Figure 11.8. WPA Pre-Shared Key (Figure 11.9) allows you to enter a strong pre-shared key. All wireless clients must also be configured to use the WPA pre-shared key in order to authenticate to the wireless network.

Figure 11.8 The WPA RADIUS Settings

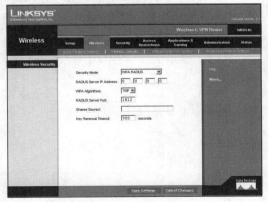

Figure 11.9 The WPA Pre-Shared Key Settings

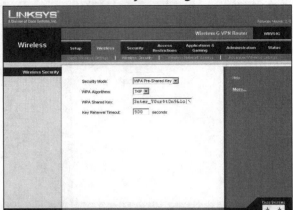

Finally, enter the RADIUS server IP address and shared secret, or the pre-shared key and choose **Save Settings** to enable WPA support.

Configuring Windows XP Wireless Clients for WPA

In order to take advantage of WPA, you must configure your wireless client. To allow Windows XP to work with WPA you must first install the Microsoft Update for Microsoft Windows XP (KB826942). This patch enables WPA compatibility in Windows XP. After installing KB826942, double-click the **Wireless Network Connection** icon on the toolbar. This opens the Wireless Network Connection Properties window, as seen in Figure 11.10. If you have a profile for your access point already set up, select it and click **Properties**. Otherwise, select Add under the Preferred Networks. The connection properties window will open.

Figure 11.10 The Connection Properties Window

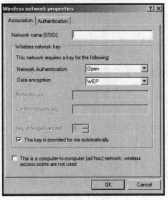

Next, enter the SSID for your access point in the **Network Name** textbox, as shown in Figure 11.11. Then, choose the type of encryption you configured your access point to use—WPA or WPA-PSK—and then the encryption standard: WEP, Temporal Key Integrity Protocol (TKIP), or Advanced Encryption Standard (AES). Finally, input the pre-shared key configured on your access point into the **Network key** and **Confirm network key** textboxes.

Figure 11.11 WPA Client Settings

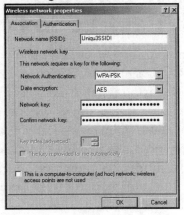

Your client setup is now complete and you can utilize your wireless network with WPA security.

Notes from the Underground...

WPA In Linux with Linuxant DriverLoader

In order to utilize WPA, you must have drivers for your wireless card that support it. Most 802.11g cards either have a WPA capable driver when they are purchased, or one can be downloaded. The problem is that these drivers are for Windows. Linux users have not been able to enjoy the benefits of WPA because there are very few card manufacturers that have released WPA drivers for Linux. Linuxant has offered a solution to this problem for many cards: DriverLoader.

DriverLoader allows you to use the Windows driver for cards based on the Atheros, Broadcom, Cisco, Intel Centrino, Prism, Realtek, and Texas Instruments chipsets in Linux. DriverLoader also supports WPA. It is available for a free trial from the Linuxant web site (www. linuxant.com/driverloader/) and a permanent license can be purchased for $19.95.

Implementing a Wireless Gateway with Reef Edge Dolphin

The first solution we'll examine is freeware. Free is always a good thing, especially in the IT industry! Reef Edge (www.reefedge.com) produces several commercial products for use in securing wireless networks, including Connect Manager. Dolphin is a somewhat scaled-down version of Connect Manager that still provides the same basic features, but is free. If you need to add an unlimited number of users, or add new user groups, you should investigate Connect Manager. The Dolphin FAQ (http://techzone.reefedge.com/dolphin/index/faq.page) provides more information on the limitations of Dolphin in comparison to Connect Manager.

Dolphin runs a hardened version of Linux and, once installed, acts almost the same as any other network appliance. The chief difference is that console and Telnet logins are not supported; all access is via the Secure Socket Layer (SSL) secured Web interface. An aging piece of Intel 586 hardware can be quickly and easily transformed into a secure wireless gateway, providing access control from the wireless network to the wired network, which we demonstrate in this chapter. Dolphin is a noncommercial product and not to be used in large implementations, but it does provide an ideal (and affordable) solution for Small Office/Home Office (SOHO) applications and serves as an excellent test bed for administrators who want to get their feet wet with wireless without opening their networks to security breaches. If you find that Dolphin is to your liking, you might want to consider contacting Reef Edge to purchase Connect Manager or an edge controller. An edge controller is a second, or satellite, machine that can be set up to support your wireless network. You will be able to easily move up to these solutions with the knowledge you gain by configuring and using Dolphin.

NOTE

SSL was developed in 1996 by Netscape Communications to enable secure transmission of information over the Internet between the client end (Web browsers) and Web servers. SSL operates between the application and transport layers and requires no actions on the part of the user. It is not a transparent protocol that can be used with any application layer protocol; instead, it works only with those application layer protocols for which it has been explicitly implemented. Common transport layer protocols that make use of SSL include: HyperText Transfer Protocol (HTTP), Simple Mail Transfer Protocol (SMTP), and Network News Transfer Protocol (NNTP).

SSL provides the three tenants of Public Key Infrastructure (PKI) security to users:

- **Authentication** Ensures that the message being received is from the individual claiming to send it.
- **Confidentiality** Ensures that the message cannot be read by anyone other than the intended recipient.
- **Integrity** Ensures that the message is authentic and has not been altered in any way since leaving the sender.

Dolphin provides some robust features that are typically found in very expensive hardware-based solutions, including secure authentication, IPSec security, and session roaming across subnets. Users authenticate to the Dolphin server over the WLAN using SSL-secured communications and then are granted access to the wired network. Dolphin supports two groups, users and guests, and you can control the access and quality of service of each group as follows:

- **Users** Trusted users who can use IPSec to secure their connection and access all resources.

- **Guests** Unknown users who are not allowed to use IPSec to secure their communications and have access control restrictions in place.

Finally, Dolphin supports encrypted wireless network usage through IPSec tunnels. Through the creation of IPSec VPN tunnels, users can pass data with a higher level of security (encryption) than WEP provides.

To begin working with Dolphin, you need to register for the Reef Edge TechZone at http://techzone.reefedge.com. Once this is done, you will be able to download the CD-ROM ISO image and bootable diskette image files from the Reef Edge download page. The server that you are using for Dolphin must meet the following minimum specifications:

- Pentium CPU (586) or later

- 64MB RAM

- 64MB IDE hard drive as the first boot IDE device

- IDE CD-ROM

- Diskette drive if the CD-ROM drive being used is not El Torrito compliant (see www.area51partners.com/files/eltorito.pdf for more information on this specification).

- Two Peripheral Component Interconnect (PCI) network adapters from the following list of compatible network adapters:

  - 3Com 3c59x family (not 3c905x)

  - National Semiconductor 8390 family

  - Intel EtherExpress 100

  - NE2000/pci

  - PCNet32

  - Tulip family

The Dolphin implementation is depicted in Figure 11.12.

Figure 11.12 Dolphin Provides Gateway Services for the Wireless Network

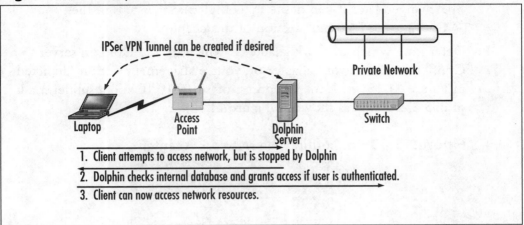

1. Client attempts to access network, but is stopped by Dolphin
2. Dolphin checks internal database and grants access if user is authenticated.
3. Client can now access network resources.

Installing Dolphin

Once you've gathered all the required items, you can begin installing Dolphin on your server. To do so, perform these steps:

1. Create the CD-ROM from the ISO image. If required, create the bootable diskette from the floppy disk image.

2. Connect a keyboard, mouse, and monitor to the Dolphin server.

3. Power on the Dolphin server and place the Dolphin CD-ROM in the CD-ROM drive. If your computer is not capable of booting directly from the CD, you will also need to use the boot diskette.

4. Select OK when prompted to start the installation.

5. Accept the EULA when prompted.

6. Acknowledge, when prompted, that installing Dolphin will erase the contents of the first physical disk.

7. Restart the Dolphin server as prompted after the installation has been completed. After the restart, you will see a long series of dots followed by this message:

```
System Ready.   IP address:   192.168.0.1/255.255.255.0.
```

This value represents the wired side of the Dolphin server and can be changed later if you desire by completing the steps in the "Configuring Dolphin" section of this chapter.

8. Determine which network adapter is which on the Dolphin server. Configure the network adapter on your management station (depicted in Figure 11.15) with the IP address of 10.10.10.10 and a subnet mask of 255.255.255.0, as shown in Figure 11.13.

Figure 11.13 Configuring the Network Adapter

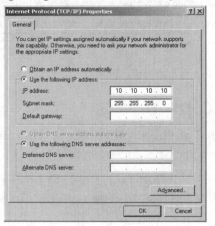

9. Connect directly using a crossover cable between your management station and one of the network adapters on the Dolphin server, ping the Dolphin server with an IP address of 10.10.10.1. If you receive an echo reply, as shown in Figure 11.14, you have located the wireless side of the Dolphin server. If you don't get an echo reply, make the connection to the other network adapter on the Dolphin server. Attempt to ping the other network adapter on the Dolphin server with the IP address of 10.10.10.1 to verify connectivity. The wired side of the Dolphin server initially has the IP address of 192.168.0.1 with a subnet mask of 255.255.255.0, as mentioned in Step 7. You can, however, change the IP addresses and subnet masks of both the wireless and wired side of the Dolphin server if you so desire, as discussed in the next section, "Configuring Dolphin."

Figure 11.14 Finding the Wireless Side of the Dolphin Server

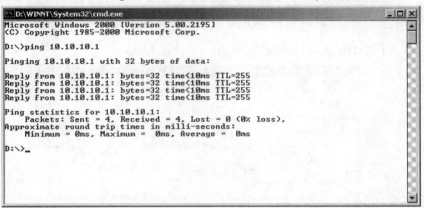

10. Configure your management station with an IP address in the 192.168.0.x range, such as 192.168.0.180, and connect it to the wired side (192.168.0.1) of the Dolphin server, preferably through a switch, but you can use a crossover cable to make a direct connection.

11. Configure your wireless client for Dynamic Host Configuration Protocol (DHCP) so that it can receive an IP address and DNS server information from the Dolphin server. (You can change the DHCP values passed out later in this procedure.)

12. Connect the AP to the wireless side of the Dolphin server (10.10.10.1). Ensure that the AP and the wireless side of the Dolphin server are configured correctly, with IP addresses on the same subnet. You should now have an arrangement like the one shown in Figure 11.15.

Figure 11.15 Making the Dolphin Connections

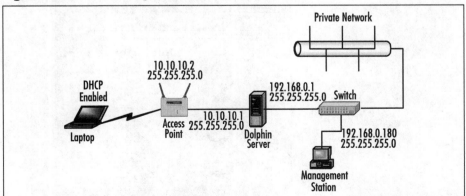

13. Force the wireless client to renew its DHCP lease and check to see that it looks something like the one shown in Figure 11.16.

Figure 11.16 Verifying the DHCP Lease

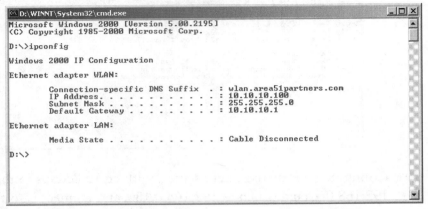

14. Ping the wireless side of the Dolphin server, from the wireless client, at 10.10.10.1 to verify connectivity.

15. Ping the wireless side of the Dolphin server again, from the wireless client, using the DNS name mobile.domain.

16. Attempt to access resources on the wired network from the wireless client. Acknowledge the SSL connection if prompted to do so (although you won't actually see any SSL-secured pages until you attempt to log in at the next step). If you see the Web page in Figure 11.17, congratulate yourself—your Dolphin installation is operating properly!

Figure 11.17 Connecting to the Dolphin Server

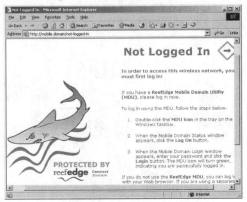

17. Log in from the page shown in Figure 11.18 using the username temp and the password temp. If login is successful, you will see the page shown in Figure 11.19. Notice that the IPSec key shown at the bottom of the page is actually your shared key that you would use to create IPSec connections.

Figure 11.18 Logging into the Dolphin Web Page

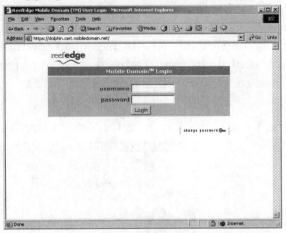

Figure 11.19 Login Is Successful

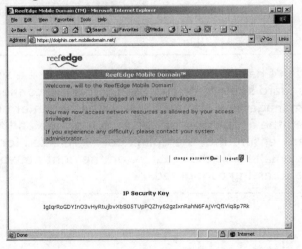

> **NOTE**
>
> Although these are the default credentials to enter your Dolphin system, it is critical that you change them once you are done with the initial configuration. After you have created your first user account, Dolphin will delete the temp account for you automatically to ensure that no one compromises the server or gains unauthorized network access.

18. Log in to the Dolphin Web management interface by entering **https://mobile.domain/admin** into your browser. You will be prompted to log in, as shown in Figure 11.20.

Figure 11.20 Logging In to the Administrative Interface

> **NOTE**
>
> If you don't have a crossover cable, you can use a switch or hub and two standard straight-through cables. Simply connect the Dolphin server to the management station through the switch or hub. Ensure that you are using the uplink port on the switch or hub and, if required by your hardware, ensure that the uplink port is selected for uplink via regular use. Also make sure that you are on the right network segment with correct IP addressing configured.

Configuring Dolphin

Your Dolphin server is now installed and operable on your wireless network. You now need to perform some configuration and management tasks before your server is ready to be placed into production. You need to add users to the Dolphin database who will be allowed to gain access to the wireless network. (Dolphin does not support RADIUS and thus must use a local user database.) In addition, you might want to change the IP addresses and subnets assigned to the Dolphin server network adapters. The following steps walk you through the process of configuring some of these options:

1. Log in to the Dolphin server by completing Steps 17–18 of the previous procedure.

2. Click the **Wired LAN** link from the menu on the left side of the window. This provides you with the capability to change the wired-side properties, as shown in Figure 11.21. In most cases, you'll need to change the wired-side IP address from the default configuration of 192.168.0.1 because this is typically reserved for use by the default gateway. Be sure to enter the default gateway and DNS server IP addresses as well as to enable wireless network clients to access network resources. After making your changes, click the **Save** button. (Note that you will have to restart the Dolphin server to commit the changes to the running configuration. You can, however, make all your changes and then restart the server.)

Figure 11.21 Changing the Wired-Side Network Properties

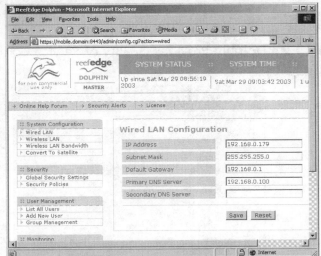

3. Click the **Wireless LAN** link to configure the wireless-side properties, as shown in Figure 11.22. You can change all these properties as you see fit. By default, the Dolphin server is configured with the domain name reefedge.com and DHCP address range of 10.10.10.10–10.10.10.253. After making your changes, click the **Save** button. If you want to configure the quality of service that wireless clients receive, click the **Wireless LAN Bandwidth** link to configure your values, as shown in Figure 11.23. After making your changes, click the **Save** button.

Figure 11.22 Changing the Wireless-Side Network Properties

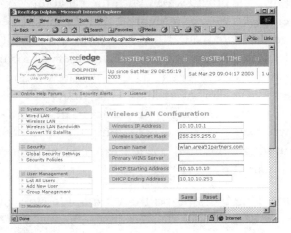

Figure 11.23 Dolphin Provides Quality of Service Controls for Wireless Clients

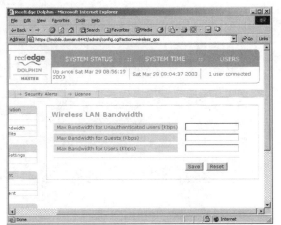

4. Create a list of authorized users for Dolphin—that is, a listing of users who can authenticate to Dolphin and then be granted wireless network access. Click the **Add New User** link to open the User Management page shown in Figure 11.24. Note that you can only choose between the users group and the guests group—Dolphin does not support creating custom groups (a limitation due to its freeware status). After supplying the required information, click **Save**. After creating your first Dolphin user, the "temp" account will be deleted for security reasons. If you want to configure additional security policies, click the **Security Policies** link to open the Security Policies For User Groups page, shown in Figure 11.25. This page allows you to configure the equivalent of a firewall rule set for your Dolphin server.

Figure 11.24 Creating Users for the Dolphin Database

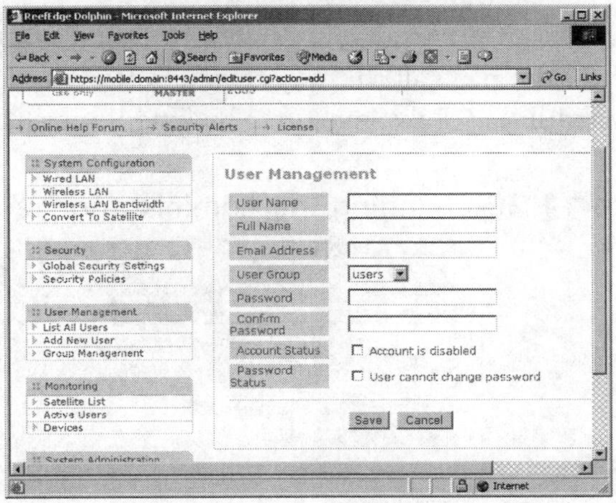

Figure 11.25 Creating or Modifying Security Policies

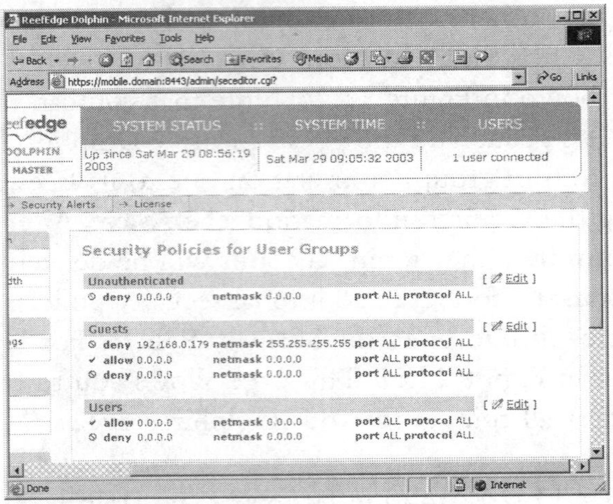

5. Change the administrative password to restart your Dolphin server. To do this, scroll the page all the way to the bottom and click the **Admin Password** link. Click **Save** after making your change (see Figure 11.26).

Figure 11.26 Changing the Administrator Password

6. Restart your Dolphin server. After Dolphin has completed loading, you will see the familiar series of dots, this time followed by the new wired-side IP address that you have configured.

Improving the User Experience

Should you not want authorized users to need to use the Web interface to Dolphin to authenticate, you can equip them with a small utility that is available from Reef Edge, and can be used to perform regular and IPSec-secured logins/logouts. The process to install and use this utility is outlined here:

1. Download the **Active TCL** package from Active State at www.actives-tate.com/Products/Download/Download.plex?id=ActiveTCL and install it onto your wireless client computer.

2. Download the **TCL TLS 1.4** package from Reef Edge's download page. Create a folder called **tls1.4** in the lib directory of the Active TCL installation path and extract the contents of the TLS 1.4 archive into this folder.

3. Download the **dolphin_status.tcl** file, also located at the Reef Edge download page.

4. Place the dolphin_status.tcl file in a convenient location on the client computer. Once Active TCL has been installed, the dolphin_status.tcl file will act as an executable and can be double-clicked to open.

5. Execute the **dolphin_status.tcl** file to get the login prompt shown in Figure 11.27. You have the option of creating an IPSec tunnel at this time as well. The tcl file will create a configuration file named *dolphin* in the same directory it is located in.

Figure 11.27 Using the Dolphin_status.tcl File to Log In

Tools and Traps...

Using Enterprise Wireless Gateways

Don't think of Dolphin as a full-featured Enterprise Wireless Gateway (EWG). However, you should consider it a wireless gateway. For a full-featured EWG, you might want to consider one of the more capable and robust (and more expensive) solutions offered from one of the following vendors:

- **Bluesocket** www.bluesocket.com
- **Columbitech** www.columbitech.com
- **Reef Edge** www.reefedge.com
- **Sputnik** www.sputnik.com
- **Vernier Networks** www.verniernetworks.com
- **Viator Networks** www.viatornetworks.com

These solutions offer the same features as Dolphin—authentication and VPN support—but they also provide many other options, such as RADIUS server support, hot failover support, and multiple protocol support (such as WAP, 3G, and 802.11). The EWG market is still in a great deal of flux as vendors try to refine their products. That does not mean, however, that you cannot create very secure solutions using today's technology. A word of caution, though: You should expect to find bugs and other errors with most of these solutions because the technology is still so new. Caveat emptor.

Dolphin Review

As you've seen in this chapter, the Dolphin product provides a very inexpensive solution for small wireless environments. It is very lightweight and has minimal hardware requirements; you most likely have an old PC stuffed in a storage room that could be turned into a dedicated wireless gateway by installing the Dolphin application on it.

On the up side, Dolphin is easy to use and configure, is inexpensive, and provides a relatively good amount of security for smaller organizations. In addition,

Dolphin supports the creation of IPSec-secured VPN tunnels between the wireless clients and the Dolphin server. On the down side, Dolphin is limited in the number of users it can support as well as the number of groups you can create to classify users. Dolphin also does not provide for the use of an external RADIUS server. These limitations, however, are clearly stated by Reef Edge because Dolphin is not intended for commercial usage. If you have a small home or office wireless network that needs to be secured by an access-granting device, Dolphin might be an ideal choice for you.

Now that we've spent some time looking at the freeware Dolphin product, let's step up the discussion and examine some more robust (and more costly) solutions that you might implement to secure a larger wireless network necessitating control over user access in a larger enterprise environment.

Implementing a VPN on a Linksys WRV54G VPN Broadband Router

The Linksys WRV54G is an access point/router combination that Linksys designed for the small office, or home user that desires a higher level of security than WEP or WPA can provide. The WRV54G offers all of the security features of other access points, but also provides the capability of setting up an IPSec VPN tunnel. A VPN tunnel allows two points to establish an encrypted session using a selected protocol. Other protocols can then be transmitted through this tunnel. A basic example of this is a Secure Shell (SSH) tunnel. A firewall can be configured to allow only SSH traffic (port 22) inbound. The client can then tunnel other traffic, such as HTTP (port 80) through the established SSH tunnel. This both encrypts the HTTP traffic, and removes the requirement to allow port 80 traffic through the firewall. Additionally, because some form of authentication (passphrase, key exchange, or both) is required to establish the initial SSH tunnel, additional user level access controls are in place.

This section describes the process of setting up an IPSec tunnel to utilize the VPN features on the WRV54G. First, we discuss the steps that must be taken on Windows 2000 or XP clients to prepare for VPN access. Then, the configuration steps that are required on the WRV54G are detailed.

Preparing Windows 2000 or XP Computers for Use with the WRV54G

There are four steps that you need to take to configure your Windows 2000 or XP computer to establish a VPN tunnel with the WRV54G.

1. Create an IPSec policy.

2. Build two filter lists.

3. Establish the tunnel rules.

4. Assign the IPSec policy to the computer.

Creating an IPSec Policy

Click **Start | Run** and type **secpol.msc** in the **Open** textbox to open the Local Security Settings screen, as seen in Figure 11.28.

Figure 11.28 Local Security Settings

Right-click **IP Security Policies on Local Computer** and select **Create IP Security Policy** to open the IP Security Policy Wizard. Click **Next** on the IP Security Policy Wizard window.

Enter a name for your security policy in the **Name** textbox (as shown in Figure 11.29) and click **Next**.

Figure 11.29 Naming the Local Security Policy

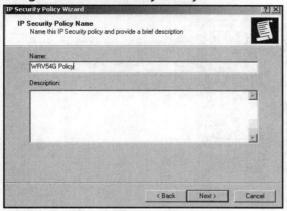

Remove the checkbox next to **Activate the default response rule,** as shown in Figure 11.30, and click **Next**.

Figure 11.30 Deactivate the Default Response Rule

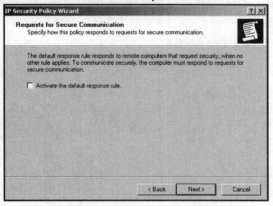

Finally, make sure that the **Edit properties** checkbox is selected, as shown in Figure 11.31, and click **Finish**.

Figure 11.31 Completing the Local Policy Creation

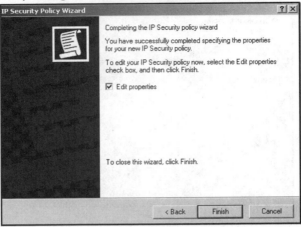

Building Filter Lists

Selecting the Edit properties checkbox before finishing the IP Security Policy Wizard opens the Properties window for your new security policy (Figure 11.32).

Figure 11.32 The Policy Properties

Deselect the **Use Add Wizard** checkbox and click **Add** to open the New Rule Properties window. By default, this window opens on the IP Filter List tab. Click **Add** again to open the **IP Filter List** window. Enter a name for the filter, as shown in Figure 11.33. Deselect the **Use Add Wizard** checkbox and click **Add**.

Figure 11.33 The IP Filter List Window

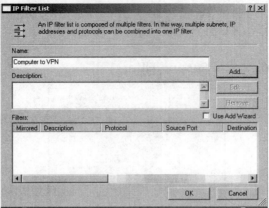

The Filter Properties window opens on the Addressing tab. Choose **My IP Address** in the Source Address field and **A specific IP Subnet** in the Destination Address field. In the **IP Address** field enter **192.168.1.0**. This represents all addresses in the range 192.168.1.1–192.168.1.255. If you are using a different range, make sure to adjust this accordingly. Enter the Subnet Mask for your network in the **Subnet Mask** field (see Figure 11.34). By default, this is 255.255.255.0. Click the **OK** button to close this window.

Figure 11.34 The IP Filter Settings

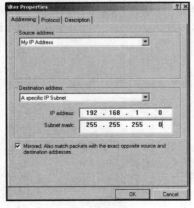

Next, click **OK** in Windows XP or **Close** in Windows 2000. This filter is used for communication from your computer to the router.

You will then need to create a filter for communication from the router to your computer. In the **New Rule Properties** window, highlight the rule you just created, as shown in Figure 11.35, and click **Add**.

Figure 11.35 Creating the Second Filter

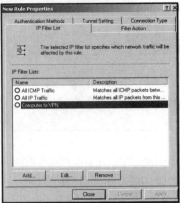

This opens the **IP Filter List** window. Enter a name for the new filter in the **Name** textbox and click **Add**. On the Addressing tab, choose **A specific IP Subnet** in the **Source Address** field. In the **IP Address** field, enter **192.168.1.0**. This represents all addresses in the range 192.168.1.1–192.168.1.255. If you are using a different range, you will need to adjust this accordingly. Enter the subnet mask for your network in the **Subnet Mask** field. By default, this is 255.255.255.0. Choose **My IP Address** in the **Destination Address** field (Figure 11.36).

Figure 11.36 The Filter Properties Window

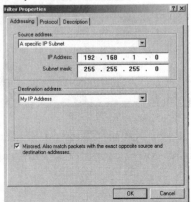

Click the **OK** button to close this window. Next, click **OK** in Windows XP or **Close** in Windows 2000. This filter is used for communication from the router to your computer.

Establishing the Tunnel Rules

The rules that are employed by the tunnels must be set up in order to properly filter traffic through the VPN tunnel. First, select the tunnel you created for communication from your computer to the router and then click the **Filter Action** tab. Next, select the **Require Security** radio button and click **Edit** to open the Require Security Properties window, as shown in Figure 11.37.

Figure 11.37 The Require Security Properties Window

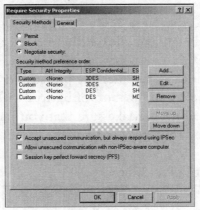

Ensure that the **Negotiate security** radio button is selected. Then, deselect **Accept unsecured communication, but always respond using IPSec** and select **Session key perfect forward security (PFS),** as shown in Figure 11.38

Figure 11.38 The Security Methods Options

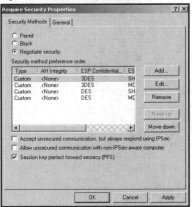

Click **OK** to return to the **New Rule Properties** window. Select the **Authentication Methods** tab and click **Edit** to open the **Edit Authentication Method Properties** window. Choose the **Use this string (preshared key)** radio button and enter the pre-shared key in the textbox (Figure 11.39). This can be a combination of up to 24 letters and numbers, but special characters are not allowed. Make sure that you remember this key as it will be used later when the router is configured.

Figure 11.39 Entering the Pre-Shared Key

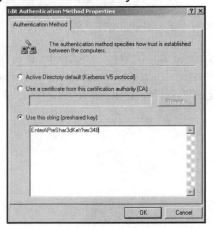

Next, click the **OK** button in Windows XP or the **Close** button in Windows 2000.

Select the **Tunnel Setting** tab on the New Rule Properties window. Select **The tunnel endpoint is specified by this IP address** and enter the external IP address of the WRV54G, as shown in Figure 11.40. This is the IP address your router uses to communicate with the Internet.

Figure 11.40 The Tunnel Setting Tab

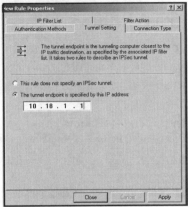

Next, click the **Connection Type** tab (as shown in Figure 11.41). Select **All network connections** if you want this rule to apply to both Internet and local area network (LAN) connections. Choose **Local area network (LAN)** if you want this tunnel to apply only to connections made from the local network. Choose **Remote access** if you want this rule to apply only to connections made from the Internet.

Figure 11.41 Select the Connection Type

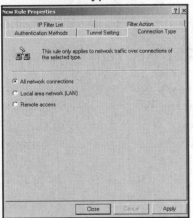

After you have selected the type of network connections that the rule applies to, click **Close**.

Another filter rule must be created to allow communication from the router to your computer. To create this rule, repeat the steps outline in this section, but enter the IP address of your computer as the Tunnel Endpoint instead of the IP address of the router.

Assigning the Security Policy

Finally, you must assign your new security policy to the local computer. In the **Local Security Settings** window, right-click the new policy that you have just created and select **Assign**, as shown in Figure 11.42.

Figure 11.42 Assigning the Security Policy

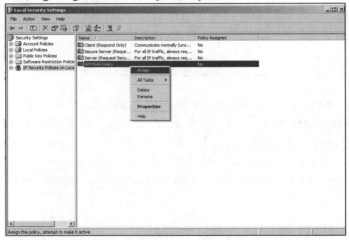

Your computer is now configured to communicate over a VPN tunnel.

Enabling the VPN on the Linksys WRV54G

Now that your computer is configured to communicate over an IPSec VPN tunnel, you must configure the WRV54G to communicate with your computer. Using your web browser, type the IP Address of the WRV54G into your address bar. This is 192.168.1.1, by default. You will be prompted for your username and password.

From the setup screen, select **Security | VPN** to display the VPN settings, as seen in Figure 11.43.

Figure 11.43 The WRV54G VPN Settings

Select the **Enabled** radio button for VPN Tunnel. Choose a name for this tunnel and enter it in the **Tunnel Name** textbox. Next, enter the IP address and netmask of the local network in the **IP Address** and **Mask** fields for the Local Secure Group. Use 192.168.1.0 to allow all IP addresses between 192.168.1.1–192.168.1.255.

Enter the IP address and netmask of the computer you just configured in the **IP Address** and **Mask** fields for the Remote Secure Group. Next, choose **3DES** from the **Encryption** drop-down box. This requires the use of Triple Data Encryption Standard encryption. Choose **SHA1** from the **Authentication** drop-down box.

Choose **Auto(IKE)** as the **Key Exchange Method** and select the **Enabled** radio button for **PFS**. This enables the use of Internet Key Exchange (IKE) and Perfect Forward Secrecy (PFS).

Finally, select the radio button next to **Pre-Shared Key** and enter the same pre-shared key you entered on your computer while setting it up.

Once you have entered these settings, your VPN setup screen should look similar to Figure 11.44.

Figure 11.44 The Completed VPN Settings

Click **Save Settings** to save your settings and establish a VPN tunnel between the WRV54G and your computer.

Implementing RADIUS with Cisco LEAP

The use of RADIUS servers to authenticate network users is a longstanding practice. Using RADIUS server dynamic per-user, per-session WEP keys combined with IV randomization is a fairly new practice. Another new addition is Cisco's proprietary offering (now being used by many third-party vendors), Lightweight Extensible Authentication Protocol (LEAP).

LEAP is one of approximately 30 different variations of the Extensible Authentication Protocol (EAP). Other variants include Extensible Authentication Protocol-Message Digest Algorithm 5 (EAP-MD5), Extensible Authentication Protocol-Transport Layer Security (EAP-TLS), Extensible Authentication Protocol-Tunneled TLS (EAP-TTLS), and Protected Extensible Authentication Protocol (PEAP). EAP allows other security products (such as LEAP) to be used to provide additional security to Point-to-Point Protocol (PPP) links through the use of special Application Programming Interfaces (APIs) that are built into operating systems and, in the case of the Cisco Aironet hardware, hardware device firmware.

LEAP (also known as EAP-Cisco Wireless) uses dynamically generated WEP keys, 802.1x port access controls, and mutual authentication to overcome the problems inherent in WEP. 802.1x is an access control protocol that operates at the port level between any authentication method (LEAP in this case) and the rest of the network. 802.1x does not provide authentication to users; rather, it translates messages from the selected authentication method into the correct frame format being used on the network. In the case of our example, the correct frame format is 802.11, but 802.1x can also be used on 802.3 (Ethernet) and 802.5 (Token Ring) networks, to name a few. When you use 802.1x, the choice of the authentication method and key management method are controlled by the specific EAP authentication being used (LEAP in this case).

> **NOTE**
>
> RADIUS is defined by Requests for Comments (RFC) 2865. The behavior of RADIUS with EAP authentication is defined in RFC 2869. RFC can be searched and viewed online at www.rfc-editor.org. 802.1x is defined by the IEEE in the document located at http://standards.ieee.org/getieee802/download/802.1X-2001.pdf.

LEAP creates a per-user, per-session dynamic WEP key that is tied to the network logon, thereby addressing the limitations of static WEP keys. Since authentication is performed against a back-end RADIUS database, administrative overhead is minimal after initial installation and configuration.

LEAP Features

Through the use of dynamically generated WEP keys, LEAP enhances the basic security of WEP. This feature significantly decreases the predictability of the WEP key through the use of a WEP key-cracking utility by another user. In addition, the WEP keys that are generated can be tied to the specific user session and, if desired, to the network login as well. Through the use of Cisco (or other third-party components that support LEAP) hardware from end to end, you can provide a robust and scalable security solution that silently increases network security not only by authenticating users but also by encrypting wireless network traffic without the use of a VPN tunnel. (You can, however, opt to add the additional network overhead and implement a VPN tunnel as well to further secure the communications.)

Cisco LEAP provides the following security enhancements:

- **Mutual authentication** Mutual authentication is performed between the client and the RADIUS server, as well as between the AP and the

RADIUS server. By using mutual authentication between the components involved, you prevent the introduction of both rogue APs and RADIUS servers. Furthermore, you provide a solid authentication method to control whom can and cannot gain access to the wireless network segment (and thus the wired network behind it). All communications carried out between the AP and the RADIUS server are done using a secure channel, further reducing any possibility of eavesdropping or spoofing.

- **Secure-key derivation** A preconfigured shared-secret secure key is used to construct responses to mutual authentication challenges. It is put through an irreversible one-way hash that makes recovery or replay impossible and is useful for one time only at the start of the authentication process.

- **Dynamic WEP keys** Dynamic per-user, per-session, WEP keys are created to easily allow administrators to quickly move away from statically configured WEP keys, thus significantly increasing security. The single largest security vulnerability of a properly secured wireless network (using standard 802.11b security measures) is the usage of static WEP keys that are subject to discovery through special software. In addition, maintaining static WEP keys in an enterprise environment is an extremely time-consuming and error-prone process. In using LEAP, the session-specific WEP keys that are created are unique to that specific user and are not used by any other user. In addition, the broadcast WEP key (which is statically configured in the AP) is encrypted using the session key before being delivered to the client. Since each session key is unique to the user and can be tied to a network login, LEAP also completely eliminates common vulnerabilities due to lost or stolen network adapters and devices.

- **Reauthentication policies** Policies can be set that force users to reauthenticate more often to the RADIUS server and thus receive fresh session keys. This can further reduce the window for network attacks as the WEP keys are rotated even more frequently.

- **Initialization vector changes** The IV is incremented on a per-packet basis, so hackers cannot find a predetermined, predictable sequence to exploit. The capability to change the IV with every packet, combined with the dynamic keying and reauthentication, greatly increases security and makes it that much more difficult for an attacker to gain access to your wireless network.

Building a LEAP Solution

To put together a LEAP with RADIUS solution, you need the following components:

- A Cisco Aironet AP that supports LEAP. Currently, this includes the 350, 1100, and 1200 models. The 350 is the oldest of the bunch and offers the least amount of configurability. The 1100 is the newest and runs IOS, offering both Command Line Interface (CLI)- and Graphical User Interface (GUI)-based management and configuration.

- A Cisco Aironet 350 network adapter.

- The most up-to-date network adapter driver, firmware, and Aironet Client Utility (ACU). You can download this driver using the Aironet Wireless Software Selector on the Cisco Web site at www.cisco.com/pcgi-bin/Software/WLAN/wlplanner.cgi.

- A RADIUS server application that supports LEAP. For our purposes, we use Funk Software's (www.funk.com) Steel Belted Radius/Enterprise Edition.

As shown in Chapter 4, our LEAP solution will look (basically) like the diagram shown in Figure 11.45.

Figure 11.45 The Cisco LEAP and RADIUS Solution

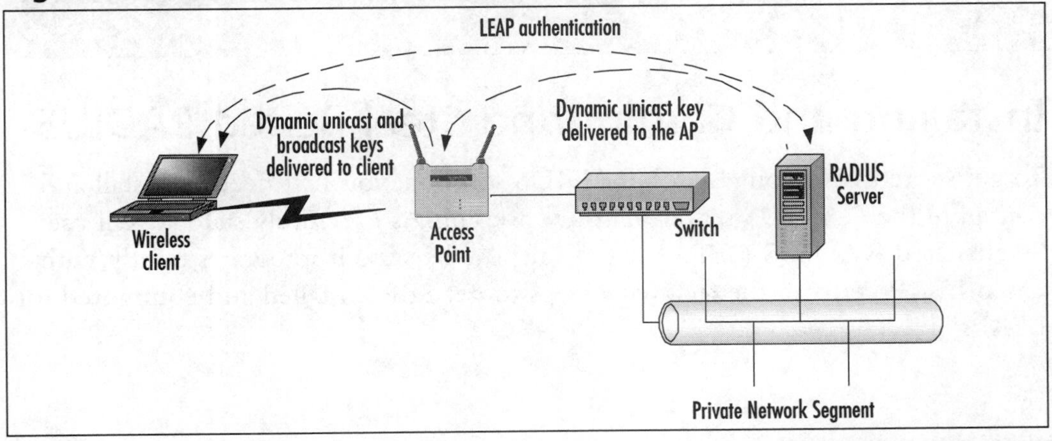

Tools and Traps...

Nothing in Life Is Perfect...

LEAP has two potential weaknesses that you need to be aware of.

The first weakness is that the EAP RADIUS packet transmitted between the AP and the RADIUS server is sent in cleartext. This packet contains the shared secret used to perform mutual authentication between these two devices. The reality of this weakness, however, is that you can mitigate its potential effects by having good network authentication policies for your wired network. Thus, an attacker would have to plug directly into a switch sitting between the AP and the RADIUS server and use a special network sniffer capable of sniffing over a switched network, such as dsniff.

The second weakness of LEAP is that the username is transmitted in cleartext between the wireless client and the AP. This opens the door to the possibility of a dictionary attack. Note that the password is encrypted using MS-CHAPv1. Your defense against a dictionary attack on your LEAP user's passwords is to implement a solid login policy for your network. For example, if you are using Active Directory and performing network authentication against it using domain user accounts, you could require strong passwords through the Password Policy options and account lockout through the Account Lockout Policy options.

For more information on configuring Active Directory for enhanced security, see *MCSE/MCSA Implementing and Administering Security in a Windows 2000 Network: Study Guide and DVD Training System* (Exam 70-214) by Will Schmied (Syngress Publishing 2003, ISBN 1931836841).

Installing and Configuring Steel Belted RADIUS

To get started with your LEAP/RADIUS solution, you first need to install and configure the RADIUS server of your choosing. As previously stated, we'll use Steel Belted RADIUS (SBR) for this purpose because it integrates tightly with Cisco LEAP. Perform the following steps to get SBR installed and configured for LEAP:

1. Download the SBR installation package from the Funk Web site (www.funk.com). You can download it for a 30-day trial if you are not ready to purchase it.

2. Provide your name, your organization's name, and your product key, as shown in Figure 11.46. Note that you can opt to exercise the 30-day trial if you desire. Click **Next** to continue.

Figure 11.46 SBR Has a "Try It Before You Buy It" Feature

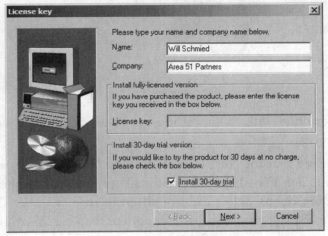

3. Select the **SBR Enterprise Edition** option on the next page, and click **Next** to continue.

4. Click **Yes** to accept the EULA.

5. Click **Next** to start the setup routine.

6. Select your installation location. Note that you will want to install both the Radius Admin Program and the Radius Server, shown in Figure 11.47. Click **Next** to continue.

Figure 11.47 Choosing the Installation Options and Location

7. Continue with the installation routine to complete the installation process.

8. Ensure that the **Yes, launch Radius Administrator** option is selected, and click **Finish**. Once the installation has completed, the Admin application opens. Select the **Local** option and click the **Connect** button. If the display you see is something like that shown in Figure 11.48, you've successfully installed SBR.

Figure 11.48 Launching the Admin Application

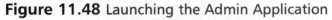

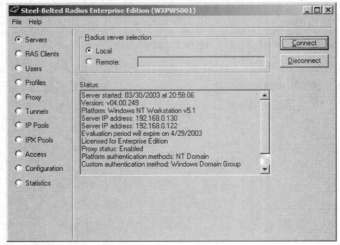

9. Close the **SBR Admin** application to begin the configuration of SBR for LEAP.

10. Navigate to the SBR installation directory and open the **Service** folder. Locate and open the **eap.ini** file for editing. For this example, we use native RADIUS authentication, meaning that users will be authenticating directly against the SBR RADIUS database. (You can, optionally, configure SBR for Windows domain authentication, as discussed later in this chapter.) Under the **[Native-User]** heading, remove the semicolon from the first three items to enable LEAP. Save and close the **eap.ini** file (see Figure 11.49).

Figure 11.49 Configuring SBR for LEAP

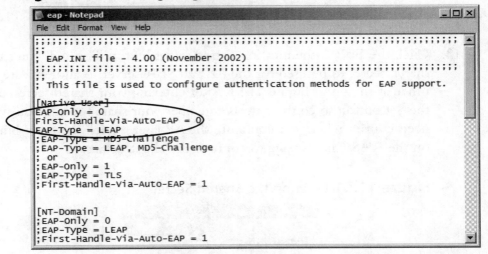

11. Restart the Steel Belted Radius service to force it to reload the eap.ini file from the **Services** console located in the **Administrative Tools** folder. Launch the **SBR Admin** application and connect to the local server.

12. Click the **RAS Clients** option to configure SBR for the Cisco Access Point, as shown in Figure 11.50. Note that the AP is the RAS client since it is performing authentication on behalf of the wireless network client. Click the **Add** button to create a new client, and click **OK** to confirm it. Next, specify the client IP address (the IP address assigned to the AP) and the type of client (Cisco Aironet Access Point).

Figure 11.50 Configuring the RAS Client Properties

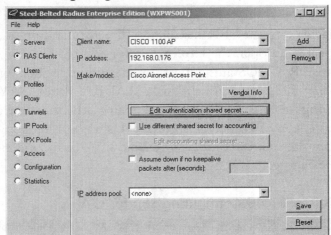

13. Click the **Edit** authentication shared secret button. This will enter the shared secret to be used for the AP and SBR server to authenticate each other, as shown in Figure 11.51. After entering your shared secret, click the Set button to confirm it. (Remember your shared secret; you will need it again when you configure the AP later.) Click the **Save** button on the RAS Clients page to confirm the client details.

Figure 11.51 Entering the Shared Secret

14. Click the **Users** option to create native users (users internal to the SBR server), as shown in Figure 11.52. Click the **Add** button to add a new username. After entering the username, click **OK** to confirm it.

Figure 11.52 Creating Native Users

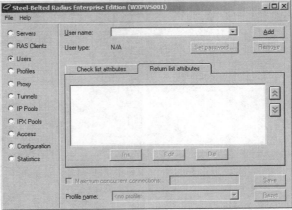

15. Click the **Set password** button to open the Enter User Password dialog box shown in Figure 11.53. You need to leave the **Allow PAP or CHAP** option selected because LEAP actually makes use of an MS-CHAPv1 derivative. After setting the password, click the Set button to confirm it. Click the Save button on the Users page to confirm the user.

Figure 11.53 Entering the User Password

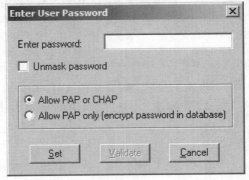

16. Click the **Configuration** option to set the authentication methods (and their order) to be used, as shown in Figure 11.54. Since we are using native users, ensure that the **Native User** option is placed first in the list. Click **Save** to confirm the change if required.

Figure 11.54 Selecting the Authentication Methods

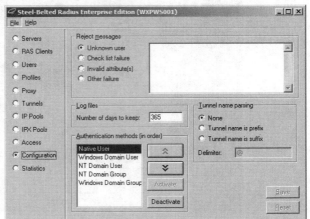

Configuring LEAP

Once you've gotten your RADIUS server installed and configured, the hard work is behind you. All that is left now is to configure LEAP on the AP and client network adapter. To configure LEAP on the AP, perform the following steps. (Note that the exact screen will vary among the 350, 1100, and 1200 APs—the end configuration is the same, however. For this discussion, a Cisco Aironet 1100 AP is used with all configurations performed via the Web interface instead of the CLI.)

1. Log in to your AP via the Web interface.

2. Configure your network SSID and enable EAP authentication, as shown in Figure 11.55. Save your settings to the AP after configuring them.

Figure 11.55 Enabling EAP Authentication

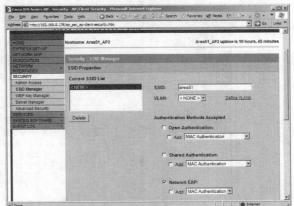

3. Enter a 128-bit broadcast WEP key, as shown in Figure 11.56. Save your settings to the AP after configuring them.

Figure 11.56 Entering the Broadcast WEP Key

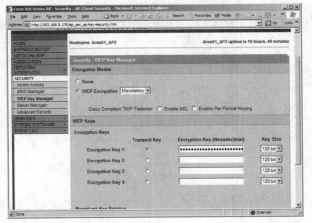

4. Configure your RADIUS server IP address and shared-secret key information, as shown in Figure 11.57. In addition, you need to ensure that the **EAP Authentication** option is selected. Save your settings to the AP after configuring them. If you want to enable a reauthentication policy, you can do so from the Advanced Security – EAP Authentication page shown in Figure 11.58. The default option is Disable Reauthentication. Save your settings to the AP after configuring them.

Figure 11.57 Configuring the RADIUS Server Information

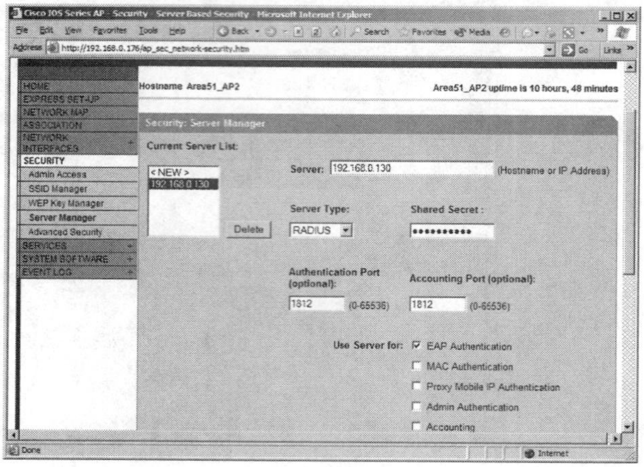

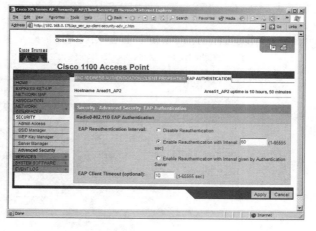

Figure 11.58 Configuring Reauthentication

To enable the wireless client for LEAP, first ensure that it is using the most recent firmware and drivers. Once you've got the most up-to-date files, proceed as follows to get the client configured and authenticated using LEAP:

1. Launch the **Cisco Aironet Client Utility (ACU)**, shown in Figure 11.59. Notice that the ACU reports that the network adapter is not associated with the AP. This is normal at this point because the AP is configured to require LEAP authentication.

Figure 11.59 Using the Cisco ACU

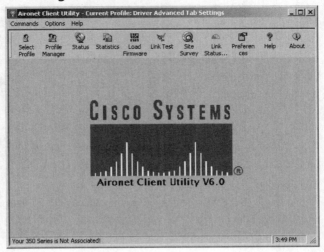

2. Click the **Profile Manager** button to create a new profile, as shown in Figure 11.60. Click the **Add** button to enter the new profile name, and then click the **OK** button to begin configuring the profile.

Figure 11.60 Creating a New Profile

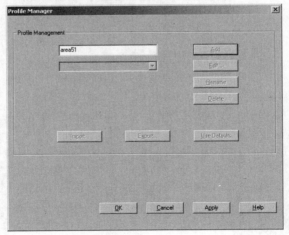

3. Enter the correct SSID for your network (as previously configured for the AP) on the **System Parameters** tab, shown in Figure 11.61.

Figure 11.61 Configuring the SSID for the Profile

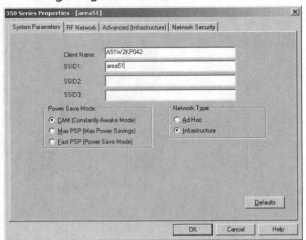

4. Switch to the **Network Security** tab and select **LEAP** from the drop-down list, as shown in Figure 11.62. After selecting LEAP, click the **Configure** button.

Figure 11.62 Configuring the Authentication Method

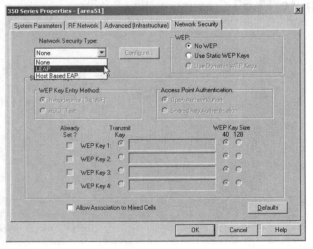

5. Ensure that the **Use Temporary User Name and Password** option is selected with the **Automatically Prompt for LEAP User Name and Password** suboption on the **LEAP Settings** page. Remove the check mark from the **Include Windows Logon Domain with User**

Name option because we are using Native mode authentication in this example. Click **OK** after making your configuration (see Figure 11.63).

Figure 11.63 Configuring LEAP Options

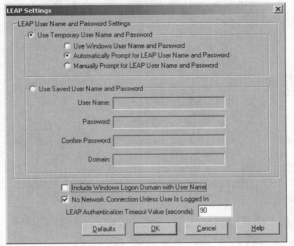

6. Click **OK** twice more and you will be prompted with the LEAP login dialog box shown in Figure 11.64. Enter your details and click **OK**. If you look at the SBR Admin application on the Statistics page, you can see successful and failed authentications. Notice that the statistics shown in Figure 11.65 represent clients that are being forced to reauthenticate to the RADIUS server fairly often.

Figure 11.64 Logging into the Wireless Network Using LEAP

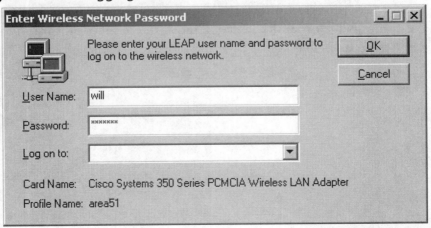

Figure 11.65 Monitoring the RADIUS Server Statistics

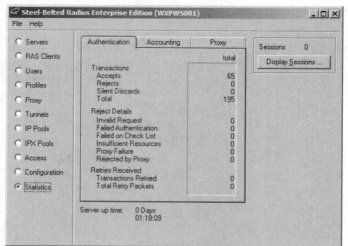

Windows Active Directory Domain Authentication with LEAP and RADIUS

In the preceding sections, we only looked at creating native users in Steel Belted Radius. As mentioned, however, you can create AD domain users and authenticate directly against Active Directory. This offers many advantages, such as preventing dictionary attacks by enforcing account lockout policies. If you want to use domain user accounts for LEAP authentication, you need only perform the following additions and modifications to the procedures we outlined earlier in this chapter:

1. Make modifications to the eap.ini file, as shown in Figure 11.66. Under the **[NT-Domain]** heading, remove the semicolon from the first three items to enable LEAP. Save and close the eap.ini file.

Figure 11.66 Modifying the eap.ini File for Domain Authentication

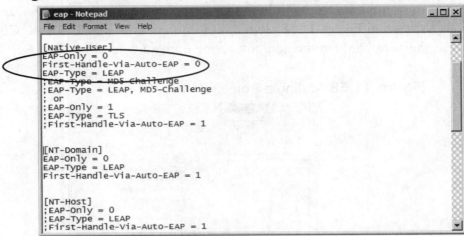

2. Restart the Steel Belted Radius service to force it to reload the eap.ini file from the **Services** console located in the **Administrative Tools** folder, Launch the **SBR Admin** application and connect to the local server. On the **Configuration** page, shown in Figure 11.67, ensure that the **NT Domain User** and **NT Domain Group** options are enabled and are at, or near, the top of the list. Click **Save** to confirm the change if required.

Figure 11.67 Checking Authentication Methods

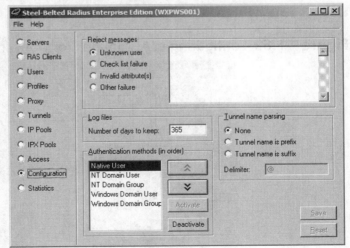

3. Go to the **Users** page and add a new user, as described previously. This time, however, you will have the option to select a domain user, as shown in Figure 11.68. Select your domain user and click **OK**. Click **Save** to confirm the addition of the domain user.

Figure 11.68 Adding a Domain User

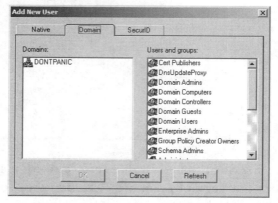

4. Open the **ACU** and edit the profile in use (the one you previously created). Switch to the **Network Security** tab and click the **Configure** button next to the Network Security Type drop-down (where **LEAP** is selected). Ensure that the **Use Windows User Name and Password** option is selected, as shown in Figure 11.69. In addition, ensure that a check is placed next to the **Include Windows Logon Domain with User Name** option.

Figure 11.69 Configuring LEAP Options for Domain Authentication

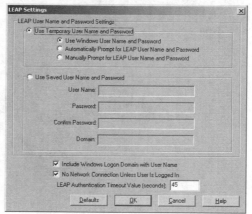

5. Click **OK** three times to save and exit the profile configuration.

6. Log in to the network using LEAP and your domain user credentials.

LEAP Review

Now that you've had a chance to examine the workings of Cisco's LEAP, you should see quite a few benefits to be gained through its use. LEAP, implemented with Funk Software's Steel Belted Radius, is an ideal and very robust security solution for a wireless network of any size. By forcing users to authenticate to a back-end RADIUS server and creating per-user, per-session dynamic WEP keys, LEAP provides greatly enhanced authentication and security for your wireless network.

LEAP addresses all WEP's vulnerabilities and is being implemented into the 802.11b standard by the Wi-Fi Alliance (www.wi-fialliance.org), which has implemented LEAP into its standards under the name of Wi-Fi Protected Access (WPA). You can read more about WPA at the Wi-Fi Alliance Web site. In addition, Cisco has licensed the LEAP technology to several third-party vendors, so you can expect to see many more LEAP-compatible devices in the near future. For example, Apple's AirPort network adapter already supports LEAP with version 2 or better firmware.

Understanding and Configuring 802.1X RADIUS Authentication

To provide better security for wireless LANs, and in particular to improve the security of WEP, a number of existing technologies used on wired networks were adapted for this purpose, including:

- **Remote Authentication and Dial-In User Service (RADIUS)** Provides for centralized authentication and accounting.

- **802.1X** Provides for a method of port-based authentication to LAN ports in a switched network environment.

These two services are used in combination with other security mechanisms, such as those provided by the Extensible Authentication Protocol (EAP), to further enhance the protection of wireless networks. Like MAC filtering, 802.1X is implemented at layer 2 of the Open System Interconnection (OSI) model: it will prevent communication on the network using higher layers of the OSI model if authentication fails at the MAC layer. However, unlike MAC filtering, 802.1X is very secure as it relies on mechanisms that are much harder to compromise than MAC address filters, which can be easily compromised through spoofed MAC addresses.

Although a number of vendors implement their own RADIUS servers, security mechanisms, and protocols for securing networks through 802.1X, such as Cisco's LEAP and Funk Software's EAP-TTLS, this section will focus on implementing 802.1X on a Microsoft network using Internet Authentication Services (IAS) and Microsoft's Certificate Services. Keep in mind, however, that wireless security standards are a moving target, and standards other than those discussed here, such as the PEAP, are being developed and might be available now or in the near future.

Microsoft RADIUS Servers

Microsoft's IAS provides a standards-based RADIUS server and can be installed as an optional component on Microsoft Windows 2000 and Net servers. Originally designed to provide a means to centralize the authentication, authorization, and accounting for dial-in users, RADIUS servers are now used to provide these services for other types of network access, including VPNs, port-based authentication on switches, and, importantly, wireless network access. IAS can be deployed within Active Directory to use the Active Directory database to centrally manage the login process for users connecting over a variety of network types. Moreover, multiple RADIUS servers can be installed and configured so that secondary RADIUS servers will automatically be used in case the primary RADIUS server fails, thus providing fault tolerance for the RADIUS infrastructure. Although RADIUS is not required to support the 802.1X standard, it is a preferred method for providing the authentication and authorization of users and devices attempting to connect to devices that use 802.1X for access control.

The 802.1X Standard

The 802.1X standard was developed to provide a means of restricting port-based Ethernet network access to valid users and devices. When a computer attempts to connect to a port on a network device, such as switch, it must be successfully authenticated before it can communicate on the network using the port. In other words, communication on the network is impossible without an initial successful authentication.

802.1X Authentication Ports

Two types of ports are defined for 802.1X authentication: *authenticator* or *supplicant*. The supplicant is the port requesting network access. The authenticator is the port that allows or denies access for network access. However, the authenticator does not perform the actual authentication of the supplicant requesting access. The authentication of the supplicant is performed by a separate authentication service, located on a separate server or built into the device itself, on behalf of the authenticator. If the authenticating server successfully authenticates the supplicant, it will communicate the fact to the authenticator, which will subsequently allow access.

An 802.1X-compliant device has two logical ports associated with the physical port: an *uncontrolled port* and a *controlled port*. Because the supplicant must initially communicate with the authenticator to make an authentication request, an 802.1X-compliant device will make use of a logical *uncontrolled port* over which this request can be made. Using the uncontrolled port, the authenticator will forward the authentication request to the authentication service. If the request is successful, the authenticator will allow communication on the LAN via the logical *controlled port*.

The Extensible Authentication Protocol

EAP is used to pass authentication requests between the supplicant and a RADIUS server via the authenticator. EAP provides a way to use different authentication types in addition to the standard authentication mechanisms provided by the Point-to-Point Protocol (PPP). Using EAP, stronger authentication types can be implemented within PPP, such as those that use public keys in conjunction with smart cards. In Windows, there is support for two EAP types:

- **EAP MD-5 CHAP** Allows for authentication based on a username/password combination. There are a number of disadvantages associated with using EAP MD-5 CHAP. First, even though it uses one-way hashes in combination with a challenge/response mechanism, critical information is still sent in the clear, making it vulnerable to compromise. Second, it does not provide mutual authentication between the client and the server; the server merely authenticates the client. Third, it does not provide a mechanism for establishing a secure channel between the client and the server.

- **EAP-TLS** A security mechanism based on X.509 digital certificates that is more secure than EAP MD-5 CHAP. The certificates can be stored in the Registry or on devices such as smart cards. When EAP-TLS authentication is used, both the client and server validate one another by exchanging X.509 certificates as part of the authentication process. Additionally, EAP-TLS provides a secure mechanism for the exchange of keys to establish an encrypted channel. Although the use of EAP-TLS is more difficult to configure, in that it requires the implementation of a public key infrastructure (PKI)—not a trivial undertaking—EAP-TLS is recommended for wireless 802.1X authentication.

In a paper published in February, 2002 by William A. Arbaugh and Arunesh Mishra entitled "An Initial Security Analysis of the IEEE 802.1x Standard," the authors discuss how one-way authentication and other weaknesses made 802.1X vulnerable to man-in-the-middle and session-hijacking attacks. Therefore, while it might be possible to use EAP MD-5 CHAP for 802.1X wireless authentication on Windows XP (pre SP1), it is not recommended. EAP-TLS protects against the types of attacks described by this paper.

The 802.1X Authentication Process

For 802.1X authentication to work on a wireless network, the AP must be able to securely identify traffic from a particular wireless client. This identification is accomplished using authentication keys that are sent to the AP and the wireless client from the RADIUS server. When a wireless client (802.1X supplicant) comes within range of the AP (802.1X authenticator), the following simplified process occurs:

1. The AP point issues a challenge to the wireless client.
2. The wireless client responds with its identity.
3. The AP forwards the identity to the RADIUS server using the uncontrolled port.
4. The RADIUS server sends a request to the wireless station via the AP, specifying the authentication mechanism to be used (for example, EAP-TLS).
5. The wireless station responds to the RADIUS server with its credentials via the AP.

6. The RADIUS server sends an encrypted authentication key to the AP if the credentials are acceptable.

7. The AP generates a multicast/global authentication key encrypted with a per-station unicast session key, and transmits it to the wireless station.

Figure 11.70 shows a simplified version of the 802.1X authentication process using EAP-TLS.

Figure 11.70 802.1X Authentication Process Using EAP-TLS

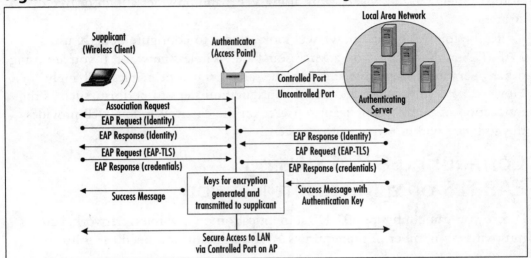

When the authentication process successfully completes, the wireless station is allowed access to the controlled port of the AP, and communication on the network can occur. Note that much of the security negotiation in the preceding steps occurs on the 802.1X uncontrolled port, which is only used so that the AP can forward traffic associated with the security negotiation between the client and the RADIUS server. EAP-TLS is required for the process to take place. EAP-TLS, unlike EAP MD-5 CHAP, provides a mechanism to allow the secure transmission of the authentication keys from the RADIUS server to the client.

Advantages of EAP-TLS

There are a number of significant advantages to using EAP-TLS authentication in conjunction with 802.1X:

- The use of X.509 digital certificates for authentication and key exchange is very secure.

- EAP-TLS provides a means to generate and use dynamic one-time-per-user, session-based WEP keys on the wireless network.

- Neither the user nor the administrator know the WEP keys that are in use.

For these reasons, using EAP-TLS for 802.1X authentication removes much of the vulnerability associated with using WEP and provides a high degree of assurance.

In the following section, we will look at how to configure 802.1X using EAP-TLS authentication on a Microsoft-based wireless network. If you are using other operating systems and software, the same general principles will apply. However, you might have additional configuration steps to perform, such as the installation of 802.1X supplicant software on the client. Windows XP provides this software within the operating system.

Configuring 802.1X Using EAP-TLS on a Microsoft Network

Before you can configure 802.1X authentication on a wireless network, you must satisfy a number of prerequisites. At a minimum, you need the following:

- An AP that supports 802.1X authentication. You probably won't find these devices at your local computer hardware store. They are designed for enterprise-class wireless network infrastructures, and are typically higher priced. Note that some devices will allow the use of IPSec between the AP and the wired network.

- Client software and hardware that supports 802.1X and EAP-TLS authentication and the use of dynamic WEP keys. Fortunately, just about any wireless adapter that allows the use of the Windows XP wireless interface will work. However, older wireless network adapters that use their own client software might not work.

- IAS installed on a Windows 2000 server to provide a primary RADIUS server and, optionally, installed on other servers to provide secondary RADIUS servers for fault tolerance.

- Active Directory

- A PKI using a Microsoft stand-alone or Enterprise Certificate server to support the use of X.509 digital certificates for EAP-TLS. More certificate servers can be deployed in the PKI for additional security. An Enterprise Certificate server can ease the burden of certificate deployment to clients and the RADIUS server through auto-enrollment of client computers that are members of the Windows 2000 domain.

- The most recent service packs and patches installed on the Windows 2000 servers and Windows XP wireless clients.

Notes from the Underground...

Beyond ISA Server

Certificates issued by a Microsoft certification authority (CA) will work for wireless authentication. However, certificates issued by other CAs probably will not work. Certificates that are used for wireless 802.1X authentication *must* contain an optional field called Enhanced Key Usage (EKU). The field will contain one or more object identifiers (OIDs) that identify the purpose of the certificate. For example, the EKU of a typical client certificate used for multiple purposes might contain the following values:

- Encrypting File System (1.3.6.1.4.1.311.10.3.4)
- Secure Email (1.3.6.1.5.5.7.3.4)
- Client Authentication (1.3.6.1.5.5.7.3.2)

The EKU of the certificate installed on the IAS server and the wireless client for computer authentication will contain a value for server authentication (1.3.6.1.5.5.7.3.1). Because the EKU is an optional field, it might be absent on certificates issued by non-Microsoft CAs, rendering them useless for 802.1X authentication in a Microsoft infrastructure. Furthermore, the certificate must contain the fully qualified domain name (FQDN) of the computer on which it is installed in the Subject Alternate Name field, and, in the case of certificates used for user authentication, the user principal name (UPN). You can confirm whether these fields and values exist by viewing the properties of the certificate in the **Certificates** snap-in of the MMC console. (Steps for

Continued

loading this snap-in are detailed later in this chapter.) There are some other certificate requirements not mentioned here that must be also be satisfied. If you would like to use a third -party CA to issue client certificates for 802.1X authentication, you should contact the vendor to see if it is supported for this purpose. If not, and you must use a third-party CA, you might need to look at solutions provided by other vendors of wireless hardware to use 802.1X.

After configuring a PKI and installing IAS on your Windows 2000 network, there are three general steps to configure 802.1X authentication on your wireless network:

1. Install X.509 digital certificates on the wireless client and IAS servers.

2. Configure IAS logging and policies for 802.1X authentication.

3. Configure the wireless AP for 802.1X authentication.

4. Configure the properties of the client wireless network interface for dynamic WEP key exchange.

Configuring Certificate Services and Installing Certificates on the IAS Server and Wireless Client

After deploying Active Directory, the first step in implementing 802.1X is to deploy the PKI and install the appropriate X.509 certificates. You will have to install (at a minimum) a single certificate server, either a standalone or enterprise certificate server, to issue certificates. What distinguishes a standalone from an enterprise certificate server is whether it will depend on, and be integrated with, Active Directory. A standalone CA does not require Active Directory. This certificate server can be a *root* CA or a *subordinate* CA, which ultimately receives its authorization to issue certificates from a root CA higher in the hierarchy, either directly or indirectly through intermediate CAs, according to a *certification path*.

NOTE

The certification path can be viewed in the properties of installed certificates.

The root CA can be a public or commercially available CA that issues an authorization to a subordinate CA, or one deployed on the Windows 2000 network. In enterprise networks that require a high degree of security, it is not recommended that you use the root CA to issue client certificates; for this purpose, you should use a subordinate CA authorized by the root CA. In very high-security environments, you should use intermediate CAs to authorize the CA that issues client certificates. Furthermore, you should secure the hardware and software of the root and intermediate CAs as much as possible, take them offline, and place them in a secure location. You would then bring the root and intermediate CAs online only when you need to perform tasks related to the management of your PKI.

In deploying your PKI, keep in mind that client workstations and the IAS servers need to be able to consult a *certificate revocation list* (CRL) to verify and validate certificates, especially certificates that have become compromised before their expiration date and have been added to a CRL. If a CRL is not available, authorization will fail. Consequently, a primary design consideration for your PKI is to ensure that the CRLs are highly available. Normally, the CRL is stored on the CA; however, additional distribution points for the CRL can be created to ensure a high degree of availability. The CA maintains a list of these locations and distributes the list in a field of the client certificate.

NOTE

It is beyond the scope of this book to discuss the implementation details of a PKI. For more information, please see the various documents available on the Microsoft Web site, in particular: www.microsoft.com/windows2000/technologies/security/default.asp, www.microsoft.com/windows2000/techinfo/howitworks/security/pkiintro.asp, and www.microsoft.com/windows2000/techinfo/planning/security/pki.asp.

Whether you decide to implement a standalone or an enterprise CA to issue certificates, you will need to issue three certificates: for both the computer and the user account on the wireless client, as well as the RADIUS server. A certificate is required in all of these places because mutual authentication has to take place. The computer certificate provides initial access of the computer to the network, and the user certificate provides wireless access after the user logs in. While the RADIUS server will authenticate the client based on the wireless client's computer and user certificates, and the wireless client will authenticate the RADIUS server based on the server's certificate.

The certificates on the wireless client and the RADIUS server do not have to be issued by the same CA. However, both the client and the server have to trust each other's certificates. Within each certificate is information about the certificate path leading up to the root CA. If both the wireless client and the RADIUS server trust the root CA in each other's certificate, mutual authentication can successfully take place. If you are using a standalone CA that is not in the list of Trusted Root Certification Authorities, you will have to add it to the list. You can do this through a Group Policy Object, or you can do it manually. For information on how to add CAs to the Trusted Root Certification Authorities container, please see Windows 2000 and Windows XP help files. The container listing these trusted root certificates can be viewed in the Certificates snap-in of the MMC console, as shown in Figure 11.71.

Figure 11.71 Certificate Snap-In Showing Trusted Root Certification Authorities

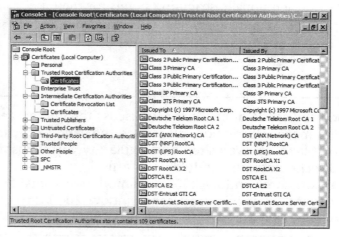

Using an enterprise CA will simplify many of the tasks related to certificates that you have to perform. An enterprise CA is automatically listed in the Trusted Root Certification Authorities container. Furthermore, you can use auto-enrollment to issue computer certificates to the wireless client and the IAS server without any intervention on the part of the user. Using an enterprise CA and configuring auto-enrollment of computer certificates should be considered a best practice.

If you put an enterprise CA into place, you will have to configure an Active Directory Group Policy to issue computer certificates automatically. You should use the **Default Domain Policy** for the domain in which your CA is located. To configure the **Group Policy** for auto-enrollment of computer certificates, do the following:

1. Access the **Properties** of the Group Policy object for the domain to which the enterprise CA belongs using **Active Directory Users and Computers**, and click **Edit**.

2. Navigate to **Computer Settings | Windows Settings | Security Settings | Public Key Policies | Automatic Certificate Request Settings**.

3. Right click the **Automatic Certificate Request Settings** with the, click **New**, and then click **Automatic Certificate Request**, as in Figure 11.72.

Figure 11.72 Configuring a Domain Group Policy for Auto-Enrollment of Computer Certificates

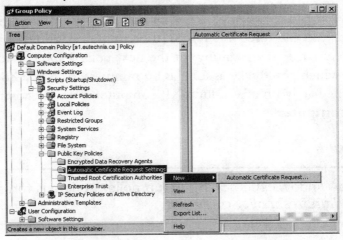

4. Click **Next** when the wizard appears. Click **Computer** in the **Certificate Templates**, as shown in Figure 11.73, and then click **Next**.

Figure 11.73 Choosing a Computer Certificate Template for Auto-Enrollment

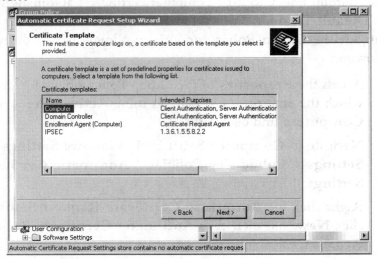

5. Click the enterprise CA, click **Next**, and then click **Finish**.

After you have configured a Group Policy for auto-enrollment of computer certificates, you can force a refresh of the group policy so that it will take effect immediately, rather than waiting for the next polling interval for Group Policy Changes, which could take as long as 90 minutes. To force Group Policy to take effect immediately on a Windows XP computer, type the command **gpupdate /target:computer**.

> **NOTE**
>
> On a Windows 2000 client, group policy update is forced by using the *secedit/refreshpolicy* command.

Once you have forced a refresh of group policy, you can confirm if the computer certificate is successfully installed. To confirm the installation of the computer certificate:

1. Type the command **mmc** and click **OK** from **Start | Run**.

2. Click **File** in the MMC console menu, and then click **Add/Remove Snap-in**.

3. Click **Add** in the **Add/Remove Snap-in** dialog box. Then, select **Certificates** from the list of snap-ins and click **Add**. You will be prompted to choose which certificate store the snap-in will be used to manage.

4. Select **computer account** when prompted about what certificate the snap-in will be used to manage, and then click **Next**. You will then be prompted to select the computer the snap-in will manage.

5. Select **Local computer (the computer this console is running on)** and click **Finish**. Then, click **Close** and click **OK** to close the remaining dialog boxes.

6. Navigate to the **Console Root | Certificates (Local Computer) | Personal | Certificates** container, as seen in a display similar to the one in Figure 11.73. The certificate should be installed there.

The next step is to install a user certificate on the client workstation and then map the certificate to a user account. There are a number of ways to install a user certificate: through Web enrollment: by requesting the certificate using the Certificates snap-in, by using a CAPICOM script (which can be executed as a login script to facilitate deployment), or by importing a certificate file.

The following steps demonstrate how to request the certificate using the Certificates snap-in:

1. Open an MMC console for **Certificates – Current User**. (To load this snap-in, follow the steps in the preceding procedure; however, at step 5, select **My user account**.)

2. Navigate to **Certificates | Personal** and click the container with the alternate mouse button. Highlight **All Tasks** and then click **Request New Certificate**, as shown in Figure 11.74. The **Certificate Request Wizard** appears.

Figure 11.74 Requesting a User Certificate

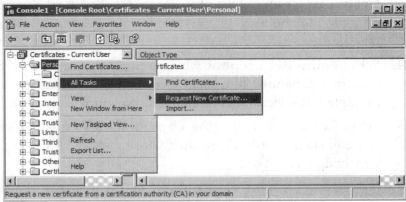

3. Click **Next** on the **Certificate Request Wizard** welcome page.

4. Select **User** and click **Next** on the **Certificate Types**, as shown in Figure 11.75. You can also select the **Advanced** check box. Doing so will allow you to select from a number of different cryptographic service providers (CSPs), to choose a key length, to mark the private key as exportable (the option might not be available for selection), and to enable strong private key protection. The latter option will cause you to be prompted for a password every time the private key is accessed.

Figure 11.75 Choosing a Certificate Type

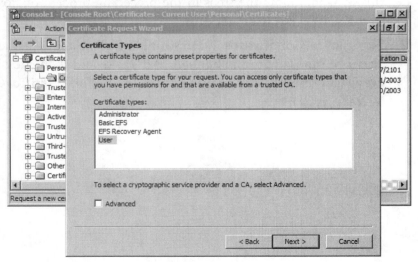

5. Type in a **Friendly Name** of your choosing and a **Description**, and then click **Next**.

6. Review your settings and click **Finish**.

You now should have a user certificate stored on the computer used for wireless access. However, this user certificate will not be usable for 802.1X authentication unless it is mapped to a user account in Active Directory. By default, the certificate should be mapped to the user account. You can verify if it has been mapped by viewing the **Properties** of the user account in **Active Directory Users and Computers**. The certificates that are mapped to the user account can be viewed in the **Published Certificates** tab of the **Properties** of the user account object.

After you configure certificate services and install computer and user certificates on the wireless client and a computer certificate on the RADIUS server, you must configure the RADIUS server for 802.1X authentication.

Configuring IAS Server for 802.1X Authentication

If you have configured RRAS for dial-in or VPN access, you will be comfortable with the IAS Server interface. It uses the same interfaces for configuring dial-in conditions and policies as does RRAS. You can use IAS to centralize dial-in access policies for your entire network, rather than have dial-in access policies defined on each RRAS server. A primary advantage of doing this is easier administration and centralized logging of dial-in access.

Installing an IAS server also provides a standards-based RADIUS server that is required for 802.1X authentication. As with configuring RRAS, you will need to add and configure a **Remote Access Policy** to grant access. A **Remote Access Policy** grants or denies access to remote users and devices based on matching conditions and a profile. For access to be granted, the conditions you define have to match. For example, the dial-in user might have to belong to the appropriate group, or connect during an allowable period. The profile in the **Remote Access Policy** defines such things as the authentication type and the encryption type used for the remote access. If the remote client is not capable of using the authentication methods and encryption strength defined in the profile, access is denied.

For 802.1X authentication, you will have to configure a **Remote Access Policy** that contains conditions specific to 802.1X wireless authentication and a **Profile** that requires the use of the **Extensible Authentication Protocol**

(EAP) and strong encryption. After configuring the **Remote Access Policy**, you will have to configure the IAS server to act as a RADIUS server for the wireless AP, which is the RADIUS client.

Before installing and configuring the IAS server on your Windows 2000 or .NET/2003 network, you should consider whether you are installing it on a domain controller or member server (in the same or in a different domain). If you install it on a domain controller, the IAS server will be able to read the account properties in Active Directory. However, if you install IAS on a member server, you will have to perform an additional step to register the IAS server, which will give it access to Active Directory accounts.

There are a number of ways you can register the IAS server:

- The IAS snap-in
- The Active Directory Users and Computers admin tool
- The *netsh* command

NOTE

Perhaps the simplest way to register the IAS server is through the *netsh* command. To do this, log on to the IAS server, open a command prompt, and type the command *netsh ras add registeredserver.* If the IAS server is in a different domain, you will have to add arguments to this command. For more information on registering IAS servers, see Windows Help.

Once you have installed and, if necessary, registered the IAS server(s), you can configure the **Remote Access Policy**. Before configuring a **Remote Access Policy**, make sure that you apply the latest service pack and confirm that the IAS server has an X.509 computer certificate. In addition, you should create an Active Directory Global or Universal Group that contains your wireless users as members.

The **Remote Access Policy** will need to contain a condition for **NAS-Port-Type** that contains values for **Wireless-Other** and **Wireless-IEEE802.11** (these two values are used as logical OR for this condition) and a condition for **Windows-Groups=[***the group created for wireless users***]**. Both conditions have to match (logical AND) for access to be granted by the policy.

The **Profile** of the **Remote Access Policy** will need to be configured to use the **Extensible Authentication Protocol**, and the **Smart Card or Other Certificate** EAP type. Encryption in the **Profile** should be configured to force the strongest level of encryption, if supported by the AP. Depending on the AP you are using, you might have to configure vendor specific attributes (VSA) in the **Advanced** tab of the **Profile**. If you have to configure a VSA, you will need to contact the vendor of the AP to find out the value that should be used, if you can't find it in the documentation.

To configure the conditions for a **Remote Access Policy** on the IAS server:

1. Select **Internet Authentication Services** and open the IAS console from **Start | Programs | Administrative Tools**.

2. Right click **Remote Access Policies**, and from the subsequent context menu, click **New Remote Access Policy**.

3. Enter a friendly name for the policy and click **Next**.

4. Click **Add** in the **Add Remote Access Policy Conditions** dialog box. Then, select **NAS-Port-Type** in the **Select Attribute** dialog box and click **Add**, as shown in Figure 11.76.

Figure 11.76 Adding a NAS-Port-Type Condition to Remote Access Policy

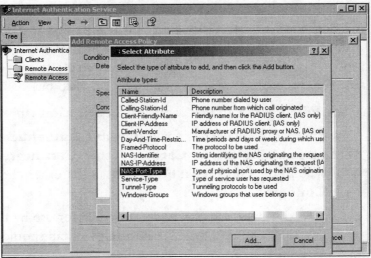

5. Select **Wireless-IEEE 802.11** and **Wireless – Other** from the left-hand window in the **NAS-Port-Type** dialog, and click **Add>>** to

move them to the Selected Types window, as shown in Figure 11.77.
Click **OK**.

Figure 11.77 Adding Wireless NAS-Port-Type Conditions

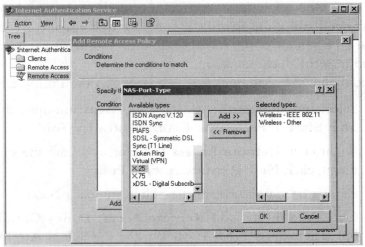

6. Add a condition for **Windows-Groups** that contains the group you
   created for wireless users after configuring the **NAS-Port-Type** conditions. Then, click **Next**.

7. Click the radio button to **Grant remote access permission if user
   matches conditions** in the subsequent **Permissions** page for the new
   policy. The next step is to configure the **Profile** to support EAP-TLS
   and force the strongest level of encryption (128 bit).

8. Click **Edit Profile** and click the **Authentication** tab.

9. Confirm that the checkbox for **Extensible Authentication Protocol**
   is selected and that **Smart Card or Other Certificate** is listed as the
   EAP type in the drop-down box. Clear all the other check boxes and
   click **Configure**.

10. Select the computer certificate you installed for use by the IAS server,
    and click **OK**. The resulting **Authentication** tab should look like the
    one in Figure 11.78.

Figure 11.78 Configuring the Dial-In Profile for 802.1X
Authentication

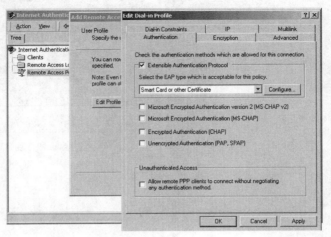

11. Force the strongest level of encryption by clicking the **Encryption** tab and then clearing all the checkboxes except the one for **Strongest**.

12 Save the policy by clicking **OK** and then **Finish**. Make sure that the policy you created is higher in the list than the default Remote Access Policy. You can delete the default policy if you like.

Finally, you need to configure the IAS server for RADIUS authentication. To do this, you need to add a configuration for the RADIUS client—in this case, the AP—to the IAS server:

13. Right click the **Clients** folder in the IAS console, and click **New Client** from the context menu.

14. Supply a friendly name for the configuration and click **Next**. The screen shown in Figure 11.79 appears.

Figure 11.79 Adding a RADIUS Client

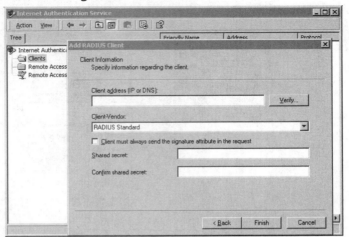

15. Configure the screen with the **Client address (IP or DNS)** of the wireless AP, and click the checkbox indicating that the **Client must always send the signature attribute in the request**. For the **Shared secret**, add an alphanumeric password that is at least 22 characters long for higher security.

16. Click **Finish**.

You can change the port numbers for RADIUS accounting and authentication by obtaining the properties of the **Internet Authentication Service** container in the IAS console. You can also use these property pages to log successful and unsuccessful authentication attempts and to register the server in Active Directory.

After installing certificates on the wireless client and IAS server and configuring the IAS server for 802.1X authentication, you will need to configure the AP and the wireless client. The following text shows the typical steps to complete the configuration of your wireless network for 802.1X authentication.

Configuring an Access Point for 802.1X Authentication

Generally, only enterprise-class APs support 802.1X authentication; this is not a feature found in devices intended for the SOHO market. Enterprise-class APs are not likely to be found in your local computer store. If you want an AP that supports 802.1X, you should consult the wireless vendors' Web sites for information on the features supported by the APs they manufacture. Vendors that manufacture 802.1X-capable devices include: 3Com, Agere, Cisco, and others. The price for devices that support 802.1X authentication usually start at $500 (USD) and can cost considerably more, depending on the vendor and the other features supported by the AP. If you already own an enterprise-class AP, such as an ORiNOCO Access Point 500 or Access Point 1000, 802.1X authentication might not be supported in the original firmware but can be added through a firmware update.

Regardless of the device you purchase, an 802.1X-capable AP will be configured similarly. The following text shows the typical configuration of 802.1X authentication on an ORiNOCO Access Point 500 with the most recent firmware update applied to it.

NOTE

For more information about the ORiNOCO device, see www. orinocowireless.com.

The configuration of the AP is straightforward and simple (see Figure 11.80). You will need to configure the following:

- **An encryption key length** This can be either 64 or 128 bits (or higher if your hardware and software support longer lengths).

- **An encryption key lifetime** When you implement 802.1X using EAP-TLS, WEP encryption keys are dynamically generated at intervals you specify. For higher-security environments, the encryption key lifetime should be set to ten minutes or less.

- **An authorization lifetime** This is the interval at which the client and server will re-authenticate with one another. This interval should be longer than the interval for the encryption key lifetime, but still relatively short in a high-security environment. A primary advantage here is that if a device is stolen, the certificates it uses can be immediately revoked. The next time it tries to authenticate, the CRL will be checked and authentication will fail.

- **An authorization password** This is the shared-secret password you configured for RADIUS client authentication on the IAS server. This password is used to establish communication between the AP and the RADIUS server. Thus, it needs to be protected by being long and complex. This password should be at least 22 characters long and use mixed case, numbers, letters, and other characters. You might want to consider using a random string generation program to create this password for you.

- **An IP address of a primary and, if configured for fault tolerance, a secondary RADIUS server** If the AP is in a DMZ, and the RADIUS server is behind a firewall, this IP address can be the external IP address of the firewall.

- **A UDP port used for RADIUS authentication** The default port for RADIUS is port 1645. However, you can change this port on the IAS server and the AP for an additional degree of security.

Figure 11.80 Configuring an ORiNOCO AP 500 for 802.1X Authentication

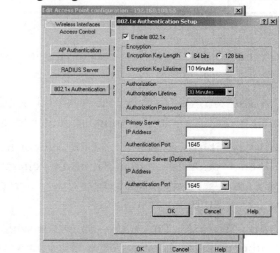

Depending on your AP, you might have to go through additional configuration steps. For example, you might have to enable the use of dynamic WEP keys. On the AP 500, this configuration is automatically applied to the AP when you finish configuring the 802.1X settings. Consult your AP's documentation for specific information on configuring it for 802.1X authentication.

Configuring the Wireless Interface on Windows XP for 802.1X Authentication

If you have been following the preceding steps in the same order for configuring 802.1X authentication, the final step is to configure the properties of the wireless interface in Windows XP. You will have to ensure that the properties for EAP-TLS authentication and dynamic WEP are configured. To do this, perform the following steps:

1. Obtain the **Properties** of the wireless interface and click the **Authentication** tab.

2. Ensure that the checkbox for **Enable access control for IEEE 802.1X** is checked and that **Smart Card or other Certificate** is selected as the EAP type, as shown in Figure 11.81.

Figure 11.81 Authentication Properties for Wireless Client

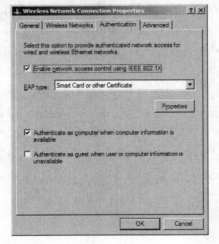

3. Click **Properties** to view the **Smart Card or other Certificate Properties** window. Ensure that the checkbox for **Validate server certificate** is checked, as shown in Figure 11.82.

Figure 11.82 Configure Smart Card or Other Certificate Properties

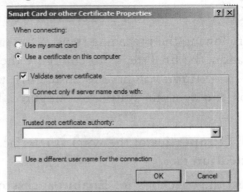

4. Select the root CA of the issuer of the server certificate in the **Trusted root certificate authority** drop-down box. If it is not already present, click **OK**. For additional security, you could select the checkbox for **Connect only if server name ends with** and type in the root DNS name—for example, tacteam.net.

5. Obtain the properties of the wireless interface and click the **Wireless Network** tab.

6. Confirm that the checkbox for **Use Windows for my wireless network settings** is selected In the **Preferred networks** dialog box. Highlight the SSID of the 802.1X-enabled AP, and click **Properties**.

7. Click the checkbox for **The key is provided from me automatically**, as shown in Figure 11.83, and then click **OK**.

Figure 11.83 Configuring Windows XP Wireless Properties for 802.1X Authentication

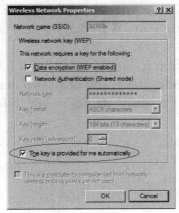

That's it. You're finished. The next time you attempt to authenticate and associate with the 802.1X-enabled AP, you might be presented with a prompt asking you to verify the identity of the IAS server certificate. By clicking **OK**, you will permit the authentication process to complete, thus allowing you secure access to the network.

Let's briefly review the steps to enable 802.1X authentication. We are assuming that you are using Active Directory, already have a PKI in place, can issue certificates from a Microsoft CA, and have installed and registered (if necessary) an IAS server. Your steps would be as follows:

1. Issue computer certificate to IAS server.

2. Issue computer certificate to wireless client.

3. Issue user certificate to wireless client user.

4. Create a Remote Access Policy on the IAS server for 802.1X authentication.

5. Configure RADIUS client settings on the IAS server.

6. Configure AP for 802.1X authentication.

7. Configure wireless client network interface for 802.1X authentication.

Although this might seem like a lot of work, the enhanced security provided by 802.1X might well justify the expense and effort of setting it up. Furthermore, much of the effort is up-front. Since you don't have to worry about frequently rotating static WEP keys, you will realize significant savings in effort and time later.

802.1X authentication in combination with EAP-TLS is not the final word in wireless security. It mitigates many of the vulnerabilities associated with wireless networks, but other types of attacks might still be possible.

Summary

Corporate or SOHO wireless networks require a level of security that goes beyond the basics. They have an obligation to protect their business proprietary and customer data. There are many different technologies that can be utilized to accomplish this. WiFi Protected Access (WPA) addresses many of the flaws inherent in WEP. WPA can utilize the Advanced Encryption Standard (AES) to encrypt wireless network transmissions.

Corporate wireless networks should never be deployed without a virtual private network. There are countless commercial VPN products available. Reef Edge Dolphin is a freeware wireless gateway that can be deployed with VPN capabilities. For SOHO users that don't have the time, or the technical staff to deploy and configure a product like Dolphin, Linksys has developed the WRV54G VPN-Broadband Router. The WRV54G provides many enhanced security features. Designed specifically with the small business in mind, the WRV54G provides complete VPN support using IPSec tunnels.

802.1X was originally developed to provide a method for port-based authentication on wired networks. However, it was found to have significant application in wireless networks. With 802.1X authentication, a supplicant (a wireless workstation) needs to be authenticated by an authenticator (usually a RADIUS server) before access is granted to the network. The authentication process takes place over a logical uncontrolled port that is used only for the authentication process. If the authentication process is successful, access is granted to the network on the logical controlled port.

802.1X relies on the Extensible Authentication Protocol (EAP) to perform the authentication. The preferred EAP type for 802.1X is EAP-TLS. EAP-TLS provides the ability to use dynamic per-user, session-based WEP keys, thereby eliminating some of the more significant vulnerabilities associated with WEP. However, to use EAP-TLS, you must deploy a public key infrastructure (PKI) to issue digital X.509 certificates to the wireless clients and the RADIUS server.

Solutions Fast Track

Implementing WiFi Protected Access (WPA)

☑ WPA was developed to replace WEP because of the known insecurities associated with WEP's implementation of the RC4 encryption standard.

☑ Many of the newer access points support WPA, some require firmware upgrades in order to enable WPA functionality.

☑ Windows XP is WPA-ready with a patch; however, you must ensure that you have WPA drivers for your wireless card.

Implementing a Wireless Gateway with Reef Edge Dolphin

☑ Wireless gateways are implemented to control access to the network by authenticating users against an internal or external database.

☑ Wireless gateways can also perform other tasks, including enforcing security by group, implementing quality of service bandwidth controls, and many other advanced security functions such as VPN tunnels and mobile IP roaming between APs.

☑ Dolphin is a freeware wireless gateway that provides authentication of users against a local database and optional support for IPSec VPN tunnels for data protection. In a small, noncommercial environment, Dolphin can be quickly and economically put into use to increase network security by controlling wireless network access.

Implementing a VPN on a Linksys WRV54G VPN Broadband Router

☑ The Linksys WRV54G is a broadband router with a built-in access point and VPN.

☑ The WRV54G was specifically designed for Small Office/Home Office (SOHO) users that require more than the basic security protection for their wired and wireless networks.

☑ To utilize the VPN features on the WRV54G an IPSec tunnel must be established between the WRV54G and any clients that access it.

Implementing RADIUS with Cisco LEAP

☑ LEAP addresses all the problems inherent in the use of WEP in a wireless network. The largest vulnerabilities come from static WEP keys and the predictability of IVs.

☑ LEAP creates a per-user, per-session dynamic WEP key that is tied to the network logon, thereby addressing the limitations of static WEP keys. Since authentication is performed against a back-end RADIUS database, administrative overhead is minimal after initial installation and configuration.

☑ Policies can be set to force users to re-authenticate more often to the RADIUS server and thus receive fresh session keys. This can further reduce the window for network attacks because the WEP keys are rotated even more frequently.

☑ The IV is changed on a per-packet basis, so hackers cannot find a predetermined, predictable sequence to exploit. The capability to change the IV with every packet, combined with the dynamic keying and re-authentication, greatly increases security and makes it that much more difficult for an attacker to gain access to your wireless network.

Understanding and Configuring 802.1X RADIUS Authentication

☑ RADIUS provides for centralized authentication and accounting.

☑ 802.1X provides for a method of port-based authentication to LAN ports in a switched network environment.

☑ For 802.1X authentication to work on a wireless network, the AP must be able to securely identify traffic from a particular wireless client. This identification is accomplished using authentication keys that are sent to the AP and the wireless client from the RADIUS server.

Frequently Asked Questions

The following Frequently Asked Questions, answered by the authors of this book, are designed to both measure your understanding of the concepts presented in this chapter and to assist you with real-life implementation of these concepts. To have your questions about this chapter answered by the author, browse to **www.syngress.com/solutions** and click on the **"Ask the Author"** form. You will also gain access to thousands of other FAQs at ITFAQnet.com.

Q: Where can I get firmware updates for my access point?

A: The Web site of your access point's manufacturer has firmware updates available. Linksys updates are available at www.linksys.com/download/. D-Link updates are available at http://support.dlink.com/downloads/. ORiNOCO updates can be downloaded from www.expressresponse.com/cgi-bin/proxim02/showFaq.cgi. Cisco updates are available at www.cisco.com/public/sw-center/sw-wireless.shtml.

Q: Where can I learn more about how VPNs work?

A: The Network Universe Web site has a good explanation of VPNs at www.dtool.com/vpns.html.

Q: Where can I learn more about wireless security?

A: Cisco has published a wireless LAN security whitepaper on their Web site, www.cisco.com/warp/public/cc/pd/witc/ao1200ap/prodlit/wswpf_wp.htm, that provides some good information about wireless security.

Q: I have heard that both WPA and LEAP are vulnerable to dictionary attacks. What does this mean?

A: A dictionary attack tries to guess the pre-shared key, password, or passphrase in use by testing it against a list, or dictionary, of words and phrases. By using strong passphrases or, in the case of WPA, long pre-shared keys you reduce your risk of being vulnerable to a dictionary attack.

Index

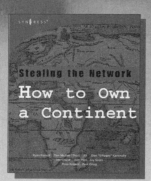